Natural Places
of the Northwest

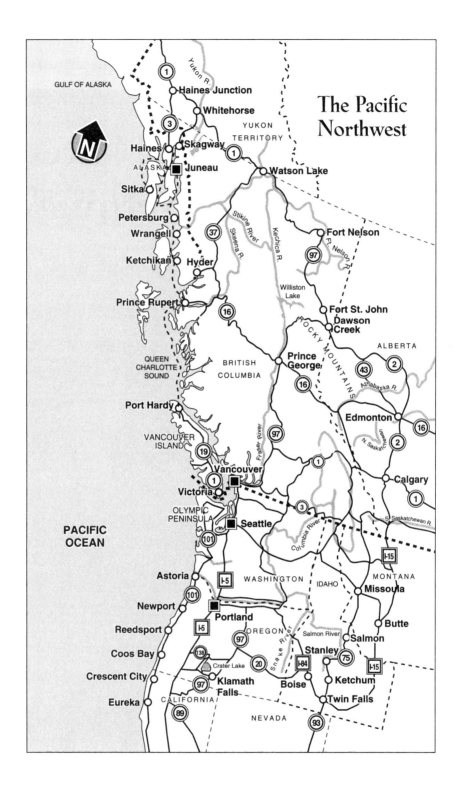

Natural Places of the Northwest

A TRAVELER'S GUIDE TO THE CULTURE, SPIRIT, AND ECOLOGY OF SCENIC DESTINATIONS

Fraser Bridges

An On-Route Communications Book

PRIMA PUBLISHING

Map: Fraser Bridges
Illustrations: Gregory G. Gersch

Library of Congress Cataloging-in-Publication Data
Bridges, Fraser.
    Natural places of the Northwest : a traveler's guide to the culture, spirit, and ecology of scenic destinations/by Fraser Bridges

      p. cm.— (Natural Places)

    Includes index.
    ISBN 0-7615-0159-2
    1. Natural history—Northwest, Pacific.   2. Natural areas—Northwest, Pacific. I. Title. II. Series: Bridges, Fraser. Natural places.
QH104.5.N6B75   1996
508.795—dc20   95-33801
                                                    CIP

96 97 98 99 00 DD 10 9 8 7 6 5 4 3 2 1
Printed in the United States of America

How to Order:

Single copies may be ordered from Prima Publishing, P.O. Box 1260BK, Rocklin, CA 95677; telephone (916) 632-4400. Quantity discounts are also available. On your letterhead, include information concerning the intended use of the books and the number of books you wish to purchase.

CONTENTS

INTRODUCTION   vii

1 Along the Pacific Coast   1

Redwood National Park   5

Oregon Coast   59

San Juan Islands   91

2 Northwest Mountains   115

The Northern Cascades   119

The Southern Cascades   151

3 Rain Forests   181

Olympic National Park   184

Vancouver Island   233

Southeast Alaska   302

4 The Ultimate Outdoors   345

Salmon River Country   349

WILDLIFE CHECKLIST   371
INDEX   384

INTRODUCTION

What was the northwest corner of North America like before the arrival of Lopez de Haro, and then George Vancouver, on the Pacific shores? This is the question I keep asking myself, as I visit what we think are the natural places of this diverse and spectacularly beautiful land. It could only have been more beautiful and more spectacular.

Only the ghosts of the previous inhabitants of the region could have known. For thousands of years, the people of the Pacific Northwest lived, alone, undisturbed by sea captains, explorers, fur traders, gold rush miners, immigrant settlers, and today's residents of the great cities. The members of Native American tribes were also the result of immigration. Before their ancestors arrived, following the land bridge between Siberia and this continent, only the wildlife was here. It was, and is, their country. All others are intruders.

But the Native American peoples managed to live in harmony with the earth and its natural bounty. Over the generations, the tribes developed an ethic that allowed them to enjoy the riches of the sea and the land but ensured that the land and its wildlife were secure from damage. The Supreme Being was the earth and all that it contained.

An Earth-Centered Existence

The concept of naturism has been around for a long, long time. The early arrivals from Asia believed in it, and many of their descendants still do. The Native Americans were farmers, raising vegetables and grains for their use. Sure, the Native Americans used the earth for their own purposes, including burning grass to enhance agriculture. The effects of this type of burning are seen today in the San Juan Islands, where meadows fringed by groves of trees support wildflowers and abundant animal life. They knew how to do it without causing an ultimate form of destruction.

One could only hope that the stewardship of the land by the people who now own and control it could have been as wise. Dams have been built on the great rivers, reducing fish stocks. And why do we use the word "stocks," as if wild chinook and steelhead are there for the farming?

During my years of travel throughout the Pacific Northwest, I have seen enormous growth: of the cities, the industrial economy based on natural resource development, and the tourism industry. Much of the success of tourism in the Northwest is due to the beauty of the area. Yet there are signs that humankind is beginning, just beginning, to realize that wildlife deserves an important place in the earth's scheme of things. One of the most felicitous decisions made recently is the decision of the National Park Service to remove dams on the once-important salmon river on the Olympic Peninsula, the Elwha. A long process of activism, recrimination, and second thought has freed the future of the Elwha, now part of Olympic National Park.

Another sign of progress (ahead to the past) is the wilderness ethic imbued in the management of the Nez Perce National Forest in Idaho. During the early 1980s, after a century of mining, timber exploitation, and clear-cutting of the magnificent pine forests of north-central Idaho, the National Forest Service adopted the new ethic of putting the health and welfare of the land first. The movement has resulted in selective logging, including horse logging, and a passion for the wilderness that has banned the use of motorized vehicles and equipment in the designated wilderness areas. If a forest ranger has to repair a riparian habitat, it is done with pack mules and travel over wilderness trails, not forest roads.

Even the current residents of the Northwest, living in such cities as Seattle, Portland, and Vancouver, are aware of the natural landscape of the region. Most of them are migrants to the area who have moved there because of the natural beauty and the sense of peace and well-being that natural environments bring. In this book, you'll find more evidence of the wilderness ethic.

A new national park is being planned for Canada's Queen Charlotte Islands. In this new rain forest park, there will be no great park lodge accommodating hundreds of thousands of visitors a year. Parks Canada and the Haida people of the Queen Charlottes are seeing to it that the South Moresby Island Preserve will stay pretty much as it is, a place of true wilderness and an island landscape of supreme beauty and inspiration.

This isn't to say that your search for real wilderness in the Northwest won't be a challenge. To see the truly "wild" wilderness, you have to wear a backpack and travel for two or three days into the far reaches of a designated wilderness area. And even then there are the remains of old mines, clear-cuts still reviving from work done a century ago. But nature has a way of restoring itself, and our children's children will see a very different landscape in selective places, thanks to planning and work now going on. We can only wish that those living today could have the natural experience of the early inhabitants. In the meantime, we'll continue to walk the nature trails, camp in organized campgrounds, stay at "wilderness" lodges, getting as much as we can out of the modern wilderness experience.

I hope that this book will steer you in a number of directions where today's outdoors can be savored and where you may feel part of the earth, and the earth part of you.

About This Guidebook

The four parts cover nine of the special places of the Northwest, from the Pacific Ocean to the western Rockies and the dramatic course of the Salmon River, and from the redwood forests of Northern California to the glaciers of southeast Alaska. There are beautiful sights to see, many trails to walk, lakes to paddle across in your canoe, and ocean bays to travel in your kayak. There are caves to explore and bears and other wildlife to meet. Each part deals with a specific region, including historical background and natural attractions.

Included in each chapter is an informal field guide, focusing on the wildlife of the area: the birds (resident and migratory), mammals, and other animals including amphibians, fishes, crustaceans, and other invertebrates. We also focus on the indigenous plants of these special places, including trees of the forests, the understory plants, and wildflowers you'll have a good chance of finding.

The chapters end with a selection of recommended places to stay, including some of the unique lodges (fishing and otherwise), historic hotels, guest ranches, campgrounds, and bed and breakfast inns, ranging from rustic to super-deluxe. The listings are marked with dollar signs for your pricing convenience: **$** is inexpensive (40 to 65 dollars per night); **$$** is moderate (66 to 100 dollars); **$$$** is deluxe (101 to 150 dollars); and **$$$ +** is super-deluxe (over 151 dollars).

This series of books, which began with the Southwest, is all about personal fulfillment and personal change. I hope that you will find your special, natural place, and that it will transport you to a different place.

PART 1

Along the Pacific Coast

From Northern California to the Canadian border, the Pacific Coast offers an amazing diversity in its topography, climate, and vegetation. The Northern California coast is often shrouded in mist and has abundant rainfall from fall through spring, providing the ideal climate for coastal redwoods to thrive. Some of the old-growth redwoods in Redwood National Park are the tallest living things on Earth.

The redwoods are seen in their northernmost habitat along the Oregon coast, but a few miles north of the California border, the coastal strip becomes covered with huge, sprawling dunes, with long, expansive beaches pounded by angry surf and pine-clad mountains sloping to meet the dunes. Farther north, the coastal region in Oregon is a more tranquil place, where peaceful beaches welcome sun lovers and tranquil farming valleys produce milk, butter, and some of the most treasured cheeses in the nation. The seas and winds rise again, approaching the mouth of the Columbia River—a watery graveyard for hundreds of ships, from the earliest days of western exploration for a passage from the Pacific to the Atlantic, to today's fragile fishing vessels.

The coastline of Washington is a study in contrasts. To the south, the Long Beach Peninsula (the longest sand spit on the

Pacific Coast) beckons travelers to stay in old-fashioned vacation towns and even to drive on the beach. The scene changes dramatically north of the peninsula, where the Olympic Mountains create their own climatic patterns, harboring the dampest temperate rain forest in the world, the Hoh, with glaciers capping the nearby Olympic peaks. To the west, the Olympic coast provides magnificent opportunities for viewing wildlife on rugged hikes along the shoreline. Here, Native American tribes live a traditional life, based on harvesting the riches of the sea.

But a few miles away lies the great inland sea—Puget Sound—sheltered from the winds and waves of the Pacific by the Olympic Peninsula. Hundreds of miles of quiet shoreline are indented by deep fjords, with wakes traced by Washington state ferries taking visitors to historic waterside towns, including those of the idyllic San Juan Archipelago, which lies at the northern reaches of the sound.

Three of these regions are featured in this chapter, while the Olympic Peninsula is covered in Part 3, Rain Forests (starting on page 181). There could be no greater contrast in moods than in the dark, mysterious depths of Redwood National Park, the bucolic landscape and tranquil waters of the San Juan Islands, and the broad, storm-dashed beaches of the Oregon coast. All are affected by the currents of the Pacific Ocean and the variable conditions brought about by the vagaries of mountain shadows, El Niño, the continental jet stream, and other unknown effects of nature.

While the San Juan Islands have remained in a largely natural state because of their relative isolation from nearby cities and industrial areas in the Northwest, the prime natural places along California's redwood coast have been preserved due to a small group of preservationists. Back in the mid-1800s, another small group of Americans, lumber company owners, regarded the redwood forests as an area ready-made for exploitation. The timber barons connived to structure fraudulent schemes that would eventually put the forests in the hands of fewer than a half-dozen companies. This unlawful activity—the "selling" of individually owned forest tracts of 160 acres, obtained for $250 per acre, to the major lumber companies—was so blatant that in 1888, the federal government was forced to investigate the land transfers and found bribery, coercion, and outright fraud.

Indictments were issued against eight people, including two north coast lumber barons, Joseph Russ and David Evans. However, only one of the eight conspirators was convicted, and the transfer of land continued for many years.

The idea of designating a redwood park on the north coast was first bandied about in the 1850s when Henry Crabb, a California assemblyman, tried to stop the sale of redwood lands. Secretary of the Interior Carl Schurz tried the same tactic in 1879, but neither request was acted upon. Throughout the ensuing years, several plans were brought forward, including one approved by President Theodore Roosevelt. Only one redwood park existed at that time: Big Basin State Park near Santa Cruz. The movement began in earnest when, in 1918, the Save-the-Redwoods League was formed in San Francisco. Beginning with transferring land to the state parks system, the League focused on establishing Humboldt Redwoods State Park in southern Humboldt County. Three northern state parks were added during the next six years.

Park development languished until the 1960s, when the League teamed with the Sierra Club and the National Geographic Society to push the concept of a federal redwood park, meeting much opposition from the north coast timber companies. Legislation was passed in October 1968, and

Tree frog

President Lyndon Johnson signed into law a Redwood National Park of 58,000 acres, about half of which was already contained in the three associated state parks included in the new park system. The timber companies reacted badly and began to cut massive parts of adjacent timberlands on the Redwood Creek drainage south of the new park . The hills above the creek were shorn of the erosion-controlling trees. Rains brought down thousands of tons of mud and debris, which rolled down the creek, threatening the Tall Trees area containing the tallest trees in the United States (and perhaps the world).

The groups that supported the park lobbied mightily in Washington, D.C., with California representative Phillip Burton writing a bill to expand Redwood National Park. President Jimmy Carter signed the expansion legislation in 1978, adding 48,000 acres of Bald Hills territory to the park. Most of the land had already been clear-cut. The amount of $400 million was paid to the lumber companies (full market value). Close to two million acres of prime redwoods had been cut. The consolation is that, for all time, enough precious redwood land has been preserved to once again allow nature to do its work in growing a mature redwood forest. Redwood National Park will be a perpetual inspiration to those who treasure natural places for their intrinsic value as well as their beneficial role in maintaining the balance of life on the planet.

The preservation of the prime natural areas along the Oregon coast is mainly the result of state and federal actions, which have resulted in a superb group of seaside and mountain ecosystems cobbled together into a significantly protected coastline, with national forests preserving much of the coastal ranges lining the Oregon coast. State parks and beaches, national recreation areas, county parks, and two national forests feature an amazing variety of coastal and forest environments, from the California border to the mouth of the Columbia River.

The three superb natural areas lie within a few hours' drive of each other, providing a perfect vacation atmosphere, whatever your interests. And nearby are other natural places that deserve attention, on and off the beaten track, endowed with a profusion of natural beauty and a sense of tranquility.

Redwood National Park

To call the tall sequoia of northeastern California "survivors" is an extreme understatement. The old-growth forests lying between Eureka and Crescent City, in the thin band of coastal land between the Pacific Coast and the Siskiyou Mountains, contain the most magnificent examples of *Sequoia sempervirens* in the world. The tallest trees grow to a height of more than 350 feet and live to a ripe old age of more than a thousand years. The tallest live along creek beds and on bottomlands, their roots dipping into gravel beds washed down the mountainsides over millions of years. They are joined in this well-watered zone by other evergreens, including Douglas fir, Sitka spruce, and western hemlock.

Living trees are accompanied by standing dead trees, which provide nesting places for many birds and animals. Huge fallen, moss-covered trunks slowly decompose, breaking down into soil that attracts seeds falling from the tall trees. The seeds sprout and become new sequoia, sometimes growing in a straight line, above the "nurse" tree, or growing in magnificent "cathedral" circles, fed by the rotted roots of a long-gone ancient sequoia. This sequence maintains the cycle of life in a forest free from disturbance.

Below the forest canopy, nurtured by the slanting rays of the sun, are smaller trees—tan oak, California hazel, and cascara. On the floor, sword and wood ferns grow in wide swaths, with salal, red huckleberry, and rhododendron in profusion.

Wildflowers grow even in the deep forest—fairybells, sorrel, violets, and trillium—while the more open areas are favored by such flowering plants as clintonia, broad-leaved lupine, Indian paintbrush, and fireweed.

What is most unusual about these associated parks, with their 200 miles of trails, is the immense diversity in landscape and wildlife found. Most people driving along Highway 101 can easily see them as coastal parks, spread along the not so pacific ocean, with long beaches, scenic bluffs with rocky headlands, tide pools, and rivers that interrupt the trails along the oceanside. But this is also a park of meadows and forests, and not just the famed redwoods for whose benefit the parks were created. There are grassy prairies spread out over the Bald Hills. Oak woodlands dot the prairie hills. Thick, deep mixed forests are found in the valleys and creek canyons, with Douglas fir, Sitka spruce, western hemlock, bigleaf maple, tan oak, alder, and many more. There are also seaside marshes in several of the creek and river estuaries, harboring shorebirds, including many transient species.

So this is not just about taking a walk among the redwoods or sitting on a beach mesmerized by the surf. Redwood National Park is about enjoying the sights, smells, and sounds of a wealth of natural experiences in an amazing range of ecosystems framed by the sea on one side and the foothills of the Coast Mountain Range on the other, with canyons and prairies that offer a diverse and interdependent group of biotic communities.

How to Get There

From the south, the parks are easily accessible by driving along Highway 101, which turns toward the coast at Leggett in Humboldt County and follows the shoreline to Crescent City. Except for the northernmost park section, all of the national and state park attractions and trails are found beside or near Highway 101.

From the north, Highway 101 crosses the Oregon border north of Crescent City. A scenic sideroad provides a shortcut to Jedediah Smith Redwoods State Park, just south of the state boundary. Highway 197, also called North Bank Road, connects

Highway 101 with U.S. Highway 199 and the village of Hiouchi. There is a state park information center west of Hiouchi.

From the east, U.S. Highway 199 leads from Grants Pass, Oregon, crossing through Jedediah Smith Redwoods State Park.

From the west, Highway 199 is the route to take (from Highway 101) to access the trails and groves in Jedediah Smith Redwoods State Park. This route also leads to several recreation areas in the Six Rivers National Forest. A forest ranger station is located in Gasquet, six miles east of Hiouchi.

Area Roads

The area encompassed by Redwood National Park and the three state parks stretches from about five miles north of Crescent City (Jedediah Smith Redwoods State Park) to the south along a narrow coastal strip—containing Del Norte Redwoods State Park and Prairie Creek Redwoods State Park—to the main portion of Redwood National Park, located south of the Prairie Creek Visitor Center on Elk Prairie. A narrow strip of seaside parkland extends down the coast to the edge of Freshwater Lagoon and Stone Lagoon. You'll find the southern Redwood National Park Visitor Center beside Highway 101, just north of the lagoons. The major national park area is inland, on both sides of Redwood Creek, and here you'll find two significant redwood stands: Lady Bird Johnson Grove and Tall Trees Grove.

Linking the state parks are small sections of the national park, which create a contiguous strip of parkland along the coast accessed by Highway 101. A former section of Highway 101, now called the Newton B. Drury Scenic Parkway, leads through Prairie Creek Redwoods State Park. Highway 101 bypasses the parklands for about 10 miles, leading inland to the towns of Klamath and Requa. Coastal Drive, another park road, follows the coastline where Highway 101 becomes the bypass route. This eight-mile scenic road can be accessed from a point just south of the Klamath River Bridge. The route meets the Drury Parkway southwest of the parkway intersection with Highway 101.

The other interior park route is Bald Hills Road, which joins Highway 101 just north of the town of Orick and the national park visitor center. With 15 percent grades, this road, while suitable for cars and pickups, is not suggested for trailers and motor homes. Bald Hills Road snakes along the hills, east of Redwood Creek, offering access to Lady Bird Johnson Grove, the Redwood Creek Overlook, and the Tall Trees Trail. Permits are required for entry to the Redwood Creek Trail and the Tall Trees area. These permits can be obtained only at the southern national park visitor center.

Native Inhabitants

The coastal tribes occupied what we know as the Humboldt and Del Norte coast for at least 1,000 years, perhaps from as far back as 5,000 years. The Yurok, Tolowa, Chilula, Wiyot, Hoopa, Mattole, and Sinkyone each had a piece of the region, living off the land and particularly the sea. In the area now preserved within Redwood National Park, the Yurok occupied the northern section on both sides of the Klamath River (the Chilula lived in the southern area, along Redwood Creek). The Yurok were grouped in 54 river and coastal communities. Riverside towns were established on terraces, high above flood level—a smarter location than the flood plain towns of the settlers. These were small, manageable communities, the largest containing only 25 houses. Salmon and acorns were the principal diet, providing an abundance of food for two meals each day. The Yurok made dugout canoes, constructed over several months, and often traded to nearby tribes, which treasured the redwood vessels.

Tools were made from bone, stone, and wood. Salmon spears were tipped with deer horn or carved hardwood. Nature, and a little effort, provided a rich storehouse of food for the tribe.

Unlike the Yurok, the Chilula did not live on the coast, but occupied the inland area near the Tall Trees of the Redwood Creek area. The Chilula were hunters and gatherers, although they did catch some fish for food. Like the Yurok, they built plank houses, usually square, with steep, pitched roofs. They also constructed square sweat houses and circular dance houses on the prairie lands of the Bald Hills. Elk and deer were hunted to provide year-round food, and acorns were also important in the Chilula diet. Clothing was fashioned from animal skins and plants. Both tribes managed the land and the forest to their (and the forest's) advantage. Each year, the Chilula burned sections of their hillsides to generate fresh vegetation, which promoted foraging by game animals and regenerated the woodlands.

It was a peaceful, sufficient life for all of the coastal tribes, until the mid-1800s. The first European explorers arrived on the coast in 1775. During the 1820s and 1830s, fur trappers and traders came through the Humboldt region, and in 1848, gold was discovered on the Trinity River, then on the Klamath. Settlement began at nearby Trinidad in March 1850, the same year that saw the first sawmill established at Eureka. The Chilula, particularly, resented the intrusion and opposed it with raiding parties, engaging in a guerrilla war through the early 1860s. While the Chilula were successful in driving set-tlers out of the Bald Hills, they eventually signed a peace treaty in 1864, resulting in their relocation to the Hoopa Reservation. By the early 1900s, only a few Chilula remained on their tradi-tional land.

Early Days on the North Coast

The modern history of this land on the California/Oregon bor-der dates from about 1850, after gold was discovered in the two major rivers and inside Oregon at the town of Gold River. Just a year after the stupendous strike in the Sierra foothills, a rush of prospectors and miners came to northwest rivers. Because of the difficulty of reaching the area by overland routes across the mountains, the miners came up the coast, disembarking at Trinidad, Union (now Arcata), Crescent City, and Eureka. San Francisco was the main staging point for the transportation of people and goods by ship. Along with the miners came service people, including merchants, saloon keepers, and muleskinners.

As in other areas, the mining boom quickly turned to bust, and local settlers took to lumbering to stabilize the economy. For more than a century, the redwoods, Douglas firs, and spruces were taken down and transported to sawmills in the smaller communities and later to larger mills in the major towns. Before World War II, logging met the demand for lumber for house construction and redwood coffins, wood for papermaking, and myriad other uses for trees. There were few employment options for the residents of this isolated, rural district (it was not until the 1920s that the Redwood Highway was constructed, providing a motor route through the region; until then, the ocean had provided the lifeline to the outside).

Then, in 1939, after decades of successful logging enterprise, Hobbs, Wall, and Company, the area's only lumber company and its largest employer, closed its mills. The dispirited residents became so angry over their impoverished state that they joined with groups in southern Oregon, in November 1941, to attempt to secede from California and form the new state of Jefferson. The border rebellion came to naught with the bombing of Pearl Harbor on December 7 and the U.S. declaration of war.

Following the war, logging was revived, and more than 25 mills were in operation in Del Norte County alone. However, the steady decline in lumbering since the 1950s and the preservation of redwood groves such as those in Redwood National Park largely decimated the mills and logging operations. Most of the commercial timber had already been cut, with only huge clearcut areas remaining to scar the landscape. More than 90 percent of the region's timberland has been harvested over the past hundred years. Lumber companies have instituted tree farms and planting schemes and are now farming their forests—to realize new product years in the future. One large redwood plant remains in Arcata, and Pacific Lumber still operates its lumber plant farther south in Humboldt County.

The original two million acres of old-growth redwood forests in northwest California have shrunk, through cutting, to fewer than 90,000 acres. By the 1960s, the original redwood forest had almost disappeared. However, the remaining stands preserve notable samples of *Sequoia sempervirens* and are the result of strong lobbying actions by several environmental groups, notably the Save-the-Redwoods League, which has been instrumental in persuading governments to preserve the outstanding groves remaining today.

North Coast Geology

The topography of the redwoods coastline is the result of plate tectonics, the grinding of the Gorda (Pacific) and North American plates. With the Gorda plate folding under the North American plate, the upper crust was folded and crumpled, and faulted into what is now called the Franciscan Formation. Over eons, the sea rose and receded, only to rise again about 5,000 years ago, covering much of the coastal land and creating the bays and indentations that are seen today. This is an extremely unstable geologic area, with frequent earthquakes centered in the ocean west of Eureka and off the Lost Coast area west of the King Range. The most recent large shake-up occurred in April 1992, when an earthquake of 7.1 magnitude off the Lost Coast caused significant damage to the communities of Ferndale and Fortuna. Additional, and more intense, earthquakes are expected over the next hundred years. Earthquake effects and fault lines can be seen throughout the Redwood National Park region.

The folding of the incoming plate has resulted in a growing mass of conglomerate—sandstone, siltstone, volcanic rock—deposited on top of the upper plate. This accumulation, largely gravel, has been augmented by rock and silt brought down from the coast mountains, and in this bed the tall redwoods grow. The most prominent geological features in the parks are the cliffs known as the Gold Bluffs. Rising to a height of about 200 feet, the bluffs are cut by creeks with some deep scouring, creating gorges, including the scenic Fern Canyon. Other features include sea stacks (sandstone rocks sitting just offshore) near the mouths of Lagoon and Wilson creeks.

Climate

This is the Humboldt coast: a cool, misty landscape, with rugged headlands poking into the Pacific; large, sheltering bays; and mountains to the east. The rain pounds the coastal lands during winter months, filling the creeks, sometimes to the flooding point. The creeks feed the mountain water into prime salmon rivers. Spring is cool, windy, and often rainy, spurring the flowers to bloom, providing the needed water table for the shallow root systems. There is no such thing as a thoroughly dry season. Summer brings little rain but much fog, as the mists flow eastward from the ocean into the coastal regions. Fall, the most amenable season for visitors, may bring some rain (mostly in the evenings), but the days are largely sunny, with spectacular sunsets lighting the golden grass on the rolling coastal hills.

The region receives an average of 70 inches of rain per year. Snow is rare, falling only on the higher ridges, including the Bald Hills in Jedediah Smith Redwoods State Park. Winter rains can be fierce, falling in torrents that sometimes cause great flooding of the creeks and rivers. The year 1955 was a banner year for rain, resulting in December floods battering several communities on the Klamath River. Other north coast communities were also affected. A more severe storm in December 1964 caused the Klamath to rise to 18 feet above flood stage. The town of Klamath was severely hit, with but one building saved from the flood's ravages.

Crescent City was less severely affected but suffered significant damage. Rainy season often extends from October through April. While damaging to humans, this abundant rainfall aided by summer mists feeds the redwoods. Nature does have a plan, not always acceptable to people who insist on building in flood plains. But without the rain and the high water table, the tall sequoia would not be found along the Pacific Coast.

As you might expect from a coastal area, temperatures are moderate year-round. Summer highs on the beaches rarely exceed 80°F, while inland temperatures can rise to 100°F. January is the coldest month, with daytime temperatures between 45°F and 50°F.

Park Wildlife

What strikes the visitor to this collection of parks is the wide range of ecological communities and the amazing range of plant and animal life contained within these very different zones. Along the coast are spruce forests and the coastal strand consisting of beaches and dunes, marshes, and lagoons. Stretching for many miles beside the Pacific, the coastal communities feature an amazing ecosystem based on salt-loving plants, water and beach insects, the shorebirds that come to feed on this insect buffet, and the mammals that emerge at night, including the gray fox, bobcats, skunks, weasels, and coyotes. Overhead, red-tailed and Swainson's hawks circle the sky, waiting to spot the right rodent for their next meal, including mice and the California vole.

The lagoons are home to bulrushes, cattails, and pond lilies. This is where you'll find the herons (great blue and green-backed) and red-winged blackbirds. The notable lagoon communities are found at Crescent Beach, near Lagoon Creek; Freshwater Lagoon, next to the southern information center, off Highway 101; and Espa Lagoon. More marshy areas are found at the mouths of several rivers and creeks along the Gold Bluffs, accessed by the Coastal Trail. Elk and beaver are often seen at the base of the bluffs, joined by marsh birds including the Virginia rail.

While the parks are noted primarily for their stands of redwoods, a major woodland community found in several park areas is dominated by the oak. Grassland prairies containing oaks are found close to the shore, notably at Elk Prairie and near the mouth of Ossagon Creek on top of the Gold Bluffs and on the uplands areas in the Bald Hills. In this higher region, you'll find both Oregon white oak and California black oak. The oaks and the occasional bigleaf maple provide shade for animals and homes for many birds, as the grasses offer protection and a home for rodents, the basic group on the prairie food chain. Gophers, voles, and mice are abundant, making it easy for hunters, among them several varieties of hawk, including kestrels and northern harriers, and turkey vultures. Roosevelt elk and black-tailed deer feed on the upland prairies and also on the lower prairie habitats, particularly on the grasslands in the Gold Bluffs area.

Over the past 10 years, the elusive marbled murrelet (or fog lark) has confounded ecologists and loggers alike. This seabird lives in coastal forests from Alaska through Northern California and, because of its rarity, has been declared an endangered species in the U.S. and Canada. They are reclusive birds that seem to live only in the canopies of old-growth forests, laying their eggs on clumps of moss and rarely building nests. The murrelcts, and their endangered state, are part of the logging disputes of the past decade. Recent studies have stated that the most successful group of marbled murrelets live in the dense forests of Redwood National Park and the three state parks. The murrelets in this area are not often seen, but

Belted kingfisher

some have been captured and equipped with transmitters for the ongoing study.

Riparian habitats are found along the many streams that bring water from the mountains to the sea. Here, broadleaf plants grow on the woodland floor, while deciduous trees including bigleaf maple, vine maple, and red alder predominate above. Along the streams you'll find low-growing lady fern, red elderberry, salmonberry, and monkeyflower. Osprey and kingfishers survey the scene looking for fish, including cutthroat trout, chinook and silver salmon, and steelhead. The best year for salmon runs in some 50 years was 1995, with the hope that the salmon population has recovered from its long decline.

Another beloved species is the banana slug. This slimy specimen is often seen along the oceanfront and on the floor of the redwood and fir/spruce forests, including the entrance to the Redwood Information Center. You can tell that a banana slug is in the area when you spot its slime trail. The invertebrate is celebrated in an annual festival that includes slug races held in mid-August at Prairie Creek Redwoods State Park.

The redwood forest has two incarnations: old-growth and severely damaged. The old-growth forest, comprised of tall *sempervirens*, features other conifers including Douglas fir, western hemlock, and Sitka spruce, plus several shorter deciduous species. The undergrowth is filled with redwood sorrel, mock azalea, rhododendron, and red huckleberry. Trillium is found in the darkest parts of the redwood forest. Poison oak, while beautiful in the fall, is one plant that needs to be remembered while departing from park trails.

Much of the land in the most recently acquired southern section of Redwood National Park is previously forested area bearing the scars of clear-cutting. Vast swaths of cleared areas are now beginning to regenerate, but the mature results will not be seen within the lifetime of anyone living today. Three hundred years from now, visitors to Redwood National Park will be in awe of the "ancient" stands of sequoia, which are now little more than barren wastes of tumbled logs and eroded hillsides.

The Parks

Covering the redwood parks area from north to south, a tour of the region begins in the most undeveloped of the parks, in the foothills of the Siskiyou Mountains, then leads south along the coast before moving inland again to the area near Orick.

JEDEDIAH SMITH REDWOODS STATE PARK

The northernmost portion of the parks system is found north of Crescent City, via Highway 199, and is the former home of the Tolowa people, who had two communities in the area. The park started as a 20-acre tract but languished until 1939, when the state obtained a little less than 7,000 acres from the Del Norte Lumber Company for the grand sum of $80,000. The park was eventually named for Jedediah Smith, the explorer, trapper, and mountain man who conducted a trek through the rugged Siskiyou Mountains—on his way to the Rockies—in 1828. The park information center, open during the summer and fall months, is found just east of Hiouchi, 4.9 miles from the Highway 101 intersection. While the park is largely undeveloped, visitors may fish, swim, camp, hike, and float down the Smith River. Interpretive walks are conducted in July and August. The park trails are described later in this chapter.

The Howland Hill Drive provides a scenic route through the park, connecting the Hiouchi area with Crescent City. The road rambles through the southern part of the park, following an old logging track. The route begins by taking South Fork Road at its junction with Highway 199, and then taking Douglas Park Road and Howland Hill Road, joining Elk Valley Road for the final couple of miles before reaching Highway 101 near Crescent City. The road is narrow, with gravel in spots, becoming a narrow one-lane road that requires caution while meeting oncoming traffic. You'll find a raft launching site along South Fork Road before meeting Douglas Park Road. The route also provides access to trailheads for the Stout Grove Loop Trail and the Little Bald Hills Trail. Howland Hill Road follows Mill Creek, past the trailhead for the Mill Creek–Nickerson Ranch Trail.

Five miles down the road is the Boy Scout Tree Trail. A mile beyond the trailhead is the Howland Hill Giant, a huge redwood to the left of the road. The road then climbs to the ridge summit, leaving the park. You may wish to take Bertsch Road to the Mill Creek Horse Trail, which connects with the Redwood National Park's Rellim Ridge Trail. Turn left onto Elk Valley Road for the final leg to Crescent City.

Hiouchi is a roadside village, providing camping supplies, a cafe, motel, gas station, and a private RV park and campground. To the east is the Smith River National Recreation Area.

CRESCENT BEACH AREA

This region of varied attractions is located just south of Crescent City, accessed by taking Humboldt Road—off Highway 101—to Enderts Beach Road, which leads south (left) to the beach. This is the part of Redwood National Park that was once the Alexander-Pozzi Ranch, a dairy farm established in 1869. A turnoff leads to the Crescent Beach Picnic Area and the Crescent Beach Trail. A fine overlook—a wooden platform jutting over the cliff—is located two miles beyond the turnoff. The road is not suitable for trailers beyond the picnic area. At the end of the road is Endert's Beach and the trailhead to the Nickel Creek Primitive Campsite. This is also the trailhead for the Coastal Trail, which leads south above the coastline to the Klamath Overlook.

DEL NORTE REDWOODS STATE PARK

An 11.3-mile stretch of Highway 101 runs through the park, from the edge of Crescent City to Wilson Creek, with the north end at the junction of Humboldt Road and Enderts Beach Road. Established in 1925, the park then encompassed a single grove of 157 acres but quickly grew to more than 2,300 acres. Logging had taken place before the park was established, and the resulting cutover land is still visible when driving across the park. This is most apparent when taking a short sidetrip along Hamilton Road (0.8 mile from the northern boundary). This road leads east, past an old railroad trestle, to the parking area for the Miller-Rellim Lodge and the trailhead for the Rellim Ridge Trail. By following this national park trail, you'll pass through clear-cut land, now in the early stage of regeneration.

The highway climbs to the top of a ridge. There's a turnoff to a short road leading east to the Mill Creek Campground. This is a wonderful campground, with 145 sites, set next to the stream. Trailheads offer hikes along the Trestle Trail, Saddler Skyline Trail (along an old rail bed), the Nature Loop Trail, Mill Creek Trail, and the Hobbs Wall Trail—a loop walk to the ridge. This is an area harvested by the Hobbs Wall Lumber Company.

Eight miles through the park, the Damnation Creek Trail crosses a ridge, leading to wonderful ocean views from a bluff. Part of the 2.1-mile (one way) trail route is along an old wagon road.

KLAMATH RIVER AREA

The Klamath River has its source in the Cascade Mountains of southern Oregon. It falls through the Coast Range on a journey of 260 miles. This is one of the great salmon rivers of the Northwest.

South of the Del Norte Redwoods Park boundary, a narrow section of the national park leads along the coast, joining Del Norte to Prairie Creek Redwoods State Park. The Klamath River cuts this section in two. The Coastal Trail leads down the coast to the river mouth. Meanwhile, Highway 101 turns inland, running outside the park boundary. The Trees of Mystery is a privately owned attraction featuring a walk through the woods (fancified with fairy-tale characters), a souvenir store, and museum. A motel and restaurant are located across the road.

Requa Road leads west to Requa. This rustic hamlet sits beside the Klamath River, with fine views of the ocean. Requa was once a busy cannery town, dating back to 1876 when a salt-fish packing operation was started. A sawmill followed in 1881. The town became an agricultural center (dairy farming), but in 1914 a great fire destroyed much of the community. The town was rebuilt, with salmon the major product for several decades. The canneries closed following the banning of commercial fishing on the Klamath in 1934. The river is still a mecca for sports anglers. The northern section of the Coastal Trail comes to an end at the Klamath Overlook. A short side trail leads down the hill to another viewpoint. There are picnic tables and restrooms at the site.

The town of Klamath has had a checkered life, plagued by local hostilities, several massive floods, and the up-and-down economy of the region. The town received a new lease on life when Highway 101 was relocated and the old Douglas Memorial Bridge was built in 1926. A new business section was built, based on the tourist and fishing trade. You'll find a gas station, RV parks, a store, tackle shop, and the obligatory burl shop—at least one is found in every community along the redwood coast.

Just south of Klamath and immediately north of the newer bridge is State Highway 169, which leads along the river across Turwer Creek to the Klamath Glen fishing resort.

COASTAL DRIVE

This dramatic drive of 8.8 miles lies west of the Highway 101 bypass, along what was the old Redwood Highway and Klamath Beach Road. Klamath Beach Road is the access road, from its intersection with Highway 101, just south of the Klamath River Bridge, to the mouth of the river. Klamath Beach Road is a two-lane highway that drops almost to river level, passing the south end of the old Douglas Memorial Bridge, which was swept away in the great flood of 1964. Its opening, in 1926, was highly celebrated, for it was the last link in the coastal highway, linking Oregon with California. Before this, the river had to be crossed by ferry. After the 1964 flood, a new, higher bridge was built a mile upriver.

Across the highway from the bridge ruin, Alder Camp Road leads southwest—an alternate route that cuts off the drive to the rivermouth, connecting with the old Redwood Highway section of Coastal Drive. If you continue on Klamath Beach Road, you'll reach an overlook, with views of the mouth of the Klamath River and the remains of Dad's Camp, an old fishing resort that eroded away thanks to the predation of the Klamath River. The small cemetery is that of the Shortman-Williams family, which owned and operated the resort. Charlie and Annie Williams founded the resort in 1914.

Coastal Drive leads south, past the Flint Ridge (primitive) Campground, and a fascinating World War II oddity. This is the section previously known as the County Wagon Road. Between the campground road and the High Bluff Picnic Area is a collection of rustic buildings known as "Farm B-71." This is a wartime radar station in disguise, built of concrete blocks with wooden planks for camouflage and with fake windows and trim. Parts of the road are narrow with gravel sections.

The drive continues to the Gold Bluffs Overlook, located at a pullout, with coastal views. Before the overlook is a road that runs to Alder Camp, a state minimum-security prison. The Coastal Trail resumes at a parking lot beside the road. The northern part of the trail leads along the beach, which is accessible at low tide only. The route enters Prairie Creek Redwoods State Park for a final mile before meeting Newton Drury Parkway. Highway 101 is reached by taking Drury Parkway (turn left) for another mile.

PRAIRIE CREEK REDWOODS STATE PARK

The most highly developed areas of the park system lie within this state park, founded in 1923 when benefactor Zipporah Russ donated 160 acres of canyon land. The Save-the-Redwoods League went into action, in 1931, when it obtained nearly 5,000 acres of adjoining land from a timber firm. The Civilian Conservation Corps established a camp on Elk Prairie and built fences, a suspension bridge, and the park visitor center. Fern Canyon was added to the park in 1965. When the Highway 101 bypass was finished, in 1992, the old stretch of 101 that ran through the park became an interior park road, the Newton B. Drury Parkway. Drury was the first secretary of the Save-the-Redwoods League.

Elk Prairie, Fern Canyon, and the Gold Bluffs are the major centers of interest in the park. Roosevelt elk are often seen on both the prairie and the grasslands above the bluffs. The story of the survival of the western elk is another triumph for the League. Following the total decimation of the eastern elk (in the 1850s) and then the grizzly bear in California (by 1910), hunters continued to shoot elk for their meat and hides. Only one small herd remained by the mid-1930s, and that herd lived on the coast near Orick. In 1948, the League convinced the state to set aside an elk refuge in Prairie Creek Redwoods State Park. From as few as 15 elk (an estimate in the 1920s), the refuge served to revive the wapiti herd. Within seven years, 1,000 elk were living in three herds, south and north of the Klamath River. The elk are seen in large groups within the park, offering close-up views of this once-endangered species. The foresight of the League has led to the establishment of other elk refuges, including the program at Point Reyes National Seashore.

Entering the park from Highway 101, along the Drury Parkway, the park visitor center and campground are found on Elk Prairie, near the southern edge of the state park area. The visitor center has a small interpretive display, a bookstore, and an information desk. Several trails lead from the prairie: along Prairie Creek, to Cathedral Trees, and along Miner's Ridge. Three short walks are available: the Five Minute Trail begins behind the visitor center, leading to several spectacular trees; the Redwood Access Trail and Revelation Trail are both easy walks and both are handicapped-accessible. The Foothill Trail, Rhododendron Trail, and the Nature Trail are also in the area. The James Irvine Trail leads across the park in a northwest direction, providing access to Fern Canyon Trail.

Two backroads take visitors to unique park areas. Just north of the visitor center turnoff, Cal-Barrel Road is a short (2.5-mile) gravel road that leads east, up a ridge and through a redwood forest, coming to a dead end. This road is open from 9 A.M. to 5 P.M. A longer route, which could provide a full day of activity, is the drive to the Gold Bluffs. The drive begins on Highway 101, north of Orick and south of the Highway 101/Drury Parkway intersection. Begin by taking Davison Road, which leads west from Highway 101. The road passes across a section of prairie sometimes occupied by elk. The Davison Ranch was recently obtained by Redwood National Park. As the pavement ends, the road climbs and then descends toward the sea. The Jogging Trail leads north at the two-mile mark. Nearly four miles from the highway, the route reaches the ocean and the entrance station to Prairie Creek Redwoods State Park. The roadway is now called Gold Bluffs Beach Road. Espa Lagoon is the first natural feature along the road, which runs northward, and below the bluffs, which are as high as 200 feet. A picnic area is located next to a pullout, 4.4 miles from Highway 101. Farther north is the Gold Bluffs Beach Campground, with more than two dozen sites in the dunes. Several trailheads are found in this area, including the entrance to the Gold Bluffs Beach Trail.

The road continues for another mile, reaching another picnic area before coming to the end and a parking lot. There are restrooms and a picnic area off the turnaround. You'll find additional trails here, including the wonderful Fern Canyon Loop Trail. This short trail, less than a mile long, leads through the fern-covered gorge, with short side trails leading to scenic points including a small waterfall, returning to the starting point by climbing to the bluff top, and connecting with the James Irvine Trail to return to the parking lot. There is no better way to spend an hour, or a day, along the bluffs and on the beach!

THE BALD HILLS

Before the 1850s, the high, rolling grasslands and oak woodlands of the bald hills were occupied by two symbiotic groups: the Chilula people and a huge herd of elk. By 1865, after the arrival of ranchers and hunters, the Chilula had retreated to the Hoopa Reservation, and the elk had been almost eliminated. Sheep farms had taken over the area. This vast area is now the southeastern portion of Redwood National Park. It contains the Lady Bird Johnson Grove and the Tall Trees Grove; both are standouts. The road climbs to over 3,000 feet, and on the way, it passes through several prairies and through several wooded coniferous areas, primarily second-growth forest, with some areas in the early stages of regeneration. Much of the Bald Hills region is oak woodland and is not seen closer to the coast.

The road is found a half-mile north of the town of Orick. At its start, it is a two-lane, paved route that crosses Prairie Creek and the last lumber operation left in the area. It quickly enters the parkland, with a paved road leading to the Redwood Creek Trail (permit required), the Tall Trees shuttle bus station, and a picnic area. The main road climbs through a thick forest, passing several old logging roads. The turnoff for Lady Bird Johnson Grove is found immediately after crossing under a wooden footbridge. The Lady Bird Johnson Grove Loop Trail features a walk through a magnificent sequoia grove (see page 24). There's a picnic area with restrooms at the trailhead.

Beyond the Johnson Grove turnoff, Bald Hills Road continues through a grove of Douglas fir and through a mixed forest before coming out into Gans Prairie. The Holter Ridge Bike Trail leads left (east) from the roadside. Redwood Creek Overlook provides fine views of the canyon, plus restrooms and a picnic area. There is an old-growth redwood forest covering some 9,000 acres, one of the largest remaining old-growth stands anywhere.

The Tall Trees Access Road, at mile 7.1, is closed to private vehicles during the busy summer months but is accessible by permit during the rest of the year. Permits may be obtained at the Redwood Information Center, on Highway 101 south of Orick. Shuttle buses are used in summer to transport visitors to the Tall Trees. At the bottom of this six-mile drive (a former logging road) is the loop trail leading to the world's tallest redwood and its companions in this ancient grove.

As Bald Hills Road continues, an old barn marks the site of the Sherman Lyons Ranch, first a pioneer farm, and then one of the largest sheep ranching operations in the region. At the 10-mile point is Johnson Road, a one-lane gravel track that leads north to the Klamath River and the village of Johnson. The main route passes Dolason Prairie, where a short road leads to a parking lot with a picnic area and toilet. Here is the trailhead for the Dolason Prairie Trail, which leads past the old Donaldson Farm site (the name was subsequently misspelled) to other trails that lead to the Tall Trees parking area.

Passing Counts Hill Prairie, Bald Hills Road reaches a height of land that provides stunning views of the prairie and Schoolhouse Peak before passing through Child's Hill Prairie. At mile 17, a sideroad runs to the Lyons Ranch Historic Site. There is a parking area from which walkers may pass a locked gate to take a walk along an old road to the first of the Lyons family's ranches in the Bald Hills area. The main road continues east, past other old barns. Lookout Road offers another walk to a viewpoint at the Schoolhouse Peak Fire Lookout (el. 3,092 feet). The road leaves the national park lands after climbing to the ridge above Coyote Creek, at the 19-mile point. It is not necessary to retrace the route for the return to Highway 101, although Bald Hills Road is the shorter route to the Drury Parkway. But there is more scenery to experience. East of the park boundary, the road forks with French Camp Road leading to the Hoopa Valley and Highways 96 and 299.

Bald Hills Road (the left fork) continues to Martin's Ferry, on the Klamath River, and Highway 101 is reached via Highways 96 and 299.

In the springtime, the Bald Hills are decorated with wild-flowers, including impressive rhododendron displays, and smaller plants, including columbine, lupine, leopard lily, trillium, delphinium, flowering currant, and many other colorful woodland flowers. The national park area preserves not only several significant redwood groves but one of the finest foothill woodland environments in the state, once the home of large elk herds and now being reclaimed as a special reserve where elk and other species may once again roam free.

ORICK AREA

Highway 101 links several points of interest along the coastline, between the national park boundary (just north of the town), and Prairie Creek Redwoods State Park, eight miles to the north. The Redwoods Information Center, at Freshwater Lagoon, marks the southern boundary, an area of expansive beaches and wetlands with boardwalks and good views of the estuary at the mouth of Redwood Creek. The highway leads north into the Redwood Creek Valley and into Orick. Once a thriving sawmill community (only one mill remains), Orick was a dairy center with a cheese factory and became famed for fishing in the 1920s. Sawmills boomed throughout the 1940s and 1950s, as the redwoods and firs were felled on the nearby hills. Orick residents and the Save-the-Redwoods League were on opposite sides of the battle to establish a national park in the area. However, lumbering had gone into decline before the park was developed, with most of the mills closing and Orick becoming a pale shadow of its former size. It now capitalizes on the tourists who come to visit the remaining redwoods; it is a shopping center for campers and others who visit the area and stay in Orick motels and eat in local cafes.

Approaching Orick from the north, a short sideroad leads to the southern trailhead for the Coastal Trail. There is a picnic area at the trailhead, and the steep road crosses Prairie Creek and passes the former site of Berry Glen, a gas station, and berry farm with a retail berry store. The pies baked by owner Jean Batrel and sold in the store by Mrs. Batrel and her husband Jack became famous. The store and berry sales continued until the 1950s, but now only overgrown buildings and berry patches remain.

The intersection with the Bald Hills Road provides access to the most heavily logged area—the source of the Orick economy for a century. Hufford Road runs west from the highway, leading to the coast just west of the mouth of Redwood Creek.

Hiking in the Parks

Hikers have the choice of spending short amounts of time on several short nature trails, most of them self-guided, or taking longer hikes to significant points of interest—superb stands of redwoods, across high-level prairies and oak woodlands, through long creek basins, or along the coastline.

SHORT NATURE TRAILS

Stout Grove Loop Trail *Access:* The trail is in Jedediah Smith Redwoods State Park. Drive east from Highway 101 on Highway 199, past the hamlet of Hiouchi to the junction with South Fork Road. Drive down South Fork Road and turn onto Howland Hill Road. The east trailhead is 2.1 miles from the Highway 199 junction. For a shorter walk around the redwood loop, drive along Howland Hill Road to the Jedediah Smith Campground. The trailhead for the short loop is at the south end of the Smith River bridge.

The Hike: The trail (1.8 mile, round trip) runs near the Smith River as it flows downstream. You'll see a curved bridge, and then the route crosses low-lying land with tan oak and alder trees. Take the right fork, part of the Stout Grove Loop Trail, descending to Mill Creek—crossed on a summer bridge—before reaching the Jedediah Smith Campground. On the return walk, take the right fork (the other side of the Stout Grove Loop) and then retrace the route to the parking area on Howland Hill Road.

Lady Bird Johnson Grove Loop Trail During Lyndon Johnson's presidency, the First Lady played a strong part in efforts to beautify the nation and to preserve significant natural areas. She visited the park at the time of its formal dedication, in 1968.

Access: Located in the southeastern section of Redwood National Park, the grove is accessed by a spur road off Bald Hills Road. From Highway 101, take Bald Hills Road (east) for 2.7 miles, and park at the trailhead.

The Hike: This easy trail crosses over Bald Hills Road to a display where trail guides are obtained. The trail runs along a ridge on an old roadway. After passing groups of rhododendron and honeysuckle, the route descends to the plaque dedicated by President Richard M. Nixon in 1969. The hillsides are covered with tall redwoods, Douglas fir, and western hemlock. The trail runs in a counterclockwise direction, leading along the semicircular ridge, and then returns to the trailhead.

Fern Canyon Loop   *Access:* Drive to the end of Gold Bluffs Beach Road. Exit Highway 101 at Davison Road, which leads westward, becoming Gold Bluffs Beach Road at the entrance to Prairie Creek Redwoods State Park. A picnic area is located at the trailhead parking lot.

The Hike: This walk is only 0.8 mile, but what a wonderful walk it is. The trail leads up a flat-bottomed canyon, with steep, fern-covered walls. From the parking lot, take the right trail, one of a pair of paths that cross Home Creek. The left trail is the Coastal Trail. The right path leads to the junction of the James Irvine Trail and the Fern Canyon Trail. Take the right trail into Fern Canyon. The most prominent fern is the five-fingered fern, although several other fern species are seen on the canyon walls. One-third mile along the trail, a short path climbs to a small waterfall. The main trail leaves the canyon floor and climbs a series of steps to the bluff top. The trail ends when it meets the James Irvine Trail. Take the Irvine Trail (left) to return to the parking lot. You'll see a side path leading left. This is a short trail, which leads to the edge of the bluff, offering a fine view of the ferny canyon below.

Five Minute Trail   *Access:* The trailhead is one of several surrounding the Prairie Creek Redwoods State Park Visitor Center. Drive from Highway 101 on the Drury Parkway to the visitor center and campground on Elk Prairie. The trail is found at the rear of the building.

The Hike: This short trail leads past several large trees, including the "Church Tree" and the "Chimney Tree" with a hollow trunk. A Yurok family once lived in the "Indian House Tree."

Short Cathedral Trees Loop   *Access:* Also at Elk Prairie, the route proceeds across the Drury Parkway, near the visitor center. The name celebrates several cathedral groups of redwoods, growing from long-dead ancestors or "nurse" trees, along with some other striking individual trees.

The Hike: This trail offers a round trip of 1.5 miles, on the Cathedral Trees and Rhododendron Trails. To start, the Cathedral Trees Trail runs beside the campground road and crosses under the Drury Parkway, with elk often seen as the trail crosses the prairie through a row of redwoods, before reaching a mature redwood forest and connecting with the Rhododendron Trail (turn right). Here you will see two great cathedral groups. The Rhododendron Trail descends to the prairie and the visitor center area.

Revelation Trail   *Access:* The trailhead is just south of the Prairie Creek Redwoods State Park Visitor Center.

The Hike: This self-guided nature trail is designed for both blind and sighted persons. A cassette guide is available at the park visitor center. The route is equipped with rope and wooden handrails. The 0.3-mile walk takes about five minutes and is an excellent nature experience for adults and children.

Radar Station Trail   *Access:* Located off Coast Drive, just south of the Klamath River; some of the most picturesque views are available by walking several short trails to the bluff tops. The trailhead is located almost exactly halfway along Coast Drive, south of Dad's Camp. There is a wide area off the road for parking. Leave Highway 101 at Klamath Beach Road and drive along the river to Alder Camp Road. Trailers and long RVs should take Alder Camp Road. Other vehicles should continue on the narrow Klamath Beach Road, to Dad's Camp, and then drive south along the coast.

The Hike: The World War II radar station—disguised as a small farm—is located just an eighth of a mile from the road. The site overlooks the ocean.

High Bluff Trail   *Access:* Half a mile south of the Radar Station Trail is High Bluff Picnic Area, from which a paved path leads to an overlook. The viewpoint sits 300 feet above the ocean, with expansive views—north and south—along the coast.

DAY-HIKES

Boy Scout Tree Trail *Access:* This is a popular trail in Jedediah Smith Redwoods State Park. Drive east from Highway 101, north of Crescent City, along U.S. Highway 199. Take a right turn onto South Fork Road and turn right onto Howland Hill Road. The trailhead is 5.1 miles from the Highway 199 junction.

The Trail: This round trip of 5.6 miles begins at a parking lot and enters a mixed forest, soon reaching a stand of tall redwoods. The route descends to cross two creeks. A side trail (at mile 2.4) leads up a hill to the Boy Scout Tree, a superb specimen with two trunks. The main trail (left) continues to its end and a waterfall.

The Hike: This easy trail has some mild climbing but is gentle enough for most people. Within a half-mile of the trailhead, the first redwood grove appears. The forest floor features displays of rhododendron and other flowering plants, including clintonia, iris, and milkmaids. As the trail passes over the top of a hill, you'll see Pacific starflower and yerba de salva, among other plants. Another redwood grove appears, with ferns blanketing the ground. Riparian plants are found as the trail crosses the two streams. Look for the large ring of burls on one of the two trunks of the Boy Scout Tree. Fern Falls offers a lovely scene—the perfect end for a nature trail.

Hiouchi Trail *Access:* The northern trailhead is at the west end of the Hiouchi Bridge, beside Highway 199, 4.1 miles from the Highway 101 junction, leading through part of Jedediah Smith Redwoods State Park.

The Trail: Leading from the Hiouchi Bridge, the trail runs two miles beside the Smith River, with the southern trailhead at the Jedediah Smith Campground. It also provides easy access to the Stout Grove Loop, which is across the river from the campground. Return to the Hiouchi Bridge by retracing your steps north.

The Hike: There is a short section containing switchbacks as the trail climbs from the Hiouchi Bridge to meet the Hatton Trail. The main trail descends, coming close to the river, and then runs through a mixed forest of redwood, tan oak, madrone (arbutus), and laurel. There's a river viewpoint before the one-mile mark and another overlook just before the two-mile mark. On the way, the trail crosses several little creeks and riverside land with more mixed forest, including redwoods. The path meets the Mill Creek Trail just before reaching the bridge to the campground. The trail ends at a beach. Across another bridge is the Stout Grove Loop Trail.

Mill Creek–Nickerson Ranch Trail   *Access:* Take South Fork Road and Howland Hill Road from the junction with U.S. Highway 199. The trailhead is 4.8 miles from Highway 199 and is a short distance north of the Boy Scout Tree trailhead.

The Trail: Covering a distance of 1.6 miles, this short trail leads along this fine creek and through a varied forest landscape. It meets the Nickerson Ranch Trail, which ascends to meet Howland Hill Road. For those who want to return to their cars quickly, the shortcut north, along Howland Hill Road to the parking area, is a half-mile's distance.

The Hike: The trail begins by leading beside Mill Creek, one of the most beautiful little water courses in the Northwest. The path passes through a mixed forest, including old-growth redwoods, with vine maple and western hemlock and an understory of ferns. A group of splendid, moss-covered bigleaf maples is seen next. Before the next climb, you may be able to spot a little-used track leading left to the creek. This was the site of an old mining operation called Nickerson "Ranch." The walk continues, as the Nickerson Ranch Trail, ascending to more redwoods, other creeks, and then to its end at Howland Hill Road.

Damnation Creek Trail   *Access:* In Del Norte Redwoods State Park, the trailhead is on the west side of Highway 101, south of Crescent City near highway milepost 16.0. You'll see a wide turnout.

The Trail: The 2.5-mile (one way) walk is somewhat strenuous, with an elevation change of 1,000 feet, some of it on an optional path to a secluded little ocean beach. It is best to plan this trip to coincide with low tide, unless you're content to stand on the bluff and gaze at the ocean (most people are). Return to your car by retracing your steps.

The Hike: Beginning with a climb from the highway, through mixed forest, the trail leads along what was a wagon road. It then drops over a ridge, and the trail descends to the ocean. The major plants are redwoods and rhododendrons, with a spruce/fir forest closer to the ocean. Look for fairybells (Hooker's and Smith's) beside the trail. The trail crosses a paved road. This is the old Redwood Highway, now used as part of the Coastal Trail. There are some redwoods as the trail approaches the bluff. Close to the sea, the trail crosses over two bridges. You'll see bigleaf maple and some alder beside the creek. The steep path leads down the cliffs to the rocky beach. This path is suitable only for the sure of foot.

Miner's Ridge Trail *Access:* Located in Prairie Creek Redwoods State Park, the eastern trailhead is at the Elk Prairie Visitor Center. The western trailhead is beside Gold Bluffs Beach Road. The visitor center is just off the Newton Drury Parkway, a short distance from Highway 101. The Gold Bluffs are reached by taking Highway 101, then turning west onto Davison Road and passing through the entrance station for Prairie Creek Park. Continue north on Gold Bluffs Beach Road.

The Trail: This 4.3-mile trail leads in a northwest direction from the Elk Prairie visitor center, beginning with the Nature Trail, which connects with the Miner's Ridge Trail. Take the right fork after crossing Godwood Creek. The path climbs to the top of the low-lying ridge and follows the ridge, ending at the Gold Bluffs Beach Campground. It provides access to the Clintonia Trail as it nears the coast.

The Hike: Along the ridge, the trail passes through stands of redwood, and a Douglas fir/Sitka spruce forest. Part of the trail runs along an old corduroy logging road. It was also the route of pack trains to the former mining operation at Fern Canyon and to another mine site farther along the ridge. There are fine views from several points on the ridge. After the trail meets the Clintonia Trail, it continues on another old logging road, descending through a harvested section of forest. You'll see old redwoods as the trail nears the ocean. Climbing above the creek, you'll see a side trail that leads right to the Hike and Bike Campground. The main trail continues across the creek to Gold Bluffs Beach Road. A suggested return trip, making a loop, is via the James Irvine Trail for a total round trip of 10.3 miles. A night's stay at a Gold Bluffs campsite makes for a fine two-day experience.

James Irvine Trail *Access:* As with the Miner's Ridge Trail, the western trailhead is at the Elk Prairie Visitor Center. The western end is on Gold Bluffs Beach Road, next to Fern Canyon and north of the Miner's Ridge trailhead. We are treating this hike as the continuation of the previous hike, beginning at the oceanside.

The Trail: There is little variation in elevation on this easy walk of 4.7 miles. You have a choice of scenery at the very start, by taking either the Fern Canyon Trail through the canyon and up to the bluff, or the Irvine Trail from its own trailhead. This trail provides access to the Clintonia Trail, which could provide the basis for a shorter loop walk to the Miner's Ridge Trail and then back to the Gold Bluffs area.

The Hike: The Irvine Trail starts on a boardwalk and ascends through alder thickets. Alexander Prairie is to the right. This was the site of a sizable tent community in the 1850s, when there was mining on the bluffs. You'll then meet the Fern Canyon Trail. The Irvine Trail crosses a bridge and passes the Friendship Ridge Trail. There is a fine view from the Baldwin Bridge as the trail crosses a scenic canyon. Home Creek lies below, and the trail wanders along the hills for three miles. There's a waterfall and bridge over another canyon. A spur trail leads to a redwood grove. Then another bridge over another canyon, with a second spur trail to the wooded creek. The path leads under two fallen logs before reaching another bridge over Home Creek, ascending to meet the Clintonia Trail, which provides access to the Miner's Ridge Trail.

Just past the highest point on the Irvine Trail, at the halfway point, is a huge redwood. The trail crosses an old boardwalk, past a long benchland through an area with many fallen trees. The trail crosses Godwood Creek three times before crossing a series of corduroy bridges in a marshy area in the final two miles of the hike. The approach to the visitor center passes through a thick, ancient forest with huge mature redwoods, Sitka spruce, and Douglas fir, mixed with tan oak, alder, maple, and western hemlock. The trail descends after passing the junction with the West Ridge Trail. You'll pass the start of the Prairie Creek Trail and cross over a bridge before reaching the visitor center.

Brown Creek–Rhododendron–South Fork Loop   *Access:* The Brown Creek trailhead is on the east side of Drury Parkway, at mile 2.9. Parking areas are located on both sides of the road, in Prairie Creek Redwoods State Park.

The Trail: This circular route uses three of the state park trails for a round trip of 3.6 miles. The Brown Creek Trail runs for about 1.5 miles, turning onto the Rhododendron Trail to hilltop views, and then via the South Fork Trail (also along a ridge) descending to the original trailhead. Options are available for longer loops, up to 8.5 miles. The shorter distance takes about two hours.

The Hike: This is one of the most rewarding hikes in Prairie Creek Park. It explores two creek canyons, great forests including maple groves, the Carl Alwin Schenck Grove (or Great Grove) of redwoods, the Frederick Law Olmstead Grove, lots of rhododendron, mock azalea, vine maple, and a dozen species of wildflowers, which line sections of the route. The hike begins at the South Fork/Prairie Creek trailhead. Take the South Fork Trail heading east through a magnificent mature redwood forest. The trail follows the South Fork of Brown Creek across a bridge and then turns left onto the Brown Creek Trail.

The trail crosses another bridge and then climbs through more ancient forest beside the creek. Early spring brings trillium flowers. The forest floor is covered with sword and deer ferns as well as salal, sorrel, and iris. A spur trail leads to the Carl Alwin Schenck Grove. Schenck, a noted forester and educator (founder of the first school of forestry in the U.S.), selected 20 huge redwood trees and named each tree in tribute to a prominent person, with the 20th in honor of his school. Famed landscape architect Frederick Olmstead is commemorated in the second major grove, found at mile one.

The Brown Trail connects with the well-named Rhododendron Trail. Turn right for the return to Elk Prairie. At 2.6 miles, the loop takes South Fork Trail (turn right). The route follows a ridge, with many lilies along the way. Here, again, is a mixed forest of redwoods and tan oak, with more rhododendrons, sorrel, huckleberries, and trilliums. The path descends with several switchbacks and meets the Brown Creek Trail. You can return to the trailhead by the Brown Creek Trail, turning left, and then retrace the first (and final) section of the South Fork Trail.

A longer trip can easily be taken by continuing along the Rhododendron past the junction with the South Fork Trail. The Rhododendron Trail descends to Elk Prairie near the visitor center. Part of the excitement of this longer trip is a climb to an elevation of 960 feet, providing several fine viewpoints. It then descends, crossing Cal-Barrel Road, and providing later access to the Cathedral Trees, Elk Prairie, and Foothill Trails, before its end by the Drury Parkway.

Tall Trees Loop Trail   *Access:* By shuttle bus or your own car. The Tall Trees are located in the southeast portion of Redwood National Park, off Highway 101 via Bald Hills Road. During summer months, private vehicles are banned, and visitors take a shuttle bus from the Redwood Visitor Center to the trailhead. During the off-season, vehicle permits are available from 8 A.M. to 5 P.M. at the Redwood Visitor Center on Highway 101. Motor homes and cars with trailers are not permitted at any time. For those with vehicle permits, drive along Highway 101 to Bald Hills Road. Drive 7.1 miles to Tall Trees Road (to the right). Open and close the gate, and drive along the old mainline logging road for six miles to the trailhead parking lot.

The Trail: The total length of the hike is 3.4 miles, with a change in elevation of 600 feet. Two picnic areas are seen at the start of the walk, in an area rich in rhododendron, huckleberry, ceanothus, salal, and tan oak, along with many other plants in the understory and forest floor.

The Hike: The trail drops after passing the junction with the Emerald Ridge Trail, as the trees get larger and the understory gets more lush. The twisty trail crosses a stream and then another creek with wonderful ferny vegetation. The trail continues to descend. There is a restroom just past the one-mile mark, and then the trail drops to the forest floor, passing a goose pen redwood with its large ground-level cavity. The trail connects with the Redwood Creek Trail. The tree thought to be the world's tallest is 250 feet to the right. Another (said to be the second tallest), with twin trunks, rises 367.8 feet. You'll also find the third, fifth, and sixth tallest trees on this 0.75 mile loop tour.

For a longer walk, we suggest that you also take the Emerald Ridge Loop, a four-mile hike that runs along, across, and in Redwood Creek until meeting the Emerald Ridge Trail. The walk begins by walking upstream from the Redwood Creek Trail crossing at the south end of Tall Trees Grove. Walk along the creek for 1.5 miles, pausing to enjoy the scenery, which includes a waterfall cascading to the creek. Late spring and early summer offer swimming opportunities. Just beyond the waterfall (about 70 yards) is the Emerald Ridge Trail. Take the trail up the hillside, passing a grove of redwoods and Douglas fir and beyond the end of Dolason Prairie Trail. Stay on the Emerald Ridge Trail, which climbs again and then drops before climbing to the top of Emerald Ridge. The route passes a burn area, ending at the Tall Trees Trail near the parking lot. Turn right to get to your car or the shuttle bus.

Hidden Beach (Coastal) Trail *Access:* The northern trailhead of this four-mile section of the Coastal Trail is at the Lagoon Creek Picnic Area, off Highway 101, one mile north of the Trees of Mystery. The southern end is at the parking lot at the Klamath Overlook, on Requa Road, 2.3 miles from Highway 101.

The Trail: We begin at the southern trailhead, leaving the Klamath River Overlook, descending on the bluffs. A spur trail leads down, close to the ocean. The main trail leads north.

The Hike: The main trail first crosses flower-filled fields (in spring and early summer). Beyond an overlook, the trail passes through alders, leads past a pond, and reenters more forest. The trail runs along an old road with great views of the coast and, on a clear day, Crescent City. This trail connects with the Hidden Beach Trail and then continues north. There's another side trail, this one leading down to Hidden Beach—a lovely, private cove decorated with large rock formations. The Coastal Trail continues northward on a grassy flat and into another thicket of alders, meeting the Yurok Loop Trail. There are tide pools at low tide. The Coastal Trail continues (left), turning toward Highway 101. The trail meets the other end of the Yurok Loop Trail and crosses Lagoon Creek. Beyond the wooden bridge, the trail forks. Going left will take you to a beach. The right fork leads to Redwood Hostel and the next (DeMartin) section of the Coastal Trail. This section ends at the Lagoon Creek Picnic Area.

Another route to this part of the shoreline is the newer Hidden Beach Trail, with its trailhead at the Trees of Mystery. The one-way trip is 2.5 miles, with an elevation change of about 350 feet. You'll be amazed and excited by the deep, thick forest, the very heavy undergrowth, several creek crossings with riparian habitats, and skunk cabbage in smelly profusion. You'll also see a recently cut area in a section of privately owned land, contrasting starkly with the protected virgin forest. Comparisons may be as odious as the skunk cabbage.

BACKCOUNTRY TRAILS

Redwood Creek Trail   *Access:* The north end—and the suggested starting point—is the Redwood Creek Trail parking lot, on Bald Hills Road, 0.4 mile east of Highway 101. The south end is the Tall Trees Grove parking lot, reached by vehicle (permit required). A summer shuttle bus makes the north-to-south trip possible, without having someone drive to the Tall Trees area. Contact the Redwood Information Center for the current bus schedule and reservations.

The Trail: This 9.5-mile trip follows the Redwood Creek Canyon along an easy backpacking route, much of it along old logging roads through stands of deciduous trees, particularly bigleaf maple and alder. From May through September, two creek crossings are accomplished on summer bridges. April and October hikers usually ford the creek at these places. Fording is difficult to impossible during winter and early spring, when the creek is usually running at a fast clip.

The trail runs through the traditional homelands of the Chilula, who had small villages along Redwood Creek. Most of the 20 villages were located on the eastern slopes. Camping is permitted on the gravel bars of the creek, of which there are many, except within one-quarter mile of the Tall Trees bridge. Dedicated backcountry hikers often leave the trail to walk the creek. Water is rarely higher than your knees during summer and early fall, making hops from bar to bar an enjoyable feature of the hike.

The Hike: The trail leads southeast through a typical Bald Hills mixed riparian forest of willows, alders, and laurels. The redwoods appear when the trail reaches the creek. The route crosses the creek on a bridge and heads south. There are four meadows in the early part of the hike, with many wildflowers and large blackberry brambles. Look for a large (empty) osprey nest on top of a redwood at the 2.7-mile mark, opposite the mouth of Elam Creek. Following the fourth meadow, the trail crosses the creek on a summer bridge. There's a gravel crossing about 200 feet north of the bridge crossing, used for fording when the bridge is removed. Red markers show the trail location on the opposite bank.

The path descends until it meets McArthur Creek, a distance of 1.75 miles from the trailhead. Another quarter-mile, and you're beside Redwood Creek. The trail hugs Redwood Creek, crossing several small creeks, moving onto the gravel bars for a while and then moving to the bank through the riparian forest. At five miles, the path climbs about 100 feet up the side of the canyon, with a high bridge over Bond Creek at about 5.5 miles. Just past the six-mile mark (there's a marker post), you'll pass a fine stand of mature redwoods, with a bench placed at the crest of the hill.

The trail descends to cross Forty-Four Creek, rising again to the trail summit at an elevation of 290 feet. A spur trail leads to the Forty-Four Horse Camp and the horse trail. The main trail continues on a section of the old logging road. Just past the 7.5-mile marker, the trail (now much narrower) passes a slide and reaches the Tall Trees Overlook. This is a great place to observe what is reputed to be the world's finest stand of virgin redwood. After another section of the logging road, the trail drops to the creek and over the second summer bridge (at mile 8.2), crossing benchland beside the creek and connecting with the Tall Trees Loop Trail (see page 32). Turn right and follow the loop to the parking lot and the shuttle bus (mile 9.5). You may wish to have a longer backcountry experience by taking the Emerald Ridge Trail, which will return you to the Tall Trees Trailhead.

Coastal Trail   *Access:* The Coastal Trail leads along the Pacific coastline, in a north-south direction through the Redwood National Park and state park sections, from just south of Crescent City to two miles north of Orick. There are entry points along the route of the trail, which is broken into seven sections. The Crescent Beach Trail runs 2.2 miles south from the Crescent Beach Information Center, along Enderts Beach. The Last Chance Section begins at the southern end of Enderts Beach Road and leads through Del Norte Redwoods State Park, connecting with the Damnation Creek Trail and continuing south from milepost 15.6. Leading farther south, the DeMartin Section continues to Wilson Creek and the American Youth

Hostel. The Hidden Beach Section is next, from the hostel or (on the lower route) from the Klamath Overlook. The higher trail leads along the bluffs. The Flint Ridge Section leads along part of Redwood National Park for 4.5 miles, from the trailhead at the north end of Coastal Drive, where there is a primitive campground with 10 sites. The Gold Beach Section leads down the shoreline of Prairie Creek Redwoods State Park, accessible by Davison Road and Gold Bluffs Beach Road. The beach is used as part of the trail, and it is best to do this section at low tide. The southernmost section is the Skunk Cabbage Trail in Redwood National Park. This five-mile hike begins beside Espa Lagoon on Davison Road. It's possible to walk 2.5 miles along the beach to the mouth of Redwood Creek.

The Trail: The entire Coastal Trail is an easy hike, along several beaches and on bluffs near the ocean, with exceptional seaside views along the entire length. With several campgrounds, including primitive sites and a developed campground (at Gold Bluffs Beach), the trail offers a backpacking hike of more than 45 miles over four or five days.

The Hike: Few visitors walk the entire length of the Coastal Trail, but many use separate sections for short and easy dayhikes. Each section has a different character. Several offer walks along park beaches. Others cross the bluffs above pounding surf. The Skunk Cabbage Trail offers a walk through huge Sitka spruce before reaching the beach. The Gold Beach Section provides the opportunity to commune (not too closely, please) with an elk herd, and to fish, with a campground for an overnight stay. Farther north, the Hidden Beach Section features a spruce/ alder forest, meadows with wildflowers, excellent bird watching, the secluded beach, and a connection with the Yurok Loop Trail. Old-growth redwoods and a primitive campground are found along the DeMartin Trail. The Last Chance Section offers just about everything, including an easy walk along the old Redwood Highway. This is one of the region's best bird-watching spots. The same area also offers spruce and alder groves and high bluffs above the Pacific. You may see a fine collection of raptors along Crescent and Enderts Beaches.

The Coastal Trail within the parks is only part of the longer California Coastal Trail, which is being developed as a 1,600-mile hiking experience—from the Oregon border to the Mexico border. At this time, about 120 miles of trail are available in northwestern California, from north of Crescent City to Humboldt Bay, near Arcata.

Dolason Prairie–Emerald Ridge Trail   Running across the prairie land of the Bald Hills, Dolason is the newest trail in Redwood National Park, offering a trip through old-growth forest, magnificent Douglas firs, wide grasslands, and former ranching lands. This is a truly wonderful experience without strenuous effort, offering the chance to stroll from ecosystem to ecosystem, lingering in deep forests, or spreading a blanket on the prairie grass for a relaxing picnic. There are few places that offer this diversity of plant life, plus the opportunity to contemplate the wonders of nature in this place of ultimate peace and tranquility.

Access: To get to the trail, drive east from Highway 101 on Bald Hills Road. The trailhead is 11.5 miles from the Highway 101 intersection. Or, take the park shuttle bus from the Redwood Information Center during the busy summer months, when you can hike the two trails without depriving a companion of a fine walk to drive your car to the Tall Trees parking lot.

The Trail: The Dolason Trail can be walked on its own for a round trip of 9.8 miles, or done in conjunction with the Emerald Ridge Trail with an additional hike of one mile to the Tall Trees parking lot, for a combined hike of 5.9 miles. This is an easier walk than returning on the Dolason Trail, as the Emerald Ridge trail descends almost all the way to the Tall Trees Grove. The shuttle bus can return you to your car. A much shorter round trip of 2.4 miles from the Dolason Prairie trailhead leads to and from the Dolason Barn, part of the former ranch property. This is the second barn you'll see on both the shorter and longer routes. The elevation change to the Dolason Barn is 540 feet, with an elevation change of 2,200 feet on the entire Dolason Prairie Trail.

The Hike: Dolason Prairie Trail offers a gentle downward stroll, high above Redwood Creek, across broad meadows, through oak woodlands and contemplative mixed forests of bigleaf maple, Douglas fir and grand fir, more redwoods, western hemlocks, bay laurels, and tan oaks. The hike begins by passing through a second-growth area and then past Douglas firs before turning onto the old K & K logging road past a meadow. The trail leaves the road, dropping into mixed woodland and coming out to enter the Dolason Prairie, close to an old barn—a former sheep shed on the Lyons Ranch. At the edge of the prairie, the trail skirts a grove of Oregon white oaks before descending into a thick forest of Douglas fir. This, and the subsequent prairie area, are fine places to stop to view spring wildflowers.

Rhododendron and clintonia, two of the region's outstanding wildflower plants, are found farther along the trail. There's a long wooden bridge that crosses the Emerald Creek Canyon (mile 4.7), climbing to the top of the gorge to connect with the Emerald Creek Trail at mile 4.9.

This is a point for decision making. The return walk along the Dolason Prairie Trail will take you up the hills you have just descended—a fairly strenuous ascent. On the other hand, you could meander down to the Tall Trees parking lot via the Emerald Ridge Trail. This final part of the hike will be one mile long.

Holter Ridge–Lost Man Bike Trail   *Access:* An 11.5-mile bicycle route is available by combining the Holter Ridge and Lost Man trails, located in the southeast portion of Redwood National Park. To reach the trailhead for the Holter Ridge Trail, drive along Bald Hills Road past the road to Lady Bird Johnson Grove to the trailhead near the Redwood Creek Overlook picnic area. The northwestern end of the Lost Man Trail is at the picnic area of the same name, off Highway 101.

The Hike: The Holter Ridge Trail follows a former logging road, atop a high ridge overlooking the Bald Hills, passing the sources of Little Lost Man Creek and several tributaries of Lost Man Creek. It runs at this elevation with great views of old-growth redwood forests, including the Lady Bird Johnson Grove, which lies far below the trail to the west. Slightly more than halfway along the circuit, the road turns sharply to the west, beginning the Lost Man Creek Trail. As the route descends, the trail meets and crosses Lost Man Creek and continues to drop, with Lady Bird Johnson Grove to the south (left). The ride can end at the Lost Man Picnic area, or it can continue to Highway 101, only one mile to the west.

Nearby Attractions

HUMBOLDT REDWOODS STATE PARK AND AVENUE OF THE GIANTS

Northern California's largest state park, Humboldt Redwoods lies along Highway 101 at the southern end of Humboldt County, between Garberville and Scotia. Access to much of its 51,315 acres is by the immensely popular Avenue of the Giants, a 33-mile road that wanders through many groves of old-growth forest. Spring and fall are by far the best seasons to explore the park.

Although close to a million people visit the Avenue of the Giants each year, very few explore the park interior, with its quiet, magnificent groves of coast redwood. Most of the park trails start from the Avenue, leading to and through groves east and west of the road. The Bull Creek Flats Trail, exploring the Rockefeller Forest, provides a wonderful tour of virgin redwoods. The 9,000 acres on Bull Creek were purchased in 1931 by the Save-the-Redwoods League, with a $2 million donation by John D. Rockefeller, Jr. The gift was matched by state funds, and the park was then established. Later, in 1955, the disastrous effects of clear-cut logging farther up Bull Creek almost ruined the creek, including terrible flooding that expanded the width of the creek and brought a wall of silt and fallen trees raging down to the protected forests. The park was expanded to include almost all of the Bull Creek watershed. Reforestation has taken place, and the upper forests are slowly recovering.

For access to the Bull Creek Flats trailhead, drive along Highway 101 to Mattole Road (South Fork/Honeydew exit). Drive west on Mattole Road to Grasshopper Road. The trail is found off Grasshopper Road, just beyond the end of the pavement. You may also gain access to the trail across the bridge from the Big Tree area, off the Avenue of the Giants. A hike along portions of the trail can take from one to four hours. The total length of the round trip is eight miles, or four miles from the Big Tree area.

The park information center is beside Avenue of the Giants, in the center of the park next to the Burlington Campground. For park information, call the district office in Eureka at (707) 946-2409 or (707) 445-6547.

Lost Coast and King Range Wilderness

One of California's most impressive, rugged, and unspoiled landscapes is in what is called the "Lost Coast." The area extends from the northwest edge of Mendocino County to just south of Ferndale in Humboldt County. Much of the area is preserved in the King Range Conservation Area and Sinkyone Wilderness State Park, which lies on the coast at the southern end of the region.

There are three ways to drive into the Lost Coast. From the south, Usal Road branches off Highway 1, three miles north of the hamlet and ghost town of Rockport. This road is unsigned and unpaved. For the first six miles, Usal Road winds and rises to more than 1,000 feet and then descends to the Usal Beach Campsite.

From the east and Highway 101, take either the Garberville or Redway exits, drive through Redway, and turn west on Briceland Road. After 12 miles of driving, turn on the left fork to the hamlet of Whitethorn. One mile past Whitethorn the pavement ends, but you can continue on the dirt road for another 3.5 miles to the Four Corners (a junction). To the left is Usal Road; to the right is a road climbing into the mountains. Drive straight ahead and you come—in another 3.5 miles—to the Sinkyone Wilderness State Park Visitor Center. This last part of the road may be impassable during winter months. The state park headquarters has trail maps and campsite information. There are camping areas at Needle Rock near the visitor center, where trails lead to the beach, and at the Jones Beach site. Drive-in campsites lie four miles south of Needle Rock, at Bear Harbor. This is where the road ends and the Lost Coast Trail begins. For advance information, write to the California Department of Parks and Recreation, Eel River District, P.O. Box 100, Weott, CA 95571.

The third access route is from the north, but this route is recommended only for intrepid drivers with four-wheel-drive or high-clearance vehicles, and then only during the dry summer and fall months. Mattole Road runs south from the Victorian town of Ferndale, past Cape Mendocino and on toward the only community on the Lost Coast.

Aside from the coastal village of Shelter Cove, the rest of the region is virtually uninhabited, with the King Mountains sealing it off from the east. Hiking, fishing, sea-watching, and camping are the reasons people come to visit the Lost Coast. Those who take the trouble to venture into this area are impressed with its rugged beauty and the truly spectacular vistas along the coastline. The Lost Coast Trail offers a 100-mile hike. Shorter walks are available on several sections of the trail, which can be reached by access roads, particularly in the southern section.

Much of the rugged mountain country of the Lost Coast is in the King Range Conservation Area. This is a perfect location for wilderness hiking. A mixture of long, rugged trails and easier walks makes this area an enjoyable recreation spot for those who like nature in the raw. Most of the trails are for experienced hikers, and almost all of the backroads are suitable only for four-wheel-drive vehicles, certainly not for large motor homes and cars with trailers.

Although it is possible to walk almost the entire 100 miles of the Lost Coast, most hikers use the southern portion, in Sinkyone Wilderness State Park. The state park trail leads 16 miles from Bear Harbor, along the shoreline to the Usal campground. Many people camp at the Bear Harbor or Needle Rock campgrounds and spend several days walking two or three sections of the trail before tackling the other trails that lead into the King Range Conservation Area.

The portion of the coastline trail from Needle Rock to Whale Gulch (4.5 miles round trip) begins from the trailhead behind the barn near the park road. A longer, nine-mile round trip is part of the trail from Bear Harbor to the Wheeler Campsite. The route leads through canyons with redwood groves and across prairie grasslands.

One of the most scenic hikes (six miles round trip) in the northern portion of the Lost Coast, starts at the mouth of the Mattole Recreation Site (via Lighthouse Road) and leads past the river mouth and waterfalls. The southernmost part of the Lost Coast Trail leads from the Usal Campsite to Anderson Gulch, a round trip of five miles through redwoods, climbing to a scenic view (at 1,300 feet), with a campsite at Anderson Gulch.

In each chapter, a short, informal field guide provides descriptions of the prominent species that live in this book's eleven Northwestern destinations. These descriptions cover many of the birds, animals, and plants you'll probably see on your visit, in addition to the resident wildlife that is rarely seen elsewhere or is unique to the particular region. We have tried to localize these listings so that you'll know where to find individual species in the destination area covered by each chapter.

Because the terrain of the redwood parks is so varied and the ecosystems so diverse, there is a real richness to the biotic scene in this part of the world: from oceanside marshes to upland riparian habitats, the old-growth redwood groves, and the prairie and oak woodlands. Two endangered birds—the spotted owl and the marbled murrelet—are resident in sufficient numbers that you could seek them out should you have enough patience.

No patience is required in spotting the Roosevelt elk (on Elk Prairie and the Gold Bluffs), the varied thrush—a resident songbird in the oak woodlands—or the American dipper, one of many shorebirds found in and beside the streams and marshes along the coastline as well as on the ocean beaches.

BIRDS

Northern Spotted Owl
Otus flammeolus

Although this owl is reclusive enough that it is rarely seen except by those who really spend some time in certain forests, it is easily identified by its eyes. It is the only large owl, except barn and barred owls, to have completely dark eyes. To differentiate, barred owls have vertical stripes on the belly, while the head of the barn owl does not look like that of the spotted owl at all.

This bird, famous for its role in disputes between environmental groups and the logging communities, lives in old-growth forests from southwestern British Columbia to northern Mexico, including the groves of Redwood National Park. Recent studies suggest that, perhaps, spotted owls may be able to exist happily in second-growth or recovering forests. There is not enough research to prove this theory. However, more spotted owls have been seen recently in California forests than was previously estimated.

Aside from its eyes, this owl has two other distinguishing features: its spotted chest and horizontal barred belly. Its voice is a series of three or four high-pitched hooting sounds, often compared to a dog's bark: *hoo, hoo-hoo;* or *hoo, hoo-hoo-whoooo.* It also sounds a longer series of fast-paced hoots (barks), rising in volume. The best place to hear spotted owls is in the mature forest up Boyes Creek, in Prairie Creek Redwoods State Park, accessed by the Cathedral Trees Trail or the Rhododendron Trail. Other owls resident in the redwood parks include the common barn owl, great horned, western screech, northern pygmy, and northern saw-whet owls.

Chestnut-backed Chickadee
Parus rufescens
This and two other members of the Paridae family (bushtit and black-capped chickadee) reside year-round in the redwood parks. The chestnut-backed chickadee lives in damp conifer forests, as well as in oaks and other shade trees located close to an evergreen forest. Like other members of this family, this chickadee is a small, plump bird with a small bill.

It has a black cap and black bib, with white cheeks, similar to other chickadees. Its identifier is its chestnut back. The same bird in central California has gray markings below its wings. It does not have a whistle. Its voice is a hoarse *chick-a-dee-dee-dee.*

Pileated Woodpecker
Drycopus pileatus
This is a large woodpecker, as large as a crow. Its back is very black, with white on the sides of the neck and a flaming red crest. It is the model for the saucy Woody of cartoon fame. The female has a black forehead, leaving a smaller red crest. This bird has a dramatic flight pattern, with great sweeping wingbeats. From the ground, the white wingbottoms are clearly seen. The holes drilled by the pileated woodpecker are large and oval shaped. Its call takes two forms: a loud *kik-kik-kik-kik-kik,* or the more varied version of the same sound, much like that created by Mel Blanc for the animated Woody.

Belted Kingfisher
Ceryle alcyon
One of only two kingfishers found in the American West (the other is the green kingfisher), this alert-looking bird with the sharp eyes has a bill like the heron and syndactyl feet, with two toes slightly joined. It lives from Alaska to the southern U.S., and it spends the winter in South America. It prefers streams and coastal bays and often builds its nest in banks. You'll see this kingfisher making steep dives into the water as it goes about its food-catching routine. Before diving, it hovers with its wings beating rapidly. It is the size of a large robin, with blue-gray feathers above, a spiky crest, and gray feathers extending across the breast. The female has a rust-colored breastband under the gray band. Its sound is a dry rattle, often heard when it is flying.

Varied Thrush
Lxoreus naevius
Robins and thrushes are members of the same family (Muscicapidae),

and the varied thrush has a look similar to the American robin, except it has an orange stripe above the eye, orange wing bars, and a band across the breast. Otherwise the two birds are similar, with a brick-red breast and dark upper. The male has a black band; the female, a gray band. The bird is a resident of the redwood parks, but has a range extending from Alaska to this region. It lives in heavy, damp forests, mainly conifer groves, and in streamside ravines and canyons.

Wilson's Warbler
Wilsonia pusilla
The wood warblers make up a very large family (Emberizadae), including warblers, redstarts, yellowthroats, the parula, and ovenbirds. Seventeen varieties of warbler are found in the redwood parks, and all are seasonal residents, most of them staying the summer, with a few holdovers into the fall. Wilson's warbler is a common summer resident, wintering in Mexico and Central America as far south as Panama. The male is golden with a grayish upper and a black cap. The female has a smaller gray cap. There's a distinct yellow stripe above the eye. It lives in riparian habitats, particularly in willows and alders. The stream canyons provide perfect living conditions. Its song is a light chattering sound, *chi chi chi chi chi chet chet,* dropping in pitch for the final notes.

Red-tailed Hawk
Buteo jamaicensis
From below, the tail of the flying red-tailed hawk seems to be a light pink. From above, the tail is a bright red color. This is a large hawk with broad wings and a wide tail. It has a dark (patagial) bar on the fore edge of the wing. The under part of this hawk is zoned: a whitish breast, with a wide band of streaks across the belly. It is easy to see when perching, with the red tail clearly visible. It is the red-tailed hawk flying over the oak woodlands and prairies, including the Bald Hills area, and perched beside the roads and on trees. Along the Pacific Coast, this bird's range stretches from Alaska to Panama. Its voice is a downward squealing sound, *keeeeer.*

Tree Swallow
Tachycineta bicolor
A common summer resident in redwood country, this five- to six-inch songbird lives in open country close to water, including marshy areas, and beside streams and lakes. It takes over holes in trees for its nest, as well as roosting in marshy reeds. It's a good candidate for birdhouse living in your yard. Its range includes Alaska, most of western and central Canada, and the U.S. The mature bird is a metallic combination of blue, green, and black above and white below. Immature tree swallows (first year) are brown above. Its voice has two different forms, a *cheet* or *chiveet,* and a twittering song: *weet, treet, weet, treet.*

Sora
Porzana carolina
This is a rail, one of several henlike marsh birds of the Rallidae family,

which are fairly reclusive but often heard. Its voice is a horselike, descending whinny. In the spring, you'll hear a different sound, a whistled *kee-whee.* When startled, it utters a sharp *keek.*

The sora has a sharp yellow bill and green legs. Its upper is brown with a gray belly and a distinct black patch on the face and throat. Immature rails do not have the black patch. A few rails live in the redwood parks year-round. The bird's habitat is generally a marshy area, including salt marshes, and on moist meadowlands. Its range is from Canada to the western and central U.S. Rails usually winter from the southern U.S. to Peru and are often not seen in this area during winter months.

American Coot
Fulics americana
This ducklike bird is found all along the U.S. Pacific Coast and from Canada to Argentina. It is a common resident of the shoreline in fall, winter, and spring, flying farther north in summer. This slate-colored bird has a blackish head and neck and a distinctive white bill. It has a divided white patch on the underside of the tail. It has large, greenish, lobed feet. It has a distinctive back-and-forth movement of the head when it's swimming, diving at times but dabbling into the surface more often than not. Its takeoff is not graceful. It labors while leaving the water, dragging its feet in the water. While most commonly seen on the ocean, it also is found on marshes, salt

bays, and ponds. Its variable sound can be a rasping *kuk-kuk-kuk-kuk, kakakakakaka,* or a divided *kaa-haa, haa-haa,* often accompanied by loud croaks.

Sanderling
Calidris alba
This is just about the cutest bird you'll find along the ocean beaches: a small black-legged sandpiper that races at a furious pace along the waterline, chasing the outgoing waves like some sort of dervish. It bears a different coloration in summer and winter. Its spring and summer plumage is a rusty brown on the head, back, and breast. In winter, it changes to a dull gray above, retaining its whitish breast, but having black shoulders below the wing. Junior sanderlings are a mottled black above. Its range is amazing for such a small bird. It lives in Arctic areas, wintering in the U.S., the British Isles, China, and also the Southern Hemisphere. Its voice is a short *twit* or *kwit.*

Black Oystercatcher
Haematopus bachmani
These large, wading shorebirds have long, flat, red/orange bills. The legs are a pinkish color. Young oystercatchers have a black tip on their tails. There are two oystercatchers of the family Haematopodidae in the western United States. The other is the American, which strays to the California coast but is rarely seen here. The black lives as far south as Morro Bay and on coastal islands to Baja California. It ranges north to

the western Aleutian Islands. It is found in the several river and creek inlets and in marshes in the redwood parks system. It eats crabs and other marine life, including sea worms.

Western Gull
Larus occidentalis
There are at least a dozen types of gulls along the California coastline, although the most seen are the glaucous-winged, Heermann's, mew, and herring gull. The latter is not widely seen in this northern region. Along with the western gull, the others are in good supply along the park beaches. In addition, you may see some less-common varieties including Thayers gull, the black-winged kittiwake, and the California gull, which is more common to the south. The western gull is seen in many incarnations, for it does not adopt its final plumage until the forth year. Juveniles are largely a mottled brown, with a yellow bill and pinkish feet. The mature gull has very dark back and wings, with very white underparts. There is a red dot on the bottom of the bill, at the tip. Its sound is a guttural croak, *kuk kuk kuk,* and also a wheezy *whee whee.*

MAMMALS

Roosevelt Elk
Cervus elaphus occidentalis
The elk is the most visible animal in the redwood parks system, and the largest herds are found in Prairie Creek Redwoods State Park, on Elk Prairie, and the Gold Bluffs

area. The western elk was renamed in commemoration of President Theodore Roosevelt, who led the campaign for the animal's preservation. These are very large deer, with thick necks and slender legs. They are brown or tan with a darker belly and rump and a yellow/brown tail. The larger males wear a dark brown mane (on the throat) and have tined antlers (six on each side for mature elk). Females lack antlers.

Rutting season is August to November, and this is a time to avoid getting too close, especially to the males who are in a bullish mood. Elk are polygamous, with one bull servicing as many as 50 or 60 cows. Calves are born in the spring with one or two born per mother. The elk inhabit the grassy prairies in the summer, moving to higher (often wooded) ground for winter.

Elk are very good at maneuvering themselves through the forest, and those who take backcountry forest trails may hear them crashing through the underbrush. Bulls are not seen with the cows and young in nonmating seasons

Elk are found along much of the northern Pacific Coast, from Northern California to western Washington and Vancouver Island, and are much more widely seen in the Rocky Mountain states. They're also called wapiti (the Shawnee name).

Mountain Lion
Felis concolor
Those of us who live in or travel often in California are aware of the

increase in the number of mountain lions in the state following the ban on hunting these native animals. The increase has brought lobbying for the renewal of hunting, which is opposed by environmentalists and the state Department of Fish and Game. There have been some recent sightings in the redwood parks. As new trails are opened in more remote sections of Redwood National Park, it is expected that humans will come into infrequent contact with these large cats, which have roamed the coast foothills for many thousands of years. One important thing to remember is that when encountering a mountain lion, a human should not run or walk away from the lion. The park rangers advise holding your ground or moving away very slowly while facing the animal. Do not play dead.

Growing to 108 inches, the mountain lion is a tawny color above and white with buff markings below. It has a long tail with a black tip. There are two whisker patches on the upper lip. It has large feet. The prints are round with four toe marks and a lobed heel pad scalloped at the front (one) and back (two). The young are born in dens, rock piles, or shelters lined with moss or other vegetation. Its range is from British Columbia and Alberta, through the Rocky Mountain states, to California and west Texas, and to the Gulf Coast states to Florida.

River Otter
Lutra canadensis
The Klamath River is one notable place to see this good-looking and popular animal. Growing to a length of about 50 inches, it has a long, dark brown body, with a slightly paler belly. The throat is a silvery gray, and it has long, white whiskers. The river otter is active during the day, swimming underwater and on the surface, raising its head high above the water to survey its territory. It does well on land, and it crosses the ground on its way to its den in the riverbank. It can and does build underwater entrances and sometimes lives in hollow logs, under piles of driftwood, and under roots.

One good sign that a river otter is near is the slide it makes on the riverbank, usually about eight inches wide. Its tracks (five toe marks and heel pad) are often three inches wide. The young are born in the spring (April and May), and they leave the nest after eight months. They feed on fish and rely on mice and other small mammals when fish are not plentiful.

Townsend's Chipmunk
Eutamias townsendii
This dark brown mammal is one of the largest of the western chipmunks, with a dull, loose coat of fur. This is not a gregarious animal, but it does move about during the day. It lives in burrows usually four to five feet in depth and only about two inches across. It's good at running up trees and does so to escape its enemies. It has vague black and light stripes from its head to the end of its body. Its ears are a medium brown on the front and gray on the back half. The tail is

long and bushy. It has a brown stripe below the ears. You'll see Townsend's chipmunks in the redwood forests, scurrying about the damp vegetation. It loves dense, humid forests, either hardwood or coniferous. This is the southernmost habitat for this species. It is found along the Oregon coast and the most southern coastal areas of British Columbia.

AMPHIBIANS

Pacific Giant Salamander
Dicamptodum ensatus
This fast-moving amphibian has smooth brown or purple skin, mottled with black. Its underside is whitish (with a yellow tint) or a light brown color. Like other salamanders, the Pacific giant emerges from eggs that are laid underwater on submerged logs. Larvae hatch and transform into salamanders during or after their second year. The new salamanders grow from about 8 inches to more than 11 inches. They live and stay on the ground, particularly in cool, damp forests near rivers and creeks—a perfect description for much of the redwood parks area. Its range is from the extreme southwestern coast of British Columbia, south along the Pacific, to Santa Cruz County. A pocket of this salamander is also found in the Rocky Mountains of northern Idaho and Montana.

Pacific Tree Frog
Hyla regilla
This small frog rarely grows more than two inches long. It has very rough skin, varying in color from black to green or light brown, and the skin often is covered with dark spots. There's a black stripe through the eye and sometimes a black triangle between the eyes. The male has a gray throat. It lives throughout Washington and Oregon, in all of California except the southeast deserts, and in western parts of Nevada, Idaho, and Montana. It is also found in southern British Columbia. Its high-pitched voice, a two-part note that is more of a squeal than a croak, is very familiar to anyone who has camped along the coast or lives in its zone. It's found from sea level to elevations of 10,000 feet.

Red-legged Frog
Rana aurora
The northern subspecies of the red-legged frog (*R. a. aurora*) is found from British Columbia to the redwood coast. It is large (growing to more than five inches), gray to reddish brown, with many solid dark blotches and specks. Farther south in California, you'll see *R. a. draytoni,* which has dark blotches with light centers. Both have a dark mask with a white border on the jaw. The underside is yellow with touches of red on the hind legs and lower abdomen. The male has larger thumbs than the female. Both subspecies like to live in damp, wooded areas and near ponds and other permanent water sources. Its voice is a series of unenthusiastic, raspy notes that last several seconds.

Roughskin Newt
Taricha granulosa

This warty amphibian has brown or black upper parts and an easily seen yellow to orange belly. When breeding, the male's skin is temporarily smooth, and its toes develop a black, hard layer. It has small eyes with almost black lower lids. Like the salamander, the newt lays its eggs on water plants or on twigs and branches that lie under the surface. Larvae transform in the fall or spring, with the spring newts larger, at about three inches. Adults are found on land and in the water, coming to land to look for insects when the air is cool and the forest floor is moist. Its habitat includes ponds, creeks, and slow-moving rivers with submerged vegetation and nearby forests. There is a slightly different subspecies (*T. g. mazamae*) in Crater Lake National Park in Oregon. The common (northern) roughskin newt is found along the coast from the Alaska Panhandle to Santa Cruz County, California.

REPTILES AND INVERTEBRATES

Pond Turtle
Clemmys marmorata

There are only two freshwater turtles found in all of the northwest Pacific Coast regions: this one and the painted turtle. The pond turtle has a dark brown or olive carapace, with darker, broken streaks radiating from the center of the shields. The plastron (the "dicky," or ventral part) is usually a dirty yellow color,

often with dark blotches. This turtle lives as far north as the British Columbia coast, the Puget Sound area of Washington, and down the Pacific Coast through Oregon and California. The painted turtle is not found in redwood country. You may see the pond turtle sunning itself near streams and standing water.

Northwestern Garter Snake
Thamnophis ordinoides

The most common snake throughout the Pacific Northwest is this small garter snake, which rarely grows longer than two feet. Different snakes of this species vary in color and pattern, ranging from a black or brown cast to the upper background color, and a green or blue tint to the background color below. It may have a well-defined red or yellowish dorsal stripe, or it may not. Lateral stripes are vague, at best. It is both a lowlands and an uplands snake, living at elevations from sea level to about 3,300 feet. In the redwood parks, this snake is seen on the lowland prairies (Elk Prairie, Gold Bluffs), and at higher locations on the Bald Hills. The park prairies are perfect for this snake, which prefers to live and hunt in grassy fields, meadows, and areas with brush, and especially around rock walls. Its preferred food is the slug, but it also feasts on earthworms, frogs, and salamanders. Rarely biting when disturbed or handled, it instead discharges a foul-smelling substance from its anal glands and may even offer a disgusting bowel secretion when frightened. Beware!

California Mountain Kingsnake

Lampropeltis zonata

This beautiful, brightly colored snake has alternating red and white rings separated by black rings. The snout and top of the head are black. It reaches a length of about two feet. While it looks somewhat like the poisonous coral snake, it is not poisonous. Besides, the coral snake lives in the desert of the Southwest. The mountain kingsnake lives in brush areas and in open woods, including the oak woodlands of the redwood parks. A constrictor, it feeds on lizards, mice, and other small mammals and invades nests to eat young birds.

Banana Slug

Ariolimax columbianus

A varied range of land mollusks are found in the coastal forests. The banana slug is an unabashed creature that travels on its self-made track of slime across park trails, boardwalks, and even the steps to the Redwood Information Center. Growing to a length of 5.5 to 6 inches, it is the largest land mollusk in the Pacific Northwest. It has an allover yellowish olive color, usually with some black spots or blotches. In some areas, this slug may be a much deeper brown color. The banana slug eats foliage and prefers to live in dense woodlands, where there is lots of low vegetation. This slug has become a sort of "pet" of the redwood parks, and an annual slug festival is held each year.

TREES

Coast Redwood

Sequoia sempervirens

This is the world's tallest tree, found only in a narrow strip along the Pacific Coast from the southwestern corner of Oregon to central California, near Santa Cruz. This is the fog belt, where the ocean mists come ashore to give these water-loving trees an almost daily bath of moisture. Its trunk is a reddish-brown, with an enlarged base, and often with burls. The bark is very thick and fibrous, furrowing as the tree ages. The inner bark is a cinnamon color. Its crown is short and narrow. The *sempervirens* grows to between 200 and 325 feet, with some giant specimens taller than 350 feet, particularly in the Tall Trees Grove in the southeastern part of Redwood National Park.

There are two kinds of leaves: most are like needles, of unequal length, to about 0.75 inch long, dark green above and a lighter green below; and on leaders, a very short concave, scalelike leaf, clustered around the twig.

California Black Oak

Quercus kelloggii

One of the most common oaks in this state, the California black is found in both the coast ranges and in the western Sierra Nevada foothills. It is a prime occupant of the oak woodlands in Redwood National Park and is also mixed with conifers. Growing to a height of 80 feet, its trunk can have a diameter of three feet. It has alternative leaves from three to eight inches long, with seven lobes (most of the time), each lobe having small, pointed teeth. The leaves are a shiny green above and a lighter yellow-green and hairy below. The distinctive acorns are long and elliptical, 1 to 1.5 inches long, with a thin, scaly cup. The acorns mature in the second year.

Bigleaf Maple
Acer macrophyllum

Some of the largest, tallest bigleaf maples are found in the redwood parks, particularly in the Bald Hills and Redwood Creek section. Some of the giants grow to 70 feet. It has the largest leaves of all the maples: opposite, six to ten inches long and wide, with five (sometimes three) long, pointed lobes. There are five veins in each leaf, which is shiny and dark green above and lighter and hairy underneath. The tree's bark is brown and furrowed with small four-sided plates. Small, yellow flowers appear in clusters in the spring, followed by long-winged keys that are brown with yellow hairs. Each key contains one seed. The bigleaf maple lives best along the banks of streams and in protected canyons with a good water supply. It is found from southwestern British Columbia to Southern California, at elevations from sea level to more than 3,000 feet in California.

Red Alder
Alnus rubra

This is the alder you'll see in profusion along creek banks, often in association with bigleaf maples and willows. With a very straight trunk, the red alder grows to a height of 100 feet, and its trunk can have a diameter of two or three feet. However, it is often found in an emerging new forest that has been damaged by fire, and many of the alders in this region are growing in the aftermath of clear-cutting. The trunk is a mottled light gray color, with smooth bark. Leaves are alternate, in three rows, about four or five inches long and slightly longer than they are wide. The oval leaves have short points at each end, with 10 to 15 veins on each side. The leaves are dark green and smooth above and a grayish green with hairs below. The red alder has tiny flowers in the spring. Male blossoms are in yellow catkins. The female are reddish, in cones. Tiny nuts form in cones, attached to two small wings. This tree is found from southeast Alaska to central California, growing in moist, gravelly, and sandy areas, usually in pure stands. There are several fine alder stands along Redwood Creek.

ARCATA

The Lady Anne
902 14th Street
Arcata, CA 95521
(707) 822-2797

This bed and breakfast home is in a well-preserved 1888 building with turrets. **($$)**

CRESCENT CITY

Best Western Northwoods Inn
655 Highway 101
Crescent City, CA 95531
(707) 464-9771

Located just south of town, a half-mile from the downtown area, this is a superior, large motel with standard rooms and one-bedroom suites, a restaurant, two hot tubs, and guest laundry. **($$)**

Crescent City KOA
4241 Highway 101 North
Crescent City, CA 95531
(707) 464-5744

This campground with full hookups for RVs and trailers, cabins, and tenting sites is spread over part of a 21-acre tract, including 10 acres of redwood forest. It is two miles from Jedediah Smith Redwoods State Park and five miles from the Smith River. Facilities include showers, laundry, store, nature trails, a playground, and propane service.

Crescent City Motel
1455 Redwood Highway South
Crescent City, CA 95531
(707) 464-5436

This otherwise standard motel has a scenic location on the beach. Rooms have patios and decks. **($$)**

Crescent City Travelodge
725 Highway 101
Crescent City, CA 95531
(707) 464-6106 or 800-255-3050

This is a standard chain motel, with easy access from the highway, and it's close to restaurants and stores. **($ to $$)**

EUREKA

Carson House Inn
1209 Fourth Street
Eureka, CA 95501
(707) 443-1601 or 800-772-1622

The 60-room motel, with one separate cottage, is next door to the old Carson Mansion. It has standard rooms and suites, some with whirlpool, plus a heated pool and sauna. **($$)**

Carter House and Hotel Carter
301 L Street
Eureka, CA 95501
(707) 444-8062

Eureka is a fine B & B town with several historic mansions converted to bed and breakfast operations. The Carter House (seven rooms), and the adjacent inn, with 23 units including rooms and suites, plus a separate cottage, is furnished with antiques, as befits a Victorian original. The ambience is both sophisticated and relaxing. Afternoon and evening tea are served, as is wine and sherry, plus a sumptuous breakfast. **($$ to $$$)**

Daly Inn

1125 H Street
Eureka, CA 95501
(707) 445-3638

Located in Eureka's Old Town, this is a colonial revival home built in 1905. It's close to restaurants and shops in the historic district, and a full breakfast is supplied. **($$)**

Eureka Inn

518 Seventh Street
Eureka, CA 95501
(707) 442-6441 or 800-862-4906

This Tudor-style gem, built in 1922, is a National Historic Landmark. Beautifully constructed with polished redwood, when that wood was very plentiful, it has a wonderful mix of period and slightly more modern design. The high-ceiling lobby is a standout. The inn has been completely renovated, with 105 rooms and suites, sauna, whirlpool, pool, and three restaurants including a delicate cafe, the fine dining room, and a German-style pub. There's also a quiet piano lounge. The rates are reasonable for such a marvelous stay. **($$ to $$$)**

FERNDALE

Ferndale is a perfect place for B & B lodging, and there are several fine inns to consider. Campsites, suitable for RVs and tents, are available at the local fairgrounds; just call (707) 786-9511.

Gingerbread Mansion

400 Berding Street
P.O. Box 40
Ferndale, CA 95536
(707) 786-4000

The nine rooms are in a restored 1899 mansion, with garden, fireplaces, and antique furnishings. Continental breakfast is served. **($$ to $$$)**

Shaw House Inn

703 Main Street
Ferndale, CA 95536
(707) 786-9958

Set on a large property, the inn is an 1854 gothic house with garden, fireplaces, and three shared-bath bedrooms out of the seven rooms available. An expanded continental breakfast is served. **($$ to $$$)**

GARBERVILLE AND AREA

Benbow Inn

445 Lake Benbow Drive
Garberville, CA 95440
(707) 923-2124

This historic inn has an abundance of atmosphere and is located two miles south of Garberville, overlooking the South Fork of the Ecl River. The rooms vary from small units with queen beds to large king bedrooms with fireplaces. There's also a garden cottage available for a price. The property features a nine-hole golf course. The inn has a cozy Victorian atmosphere and a popular dining room. The inn is nonsmoking. **($$$)**

Benbow Valley RV Resort

7000 Benbow Drive
Garberville, CA 95440
(707) 923-2777

Located two miles south of Garberville, this is a deluxe RV park with its own nine-hole golf course, paved RV sites, full hookups, a cafe, and other amenities such as swimming pools and whirlpool, showers, store, laundry, playground, and a game room including bumper pool and table tennis.

Dean Creek Resort

4112 Redwood Drive
P.O. Box 157
Redway, CA 95560
(707) 923-2555

For campers who require full hookups, Dean Creek Resort in Redway has serviced sites on the river, with hookups, cable TV, a whirlpool, and a sauna. There is also a standard motel at the resort. **($)**

Hartsook Inn

900 Highway 101
Piercy, CA 95587
(707) 247-3305

A few miles south of Garberville, in the village of Piercy, the Hartsook Inn has 62 cabins set in the forest next to Richardson Grove. **($)**

Humboldt House Inn

701 Redwood Drive
Garberville, CA 95542
(707) 923-2771

Accommodations in the town of Garberville tend to be standard motels, but this is superior to most. It's a Best Western operation at the north end of Redwood Drive (the main street) with 75 units, including suites, a swimming pool, and whirlpool. Continental breakfast is served to overnight guests. **($$)**

Miranda Gardens Resort

6766 Avenue of the Giants
Miranda, CA 95553
(707) 943-3011

For an old-fashioned overnight experience, these cabins set in the redwoods may be just the thing. North of Garberville on the scenic road, the resort has cottages and motel units, a heated pool, whirlpools, and fireplaces in some cottages, and barbecue units. Tennis courts, restaurants, and park redwood groves are nearby. **($ to $$)**

River Rose Cottage

P.O. Box 418
Garberville, CA 95542
(707) 923-3500

For a romantic getaway in a hideaway, you can rent this private cottage set off Sprowel Creek Road beside the river, a half-mile from downtown Garberville. The bedroom has a double bed, and the living room has a pullout queen sofa. A full breakfast, at the nearby Woodrose Cafe, is part of the package. **($$)**

KLAMATH AND REQUA

Camp Marigold Motel and RV Park
16101 Highway 101
Klamath, CA 95548
(707) 482-3585

Four miles north of the Klamath River Bridge, the motel has housekeeping cabins and six rooms inside the lodge. Breakfast is served. **($$)**

There are RV hookups, tenting sites with picnic tables, showers and flush toilets, and a laundry. Camp Marigold is set on 3.5 acres with a garden, next to the redwood forest, with hiking trails, and the Trees of Mystery are close at hand.

Camper Corral
Highway 101
Klamath, CA 95548
(707) 482-5741 or 800-701-7275

Located beside the Klamath River at the north end of the Highway 101 bridge, this campground has 100 pull-through sites, and a large, grassy tenting area, modern restrooms, store, laundry, recreation hall, and planned activities. Klamath River jet boats leave from the campground.

Chinook RV Resort
17465 Highway 101
Klamath, CA 95548
(707) 482-3511

There are 72 sites with full hookups and a tenting area on the river with showers, laundry, store, and liquor store.

Motel Trees
Highway 101
(Redwood Highway)
(707) 482-2251 or 800-638-3389

Four miles north of Klamath (and just north of the Requa turnoff) is this modern motel, across the road from the Trees of Mystery attraction. The motel has 23 units, tennis courts, a lounge, and restaurant. **($$)**

Redwoods Hostel
Wilson Creek Road
Klamath, CA 95548
(707) 482-8265

Located north of Klamath and the Trees of Mystery, the Redwoods Hostel offers inexpensive lodging just south of the national park boundary. Wilson Creek Road is found across Highway 101 from a roadside picnic area. This is a large restored ranch house built in the late 1870s by Louis and Agnes DeMartin. Ten children were raised in this home, which also served as an overnight and lunch stop for travelers. A meal cost 25 cents in the early years. Overnight lodging in the hillside hostel costs a little more, but not much. **($)**

Requa Inn
Klamath, CA 95548
(707) 482-8205

This fascinating inn is located one mile off Highway 101, north of Klamath and west of Requa, with 16 rooms in a historic building overlooking the Klamath River. The nightly charge includes a full breakfast. **($$)**

Riverwoods Campground

1661 West Klamath Beach Road
P.O. Box 589
Klamath, CA 95548
(707) 482-5591

The campground is two miles west of the highway, featuring oversized RV and trailer sites with full hookups and individually shaded tent sites with fire rings and picnic tables. There are showers, hiking trails, a store (with ice and tackle), and firewood is available for sale or free to gather.

ORICK

Park Woods Motel

121440 Highway 101
P.O. Box 61
Orick, CA 95555
(707) 488-5175

This ordinary motel has housekeeping rooms and is occupied by lots of anglers in season. **($$)**

Rolf's Prairie Creek Motel and Park Cafe

Highway 101
Orick, CA 95555
(707) 488-3841

This is a standard motel, designed with kitchens—for anglers—plus a cafe where German specialties are served along with game (elk, buffalo, boar) and barbecue. **($$)**

PETROLIA

Mattole River Resort

42354 Mattole Road
Petrolia, CA 95558
(707) 629-3445 or 800-845-4607

Petrolia is well off the beaten track, southwest of Eureka in the area known as the Lost Coast. It is inland, and you reach it by taking Bull Creek Road from Highway 101 north of Garberville and turning north onto Mattole Road. Another route starts at Ferndale, leading south along Mattole Road to the coast at Cape Mendocino and then moving inland to the village of Petrolia. The resort features cabins fully equipped with kitchenettes; some units hold as many as six adults. It's about 60 miles away from the nearest town, set beside the river (famous for steelhead), between the ocean and the King Range Conservation Area. **($ to $$)**

REDWOOD NATIONAL AND STATE PARKS

There are no lodges or other indoor accommodations within the park boundaries. However, motels are available in the nearby communities, including Crescent City, Orick, Klamath, Requa, and Trinidad, as well as farther away in Eureka and the Garberville area. All campgrounds operate on a first come, first served basis.

Elk Prairie Campground

Located in Prairie Creek Redwoods State Park, the large campground has RV and tent sites with showers and a dump station, and it offers handicapped access.

Freshwater Lagoon Spit

This is the only vehicle camping area in the federal park lands, providing separate areas for RV and tent camping next to Highway 101 at the southern edge of the park.

Gold Bluffs Beach Campground

This developed campground is located on Gold Bluffs Beach Road, in a dunes area near the ocean and under the bluffs. The size limit for cars with trailers and RVs is 24 feet. The campground offers solar showers.

Gold Bluffs Environmental Camp

This primitive camping area is on Davison Road, 3.2 miles from Highway 101. There are several sites, each accommodating up to eight campers, with a short hike to the sites from the parking area. Campers are required to carry out all garbage, and there is no water. Register at the Elk Prairie Entrance Station to obtain the gate lock combination.

Jedediah Smith Campground

Located in an extremely scenic campground location beside the Smith River, in Jedediah Smith Redwoods State Park northeast of Crescent City, this large campground has tent and RV sites, dump station, showers, and handicapped access. Several park trails fan out from the campground.

Mill Creek Campground

Located in Del Norte Redwoods State Park, south of Crescent City, 145 wooded RV and tent sites are at the bottom of Mill Creek Canyon. The campground has showers, dump station, and handicapped access.

SHELTER COVE

This little community on the Lost Coast is a prime spot for ocean fishing, and it offers accommodations for those who want to explore the Lost Coast, but don't want to camp in primitive campgrounds.

Marina Motel

533 Machi Road
Shelter Cove, CA 95589
(707) 986-7432

This is a nine-unit motel, with rooms facing the ocean, in addition to trailer units with kitchens. These units are beside the marina that services sport anglers with gas, supplies, and bait. **($$)**

Shelter Cove Beachcomber Inn

7272 Shelter Cove Road
Shelter Cove, CA 95589
(707) 986-7733

This motel is operated by the long-time leading family in this seaside village, the Machis. The inn has units with brass beds, fireplaces, stoves, and kitchens. **($$)**

Shelter Cove Campground

492 Machi Road
Shelter Cove, CA 95589
(707) 986-7474

The campground has 100 serviced sites, with full hookups, plus a tenting area, propane service, ice, and showers. There's a market and deli serving fish and chips, sandwiches, and other dishes.

Shelter Cove Motor Inn
205 Wave Drive
Shelter Cove, CA 95589
(707) 986-7521

All of the rooms face the ocean, with wonderful views of the crashing surf. Each room has a refrigerator with ice, plus in-room coffeemakers and satellite TV. Fishing guides are available. **($$)**

TRINIDAD

Trinidad is a picturesque community close to the southern boundary of Redwood National Park, near Patrick Point State Park and the Humboldt Lagoons area. Trinidad State Beach is just west of the small town, which has become an artist's colony.

Big D RV Park and Campground
3883 Patrick's Point Drive
Trinidad, CA 95570
(707) 677-3436

One of five private campgrounds on Patrick's Point Drive, Big D has hookups for RVs and trailers, plus tent sites.

Deer Lodge Motel and RV Park
753 Patrick's Point Drive
Trinidad, CA 95570
(707) 677-3554

This standard motel has a campground, suitable for RVs and trailers. **($ to $$)**

Lost Whale Bed and Breakfast Inn
3452 Patrick's Point Drive
Trinidad, CA 95570
(707) 677-3452

With a similar New England colonial look, this B & B has four ocean-view suites. **($$ to $$$)**

Trinidad Bed and Breakfast
Trinity and Edwards Streets
P.O. Box 849
Trinidad, CA 95570
(707) 677-0840

This is a Cape Cod–style home, on Edwards Street. The house has four rooms with views of the bay and expanded continental breakfast. **($$)**

Oregon Coast

Sherlock Holmes never visited the Oregon coast, but he probably would have uttered, "Elemental, my dear Watson!" to his friend the doctor. Sunny and beach-full in summer and storm-tossed in winter, the Oregon coast is a truly elemental place, where the great gray whales pass high rocky headlands on their migrations. Hundreds of thousands of visitors come here yearly to savor the wild mountain rivers, forest lakes, trails, massive sand dunes, wildlife marshes, wide beaches, and peaceful agricultural valleys; they sense that along this narrow, 300-mile stretch of natural wonder, the earth's primal forces have created just about the perfect natural environment.

From the Klamath Mountains sitting slightly inland at the southern end of the state to the continuous peaks of the Coast Range, this is an endless landscape of rugged beauty. The narrow strip of land between the mountains and the sea offers a wonderfully diverse series of environments, including rocky cliffs; haystacks and seastacks lashed by the surf; and rivers that swiftly flow from mountain ranges into estuaries that harbor many species of birds. Then, there are the spectacular shifting dunes, sprawling against the ocean along the southern coast, playing counterpoint to the flat and more placid recreational beaches of the central and northern coast.

To the south, between Coos Bay and Port Orford, the coastline changes from dunes to steep mountains, which dip their toes in the Pacific. Little towns hug the coast, and the Siskiyou

National Forest provides exciting trails to hike and rivers to raft. Closer to the California border, the Klamath Mountains were once (100 million years ago) an offshore island, severed from the mainland by unknown forces. The sea between the mountains and the coast gradually filled with sediment, putting the mountains back on the mainland. They are now located about 60 miles east of the coast and at least 50 miles north of where they once were.

The Oregon coast has long been a psychic refuge and vacation retreat for Oregonians, and more recently it has become a travel destination for people from afar. All of this vacation activity has created sizable beach communities, bringing the usual congestion, noise, and other human trappings, including wax museums, microbreweries, beachside motels, and chic boutiques found in resort communities. Yet a five-minute drive or a 30-minute walk from any of the towns will take you into pure, natural landscape—free from distraction and offering a blissful sense of quiet and peaceful solitude.

Whatever humankind has tried to do to the Oregon coast, just around the next corner is the elemental wilderness. Much of this natural wonder is the result of protection by agencies such as the National Forest Service, and the Oregon state parks department. Many miles of the Oregon coast and much of the nearby mountainsides are now set aside for scenic and habitat protection. And most of this was accomplished long before spotted owls became a regional obsession.

The coast is at its most elemental after the summer tourists depart for their urban pursuits. Several communities vie for the sobriquet of "storm-watching capital of the world." Winter is the time of year when the Pacific storms rage against the coastline, bringing windy tempests and huge waves that crash over the seastacks like some sort of avenging fury. Through all of this storm activity, the gray whales pursue their methodical and timeless journeys to their winter and summer habitats, first moving south to warmer and more peaceful waters to mate, and then returning to their north Pacific home. Fall and spring bring migratory birds that rest in the estuaries. Snow falls in the mountains, melting to bring life-sustaining moisture to the valleys. This is a place where the annual cycle of life is so pronounced that even the most blasé visitor can't miss it.

Early Days

Meriwether Lewis and William Clark had spent a long year (and almost spent themselves) when they found the Columbia River and began the fast descent to the Pacific Ocean. Native Americans stood on the high cliffs above the tiny boats, watching the intrepid explorers shoot the rapids in a hurry to finish their journey across more than half of the continent.

In 1803, Meriwether Lewis, private secretary to President Thomas Jefferson, was assigned the task of finding a transportation route to the Pacific, across the western lands that Jefferson considered to be of supreme importance to the future of his nation. Lewis chose Army Major William Clark to be the cocaptain of the expedition. They had waited out the winter of 1803–1804 on the banks of the Mississippi, across from the mouth of the Missouri.

On Monday, May 14, 1804, the two leaders and their crew of experienced frontiersmen set sail up the Missouri on their voyage of discovery. It took them until the next spring (June 1805) to reach the Great Falls of the Missouri, in what now is Montana. They then crossed the ranges of the Rocky Mountains, through Yellowstone country, across the Bitterroots into Idaho, down the Lemhi and Salmon Rivers, meeting the Nez Perce people. But the Salmon River was too dangerous and so the explorers headed east, away from the coast, once again traversing the Bitterroots, meeting members of the Flathead Nation in August. They were on horses, looking for the final route into northern Oregon. Once again they traveled west, meeting the Nez Perce for a second time, and storing their horses with the peaceable nation before making the final dash to the Pacific.

The explorers reached the Snake River, in November, and then the Columbia. They shot down the mighty Columbia, portaging over difficult rapids, but shooting the final rapids in their eagerness to end their journey. Lewis's first sighting of the ocean was on November 7, 1805. A few hours later, they had reached the coast.

They spent a rainy winter on the northern Oregon coast, constructing a makeshift fort near the present-day city of Astoria. They set out on their return journey, arriving to a tumultuous welcome in St. Louis in September 1806.

The journey of Lewis and Clark was the epic event that served to open the American West to transportation and colonization. The Oregon coast became an important part of the nation. Astoria was founded as a fur trading fort, after another group of adventurers—the Astorians—were sent to explore the west by John Jacob Astor. The forests along the Oregon coast provided timber for the construction of the great cities of the Northwest. Ports were built and business commenced, opening up the whole Pacific coast of the United States to trade and commerce.

If only Lewis and Clark had taken the time to travel south, along the coast, they might not have returned to St. Louis so quickly. What they missed was one of the most beautiful and wild landscapes in the world.

Native peoples had lived along the Oregon coast for more than a thousand years before the arrival of European sea captains and American settlers. The Tillamook lived to the north, meeting Lewis and Clark during their winter at the mouth of the Columbia. Far to the south, immigrant settlers from the east encountered several tribes, including the Modoc, Paiute, and Klamath. For good reason, the tribes became hostile to eastern settlers during the great migration of 1843, and the Klamath country became a battleground for the next two decades. Finally, after years of unfriendly relations, the Treaty of 1864 was signed between Klamath, Modoc, and Paiute leaders and the U.S. government.

The three groups, designated the Klamath tribe, were forced to live with each other in a combined reservation. The Modoc fought the idea and under an aggressive chief, called "Captain Jack," rebelled against the army based in Fort Klamath. As in all other "Indian wars," the Modoc won a few battles but lost the war. On June 1, 1873, Captain Jack surrendered after being betrayed by some of his tribesmen, who were tired of fighting.

The Modoc were shipped across the country to a reservation in what is now Oklahoma. Fort Klamath was abandoned in 1889. The Klamath Indian Reservation, which once was spread over 1,800 square miles, was reduced in size by 1961 to less than 1,350 acres. The forest industry had taken over much of the reservation area near Crater Lake. In the early 1890s, a federal law allowed tribes to take individual pieces of land for each member, and more than 75 percent of the tribal members took their claims, with the surplus land designated to benefit the tribe as a whole. In 1954, the assets of the tribe were liquidated, and each member of the tribe received a cash payment of $43,500.

The Oregon coast had long ceased to be a place for hunting and gathering by the native people of the region. Little seaside towns sprang up as fishing ports were established. In the first half of the 1900s, residents of the big inland towns and the city of Portland began traveling to the coast for recreation and rest. Tourism replaced fishing as the major industry. Two major national forests had been established to manage logging operations in the public lands of the Klamath and Coast Ranges. The forests also became prime places for recreational pursuits, with several tiny rustic villages established within the forests.

The coast, with its magnificent beaches, rocky heads, sprawling dunes, and seastack and haystack rocks, was considered a state treasure. In 1967, the state legislature declared the entire coastline public property to be managed by the state parks department for the benefit of all. From Astoria to Brookings, anyone may walk along the shoreline and across the headlands, hike the dunes, and relax on a beach, at any time.

Oregon Dunes

For nearly 50 miles, from the mouth of the Siuslaw to Cape Blanco at Coos Bay, the largest area of dunes in the country lies between the Pacific Ocean and the Coast Mountains. In places, the dunes extend 2.5 miles inland, and some are as high as 500 feet. In 1972, 32,186 acres of dunes, forest, streams, and lakes were set aside as the Oregon Dunes National Recreation Area (NRA).

These dunes are at least a million years old, but the production of the sand began at least 20 million years ago. The sand is the product of erosion, mainly of volcanic material from the Cascade Range, and later from the Klamath Mountains. The granitic material from the Klamath Range was laid down, alternately, with the sediment from the Cascade volcanoes, carried by ocean currents. In those early millennia, the dunes were covered by the sea. Before recent history, there was one set of dunes that stretched from the mountains to the shore.

Now there are two: the back dunes remaining from an earlier era, and the fore dunes, which are the result of importation of European beach grass around the turn of the century. The grass was planted to stabilize the dunes and adapted so successfully that it keeps up with the shifting sand, surviving burial, and spreading to the extent that if allowed to grow unchecked, the grass will cover the whole dunes area within the next hundred years. While there are vast stretches of dunes not presently covered with grass, much deliberation has taken place to determine whether intervention is necessary to preserve the dunes in something resembling their original state. For now, the beach grass continues to grow on the back dunes, while the ocean is building the lower fore dunes.

There are hard choices to be made. Eradicating beach grass with defoliants will destroy native plants and will affect the dunes' fauna, of which there is an amazing abundance. Letting the grass continue to grow will destroy the natural appearance of the dunes and prohibit the winds from carrying out their natural shifting of the sand—constantly creating new dunes architecture. The state of Oregon continues to wrestle with the problem.

The dunes are not made of just sand. There is water, coming down from the mountains, emptying into the ocean and creating marshy estuaries, which harbor waterbirds and amphibians, among many other animals. The snowy plover, an endangered shorebird, counts on the availability of ocean debris, including driftwood, on sand spits near the river mouths in order to breed. The osprey, found along the length of the dunes, rests on dead trees buried by the dunes. The great egret lives along banks, where the rivers meet the ocean.

A host of native plants grows on the dunes, now in danger of being overshadowed by the imported beach grass. Trees include the little shorepine, a type of lodgepole pine, that grows on windy knolls of sand. In more sheltered places, you'll find Douglas fir, Sitka spruce, western hemlock, and western red cedar. The abundant Scotch broom, seen in many places along the coastal highway, is not a native. It too was brought into Oregon to stabilize the sand during road building.

This is clearly not a wilderness preserve. There are too many people around for that, and the entire dunes area is, after all, a national recreation area. But there are sections of the dunes where a person can climb to the top of a high dune, look around, and see no one else, with the sea and mountains providing stirring backdrops. In this coastal area of Oregon—a heavily touristed region, where the primeval wilderness disappeared before 1900—this is as good as it gets. And it is good indeed.

Dunes, all dunes, are shrouded in an air of magic and mystery. The sand is constantly shifting, borne by breezes, often imperceptibly, creating a new dunescape. You can never count on seeing exactly the same scene twice, and so the present view is a once-in-a-lifetime experience. Another mystery is the abundant wildlife on and in the Oregon Dunes. There is a rich collection of plants, mammals, birds, amphibians, and insects that inhabit the dunes or live beside the dunes where the rivers meet the sea. This is not a sterile environment but an amazingly prolific ecosystem.

EXPLORING THE DUNES

The dunes are found south of Florence and north of the neighboring communities of Coos Bay, Charleston, and North Bend. They lie along the coast, with the estuaries of three major river valleys connected by two long stretches of sand. The Siuslaw River marks the northern boundary of the dunes, at Florence. The Umpqua River flows into Winchester Bay and the ocean, at the town of Reedsport, halfway along the stretch of dunes.

You'll find the recreation area headquarters and information center located west of Highway 101 in Reedsport. For information on dunes facilities and recreational opportunities, contact Oregon Dunes National Recreation Area, 855 Highway Avenue, Reedsport, OR 97467, or call (503) 271-3611 or (503) 271-3614. Off-road vehicle permits can be obtained at this office.

U.S. Highway 101, the coastal highway leading north from California, provides the main link to the national recreation area trails, viewpoints, campgrounds, and other facilities.

Parts of the dunes area are open to off-road vehicles. Rental shops are located at several points along the highway and in the towns. South Jetty Road, across the river from Florence, leads to a popular off-road staging area. Campgrounds in the stretch between Florence and Coos Bay (on and off the dunes) are operated by the recreation area, the state parks department, and the Siuslaw National Forest, which manages the dunes area. Many campgrounds are open year-round.

To provide some organization for a tour of the dunes, we list the following attractions from north to south, including several commercial attractions that appeal to families.

Fore Dunes–South Jetty Road Highway 101 leads south across the Siuslaw River Bridge. Less than a mile from the bridge, South Jetty Road runs west to the fore dunes area. This is a popular place for off-road vehicles (ORVs), and windsurfers are fond of testing the winds off the south jetty.

Sandland Adventures Two miles south of the Siuslaw bridge, Sandland offers four-wheel ORV rentals, or a guide will take you on a tour of the dunes. You'll find other amusements here, including bumper boats, go-carts, and miniature golf.

Jessie Honeyman State Park Open year-round, this 522-acre park includes three lakes: Woahink (on the east side of the highway), Cleawox, and Lilly. There is a large, year-round camping operation, suitable for tents, trailers, and RVs, and it includes several yurts. Day-use facilities are based on Cleawox Lake, including rental boats, a store, picnic areas, and swimming beaches. A trail around this lake is wheelchair-accessible. There are boat ramps, as well as picnic areas and swimming at Woahink Lake.

Sand Dunes Frontier This is another commercial "theme park," offering open-air bus tours of the dunes, dune buggy rides, and ORV rentals. Also included are miniature golf, a shooting gallery, a nature trail, and the usual refreshment stand.

Siltcoos Lake The small lake lies east of the highway, with camping at Tyee Campground. This small facility is operated by the national recreation area. The short road leads on to the Westlake Post Office and boat ramp.

Siltcoos Recreation Area This is part of the national recreation area. On the east side of the highway, you'll find hiking trails leading to Siltcoos Lake. There are six walk-in campsites beside the lake. On the west side, the road runs past four campgrounds: Lagoon, Waxmyrtle, Lodgepole, and Driftwood. This is off-road vehicle country, and the campgrounds are popular with the dune buggy crowd, but there are dune trails where only walkers are allowed. The road comes to an end near the beach.

Carter Lake Campground   This is another Oregon Dunes NRA campground, more primitive than the state park campgrounds, but suitable for cars and RVs. As with the other NRA campgrounds, this one has trails leading through the dunes. Many people just take off on their own cross-country explorations.

Oregon Dunes Overlook   You'll find the overlook nine miles south of Florence. A park road leads a quarter-mile to a parking lot. Viewing from the overlook is one of the best ways to get a feel for this vast area. Stairs, and an 80-foot wheelchair ramp, lead to the high viewing platform for a panoramic look at miles of dunes. A marked one-mile trail across the dunes leads through a shorepine grove to the beach.

Tahkenitch Lake   A boat ramp is found along the highway, three miles south of the overlook. A half-mile farther south is a medium-size campground and another boat ramp. This is a popular stop for anglers, but there is no drinking water at the campground. A larger campground is located across Highway 101, operated by the Oregon Dunes NRA. There is a wheelchair-accessible fishing pier.

Reedsport   This little town has a working harbor with a crab dock over Winchester Bay. The information center for the Oregon Dunes National Recreation Area is located at the north end of town. The waterfront boardwalk was built in the spring of 1993. You could take a scenic sidetrip east, along State Route 38, beside the Umpqua River. There are fishing points along the river. A loop road leads from the community of Winchester Bay (south of Reedsport), to Windy Cove County Park (day-use and camping), and the former U.S. Coast Guard Station, containing historical exhibits on the region and the Umpqua Lighthouse. Across the road from the lighthouse, which is still operational, is the Umpqua River whale-watching station, a fine place to observe the whales that pass by during their semiannual migrations. Two miles down the loop road, Umpqua Lighthouse State

Park offers overnight camping, plus picnicking and other day-use facilities.

William M. Tugman State Park Located on Eel Lake, the park offers a developed campground, including sites for tents, RVs, and trailers (up to 50 feet). There is also a hiker-biker campground. This is a handy place to stay. As no reservations are taken, the park often has spaces when other RV parks do not. There is a fishing dock, accessible to wheelchairs.

North Eel Creek Campground Back in the Oregon Dunes NRA, this large campground has sites for tents and RVs. This is an excellent place to walk over miles and miles of dunes, which stretch as far as the eye can see.

Spinreel Campground This Oregon Dunes NRA campground provides access to Tenmile Creek and is a favorite of dune buggy drivers. This is another area open to off-road vehicles.

Horsfall Dunes and Beach This is the southernmost area in the Oregon Dunes. Access to a huge dunes area and a beach is via Horsfall Road, which passes three recreation area campgrounds, ending at a beach parking lot. The first campground along the access road is Horsfall, designated for ORV people. Bluebill is the next campground, a small, quieter facility. The third is Wild Mare Horse Camp, with a corral at each of the campsites. People without horses are also welcomed. You can also camp in the parking lot at the beach.

DUNES TRAILS

There are several hiking trails in the dunes that do not connect directly to the beach. One of the most popular is the Bluebill Trail that circles the 40-acre Bluebill Lake. To get to the trailhead, drive 2.5 miles east of Highway 101 on Horsfall Beach Road at the southernmost end of the national recreation area (just north of Coos Bay). There's a horse camp in this area in addition to tent and trailer sites at Horsfall Beach Campground.

The Umpqua Trail is accessed from Eel Lake Campground, near Lakeside, eight miles south of Reedsport. This trail leads through an evergreen forest and breaks out into open sand. The magnificent, high dunes are at least a half-mile wide at this point.

THOSE OFF-ROAD VEHICLES

A word to nature-loving purists: You may be annoyed, even outraged, by the presence of commercial "theme parks" and off-road vehicles on what should be seen as pristine dunes, bathed only in the quiet whispers of off-shore breezes, and not by the sounds of little buglike moving things that buzz like huge, angry mosquitoes and belch noxious fumes. Approximately half of the Oregon Dunes National Recreation Area is open to dune buggies and the other types of off-road vehicles that run up and down the dunes, making noise and scarring the sand. That leaves at least half of the dunes for the rest of us, in as pristine a state as European beach grass will allow, and there to be hiked, sifted through fingers, scuffled by feet, lain upon, picnicked on, and otherwise admired.

And if it's any consolation, it seems the effect of buggies running across the dunes is slight to nil, and the NRA prohibits dune buggies from driving over areas with natural vegetation. If this were not true, many otherwise peaceable naturalists might be joining the other NRA to correct the problem. Nature has a way of quickly repairing the scars, for that's what shifting sand is all about. Even your own footprints will probably have disappeared by the day after your dunes encounter. So, if you're likely to have your psyche upset by dune buggies, plan your visit for those areas where only visitors on foot are welcomed. Either that, or take a horse and leave a few longer-lasting reminders (including fertilizer for the beach grass) on the almost-pristine sands.

North Oregon Coast

The 168 miles of coastline north of the Oregon Dunes is the historic area discovered by Lewis and Clark, and it is much loved by summer visitors from Portland and other nearby cities. Astoria, at the mouth of the Columbia River, is a city filled with history, from the prehistoric encampments through the fur trading period and the days when the Columbia River was a major trading thoroughfare. The historical attractions of the Astoria area include a reconstruction of the Lewis and Clark winter encampment (Fort Clatsop) and a Civil War bastion (Fort Stephens), which was built to keep potential Confederate invaders out on the ocean or blasted off it with cannons. The fort is now included in a state park, located 10 miles west of Astoria, with nature trails, swimming in Coffenbury Lake, and the trailhead for the Oregon Coast Trail located at the south jetty in the northwest corner of the park. The trail, not yet completed, offers long stretches of hiking trail along the state's ocean beaches and headlands. Fort Stephens has a large camping facility, with RV and trailer sites accommodating vehicles up to 69 feet long. To make camping reservations, write Fort Stephens State Park, Hammond, OR 97121.

SOUTH FROM ASTORIA

You'll encounter mixed attractions, including a few delightful forest walks in the Siskiyou National Forest, a dozen towns of varying sizes along the beaches and slightly inland in the agricultural valleys, and notable state parks that serve to protect the seashore while offering bits of Oregon history (including several lighthouses) and fascinating natural environments. This is the coastal area known for haystacks and seastacks, the huge rocks rising offshore.

Ecola State Park provides the first major access to the oceanside. Located 28 miles south of Astoria, the park offers wonderful views of the ocean and beaches, all the way south to Oswald West State Park. This park has 3.5 miles of walkable beach, plus fine stands of Sitka spruce and western hemlock. Elk and deer live in the park. Within the park, the Tillamook Head Trail runs six miles between the towns of Seaside and Cannon Beach. The park includes a walk-in campground at Indian Creek.

Highway 101 continues southward, through the town of Seaside, and then past Cannon Beach and the Tillamook Rock Lighthouse (decommissioned) a mile offshore. Just south of the Clatsop/Tillamook county line is Oswald West State Park, named in honor of the state governor who proclaimed the Oregon beaches to be publicly accessible. This park includes most of Neahkanie Mountain (with a trail) and Cape Falcon. A quarter-mile hike leads tenters to a number of primitive campsites in the forest. The park is well known to surfers. You'll find a series of scenic viewpoints along the highway. Neahkanie Beach is in the southern portion of the park at the base of the mountain.

South of the town of Manzanita, Nehalem Bay State Park is reached by an access road leading west for three miles. The park extends to the tip of the spit enclosing Nehalem Bay, with large campgrounds, camping in yurts, a horse camp with corrals, and a hiker-biker camp. No reservations are taken. There is a boat ramp at the nearby town of Nehalem.

Manhattan Beach Wayside Park, 48 miles south of Astoria, is a day-use picnic area on the beach. Tillamook County maintains a campground beside Lake Lytle, two miles south of the wayside. The highway continues through Rockaway Beach (the town), and then through three small towns on the eastern shore of Tillamook Bay (Barview, Garibaldi, and Bay City). It then leads inland a few miles to the town of Tillamook—a mecca for cheese lovers with the huge Tillamook Cheese Factory (specializing in Cheddar) and Blue Heron Cheese (housed in an old Dutch dairy barn, dedicated to making Brie and Camembert). Both cheese factories welcome visitors for tasting and buying.

THREE CAPES AREA

The Three Capes Scenic Loop is a route leading west from Highway 101 to an exceptionally beautiful piece of coastline, which includes Cape Meares, Cape Lookout, and Cape Kiwanda. Cape Meares State Park is a large day-use park offering picnicking, beach activity, and a visit to the historic Cape Meares Lighthouse. Three Arch Rocks National Wildlife Refuge is a prime birding area, known for the largest flock of puffins on the Pacific Coast. Cape Lookout State Park has camping within its 1,974 acres. This is one of the state coastal parks that take campsite reservations between Memorial Day and Labor Day. For information on availability and to make reservations, call the state parks department at 800-452-5687 (in-state and out of Portland), or (503) 731-3411 (in Portland and out of state). Two parks encompass the Cape Kiwanda area: a Tillamook County park includes the parking area; the state park contains the cape. There's a huge haystack offshore. As the Three Capes Loop passes Pacific City, the route provides access to Bob Stroud State Park. This day-use park offers exciting walking on a section of dunes on Nestucca Spit.

Tufted puffin

The Cascade Head Experimental Forest is found along the historic (former) Highway 101, which leads off the newer 101, just south of the town of Neskowin. The forest headquarters office provides information on silvaculture. Another sideroad, this one three miles south of Neskowin, leads to Cascade Head.

ENDLESS BEACH

The stretch of coast south of the three capes contains the popular Lincoln County beaches, a continuous 60 miles of white, sandy beach, with a succession of state beach parks and beach-side tourist towns, including Lincoln City, Gleneden Beach, Depoe Bay, Otter Rock, Newport, Seal Rock, Waldport, and Yachats (pronounced YA-hots). Halfway down this strip of beach is Newport, positioned on Yaquinna Bay, the home of the Oregon Coast Aquarium and the Hatfield Marine Science Center next door. Keiko, the orca star of the *Free Willy* movies, has migrated from Mexico and is now in residence in an upscale killer whale home in the Oregon Coast Aquarium. The science center sponsors daily dock and estuary walks during summer. The aquarium, with its displays of marine animals plus a seabird aviary, charges an entry fee. Entry to the science center is free. The major section of the Siuslaw National Forest appears just south of Newport, where it is two miles inland. By the time you reach Yachats and Cape Perpetua, Highway 101 is into the forest, with access to scenic trails and Forest Service campgrounds.

Crossing the Lincoln/Lanc county line, we're now 168.5 miles south of Astoria—more than halfway down the Oregon coast—and at an unsigned beach access point, one of many along the coast that provide paths onto secluded stretches of ocean beach. This beach is noted for a sea "horn," a spout of water shooting through holes in the rock. There are other horns to the south. Neptune State Park (another mile) has picnic tables and restrooms. Less than a mile south is a short road to the Cummins Ridge Trailhead. This is a prime, 18.6-mile hiking loop in the Siuslaw National Forest.

A small wayside park is located at Bob Creek. Again, there are no facilities, but a short stay here is recommended. Mussels are in plentiful supply on the rocks at low tide, and the creek mouth is a home for ducks. Harlequin ducks have been seen here. Four miles south of Bob Creek, Ocean Beach State Park offers picnicking in a small wayside area next to another beach. The Forest Service operates Rock Creek Campground, a small but extremely scenic site in the forest, about a quarter-mile from the highway.

Two major state parks are located just north of Florence. Carl G. Washburne State Park comprises 1,800 acres of beach (more than a mile long) and shoreline vegetation. China Creek and Cape Creek flow through the park, offering wildlife habitat. You can explore tide pools and view elk at a distance. A day-use area with picnic tables and restrooms is located west of Highway 101. A campground is east of the highway, with additional walk-in sites and a hiker-biker camp. The campground is open year-round. Devil's Elbow State Park is adjacent to the Hecata Head Lighthouse. The park is a day-use facility for picnicking and walking along the seafront. The historic lighthouse is open for tours Thursday through Sunday from noon to 5 P.M. during the summer months.

For most visitors, a weekend or a week on the northern Oregon coast is spent on the beach or driving to the scenic parks and viewpoints. For those who wish to venture off the beaten track, there are many trails in the Siuslaw National Forest and portions of the Oregon Coast Trail. The latter will take you between the well-traveled parks and viewpoints, providing a private perspective on this impressive coastline.

South Oregon Coast

The southern 150 miles of Highway 101 covers an amazing range of coastal features, in addition to the Siskiyou National Forest, which is found to the east of the highway for 80 miles. Coos Bay is the largest ocean port in Oregon, a shipping way station for lumber and other resource materials. The city is located on Coos Bay, with North Bend and Charleston to the north and south, respectively. Charleston is the historic community, resembling a typical New England seaport village, only it's here on the Pacific Coast. The communities are just south of the Oregon Dunes National Recreation Area.

HEADLANDS AND BEACHES

As Highway 101 leads south from Coos Bay, the Cape Arago Highway (State Route 240) provides a loop drive to the coast and several natural attractions. The route passes the Charleston Boat Basin and the historic downtown area before the junction with Seven Devils Road, which leads south to the South Slough Estuarine Reserve. The reserve is probably the Oregon coast's best point to observe waterfowl in great numbers. Ten miles from Highway 101, Bastendorff County Park has a large campground plus day-use facilities, including picnic areas perched overlooking the ocean. Sunset Bay State Park also features camping and picnicking. The large campground at Sunset Bay is one of the facilities available through state parks reservations during the summer months: 800-452-5687 (in-state and out of Portland), or (503) 731-3411 (in Portland and out of state).

Shore Acres Botanical Gardens State Park is a memorial and tribute to Louis Simpson, a real-life timber baron who built an estate on the property. The mansions are gone (one burned and the other was torn down), but the extensive gardens remain and are open to the public, ablaze during evening hours with a multitide of more than 150,000 lights twinkling during the winter holidays. The park has a storm shelter on a scenic ocean viewpoint, and you can pick up a portion of the Oregon Coast Trail in the park.

Cape Arago State Park—on the same loop road—has a trail that leads north along a ridge where sea lions and seals are seen on the rocks that comprise the Oregon Islands National Wildlife Refuge. This portion of the shoreline is noted for its fierce winter winds and raging surf, and this park is probably the best place to see winter storms. Storm watching has become an important annual event for many visitors, who come to experience the brutal effects of the wildest of Pacific seasons. The park has picnic areas.

The Cape Arago Highway eventually rejoins Highway 101. Bullard's Beach State Park has a large campground with full and electrical hookups for RVs and trailers, plus tent sites and a few yurts in which to stay. The park also has hiker-biker and horse campsites, and includes four miles of beach with dunes and forest, with access to the Coquille River north jetty and lighthouse. The campground is open year-round and reservations are not required.

The town of Bandon is another cheese lover's haven, with a factory producing distinctive Cheddars. There is a retail store on Highway 101. South of town is the Beach Loop Drive, passing Bandon Rocks, a small wayside picnic park, and Bandon State Park. There is no camping along this road, but the beaches are fine and generally uncrowded, with an impressive display of offshore rocks.

Other smaller parks lie to the south along Highway 101. The road to Cape Blanco is found 26.5 miles south of Bandon. Located five miles west of Highway 101, Cape Blanco State Park has a campground and also a lighthouse located at the westernmost point in Oregon. The campground has electrical hookups, hiker-biker areas, and a horse camp. Inside the park is the historic Hughes House, built for a pioneer family in 1898. Tours of the home are available from May to September: Thursday to Monday from 10 A.M. to 4 P.M., and on Sundays from noon to 4 P.M.

South of the small town of Port Orford, Humbug Mountain State Park offers a three-mile hiking trail to the summit of the mountain, at an elevation of 1,750 feet. Another trail links the park campground (no reservations necessary) and picnic areas.

ROGUE RIVER COUNTRY

The southern end of the Oregon coast is a combination of Oregon and California landscape. The Siskiyou Mountains touch the sea for much of the last 40 miles, with the Klamath Range slightly inland. In the center of this forest area is the small town of Gold River. This is where the Rogue River reaches the sea after tumbling down the mountain slopes from its source, a series of springs near Crater Lake. Brookings and Harbor, two towns on either side of the mouth of the Chetco River, are close to the California border.

There's a unique mix of vegetation found in southwestern Oregon, including redwoods that have sneaked into the state from nearby California, myrtle, and huge Douglas firs. You can experience this ecosystem by visiting Loeb State Park, located inland from the town of Brookings. The park was created to preserve a grove of virgin myrtle trees. A short trail follows the Chetco River through the extremely dense grove and leads to a Forest Service trail that climbs through a grove of tall Douglas firs and then into a coast redwood forest. These trees are at the north end of their range. It's easy to see why early explorers of this region dreamed of the legendary Sasquatch, or Bigfoot, living in these incredibly dense and moist forests.

The town of Gold Beach is named for the gold discovered here in the mid-1800s. The town offers camping, ocean and river fishing, and the famous jet boats that take visitors up the Rogue for an unforgettable trip. They are successors to the early mail boats that ran mail and supplies to mining and lumber camps along the river. Today, the Wild and Scenic Rogue is protected, from Lobster Creek about ten miles upriver to Grants Pass. The Illinois River, which flows into the Rogue just downstream from the wilderness reserve, is also part of the Wild and Scenic River system. It is classified as wild for 30 miles, and another 18 miles is designated as scenic. Both rivers are descended by rafters and kayakers.

Rogue River Trail The Rogue is a prime rafting river, and the Siskiyou National Forest's Rogue River Trail is one of the best ways to experience the Oregon wilderness while catching the historical flavor of the area, as it parallels the river from near Grants Pass to a point about 31 miles from Gold Beach.

Access: Drive along U.S. Highway 101 to the town of Gold Beach. Take Jerry's Flat Road (also known as Forest Road 33) along the south side of the Rogue River for 31 miles, past the little river resort community of Agness, and onward past a river crossing. After crossing the bridge, turn right, and continue upriver for another four miles. The trailhead is located at Illahe, near Illahe Lodge.

The Trail: The trail is 40 miles long, climbing beside the river as it winds through the forest, past the community of Marial, to its end at Grave Creek, on the Rogue, about 24 miles from Grants Pass and Interstate 5. The elevation change from beginning to end is only 200 feet, but the various ups and downs require five days to do the hike. There are abundant campsites along the route. Trail maps are available from the Forest Service ranger stations in Gold Beach and Grants Pass. Ask for Trail #1160.

The Hike: This trail offers a great deal of quiet solitude, and except for rafters passing on their way down the river, you'll see few people on the trail. Wildlife is apparent along every section of the trail. To avoid plundering by bears, be sure to hang your food out of reach. The trail passes Illahe Lodge, and at mile one, it enters the Wild Rogue Wilderness. There is a wonderful waterfall at Flora Dell Creek, and those who stay at Illahe Lodge often do this portion of the longer trail as a day-hike. The round trip from the lodge to the falls is nine miles, and the elevation change is only 50 feet.

Clay Hill Lodge is at mile six, and Camp Tacoma, with tent sites, is another mile. This campground is located near Tate Creek. You'll see remains of the old gold mine at Solitude Bar (mile eight), and at Bushy Bar (mile nine). Blossom Bar (with campsites) is at mile 13, the location of a stamp mill that once processed ore from the area mines. At mile 16, the trail leaves the forest temporarily, on a Forest Service road, to pass the town of Marial, and the historic Rogue River Ranch. There are more campsites at East Mule Creek. A literary relic is seen at Winkle Bar (mile 22). The log cabin here was once owned by western author Zane Grey.

Numerous campsites are located along the route between Winkle Bar and the eastern trailhead. More mining ruins from the 1851 gold rush are found at mile 37. Reaching Whiskey Creek, you'll see a miner's cabin dating back to 1880. Rainie Falls is at mile 38, and the end of the trail is at mile 40. You're 24 miles from Grants Pass.

BIRDS

Common Murre
Uria aalge
One of the largest colonies of this black and white seabird is found on the rocks of the Oregon Islands National Wildlife Refuge, in the Three Capes area. This is one of the larger members of the auk family. In summer, the entire head and neck are black, with white below. In winter, the cheek, throat, and neck are white, and a black line curves down behind the eye. It stands upright, like a penguin. Its habitat is the open sea and gulfs. Murres catch their fish at sea and return to land only to rest. It ranges widely over the Western Hemisphere, wherever cold currents bring a good supply of fish. Along the Pacific Coast, the murre is seen as far south as California and as far northwest as the Aleutians. Its voice is like its name—a long moan: *aaarr-r-r-r.*

Snowy Plover
Charadrius alexandrinus
This waterbird is endangered on the Pacific Coast and is the subject of much study by biologists. Its habitat includes mud or salt flats and also sandy shores. It is seen in small numbers in several estuaries between the Oregon Dunes. It is a small whitish or sandy bird, with an incomplete breast band and also an eyeline that is not all there. Its bill and feet are darker than the semi-palmated plover, which has yellow feet. The snowy is found along the Pacific Coast from southwestern Washington to Baja California. Its voice is a deep *krut* and also a whistled *ku-wheeet.*

Tufted Puffin
Fratercula corniculata
You'll find this pigeon-sized seabird along the Oregon coast, particularly in Cape Meares National Wildlife Reserve, where it sits upright on sea cliffs. It has a stubby, black body, a white face, and yellowish tufts hanging behind its eyes. Its large, orange bill is parrotlike. In winter the bill changes to a dusky color and the tufts disappear. Like the murre, this bird feeds at sea and comes to the cliffs to rest. It lives alone or in colonies. A few tufted puffins are on the Oregon coast. It is seen in much greater numbers on the Alaskan and British Columbia coasts. It winters as far south as California. It doesn't make much of a sound, except for a growling note when it is on or near the nesting place.

Tundra Swan
Cygnus columbiana
One of the best places to see this beautiful bird is the dunes area of the Oregon coast during winter months. It's also called the whistling swan and is well known for its high-pitched whistle, *wow-wow,* usually heard from high in the sky as the flock descends to its

overnight resting place. It is a large white swan, with its neck held straight and stiff. The black bill often has a small yellow spot near the eye. The immature whistler has a grayish-brown color, with a pink bill. It breeds near the Arctic coast between the Bering Sea and Hudson's Bay. It winters along the Pacific Coast and is often seen inland, floating on small ponds as far east as the Sierra Nevada foothills.

Cinnamon Teal
Anas cyanoptera
This male duck has an overall chestnut brown color, with a distinctive light blue patch on the front edge of the wing. The female is a mottled brown, with blue on the forewing. Both male and female have a large bill. When flying, the cinnamon and blue-winged teal look quite the same. The cinnamon teal inhabits fresh ponds and marshes. Its range is from southwest Canada to Mexico.

MAMMALS

California Sea Lion
Zalophus californianus
The huge sea lion has become a steady fixture at docks along the Pacific Coast, including the Fisherman's Wharf section of San Francisco Harbor. It is seen along the coast as far south as Baja California and as far north as Vancouver, B.C. It is a steady sight

along the Oregon coast. Buff to brown (looking darker when wet), the male grows to a length of eight feet, while the female is somewhat smaller, growing to about 6.5 feet. The male has a high forehead. There aren't as many California sea lions as there used to be. They were hunted for their blubber and were also a prime ingredient in dog food. They are now protected by law. They live along rocky beaches and in caves, including the Sea Lion Caves, a commercial attraction in southern Oregon. Unless there is an easier supply of fish (as in fishing harbors), it prefers to live on islands. It leaves the northern coast to breed in California's Channel Islands and along Baja California.

Gray Whale
Eschrichtius robustus
This giant of the sea is seen migrating along the Oregon coast, part of its annual round-trip journey to breed in the winter calving grounds of Baja California. In spring, they return to their summer feeding grounds in the Arctic. Unlike other whales, their spout is finely dispersed, more like a cloud of mist. If you happened to fly over a gray whale, you'll see a huge torpedo shape tapered at both ends. It is mottled gray, but often appears lighter when it surfaces. The back has a low hump two-thirds of the way down the body, with serrated ridges behind the hump. It migrates in coastal waters close to the shore.

TREES, SHRUBS, AND UNDERSTORY PLANTS

Port Orford Cedar

Chamaecyparis lawsoniana

This gray-green native tree of southern Oregon and northwestern California is also called Lawson cypress. It is a coastal tree, with Coos Bay its northernmost habitat. It is a strong feature in the lower-level forests of the Siskiyou Mountains, where it is found with Douglas fir and myrtle. It is also cultivated and sold in other areas of the Pacific Northwest, and it is seen in many yards and parks. The branches are distinctive, growing straight from the trunks and then drooping just before the tips. The cones are globular, with many scales. It grows to a height of about 160 feet and has a lemony odor.

Incense Cedar

Calocedrus decurrens

The incense cedar is used as a Christmas tree in Oregon and California, and it is common in the Cascades of southern Oregon and in the Siskiyou Mountains. It is grown by tree farmers out of its native range, particularly in Oregon's Willamette Valley and California's Central Valley. Quite unlike the more widespread western red cedar, its leaves are longer than they are wide. The branches are slender and drooping. The foliage is a darker green than the western red, and the foliage has a distinctive (some say disagreeable) odor. The cones are also different, growing to almost an inch long, and are made up of six scales, two of which are seed-bearing. When separating, the cones look like duck bills. Used commercially to make pencils, the incense cedar grows to a height of 130 feet.

Madrone

Arbutus menziesii

People in British Columbia call it arbutus, while people below the border call it madrone. It is one of the coastal trees that mixes with coniferous species, including Douglas fir, Sitka spruce, hemlock, and cedar. It is quite a distinctive tree, with evergreen leaves and a reddish-brown bark that cracks and peels away from the trunk and branches. The leaf blades are oval-shaped and dark green and shiny above, and much lighter below. It bears flowers, in clusters, in May and June. The berries are bright orange-red, ripening in the fall, often holding on to the tree well into winter. Madrones are helped to reproduce by birds, who eat the berries, scattering the seeds at a distance from the host tree.

Oregon (or California) Myrtle

Umbellularia californica

Some botanists insist that this tree should be called the "Pacific laurel," because it is closely related to the laurel or bay tree. A visitor to the southern Oregon and Northern California coast sees many myrtlewood stores along the highway, selling furniture and highly polished gewgaws made of this hard, gnarled tree. Myrtle trees that grow in the open usually have twisted, gnarled trunks. They grow to a height of 65 feet, with evergreen, lance-shaped leaves. When torn, the leaves smell like camphor. It bears small flowers, followed by round fruits about an inch long, with just one seed. There is a fine stand of myrtle in Loeb State Park, near the town of Brookings.

Sugar Pine
Pinus lambertiana
This is a close relative of the western white pine, except that the sugar pine has longer cones (from 10 to 17 inches) and pointed needles. It is found in the southern Cascades and in smaller numbers in the Siskiyou and Klamath Ranges. It is also related to the whitebark pine, which grows in the southern British Columbia mountains and on the Olympic Peninsula. The sugar pine is seen slightly inland from the Oregon coast, in mountain groves along with Douglas firs, oaks, and madrones. They are also found along the course of the Rogue River and at elevations as high as 4,600 feet.

Pacific Rhododendron
Rhododendron macrophyllum
There is nothing more pleasing than to visit the Oregon Dunes and to come across a rhododendron spread across the sand with a showy display of its bright pink

tubular flowers, surviving in what must be a hostile environment. Its evergreen leaves are large and leathery. The flowers are borne in rounded clusters. The color of Oregon rhodos ranges from a light pink to rosy purple. You may see the odd white-flowered plant. The Pacific rhododendron grows along much of the coastline, from southwestern British Columbia, where it grows wild in the B.C. Cascades, to the Oregon and Northern California coast where there are large groves of rhododendron shrubs. The plant grows in acidic soils or in shady evergreen forests, where the trees enhance the acidic properties of the soil. You'll see mass displays of rhodos in late spring and early summer.

Tan Oak
Lithocarpus densifloras
Found in California redwood forests as well as in the Rogue/Chetco Rivers area near the Oregon coast, the tan oak is not an oak at all. It is an evergreen shrub that populates the understory of dense conifer forests. It grows to about eight feet, with a round top and round-tipped, alternate leaves. The brown or gray bark is smooth. It bears male and female flowers on the same plant. The male flowers exude a foul odor. One to three female flowers grow at the base of the male catkin or in separate catkins. This tree lives on rocky mountain slopes and ridges, at elevations from 2,500 to 11,000 feet. Southern Oregon is its northern limit. It is widely found in the Sierra Nevada and is seen in quan-

tity in Redwood National Park, across the California border.

WILDFLOWERS AND GRASSES

Henderson's Checker-mallow
Sidalcea hendersonii
This taprooted perennial grows from a short rhizome, bearing a deep pink flower (something like small hollyhocks) on hollow, leafy stems. The stalks grow to a height of about five feet. This wildflower is found only along the southeastern coast of Vancouver Island and south along the narrow Pacific coastline, and in Oregon, as far south as the mouth of the Umpqua River. Other checker-mallows grow farther inland, including such places as the Willamette Valley (rose checker-mallow) and the southern Cascades (meadow checker-mallow). Henderson's is also called marsh hollyhock, and its botanical name is somewhat similar. It grows in tidal marshes and wet meadows at low elevations.

Darlingtonia
Darlingtonia californica
Another water-loving plant, the darlingtonia (also called the pitcher plant and the cobra lily) is found in sphagnum bogs in Northern California as well as in the Siskiyou Mountains and along the coast as far north as Florence. Darlingtonia Wayside Park, beside Highway 101, is a protected bog environment that has a fine display of this flower. It is the only member of the pitcher plant family found on the West

Coast. The plant has quite a beautiful structure, with leaves growing upright to a length of more than 19 inches and a creeping stem. The leaves are tubular, rising to a hood that droops over the opening. Hanging from the hood is an appendage that looks like a whale's tail. The plant bears yellowish-green flowers, singly, on a stalk that is higher than the leaf tops. The fruit is a capsule, a little more than an inch long.

Globe Gilia
Gilia capitata
Unlike the beautiful red skyrocket gilia that grows in the southern Cascades, the globe gilia is an annual, with tiny light blue flowers that are forked in dense, ball-shaped heads. The flowers grow from short stems found at the ends of upright leafy stems. The stem leaves are arranged alternately, with one or two lobes, which have narrow segments. The fruits are capsules, each with three chambers and one to three seeds per chamber. This gilia grows in dry to moist meadows, on rocky slopes, forest clearings, and roadsides, mostly at lower elevations.

European Beach Grass
Ammophilia arenaria
This grass, which is taking over the Oregon Dunes, was imported from Europe around the turn of the century. It was planted to control the movement of sand, including stabilizing roadsides. It is well adapted to this work, being an excellent sand-binder. The problem is that

this grass changes the entire topography of the dunes, in particular causing the creation of a whole new set of fore dunes, closer to the ocean. This is a tough perennial grass, growing in tufts connected by deep, creeping rhizomes. The narrow and very stiff leaves are rolled inward. The flower cluster (inflorescence) is a stout spike, with soft, hairy bracts (glumes and lemmas). In its natural environment, European beach grass is the main ground cover plant on rocky, treeless islands and along ocean shores, where rocky or sand beaches meet the forest.

Douglas Iris
Sisyrinchium angustifolium
Douglas iris, also called grass-widows, is found in moister areas at the edges of the dunes and throughout the coastal areas of southern Oregon. In the Northwest, it is primarily a Columbia Gorge wild-flower, and it is also found on Whidbey Island, but not on the nearby San Juan Islands. It has a beautiful flower, with satiny, reddish sepals and petals. The color does vary from location to location. Many grass-widows in southern Oregon have a salmon tinge; a few may be white. This plant, like many others including the Douglas fir, was named for the early 19th-century Scottish botanist who explored the flora of the Pacific Northwest.

Cardwell's Penstemon
Penstemon cardwellii
This low shrub has a limited range, which includes the Cascade Range

in Washington and Oregon, and the other southern Oregon mountains: the Klamath and Siskiyou Ranges. This low shrub grows to a height of about 11 inches, producing bright purple to deep violet flowers with long, woolly anthers. Flowers grow up the stalks in small terminal clusters and in the axils of the upper leaves. It also bears a capsule fruit. It grows on the edges of open forests and along rocky slopes at middle elevations.

Coast Penstemon
Penstemon serrulatus
This perennial has a much wider range than Cardwell's, growing as far north as Prince Rupert, B.C., and throughout the Olympic Peninsula and the Cascade Range. It has a branching, woody base and several hairy stems. The sawtooth leaves are opposite, with the lower leaves smaller than the upper leaves. The flowers are a deep blue to dark purple, much like Cardwell's, and the trumpet shape of its flower is also similar. The coast penstemon grows on streambanks, on moist, rocky slopes, and in gullies from low to middle elevations. It is seen along the Rogue River Trail and along the other streams that flow into the Pacific in Oregon and Washington.

Silverweed
Potentilla anserina (ssp. *pacific*)
Unlike other cinquefoils found along the Pacific Coast, silverweed is recognized by its long runners and flowers that grow alone at the end of its leafless stalk. Its yellow flowers have five oval petals. The

plant is a perennial herb that grows from its rooted runners. The popular name comes from the plant's gray, hairy appearance. Silverweed has been a food source on the Pacific Coast. The roots were eaten, either prepared fresh or from the dried state. The Haida made a tea from boiled roots. Others used the silverweed for medicinal purposes, boiling the roots and mixing the pulp with oil to make a poultice.

Douglas iris

WHERE TO STAY

The Oregon coast has thousands of places to stay, including deluxe resorts, rustic cabins, hotels, motels, bed and breakfast inns and homes, forest lodges, coastal fishing lodges, private RV parks and campgrounds, and public campgrounds operated by state and county parks departments and the U.S. Forest Service. Public campgrounds are noted earlier in this chapter. Following is a short selection of some of the more distinctive places to stay in the Oregon Dunes area and south of the dunes in the Rogue River region. For more places to stay along the Oregon coast, a good place to start is by contacting local chambers of commerce, or subscribing to *Oregon Coast* magazine, P.O. Box 18000, Florence, OR 97430-9970, or call 800-348-8401.

AGNESS

Lucas Pioneer Ranch and Lodge
03904 Cougar Lane
P.O. Box 37
Agness, OR 97406
(541) 247-7443

This old country inn, in a little riverside town along the Rogue River in the Siskiyou National Forest, is known for its relaxing atmosphere. This is mainly a cabin operation, with a few rooms in the lodge building. Some cabins have kitchen facilities. The dining room here is noted for its tasty and filling meals and its informal ambience. Agness is east of the town of Gold River, via Jerry's Flat Road. **($ to $$)**

BANDON

Bandon RV Park
935 Second Street South East
Bandon, OR 97411
(541) 347-4122

This medium-size RV and trailer park is on Highway 101, with hookups and showers. Restaurants are nearby.

Inn at Face Rock
3225 Beach Loop Road
Bandon, OR 97411
(541) 347-9441 or 800-638-3092

This seaside resort is located on the beach, near Bandon's golf course. The large resort motel has ocean-view suites with kitchens and fireplaces as well as standard rooms, a restaurant, whirlpool, and horseback riding. **($$ to $$$)**

New Gorman Motel
1110 11th Street South West
Bandon, OR 97411
(541) 347-9451

A two-story motel at Coquille Point, it is perched atop a headland, looking down on a rugged beach and haystack rocks. There is access to the seashore. Rooms have fireplaces and whirlpool baths. **($$ to $$$)**

Sunset Oceanside Accommodations

1755 Beach Loop Road
P.O. Box 373
Bandon, OR 97411
(541) 347-2453 or 800-842-2407

When you call Carl and Judy Densmore, you'll be able to book motel units, cabins, or condos, with a wide range of accommodations and prices. The buildings are perched just above a beach, and many rooms have ocean views. Facilities include a restaurant and lounge, microwave ovens, and whirlpool. **($$ to $$$ +)**

Youth Hostel

375 Second Street
Bandon, OR 97411
(541) 347-9632

One of the international hostels, this is the place for those who desire basic accommodations and prefer a communal atmosphere. It's open to all ages, with a few family rooms available. **($)**

BROOKINGS AND HARBOR

Beachfront Inn

16008 Boat Basin Road
P.O. Box 2729
Brookings Harbor, OR 97415
(541) 469-7779 or 800-468-4081

This Best Western motor hotel is (as the name suggests) on the beach (in the fishing port area) with rooms, suites (with whirlpool baths), and kitchens. All rooms have refrigerators and microwave ovens. There is a swimming pool, whirlpool, and sundeck with a view. **($$)**

Best Western Brookings Inn

1143 Chetco Avenue
Brookings, OR 97415
(514) 469-2173

This medium-size motel has standard units, suites, and a restaurant with lounge. It's located on Highway 101. **($$)**

COOS BAY, NORTH BEND, AND CHARLESTON

Charleston Marina RV Park

7984 Kingfisher Drive
Charleston, OR 97420
(541) 888-9512

This is a large RV park with full hookups for RVs and trailers, tenting sites, laundry, and propane service.

Coos Bay Manor

955 South Fifth Street
Coos Bay, OR 97420
(541) 269-1224

In this colonial-style house, each room is decorated in a different style. **($$)**

Lucky Logger Park

250 East Johnson Avenue
Coos Bay, OR 97420
(541) 267-6003

This is a medium-size campground in Coos Bay with full hookups, close to downtown.

Seaport RV Park
5050 Boat Basin Drive
P.O. Box 5750
Charleston, OR 97420
(541) 888-3122

This small campground has hookups, propane service, and laundry.

This Olde House
Bed and Breakfast
202 Alder Avenue
Coos Bay, OR 97420
(541) 267-5224

This Olde House is a Victorian home, built around the turn of the century. There are antique furnishings throughout the house, and the ambience combines coziness with the aura of history. **($)**

GOLD BEACH

Best Western Inn
of the Beachcomber
1250 South Highway 101
P.O. Box 1453
Gold Beach, OR 97444
(541) 247-6691

This medium-size motel is on the beach, with good views, an indoor pool, and hot tub, and restaurants nearby. **($$)**

Endicott Gardens
Bed and Breakfast
95768 Jerry's Flat Road
Gold Beach, OR 97444
(541) 247-6513

This B & B home is in the wooded part of town, with an extensive garden and private rooms. **($$)**

Gold Beach Resort
1330 South Ellensburg
Gold Beach, OR 97444
(541) 247-7066 or 800-541-0947

This full-service, medium-size resort operation has oceanfront units with balconies plus condo-style accommodations. The rooms have queen and king beds and refrigerators. VCRs and movies are available. There is an indoor swimming pool and a whirlpool. **($$)**

River Bridge Inn
1010 Jerry's Flat Road
Gold Beach, OR 97444
(541) 247-4533 or 800-759-4533

Located on the forest road that leads to Agness and Rogue River attractions, this is a modern 50-room motel overlooking the river, with whirlpools and free coffee. **($$ to $$$)**

FLORENCE

Best Western Pier Point Inn
85625 Highway 101
Florence, OR 97439
(541) 997-7191 or 800-4-FLORENCE

This is a medium-size motor hotel on the main highway route, at the edge of downtown Florence. Rooms have microwave ovens. There is a pool, and continental breakfast is served. **($ to $$)**

Blue Heron
Bed and Breakfast
6563 Highway 126
P.O. Box 1122
Florence, OR 97439
(541) 997-4091

This B & B is located on the Siuslaw River, two minutes' drive from downtown Florence. The relaxing inn has rooms with private baths, and large living and dining rooms, with a river view. Full breakfast is served to overnight guests. **($$)**

Mercer Lake Resort
88875 Bay Berry Lane
Florence, OR 97439
(541) 997-3633 or 800-355-3633

This small RV campground is attached to a small motel with kitchenette rooms. **($ to $$)** The campground has pull-through spaces with hookups, showers, laundry, propane, and fishing and swimming nearby.

Rhododendron Trailer Park
87735 Highway 101 North
Florence, OR 97439
(541) 997-2206

This small RV park has full trailer and RV hookups.

NEHALEM

While Nehalem is far to the north of the Oregon Dunes, we have included this little resort near the Three Capes Loop and the Central Coast attractions.

Wheeler On-the-Bay Lodge
580 Marine
P.O. Box 326
Wheeler, OR 97147
(541) 368-5858
http://www.pacifier.com/market

This longtime inn on the Wheeler bayfront has its own dock, and the property has been declared by the state to be a wildlife viewing area. This is a wonderful place to see birds and other marine life. All of the lodge rooms have fireplaces, refrigerators, microwave ovens, VCRs, and coffee machines. Some rooms have spa baths. There's a video store on-site. The inn has expert fishing guides on hand to take you out on the ocean. This is one of the few Oregon resorts with its own Internet address. **($$ to $$$)**

NEWPORT

Embarcadero Resort Hotel and Marina
1000 South East Bay Boulevard
Newport, OR 97365
(541) 265-8521 or 800-547-4779

The hotel and marina are located on the bayfront, with restaurant and lounge, indoor pool, a large whirlpool, and a sauna. The resort has one- and two-bedroom suites with fireplaces and kitchens. Fishing charters are arranged. **($$ to $$$)**

Pacific Shores RV Resort
6225 North Coast Highway (101)
Newport, OR 97365
(541) 265-3750 or 800-333-1583

This huge RV park is located two miles north of downtown Newport, with full hookups, heated pool, whirlpool, and sauna.

Sylvia Beach Hotel
267 Cliff Street
Newport, OR 97365
(541) 265-5428

This is a notable bed and breakfast inn, a European-style hotel that attracts visitors with its unusual ambience. It's oriented to book lovers, with each room dedicated to a different author. Some of the rooms have fireplaces, and the hotel serves a full breakfast. **($$)**

PORT ORFORD

Castaway-by-the-Sea Motel
545 West Fifth Street
P.O. Box 844
Port Orford, OR 97465
(541) 332-4502

This small motel is located one short block off Highway 101. It has basic accommodations. **($)**

Shoreline Motel
206 Sixth Street
Port Orford, OR 97465
(541) 332-2903

This small motel is located at Battle Rock Beach, with standard rooms

(microwave ovens), restaurant, and lounge. **($)**

REEDSPORT

Best Western Salbasgeon Inn
1400 Highway 101
Reedsport, OR 97467
(541) 271-4831 or 800-528-1234

This modern motor hotel has an indoor pool, rooms with microwave ovens, and a laundry, and it is close to restaurants and shops. **($$)**

Coho RV Park and Marina
1580 Winchester Avenue
Reedsport, OR 97467
(541) 271-5411

This combination marina and camping facility has a medium-size RV park, including full hookups for trailers and RVs, paved sites, and showers.

San Juan Islands

Most travelers to the San Juan Islands visit one or two of the inhabited islands, stay at a resort for a day or two, and then catch a ferry back to the mainland. I've been guilty of the same detachment when staying at Rosario over a Christmas holiday, or stopping for a one-day layover while on the way from the Washington mainland to Victoria, B.C.

The islands have a climate much different from that of the neighboring Cascade Mountains or the Olympic Peninsula to the south. The two neighboring mountain ranges produce weather patterns that give the islands a year-round moderate climate. The San Juans receive an average of 247 sunny days each year. Summer temperatures rarely rise above 80° F, while winter temperatures fall to about 30° F. Snow is rare, and spring and fall temperatures fall in a delightful range. Rainfall averages 29 inches a year, mainly as a soft mist throughout November, December, and January.

This archipelago of 237 islands is one of the most peaceful places on earth—a marine sanctuary for birds, other animals, and humans wanting to get away from stressful mainland life. The water between the islands is a playpen for young orcas. Rocky tide pools reveal myriad invertebrates. Little wooded islands, left to themselves, provide high nesting places for bald and golden eagles. Loons bob on the placid waters. Dall's porpoises arc gracefully as they take a look above the surface of this northern extension of Puget Sound. These are just about the best canoeing and kayaking waters along the Pacific Coast, sheltered from ocean winds by the larger islands in the archipelago.

If we were to take an earlier view of the origins of human life, the San Juans would be the ideal place to begin history. The Lummi, who first inhabited the islands, believed that human life began in the wilderness of San Juan Island. They considered the islands to be sacred places. They still are, for reasons that can only be understood while visiting the quiet bays and secluded islands of this tranquil, life-restoring corner of the nation.

The Lummi lived an independent and tranquil life on the islands, long before the 1770s, when Spanish ships appeared on the horizon. Explorers Perez Heceta and Lopez de Haro arrived to chart the waters in what would become Puget Sound, returning through the 1780s. England's Captain George Vancouver charted the inner channels in 1841, with Vancouver's reports creating a good deal of interest on the part of eastern Americans. A subsequent expedition was led by U.S. Captain John Wilkes in 1841.

The islands were prized by both the Americans and the British, resulting in a series of conflicts that could only be settled by hiring an international mediator. The unlikely sage was Kaiser Wilhelm of Germany, who decided that the islands were American. Otherwise, the San Juans would now be part of British Columbia.

A silly but not insignificant "battle" in United States and British history was "fought" on San Juan Island in the 1850s. The Pig War started when an American farmer shot a Hudson's Bay Company pig that was rooting through his potato patch. The incident brought British troops, who also camped on San Juan Island but were a fair distance from the American fort. The "war" was nothing more than a standoff, from the beginning, even though the British maintained a sturdy fort at Victoria, just in case. Each side claimed the islands for their nation, ending only with the kaiser's Solomonic placement of the international boundary through Haro Strait. The two garrison sites—"British Camp" and "American Camp"—are now parts of a national park that commemorates the period of conflict.

For those who believe that Britain and Canada were unjustly cheated out of these lovely islands by the kaiser's ruling, Canada has a similar archipelago just north of the San Juan group: British Columbia's Gulf Islands. They share much of the tranquil magic of their southern neighbors and also are wonderful places to visit.

Of the four developed islands, San Juan is the most populated, with the town of Friday Harbor as the county seat. The site of Moran State Park, Orcas Island is known for several vacation resorts placed at water's edge on this upside-down U-shaped island. Lopez Island has a few places to stay, including a park, and offers relaxed touring, while smaller Shaw Island has a county park and a few residents and is free of commerce.

How to Get There

Washington state car ferries bring visitors to the four largest islands from Anacortes and from the Victoria, B.C., area. Sixty miles north of Seattle, via Interstate 5, State Route 20 leads west to Anacortes. The ferry terminal is on a point of land beyond the town. Car ferries leave here on a regular daily schedule, with ferries added during summer months. In addition to the state ferry system, private enterprises operate ferries between the mainland and the islands.

WASHINGTON STATE FERRIES

At the north end of Puget Sound (the Gulf of Georgia) is a ferry service from Anacortes, which stops at four of the San Juan Islands (Lopez, Shaw, Orcas, and San Juan). All ferries do not stop at all of the islands. Once a day (more often during summer months), the ferry continues to Sidney on Vancouver Island, permitting travelers to drive to Victoria and points north on Vancouver Island. The first ferry leaves Anacortes at 6 A.M. with at least nine sailings during the day. The ferries cruise to the four developed islands, with some exceptions when the ferries don't land at them all. In order of ferry landing they are: Lopez, Shaw, Orcas, and San Juan. Some of the ferry runs end in Sidney, on Vancouver Island. It takes some planning to get to Anacortes (or Sidney) at the right time to catch a ferry. There may be long lines at the Anacortes terminal during the busy summer months.

For information on all state ferries, call the following numbers. Schedules: (206) 464-6400 or 800-84-FERRY (statewide), or (604) 381-1551 (Vancouver Island/Vancouver, B.C.). Vehicle reservations are recommended during summer months from ferries leaving Orcas and San Juan Islands. Call (360) 376-2134 (Orcas) or (360) 378-4888 (Friday Harbor).

Bellingham to the San Juans   The Island Shuttle Express is a passenger and bike ferry that cruises from the Cruise Terminal building, on Harris Avenue in the northwestern Washington city of Bellingham, to Orcas and Friday Harbor. The service operates from late May to the end of September, with one round trip daily. For information, call (360) 671-1137.

FLYING TO AND FROM THE ISLANDS

Four air services fly to and from the main islands (San Juan and Orcas). On the mainland, at Anacortes, West Isle Air will fly you to either island from 4000 Airport Road. For reservations, call 800-874-4434. If you wish to fly from Seattle/Tacoma or Oak Harbor (Whidbey Island), call Harbor Air Lines at 800-359-3220. From Bellingham and Anacortes, with connections to Seattle/Tacoma, call West Isle Air at 800-874-4434.

San Juan Island

San Juan has the most varied terrain of the archipelago—with small mountains, agricultural valleys, and a stunning coastline accessible by car or bicycle. The rocky shores of this island have tide pools that reveal an incredible array of crustaceans and other marine creatures.

The earliest settlement was San Juan Town, located at the southwest edge of the island, where the American Camp portion of the San Juan Islands National Park commemorates the early history of the island. You won't find much of this settlement remaining, and most of the island activity takes place in the town of Friday Harbor, a small community with a population of about 1,000 (visitors often outnumber residents). The University of Washington operates two scientific facilities that are open to the public. North of Friday Harbor is the marine laboratory where tours are available. A 200-acre biological preserve on False Bay offers a fine opportunity to observe intertidal life at low tide.

The San Juan Historical Museum, at 405 Price Street, is a homestead from the 1890s, containing displays of local pioneer artifacts. It's open from Wednesday through Saturday, 1 P.M. to 4:30 P.M., from early June through Labor Day. One of the best whale-watching locations on the Pacific Coast, San Juan Island celebrates its fortunate location at the Whale Museum, located in the second-oldest building in Friday Harbor at 62 First Street North. The museum is devoted solely to whale life and features a two-thirds scale skeleton of an orca and a life-size model of a baby humpback whale. Exhibits include data on the orca pods that feed in the waters off the San Juans. The museum is open from 10 A.M. to 4 P.M. during summer (an admission fee is charged).

Art galleries, bookstores, cafes, and grocery stores are found on Spring Street and connecting streets. The National Park Service operates a visitor center on Spring Street, where you can obtain a map for the historic walking tour of the town. Cycling is a favorite way of getting around the island, and bicycles can be rented from Island Bicycles at 380 Argyle; call (360) 378-4941. Many visitors leave their cars on the mainland and use bicycles to tour the island. Mopeds provide another way to get around, and they are available from Suzie's Moped at Churchill Square just above the ferry departure lanes; call (360) 378-5244.

Fifteen minutes' drive from Friday Harbor, the resort at Roche Harbor is one of the region's most unusual and fascinating vacation haunts. In its first incarnation, it was a Hudson's Bay trading post, servicing the nearby British encampment until limestone was discovered in the surrounding hills and 13 quarries were developed. Then a lime and cement shipping operation was started in the mid-1800s. The property and business changed hands several times until the early 1880s, when Roche Harbor was purchased by magnate John S. McMillin, who turned the operation into a multimillion-dollar mining and shipping industry.

By 1886, McMillin had built a complete village with a hotel (Hotel de Haro), houses for his workers, and a church. His limeworks were the largest lime operation west of the Mississippi, and ships carried the lime to ports down the Pacific Coast until the operation closed in 1956. With a penchant for building monuments to himself, McMillin constructed a dramatic and eerie mausoleum in the woods near the village for the burial of himself and his family.

In 1956, the Tarte family purchased the whole village, and they have turned it into a resort that includes a large marina, an excellent restaurant, the Victorian Hotel de Haro (looking exactly as it did in the early days of the century), and condominium units that provide modern accommodations for visitors. In front of the hotel is a formal garden in the English style. To the west of the resort, across the Puget Sound waters, are several state park islands. A hike to the south takes you to British Camp and the Mount Young Trail. The resort has its own paved airstrip.

Roche Harbor celebrates its past with special observances, including a daily lowering of the colors at sunset. Flags are lowered while the national anthems of Britain and Canada are played. The American flag is lowered to the strains of Sousa's "Stars and Stripes Forever." This marks the end of the day and the start of party time on the many visiting boats and in the resort's bar. This festive atmosphere provides quite a contrast for the visitor who has spent the day in quiet reflection while canoeing through the islands' calm inland waters.

American Camp is located near the southeast end of the island, accessed by driving down Cattle Point Road. This national park site has a great walking beach, a one-mile historic trail to the American redoubt, and the site of the Hudson's Bay farm—the home of the fated wandering pig that nearly brought the British and American sides to combat. Cattle Point, at the tip of the island, has its own picnic park and beach.

SHORELINE PARKS

False Bay is indeed false, half of the time. At low tide, the water disappears to leave a mud flat with tide pools. This is one of the University of Washington's biological research sites; it's open to the public.

Lime Kiln State Park offers picnicking and a view of the Lime Kiln Lighthouse. This is the nation's only whale-watching park, and one often sees pods of killer whales feeding on the salmon that stop here on their way to the mouth of the Fraser River. Whale watching—from land—is probably at its best here. In addition to pods of orcas, you can expect to see minke whales and porpoises just offshore.

San Juan County Park, to the north, is on Smallpox Bay; scuba diving, beachcombing, and picnicking are popular activities in this park. On the northeast side of the island is the

Reuben Tarte Picnic Area, on a tombolo—a small rocky peninsula that connects two coves.

Orcas Island

Orcas Island takes its name not from its whale shape but from the 1792 viceroy of Mexico. East Sound, the channel that nearly cuts the island in two, creates wonderful views from anywhere along its coastline.

The most prominent landmark on the island is Mount Constitution, the highest point in the archipelago. Much of the mountain, including the summit, is part of Moran State Park, given to Washington by Robert Moran, the World War I shipping and ship-building magnate who built the estate that became the Rosario Resort. From the summit of Mount Constitution you can see the entire archipelago, north to Vancouver Island and south to the Olympic Peninsula. On a clear day (and there's a good chance you'll have one), you'll be able to see Mount Rainier to the southeast and Mount Baker to the east.

Moran State Park offers several walking and hiking trails by which the visitor can experience the island wilderness. Although Orcas is mostly a busy place, getting off the roadway into the forested areas of the park provides a sense of what island life was like before the arrival of resorts, restaurants, and sightseeing excursions.

It's a five-mile trip to the summit of Mount Constitution from the park entrance, and it is possible to drive all the way on a paved road. Even hardy cyclists have a challenge attempting the steep roadway. Hiking trails start at mid-mountain, leading to the summit and a viewing tower built during the Depression from a design commissioned by Robert Moran, who had seen this type of stone lookout tower in the Caucasus Mountains.

Mount Constitution is only one of several attractions in this large park. Cascade Falls is an impressive waterfall. Mountain Lake, near the summit, is a fishing lake; a 3.6-mile walking trail circles the lake. Twin Lakes are small and secluded lakes that are reached by walking beyond Mountain Lake on the Mount Constitution Trail.

At the bottom of the mountain is Cascade Lake, which you pass just after entering the park. Developed campsites are in this low-level area, which attracts people for its boating, canoe-ing, and fishing, plus swimming and hiking opportunities.

Eastsound, the island's largest community, is situated on the thin, sandy piece of land that joins the two halves of the island. The village has retained its period charm over the years, and it has a tranquil, laid-back ambience. The ferry landing is in Orcas at the island's southeast corner.

The "tail" of the whale-shaped island is at Obstruction Pass, where there is a small park with a public beach. Nearby, Doe Bay Village features a "hot" spring resort near the tiny town of Olga. Two of the three mineral baths contain hot sulphur water. The other pool is cold. This is a cold spring—the water is heated without the help of nature. The resort has accommodations in cabins along 2,000 feet of waterfront. There are fine views from the tubs and the resort's redwood decks, and the management also offers guided kayak tours to a nearby wildlife sanctuary.

The most accessible public beach on the seashore is at Obstruction Pass on the southeast side of the island—a half-mile walk from the road. This is a scenic, secluded beach with a small camping area and a picnic site. There is also a short stretch (60 feet) of beach just north of Eastsound at the end of North Beach Road. Several other beaches around the island are accessible by boat.

Lopez Island

Lopez is normally a day's adventure for most travelers. It's a handy stop as the first ferry landing on the San Juan Islands ferry trip, permitting tourists to drive off the ferry and spend a few hours on the island, and then go on to stay on Orcas or San Juan. There are two parks on the island, which are quite different from the natural areas on the larger islands.

The gentle landscape of Odlin County Park, on the west side of the island near the ferry landing, features 82 acres of woods and beach with picnicking and boating opportunities. A small campground is located in the park (30 sites) and with only one resort hotel and a couple of bed and breakfasts on the island, this is where many people stay.

Spencer Spit State Park offers a different view of the ocean from the northeast side of the island. With a mile-long sandy beach, Spencer Spit provides walking trails, a covered picnic area, and 42 campsites. The spit connects Lopez with Frost Island at low tide; popular pastimes here include clamming, fishing, and crabbing. The public campsites are perfect as bicycle camps. The campsites, however, are fairly primitive and don't offer much in the way of conveniences.

Lopez Village is in the north-central section of the island, and there are cafes and stores here for obtaining camp supplies and picnic food. The slow and out-of-time ambience of the island is characterized by the down-home restaurants and the soda fountain at the Lopez Island Pharmacy.

Shaw Island

Shaw is the smallest of the islands served by the ferry system, and it is the least visited. It has no overnight accommodations except for a few campsites, so most visitors have to plan for a visit and then catch a later ferry to another island or back to the mainland. There is no restaurant on the island.

Shaw lies in the center of the group of islands and thus has sheltered water all around. The island is eight square miles in size, and 100 people live there year-round. The only commercial enterprise open to the public is the Little Portion Store beside the ferry landing. The store, post office, and the ferry landing are operated by Franciscan nuns. The Shaw Island Historical Museum is a log cabin across from the historic one-room schoolhouse, at the corner of Blind Bay Road and Hoffman Cove Road; it's open on Saturdays and Mondays.

Shaw County Park is located at the south end of the island. It has one of the best beaches in the San Juans, and this is one of the few places in the island chain where the water gets warm enough for swimming. There are 12 campsites, a boat ramp, toilets, and drinking water. Nature trails lead along the shoreline and through the woods.

Uninhabited Islands

The four developed San Juan Islands are long inhabited. With a few exceptions, there are few locations on San Juan, Orcas, and

Lopez islands that have not seen changes by human hands. The backcountry of Mount Constitution is the major exception, and there you can escape on a path into the wilderness, where you can spot belted kingfishers, Vaux's swifts in the virgin forest, eagles setting down on treetops, plus ospreys, common loons, and dippers.

Most of the islands of the archipelago are accessible only by private boat, and many visitors rent motorboats, canoes, and kayaks to see the "real" San Juan Islands. The chain of little, uninhabited islands starts just west of Anacortes. Cypress Island, north of Anacortes, has a large natural resource conservation area, with most of the island preserved by the state. Like most of the undeveloped islands, Cypress has no public facilities or visitor program.

There are state parks where visitors are permitted. The Northern Puget Sound State Parks system includes Socia, Matia, Patos, and Clark Island State Parks, located north of Orcas Island. Turn and Poesy islands are state parks to the southwest and southeast of Orcas. Blind Island State Park is north of Shaw Island, at the entrance to Blind Bay. James Island State Park is east of Decatur Island. These state park islands have campsites and pit or vault toilets.

The San Juan Islands National Wildlife Refuge takes in 83 small islands that are nesting and resting sites for many birds. Matia and Turn Islands are also part of the national wildlife refuge, and these are the only islands in the refuge on which people are allowed to land. Colville Island is noted for its sea birds, including double-crested cormorants, which you can observe while paddling by.

The Nature Conservancy manages the San Juan Preserve System. While all of its preserves can be reached by boat (and only one from land), Yellow Island Preserve is the one island on which people are permitted to land. This island is near the northwestern shore of Shaw and near the southwestern shore of Orcas. The 10-acre island features exquisite wildflower displays in spring, including blue camas, Indian paintbrush, lilies, and buttercups. As if this weren't enough, the shore offers superb wildlife viewing of porpoises, minke whales, orcas, bald eagles, and many species of ducks. This is one island where disinterest by early settlers meant that native vegetation was not

Dall's porpoise

threatened by imported species. Largely a grassy island, benign neglect has made it almost a modern miracle.

Island Hiking

The San Juan Islands are small and are not conducive to backcountry hiking. Backcountry activity is better done in a kayak or canoe, by paddling to an outlying island and camping in a primitive marine campsite. Short nature trails include a half-mile walk to Bell Point on San Juan Island, reached from British Camp (see Mount Young Trail, below), and the Nature Trail at Jakle's Lagoon, from American Camp, at the southern site of the national park.

The following short hikes (the longest is three miles) will take you to a variety of natural areas, although you can't help meeting other people along the way. Because of their size and the number of summer visitors, these are sociable islands. Fall, winter, and spring all offer calmer moments to fully experience the beauty of the islands without a lot of distraction.

Mountain Lake to Cascade Lake This is one of several hikes available in Moran State Park on Orcas Island. Because this hike is either a steep descent or a steep climb down or up the side of Mount Constitution, I suggest that it be done from top to bottom. The hike is a three-mile trip, with little exertion required (if you're coming down the mountain). To get to the trailhead, drive into the park and turn uphill 1.5 miles past the entrance on the road to Mount Constitution. Drive one mile and turn right onto a sideroad leading to Mountain Lake. The trailhead sign is off the right side of the road.

The path wanders for a while through forest, moving below the dam in the first mile. The trail begins to descend, leading beside and across the creek. At 1.5 miles, the trail leaves a meadow, with stands of alder, leading onto an old road. The trail leaves the road at a sign pointing to Cavern, Rustic, and Cascade Falls. There are a number of switchbacks before reaching the first falls, and then passing through a rich forest of Douglas fir and cedar. The second falls are reached at mile 1.75. The largest of the falls, Cascade, is reached in a minute or two. There are views of the three-tiered waterfall, the largest in the park.

To complete the hike, take the lower trail, which has a wooden railing, descending through virgin forest and connecting with the paved highway. Turn right for 100 yards (an osprey nest sits on top of a tree trunk). Another road (off the parking area) leads to the campground and park ranger station.

Twin Lakes Trail   This 2.25-mile (one way) walk also begins at Mountain Lake on Orcas Island, but it heads in the opposite direction, with an elevation change of 200 feet. The trailhead is to the left of the boat ramp in Mountain Lake Campground. The trail leads along the west shore of the lake, close to the water, and past several picnic spots. Passing a blowdown area devastated by a violent wind storm, it leads to a meadow, which is the site of an earlier home. After a little more than a mile, the trail leaves the lake and comes to a junction. The right trail continues a loop around Mountain Lake; the left fork leads to Twin Lakes.

The path now climbs through forest, reaching another junction. The vegetation here is a wonderful mixture of tall, old Douglas firs and younger hemlock, with a bed of ferns and flowers. Deer are often seen in this wooded area. Turn right to reach the two lakes. Walk on a bridge over the stream that joins the two lakes. You then have a choice of making a loop around either or both lakes. A walk around either lake offers a stroll of about a half-mile. You can also take the left trail, which leads to the stone observation tower and the summit parking lot.

Mount Young Trail   This isn't much of a mountain, but its summit is the highest point on San Juan Island, and from it you have wonderful vistas of water and other islands. The top of Mount Young was sculpted by glaciers into a smooth, rounded shape. From the Friday Harbor ferry terminal, take the road toward Roche Harbor. Turn left (south) toward British Camp. The restored buildings of the British garrison are open to the public and are part of the national park. The trailhead is at the end of the parking lot.

The trail leads through trees to the highway and to a cemetery. The men of the Royal Marine Light Infantry buried here were not casualties of the Pig War, but died from drowning and other causes. Beyond the cemetery, the trail ascends through maples and madrones (arbutus) to a sign board that interprets geological points of interest. This overlook is just below the summit. The total trip to the summit is one mile long, and the walk down to British Camp seems even shorter.

South Beach Trail   This trail, leading from American Camp, on the southern shore of San Juan Island, takes you to a beach with tide pools and fine views of the Olympic Mountains and the Strait of Juan de Fuca. The one-way trip is 1.5 miles, starting from Pickett's Lane, which branches south, off American Camp Road. There is a parking area with picnic sites beside the beach. The hike is along the beach, and you have a choice of walking east to Cattle Point and a lighthouse, or west to Grandma's Cove. In addition to beach scenes, you'll see lots of birds and the grassy vegetation that covers much of San Juan Island. This is not necessarily natural growth—the inhabitants of the islands often used fire to regenerate the vegetation.

This is a place for observing shorebirds—plovers, gulls, turnstones, yellowlegs—and even the turkey vulture (this of course is not a shorebird but one of several raptor species found here, including hawks and eagles). A picnic area sits around the bend from the lighthouse, and tide pools are revealed at low tide.

Jakle's Lagoon is located directly across the peninsula from South Beach, on the other side of Mount Finlayson, and is also accessed by trail from American Camp.

BIRDS

Long-billed Curlew
Numenius americanus
One of the most identifiable shore-birds of the West Coast, its long, down-curved bill gives it away. It is large, for a shorebird, with brown, mottled neck and wings and cinnamon wing linings usually seen from above. Its summer habitat includes southwestern Canada and the western United States, including the shoreline of the San Juan islands. It winters in the southern U.S. and Guatemala. It prefers tidal flats, beaches, and salt marshes. Its voice is a loud, rising *cur-leee* and a fast-paced whistle: *kli-li-li-li.* It also has a song, from which the bird received its name: a beautiful, trilling *curleeeeeeeuuuu.*

Dunlin
Calidris alpina
This is another bird that prefers to forage on tidal flats. You might look for dunlins at False Bay on San Juan Island. It is sometimes confused with the sanderling, but this bird is the larger one, with a downward curve at the end of its bill. It also has a hunched position when feeding. In summer, it is a rusty red above, with a black patch across the belly. Its winter appearance is closer to the sanderling, with gray across the belly. However, it is darker than the sanderling. It spends its summers in the Arctic regions, and comes to this area for a winter stay. It looks for its food in muddy pools, beaches, and tidal flats. Its voice is a rough, nasal *cheezp,* or *treezp.*

Western Grebe
Aechmophorus occidentalis
The largest of the grebes seen in the western U.S. and Canada, the western grebe has a slate-black head, neck, and body, with white below. It has a long, yellow bill. Its long wing stripe is not seen when its wings are folded. This species is known for its dramatic mating customs. Hundreds of paired grebes gather together, flying fast over the water. The population has declined over the past 50 years because it is susceptible to the infusion of insecticides in its food chain and the presence of oil on its feeding grounds. Its summer range extends to large lakes in Canada and the western U.S., from British Columbia to Southern California. It winters along the Pacific Coast, from central B.C. to Mexico, and on some inland lakes. Its voice is a loud *kr-rr-rick.* Look for the western grebe on the lakes in Moran State Park on Orcas Island.

Pigeon Guillemot
Cepphus columba
A member of the auk family, this bird is pigeon-sized, living on rocky coastal areas close to shallow in-shore waters where it feeds. In summer, it is black, with a large

white wing patch that bears two black stripes. The underparts are white with light brown barring on the flanks. The feet and bill lining are bright red. These auks do not live together in colonies but separate themselves by pairs. They feed on small fish, which they catch by diving. It is found along the coast from western Alaska to Southern California, and it winters offshore. Its voice is a single, high whistle.

Curlew Sandpiper
Calidris ferruginea
Although the appearance of this fine-looking bird in the San Juan Islands is considered accidental, it is sometimes seen here. Its normal range is farther north, in Alaska, and in Asia. In spring, it has dark russet feathers on its head, breast, and belly. In fall, the breast takes on a grayish tinge. It is best identified by its white rump. Its call is a pleasing, fluid *chirrip*.

Western Sandpiper
Calidris mauri
This "peep" is small but a bit larger than the least sandpiper (*Calidris minutilla*). It has a long, black bill, slightly down-curved at the end. In spring, it is rusty red above and white below. In fall, it is gray above and white below. Its legs are always yellowish. A large number of western sandpipers migrate through Puget Sound, resting on mud flats in the San Juan Islands in spring and fall. They breed in the coastal tundra of Alaska and winter on the Pacific Coast from California to Peru. You'll see them in large

groups, feeding on the flats at low tide and moving to high ground when the tide comes in. Its voice is a high, raspy *keeep*.

Greater Scaup
Aythya marila
This bay duck has a black head, breast, back, and tail, and white sides and underparts. The black parts have a dull green tinge. Its gray bill is tipped with black. Its range extends to Alaska, Canada, and northern Eurasia, while it winters along the coast to California, the southeastern U.S., the Mediterranean, and China. Its habitat includes salt bays, estuaries, lakes, and rivers.

Vaux's Swift
Chaetura vauxi
Out of a total of 73 world species, only four swifts are found regularly along the Pacific Coast. Vaux's is a small, dark bird, much like a swallow, with no noticeable tail until it is spread. It has the typical "twinkling" flight that identifies all swifts. It produces an interesting optical illusion: When flying, it seems to beat its wings alternately (it doesn't). The narrow wings are usually bowed when flying. It ranges from western North America to Venezuela and is seen over lakes, rivers, and woodlands. Its voice is a loud chippering, or ticking, note.

MAMMALS

Dall's Porpoise
Phocoenoides dalli
This charmer (also called Dall porpoise) is often seen in the waters

outside and between the San Juan Islands. Growing to a length of seven feet, it has a small head and very small flukes. It is black, with a large, white oval patch below the dorsal fin. Some Dall porpoises are entirely black. The triangular dorsal fin is usually white above and black below. They are the most common porpoises in the waters of Alaska, British Columbia, and Puget Sound. They are seen in small pods of up to 20. Known as very fast swimmers, they often swim into drift nets. Orcas and sharks hunt them for food. Their range is from the Bering Sea to Puget Sound, and as far south as Baja California.

Northern Elephant Seal
Mirounga angustirostris
This blubbery giant is the largest meat-eating aquatic creature in North America. Brown or light gray above, it is lighter below. It grows to a length of 21 feet (males) or 11 feet (females). The adult male has a large snout (or trunk), which droops over its mouth. This snout is inflated during the mating season. Its hind flippers have two lobes. It breeds from California's Farallon Islands to islands off Baja California and on the Año Nuevo Preserve just north of Santa Cruz, California. Almost wiped out by the whaling industry, the species has grown from only 20 seals that remained off Baja California. The herd has rapidly increased to more than 70,000 seals.

Minke Whale
Balaenoptera acutorostrata
The smallest baleen whale found in North American waters, the minke is often seen leaping through the air, or breaching, around the San Juan Islands. This whale grows to a length of 33 feet. Its body tapers toward the rear. It is dark gray above. The belly and undersides of its flippers are white. Sometimes, crescents of white are found on its upper side, in front of the flippers. It has a tall, crescent-shaped dorsal fin. There are grooves along the throat and chest. It moves from the Bering and Chukchi Seas to the waters of South America. It is also found in the Atlantic Ocean.

INVERTEBRATES AND CRUSTACEANS

By-the-Wind Sailor
Velella velella
This unusual floating sea creature is four inches long and three inches wide. It lives only on the surface of the ocean. Blue and transparent on the outside, its oval, cartilage-like skeleton is filled with pockets of gas that keep it atop the water. There is a vertical crest along the top, which serves as a sail, allowing it to use the wind to steer itself. It has many blue tentacles around its rim and a feeding tube surrounded by rows of reproductive bodies. Its range is primarily in the warmer waters of the Atlantic and Pacific Oceans, although it is seen in the sheltered waters of the San Juans. It is often driven ashore in large numbers in the spring. The tentacles have stinging properties, but are harmless to people.

Moon Jellyfish
Aurelia aurita

This mildly toxic jelly has a saucer shape, about 16 inches wide. It is whitish and translucent. It has a large number of tentacles, like a fringe, and short feeding tubes that expand with frilly margins. Its reproductive organs are round or horseshoe-shaped—yellow, pink, or violet on females and yellowish-brown, rose, or whitish on males. You'll see the moon jellyfish washed on shore after storms, from Alaska to Southern California. It is also found on the Atlantic Coast. It floats on the surface of the sea, usually just offshore.

Sea Gooseberry
Pleurobrachia bachei

Also called "cats eyes," the sea gooseberry is a jellyfish that doesn't sting. It is transparent and iridescent, about one inch wide, a little over one inch high, and somewhat egg-shaped. It has two tentacles that extend far beyond the body and can retract completely into the body. The stomach, pharynx, tentacles, and sheaths are white, pink, yellow, or light brown. It is usually seen in large clusters near the shore, from Alaska to Baja California. It uses the long, sticky tentacles to catch its prey: larvae, fish eggs, and small crustaceans.

Purple Dwarf Olive
Olivella biplicata

This sand-dwelling seashell grows to a height of 1.5 inches. Stout and oval-shaped (slightly larger than a real olive), this creature has a sharp, conical spire, gray to white, with a thin, dark line below the suture, the line that separates adjoining whorls. It has a thin outer lip, usually light purple, with a brown margin. It lives on sand, from the low-tide line to water 150 feet deep. Its range is from Vancouver Island to Baja California. Young shells are often tinged with purple. They tend to bury themselves during the day, coming out on the surface after dusk.

WILDFLOWERS

Blue Camas
Camassia quamash

Also called common camas, this plant is found in moist meadows from southern British Columbia to Northern California and east across the Rocky Mountain states. Several towns are named for this plant in the western Rockies, because of its showy appearance in meadows. You'll see the camas on the Yellow Island Preserve, and even on the populated islands of the San Juans. Its star-shaped flowers are blue, from light to violet. There are six petal-like segments. The lower segments curve out from the stem more than the upper segments. The plant flowers from April to June. Its leaves grow to a length of 19 inches. The plant can be 20 inches tall. It is sometimes so profuse that it completely carpets large meadows. Native Americans, including the Nez Perce, roasted the bulbs for food and boiled them to make a syrup.

Red Columbine
Aquilegia formosa

This member of the large buttercup family likes open fields, meadows, and fields with shrubbery and brambles. It is also seen along the road and in open forests. Often growing to a height of 25 inches, the plant bears hanging red and yellow flowers that are very attractive to hummingbirds. Like other columbines, the flowers have large sepals and smaller petals. The petals have long, sac-like spurs. The fernlike basal leaves are positioned on long stalks.

Chocolate Lily
Fritillaria lanceolata

Growing from a bulb, this perennial herb has a distinctive dark purple flower mottled with greenish-yellow flecks. The bent-over flower is bell-shaped, about 1.5 inches long. The fruits that follow the flowers are six-angled capsules with wings. Inside are many flat seeds. The chocolate lily prefers to grow in open places, like grassy meadows and open woodlands. It grows profusely near the sea and also is found in mountain meadows, almost to the subalpine level. The bulbs were eaten by regional native peoples, including the Squamish and Straits Salish, who compared the taste with that of rice, except slightly bitter. These flowers are also known as "mission bells" or "checker lily."

WHERE TO STAY

The idyllic atmosphere of the San Juan Islands brings many visitors to the archipelago during the summer months and a steady stream of nature lovers year-round. More than a hundred hotels, motels, lodges, and resorts are available to the visitor, including many distinctive bed and breakfast inns. Campgrounds include private camping and RV parks and several county and state parks. For information on all of these accommodations, contact San Juan Islands Visitor Information Service, P.O. Box 65, Lopez, WA 98261, or call (360) 468-3663.

LOPEZ ISLAND

Blue Fjord Cabins
Route 1, Box 1450
Lopez, WA 98261
(360) 468-2749

Located on Jasper Cove, this rustic little resort has several cedar log cabins (for two), with kitchens, decks, and fireplaces. Nature trails lead from the property, including one to the beach. **($$)**

Inn at Swifts Bay
Route 2, Box 3402
Lopez, WA 98261
(360) 468-3636

This Tudor-style bed and breakfast sits on three wooded acres with a private beach a short walk away. The inn has rooms with private baths and shared bath, plus a whirlpool at the edge of the woods. Full breakfast is served. No children are allowed. **($$ to $$$)**

Islander Lopez Resort
197 Fisherman Bay Road
P.O. Box 459
Lopez, WA 98261
(360) 468-2233 or 800-736-3434

On Fisherman Bay, just a short drive from Lopez Village, the resort includes standard rooms (some with kitchens) and several cabins. Facilities include a marina with mooring, sail and motorboat charters, bike rentals, a swimming pool and hot tub, a restaurant, and a cocktail lounge. **($$)**

MacKaye Harbor Inn B & B
Route 1, Box 1940
Lopez, WA 98261
(360) 468-2253

This 1920 home is set in gardens, in an unspoiled setting. Rooms have private and shared baths. The beach and open water provide visual excitement and a place to relax. Full breakfast is served. Kayaks and bicycles are available for rent. **($$)**

Odlin County Park Campground
Route 2, Box 3216
Lopez, WA 98261
(360) 468-2496

The campground, basic at best, is part of an 80-acre park set beside a beach. Facilities include a boat launch, dock, pit toilets, and drinking water. Reservations are made for groups and those with a three-night minimum stay.

Spencer Spit State Park Campground
Route 2, Box 3600
Lopez, WA 98261
(360) 468-2251

This medium-size campground is set on 130 acres, with one mile of waterfront. Facilities include flush toilets, water, and mooring buoys.

ORCAS ISLAND

Doe Bay Village Resort
Star Route, P.O. Box 86
Olga, WA 98279
(360) 376-2291

The rustic resort features cabins and a hostel-style dormitory, plus camping on its 60 acres of waterfront property. There are mineral baths, a store, and cafe. **($ to $$)**

Landmark Inn
Route 1, P.O. Box A-108
Eastsound, WA 98245
(360) 376-2423

This is a modern, condominium-style resort that also has motel units, featuring views of the sound. Some units have kitchens, fireplaces, and private decks. **($$ to $$$)**

Lieber Haven Marina Resort
P.O. Box 127
Olga, WA 98279
(360) 376-2472

Olga is a small village south of Eastsound, close to Moran State Park and Doe Bay. There are beach-front cottages with kitchens and fireplaces. The resort is closed between December 1 and February 14. Children are welcome, and there is a two-night minimum stay. **($$ to $$$)**

Moran State Park Campground
Star Route, P.O. Box 22
Eastsound, WA 98245
(360) 376-2326

Located 15 miles from the ferry landing at Orcas, this is the largest campground on the island. The sites near Cascade Lake are suitable for tents, RVs, and trailers. The lake provides opportunities for water activity, including swimming, boating, and canoeing. This is a large campground, set in the woods, with boat rentals, showers, and nearby hiking trails. Reservations are necessary from Memorial Day to Labor Day, and reservations must be made by mail. Write or call for an application.

Obstruction Pass State Park Campground
no telephone number or reservations

A small number of campsites are available at this primitive campground, accessed by a half-mile trail or from the beach. There is no drinking water available. The park is 19 miles from the Orcas ferry landing.

Orcas Hotel
P.O. Box 155
Orcas, WA 98280
(360) 376-4300

This bed and breakfast inn is on a hill overlooking the island's ferry landing. It's a beautifully restored Victorian with rooms decorated in period style. The hotel's English pub and period dining room both serve food. **($$ to $$$)**

Outlook Inn
P.O. Box 210
Eastsound, WA 98245
(360) 376-2200

A restored, historic building, this large but cozy inn has rooms with private and shared baths, a lounge, and a Victorian dining room specializing in West Coast seafood. **($$)**

Rosario Resort
1 Rosario Way
Eastsound, WA 98245-2222
(360) 376-2222 or 800-562-8820

This famed resort is focused on the Moran Mansion, an authentic piece of island history. Robert Moran made a fortune building ships for the Klondike Gold Rush and later built the first U.S. battleship, the *U.S.S. Nebraska*. Moran moved to Orcas Island in 1905 after doctors told him that he had only a year to live. He began building a large mansion for his family and brought his shipwrights to the island to build the house. It was constructed like a ship—with teak and mahogany interior finishings. Moran lived there until his death in 1942, 34 years after his doctors had forecast his immediate demise.

Rosario is now a holiday resort, and it deserves its superb reputation. The mansion includes a stepped dining room with good views and excellent cuisine. The music room features a pipe organ played daily for the enjoyment of guests. Accommodations range

from cottages to modern motel-type rooms and condominium suites. There's an outdoor swimming pool, a store, marina, and cafe. **($$ to $$$)**

Turtleback Farm Inn
Route 1, P.O. Box 650
Eastsound, WA 98245
(360) 376-4914

This bed and breakfast farmhouse is furnished with antiques, with a quiet, rural pond and garden setting. Full breakfast is served. Children are allowed by arrangement. **($$ to $$$)**

West Beach Resort
Route 1, P.O. Box 510
Orcas Beach, WA 98245
(360) 376-2240

This marina resort has housekeeping cottages with fireplaces on the waterfront, plus a campground and RV park with trailer sites and full hookups, showers, laundry, boat launch, and rentals. There's a store, propane service, and moorage. **($ to $$)**

SAN JUAN ISLAND

Blair House Bed and Breakfast
345 Blair Avenue
Friday Harbor, WA 98250
(360) 378-5907

In a country setting on the edge of Friday Harbor, this bed and breakfast home is surrounded by Douglas firs, with rooms (private and shared baths) and a cottage. Facilities include pool and hot tub. Children over 12 years of age are allowed. **($$ to $$$)**

Duffy House
Bed and Breakfast
760 Pear Point Road
Friday Harbor, WA 98250
(360) 378-5604

A restored 1926 Tudor home in an orchard overlooking Griffin Bay, this B & B has resident eagles. Facilities include private baths and private beach. **($$)**

Hillside House
Bed and Breakfast
365 Carter Avenue
Friday Harbor, WA 98250
(360) 378-4730 or 800-232-4730

Just off Guard Street, this B & B home is located above the town, with a quiet setting, private and shared baths, and full country breakfast. Children over 10 years of age are allowed. **($$)**

Inn at Friday Harbor
410 Spring Street
P.O. Box 339
Friday Harbor, WA 98250
(360) 378-4351 or 800-752-5752

Located on Spring Street, this motel has large rooms, queen units, some with kitchens, plus an indoor swimming pool and whirlpool. **($$)** This ownership also has an all-suite hotel, with kitchenettes, plus a restaurant, lounge, beauty salon, and gift shop. The same reservation numbers apply. **($$ to $$$)**

Island Lodge
1016 Guard Street
Friday Harbor, WA 98250
(360) 378-2000 or 800-VAC-ISLE

Located a half-mile from the ferry landing, this motel has standard and housekeeping rooms and suites, a sauna, whirlpool, and barbecue area. Children are welcome. **($ to $$)**

Lakedale Campground
2627 Roche Harbor Road
Friday Harbor, WA 98250
(360) 378-2350

Open from April to mid-October, this campground is 4.5 miles from the ferry landing, with a large tenting area and more than a dozen RV sites with power and water hookups. Other facilities include a dump station, showers, and flush toilets.

Olympic Lights
4531-A Cattle Point Road
Friday Harbor, WA 98250
(360) 378-3186

An outstanding B & B inn, Olympic Lights is set beside the sea near British Camp, with a clear view of the Olympic Mountains. Rooms have private or shared baths. A full breakfast is served. This Victorian farmhouse on Cattle Point Road is a perfect base for beach walking and exploring the parks on the west shore of the island. **($$)**

Pedal Inn Campground
1300 False Bay Drive
Friday Harbor, WA 98250
(360) 378-3049

This campground is perfect for cyclists, set in a scenic area five miles from the ferry landing. It is open May through October, with hiker-biker sites. Facilities include showers, laundry, and a small store.

**San Juan County
Park Campground**
380 Westside Road
Friday Harbor, WA 98250
(360) 378-2992

Situated on the beachfront, 12 miles from the ferry landing, the campground has a boat ramp, flush toilets, and drinking water. Reservations are advised and must be made between January and June (for summer camping).

San Juan Inn
50 Spring Street
P.O. Box 776
Friday Harbor, WA 98250
(360) 378-2070

This bed and breakfast inn is located on Spring Street in the middle of the downtown area, close to the ferry landing. It's a charming Victorian building furnished with brass and wicker, with shared and private baths, and a "continental-plus" breakfast. **($$)**

States Inn
2039 West Valley Road
Friday Harbor, WA 98250
(360) 378-6240

A larger bed and breakfast, this country inn is located in a peaceful setting. All rooms have private baths and bear the names of different states. **($$ to $$$)**

Town and Country Trailer Park
595 Tucker Avenue North
Friday Harbor, WA 98250
(360) 378-4717

This medium-size campground, one mile from the ferry landing, has RV sites with full hookups, plus tenting sites, showers, and laundry.

Wharfside Bed & Breakfast
P.O. Box 1212
Friday Harbor, WA 98250
(360) 378-5661

This unique B & B is on the *Jacquelyn,* a 60-foot ship docked at Friday Harbor. One of the cabins has a private head. Breakfast is served in the main salon, or on the poop deck if weather permits. **($)**

SHAW ISLAND

While Shaw is nice to visit (until the next ferry arrives), you have to be serious about enjoying primitive campsites to stay here. There are no motels or B & B inns on the island, and while the campground has drinking water, it is otherwise basic. However, the bucolic island setting and the water beyond the island attract nature lovers to stay while canoeing, kayaking, and cycling.

South Beach County Park
P.O. Box 86
Lopez, WA 98261
no telephone

This is the only place to stay on Shaw Island, and it's a small campground on 30 acres, three miles from the ferry landing. The site includes a beach, boat launch, water, and pit toilets. No reservations are taken.

PART 2

Northwest Mountains

From the northern Washington coast, you can see a magnificent, conical, snow-capped volcano, as perfectly shaped as any North American mountain. This is Mount Baker, the northernmost Cascade volcano in the United States. Mount Baker, and the adjacent peaks of what we call the "American Alps," provided a formidable barrier for those who wished to cross from the east to reach the Pacific Coast. Lewis and Clark had an easy trip through the Cascades, mostly by luck, as they had stumbled on the Columbia River, which had cut through the high wall of the mountain range a few millennia earlier. But Native Americans rarely crossed this wall, content to summer on one side or the other, in winter moving down to the coastal estuaries or the eastern Washington desert.

The Cascades are a different kind of mountain range, including long stretches of ragged peaks joined by high walls of granite, and the most impressive collection of freestanding volcanoes in the Northern Hemisphere. Sitting off the Pacific Coast in a north-south line, the volcanoes include Mount Baker, Mount Rainier, and Mount St. Helens in Washington; Mount Hood in Oregon; and Mount Shasta and Mount Lassen in Northern California.

The volcanoes are past and future vents on the Rim of Fire, which curves around the north Pacific Coast from California to

Alaska, across the Aleutians, and south through Siberia and Japan to the volcanic islands of the South Pacific. While all of the Cascade volcanoes have erupted during the past thousand years, the most memorable recent occurrence was the 1980 eruption of Mount St. Helens in southern Washington. The explosion blew 1,300 feet of rock off the mountain top and and caused widespread devastation to forests and other life on its slopes.

Not only do they expect a major earthquake within the next few decades (the "big one"), the people of the Pacific Northwest can expect some major action along the Rim of Fire sometime in the intermediate future. As this book is written, volcanologists are predicting increased activity for Mount St. Helens. In addition, a major eruption of Mount Rainier, near Seattle, is expected within the next hundred years. Mount Lassen, the southernmost Cascade volcano, is in a constant state of boiling and bubbling.

Of these volcanoes, Mounts Lassen and Rainier are in national parks, while Mount St. Helens is designated a special kind of national volcanic monument (come and look at the damage). The other volcanoes are within national forests, each with wilderness areas that attract hikers and geology buffs as well as a few spiritualists. Mount Shasta has long been considered by Native Americans to be a sacred place of transcendent importance. In recent years, a modest tourist industry has been developed at the base of the mountain, including the opening of a hot spring bathhouse-cum-meditation center, only one of several New Age centers that recognize the power of the mountain while bowing to crasser commercial instincts.

The western front ranges of the Rocky Mountains lie a hundred miles east of the Cascades. The ranges—Sawtooth and Bitterroot—are separated from the Cascades by semidesert lands in Washington and Oregon and the amazing rippling forms of the Palouse hill country, where the Snake River separates Idaho from the two western states. The Sawtooth Wilderness is one of America's prime recreational wilderness areas, a land of forests, rivers, and lakes, framed by the jagged teeth of the Sawtooth peaks. The Bitterroots (featured in Chapter 9) mark the western edge of the Nez Perce National Forest, home to three major wilderness areas.

All of these major ranges offer a wealth of opportunity for visitors, from hiking and backcountry camping to canoeing, kayaking, and otherwise floating down Idaho's mighty Salmon and Clearwater Rivers; taking a walk around 14,411-foot Rainier, a journey of 93 miles that takes hikers at least a week to complete; fishing in placid alpine lakes in the Sawtooth Wilderness; getting steamed near boiling pits of mud on the side of Mount Lassen; or staying in an alpine inn on almost any of the mountains, including the restored lodge at Oregon's Crater Lake, the remains of another ancient volcano.

There is a power to mountains. It's the kind of power that brought fear to the hearts of the Native American inhabitants, who handed down tales of strange disappearances and other calamities from generation to generation. It's the same power that brings excitement, with a continued sense of risk, to today's mountain visitors—8,000 of whom attempt to climb Rainier each year. Yet mountains are also thought to have the power to mend the soul and heal the body and the mind. Shasta is that kind of "magic" mountain.

Glacier lily

For those with less of an interest in mountain spirituality, the Sawtooths, including the slopes of the famed Sun Valley Resort, provide fine skiing. The Bitterroots offer some of the best wilderness camping and river tripping in the nation, as well as hot spring pools that existed long before Lewis and Clark stumbled their way through that range and welcome us today for a therapeutic soak. And there's no more relaxing preoccupation than sitting in a canoe or boat while fishing the lakes of the northern Cascades. Whatever your inclination, these Northwest mountains have the power to influence our lives. It is there, all the time: in the tiny wildflowers of the alpine tundra; in deep valleys carved by creeks and rivers; on the snow-capped rim of an ancient volcano. It remains for humans to be aware of the power and to take advantage of it. Some of us call it recreation; others call it re-creation.

The Northern Cascades

The Cascades form a massive barrier down the length of the state of Washington. What was once a barrier for Native Americans and pioneers is also a climate barrier. As the warm, moist winds blow inland from the Pacific Ocean, they meet the western wall of the Cascades. Trapped by the wall, the winds rise, trying to escape, and instead they cool and precipitate snow and rain.

Seattle is considered by many to be one of the wettest cities on earth, which is debatable, but a few thousand feet above the warm and drizzly cities of the Pacific Northwest, the Cascades trap an amazing amount of snow. Between the rain and snow, an average of 100 inches of precipitation falls each year at the 5,500-foot level. Snow on the sides of Mount Baker or Mount Rainier accumulates to a depth of about 20 feet before the spring sun begins its slow melting process. Both Baker and Rainier poke their cone-tops above the clouds, creating their own high-level weather most of the time. Snow lasts until (and sometimes through) summer in the alpine regions.

In this chapter, we explore the virtually unvisited North Cascades National Park, then visit Mount Rainier National Park, a popular destination for thousands of summer visitors, and end with a short sidetrip to Mount St. Helens to view the effects of the most recent large Cascades eruption.

All of the moisture descending on the western Cascade slopes makes for thick, rich forests. The Douglas fir, western hemlock, and western red cedar forest make up the lowest (transition) zone, with its understory of ferns and mosses, plus huckleberries, Oregon grape, and devil's club. Vine maple fills in the spaces above the ground cover shrubs and wildflowers including trilliums, dogwood, and beadruby.

Slightly higher, about 3,500 feet, the Canadian (Hudsonian) zone takes over with western white pine and western hemlock, interspersed with amabilis fir (usually called noble fir in these parts). There is a wider variety of shrubs on the forest floor at this level, including salal, blackberry, and blue huckleberry.

The subalpine region rises from about 5,000 to 6,500 feet. Stands of trees are divided from others by meadows, with more space devoted to meadows as the elevation rises. The trees here include Alaska cedar, subalpine fir and/or Engelmann spruce, whitebark pine, and mountain hemlock. The meadows are carpeted with wildflowers in the early summer (depending on when the snow departs). The first arrivals, as soon as the snow melts, are the lilies (glacier and avalanche) and anemones, plus marsh marigolds and others. Later in the summer, these are replaced by blue lupine, monkeyflowers, paintbrush, and valerian, among many others.

The highest biotic zone in the northern Cascades is the alpine, from 6,500 feet to the mountain peaks. There are few trees here, with the exception of a few struggling and stunted subalpine firs or pines. Most of this zone features broken rock on talus slopes, snowfields, and the glaciers. But there is life here too, including heathers, daisies, stonecrops, shrubby cinquefoil, and moss campion. Even here, on the blowy, rocky slopes, are alpine phlox, white anemones, and saxifrage.

Glaciers mark the end of plant life, except for the hardy lichens and mosses that survive in sheltered places, sometimes warmed by geothermal activity.

From the valley floor and river estuaries—near sea level—to the flowery subalpine meadows, the northern Cascades provide a home for more than 50 mammals and more than 200 varieties of birds. Roosevelt elk and black-tailed deer (a variation of the mule deer) are often sighted on a walk along park trails. Mountain goats may be seen, high on the rocky slopes in both North Cascades and Mount Rainier National Parks. Douglas squirrels, golden-mantled ground squirrels, and Townsend chipmunks run across the forest floors. Marmots and pikas live at the higher alpine level.

The symbiotic relationship between the tall mountains and the Pacific winds have created a unique moisture-laden environment that nurtures abundant life on these emerald-green slopes of the northern Cascades. It is an ecosystem vastly different from that of other western U.S. mountain ranges: the Sierra Nevada with its oak woodland foothills and piney subalpine; the ponderosa pine forests of the Bitterroots and the Sawtooths; the much drier mountains of the southern Cascades; or even the eastern slopes of the same Cascade mountains that are blocked from ocean moisture.

The northwestern Cascade forests are not rain forests, but they are the closest thing to it without actually being rain forests. Here, the perfect amount of moisture, falling on a spectacularly textured landscape of both steep and more level mountain slopes, deep river canyons, wide valleys, lakes, melting glaciers, and the moderate temperatures, all combine to produce a varied and thriving aggregation of plant and animal life.

After you've finished enjoying the natural places in the North Cascades (could you ever?), you can jump in your car and drive to Seattle for the nation's best cup of cappuccino, unless you're brewing your own percolator of joe on a mountain

Pika

somewhere. For at that moment, the coffee from your rustic camp percolator will be the best cup of coffee in America.

North Cascades National Park

Sitting on flat land in the wide valley of the Skagit River, the sleepy little town of Sedro Wooley (a joining together of two villages, Sedro and Wooley) serves as the headquarters for North Cascades National Park. Aside from an annual celebration or two and the site of the park headquarters and visitor center, this little rural town is of faint importance to the visitor. It is a half-hour's drive from the town to the park boundary, via the North Cascades Highway, and it has some basic motel accommodations.

The park is one of the least-visited federal park areas, and while millions visit the Grand Canyon each year, stumbling over each other in the furious rush to be the first from their bus to peer over the brink, only a few thousand come to the northeastern corner of the nation to take in the equally stupefying wonders of the northern Cascade Mountains. And if hordes arrived, there would be no place to stay. Only two small resort operations are found inside the park: at Ross Lake, beside Ross Dam on the North Cascades Highway, and at the south end of the park at North Cascades Lodge. However, there are small towns on each side of the park (via the highway), and there are numerous campsites along the highway, in addition to those along Cascade River Road, an unpaved route that leads southeast from the village of Marblemount.

Actually, these peaks are not the northernmost of the Cascades. Those are in Canada, immediately north of the international border. If you want to experience the complete series of ranges, you have to drive to Vancouver, B.C., take the Trans-Canada Highway (#1) to the town of Hope, B.C., then make a right turn, heading east into the Cascades to Manning Provincial Park. Here, a road to a mountaintop will deliver you to a spectacular view of the northernmost Cascades. You can also walk to the Canadian mountains over the northern portion of the Pacific Crest Trail, hiking north from the North Cascades Highway, along the shore of Ross Lake, around the base of Desolation Peak, and across the border into Manning Provincial Park.

Consisting primarily of the Picket Range of the Cascades, the mountains in North Cascades National Park are completely unlike the freestanding volcanoes to the south and west. This is a range of upthrust mountains, with huge vertical walls, jagged peaks, glaciers, and greenish-blue lakes, all contributing to a landscape that has been dubbed the North American Alps. The geology of these mountains is the result of a combination of plate tectonics and volcanism, brought about by the usual culprits: the mainland and Pacific plates, and the Rim of Fire lying deep underground and escaping long ago to help shape the mountains. Mount Baker (not part of the park, but within the adjacent Mount Baker–Snoqualmie National Forest) is the nearest volcano. This beautiful mountain sits immediately west of the park boundary.

How to Get There

The park area is divided into three sections. The large northern and southern portions (called "units") are separated by the Ross Lake National Recreation Area, through which the North Cascades Highway runs. The recreation area is the most-visited portion of the park complex, providing campgrounds, short trails, and recreational facilities on the lake.

From Seattle (115 miles from the park) or from the Canadian border at Blaine, take Interstate 5 to Washington Route 20, also known as the North Cascades Highway (exit 230). From the east, take Route 20 south of the community of Mazama.

To reach the park headquarters from the north, drive south on Interstate 5, and turn east onto Cook Road at interstate exit 232. From the south, take Interstate 5 to State Route 20 (exit 230) and drive through Sedro Wooley. There is also a park information station at Marblemount, 6.5 miles west of the park boundary.

To get to the south end of the park takes some advance planning. North Cascades Lodge is located north of Lake Chelan, inside the park. If you don't mind some hiking, you can drive southwest on Cascade River Road from Highway 20 at Marblemount. This route comes to an end, and you have to hike over Cascade Pass to reach Stehekin River Road. Otherwise, you drive to the town of Chelan, at the southern end of Lake Chelan via U.S. Highway 97, and then take a four-hour ferry ride to the north end of the lake. This park section is the Chelan National Recreation Area. You can also take a chartered float plane from Chelan. No wonder that most motorized visitors use the North Cascades Highway as their axis for visits to the park.

PARK ESSENTIALS

Park headquarters are at 2105 Highway 20, Sedro Wooley, WA 98284; (360) 856-5700. Other information centers are located at the North Cascades Visitor Center, near Newhalem, and at the Golden West Visitor Center in Stehekin. Both centers have exhibits and audio-visual programs. There are also ranger stations in the park units, offering information on trails and campground facilities.

Campgrounds are located along the North Cascades Highway (Route 20) and backcountry locations along major trails. There are campgrounds in the Lake Chelan National Recreation Center, south of the south park unit. Ranger-led interpretation walks are available during summer, at Newhalem, Stehekin, and Colonial Creek campgrounds.

Food and lodging are available at Ross Lake Resort and in Stehekin at North Cascades (Stehekin) Lodge. Food stores are located in Newhalem and Marblemount, both on Highway 20.

ROSS LAKE NATIONAL RECREATION AREA

Highway 20 is a relatively recent route, completed in 1972. It follows the narrow recreation area corridor, traverses the route of the Skagit River, through the little town of Newhalem (inside the park), and skirts first the shore of Diablo Lake and then the south shore of Ross Lake. Diablo is another little town in the recreation area bypassed by the highway. The highway is closed during winter months, from mid-November to mid-April, usually between Ross Dam and Washington Pass. The latter is beyond the eastern park boundary in the national forest. Washington Pass provides unusual views of Liberty Bell Mountain and the Early Winter Spires from an elevation of 5,483 feet.

As you drive east from the park boundary, Goodell Creek Bridge provides a fine view of the Picket Range. The three dams on the river are the property of Seattle City Light, the civic power company that provides electricity to light the Space

Needle and the rest of Seattle. The towns of Newhalem and Diablo are also owned by City Light. The company provides an unusual four-hour Skagit Tour, including a cruise on Diablo Lake. You can also catch a City Light tugboat cruise between Diablo and Ross Dams. This one-hour trip begins near the Diablo Lake Resort.

The village of Diablo is off the highway, at milepost 126. A replica of the original waterwheel, installed by the pioneering Davis family, is found next to the Diablo powerhouse. Lucinda Davis and her family settled here in 1901, establishing a road-house to service the miners who arrived here during two gold rushes. There was little gold and the mining period was abortive, but dam-building brought permanent workers and the two communities, as well as the building of a railway to transport materials through the mountains for the creation of Ross Lake.

Farther east along the highway, at milepost 132, Diablo Lake Overlook provides more views: of Colonial Peak to the southwest (el. 7,776 feet), and Sourdough Mountain (to the north, with a lookout tower). Drive another 22 miles, and you reach Washington Pass. The lookout is to the north. Ross Lake Resort is located on the western shore of the lake, near the dam site. There are 17 boat access and marine campsite areas located around Ross Lake. The only vehicle access to Ross Lake, which has a boat launch, is at the extreme north end of the lake, accessible only through British Columbia from an access road near the town of Hope. Canoeists and kayakers have an easier time, dipping into the water of Diablo Lake at Colonial Creek Campground, then portaging around Ross Dam on a one-mile jeep trail and entering Ross Lake.

Ranger stations provide information to visitors in Newhalem and at Colonial Creek. Campgrounds are located at Goodall Creek, Newhalem, and Colonial Creek.

Highway 20 Day-Hikes   There's a very short nature trail at Newhalem, offering a view of the midmountain forest. The trail starts at the suspension bridge at the end of Main Street. The forest here is in the Canadian zone, with a mixture of hemlock and western red cedar.

The Thunder Woods Nature Trail begins at the Colonial Creek Campground. This is a one-mile loop walk through a cedar grove, with many old-growth western red cedars, many of them more than 300 years old. For an extra bit of hiking, walk along the first section of the Thunder Creek Trail, which runs for 19 miles, ascending to 6,300 feet (see page 128).

CASCADE RIVER ROAD

This is the only road that enters the park's southern unit from the west, running through the national forest before reaching the park boundary. The road leads from Highway 20 at Marblemount (across from the Log House Inn). The pavement soon disappears, as the road climbs and winds through the mountains, past camping areas, to end at a parking lot and picnic area at an elevation of 3,600 feet. The picnic area is situated between Johannesburg Mountain (el. 8,200 feet) and Boston Peak (el. 8,894 feet) to the east. The Park Service does not recommend the final few miles of this road for travel by trailers.

The trail to Cascade Pass begins at the parking lot, leading 3.75 miles to an elevation of 5,384 feet. This is a traditional Native American route, used by the Chelan and Skagit to traverse the mountains between Lake Chelan and the Skagit Valley. The trail begins in the lowland forest and climbs into subalpine forest and meadows, which have a beautiful display of wildflowers in the early summer. Most visitors use the trail only as far as the pass. You may choose to use the trail as a walking route to the Stehekin Valley, by hiking to the pass and then descending to the village of Stehekin and Lake Chelan via Stehekin Valley Road.

STEHEKIN VALLEY

Most people arrive at the north shore of Lake Chelan by boat (their own), or by taking a four-hour ferry ride from the south shore of the lake. Charter seaplane flights are also available.

Stehekin is a tiny pioneer community inside the Chelan National Recreation Area (NRA)—a scenic tourist hideaway with no access road from the outside. It was settled in the early years of the 20th century, when miners came through the area and spread word about its beauty, attracting tourists who required hotels to stay in. There are several ways to enjoy a vacation here.

This is the only national park area that I know about that offers backcountry camping without carrying a backpack. A shuttle bus takes campers to eight backcountry campsites and comes back to transport them back to Stehekin. There are two developed campgrounds in the NRA: Harlequin and Purple Point. These campgrounds have tent sites only, and there are showers near Purple Point. There are also several places to stay, in relative comfort, including North Cascades (Stehekin) Lodge, Silver Bay Inn, and Stehekin Valley Ranch—an operation with 10 tent-cabins and shared showers.

Stehekin Day-Hikes   There are short trails near the Lake Chelan landing, including the Imus Creek Nature Trail (0.75 mile), and the McKellar Cabin Historical Trail, which begins near the post office.

The Agnes Gorge Trail offers a five-mile round trip on a level track. Take the shuttle bus to High Bridge, near the junction with the Pacific Crest Trail, and walk across the bridge to the Agnes Gorge trailhead. The gorge has a depth of 210 feet, and Agnes Mountain (el. 8,115 feet) is a prominent fixture. The bus returns, on a fixed schedule, to pick up hikers for the return to Stehekin.

Horseshoe Basin Trail leaves from the Cascade Pass Trail. This steep walk of 3.75 miles passes at least 15 waterfalls, with fantastic views all along the way. At the end of the trail is the old Black Warrior Mine. You'll need a light in order to enter the mine tunnel.

BACKCOUNTRY HIKING

More than 350 miles of trails loop through the north and south units of the park and follow the shore of Lake Ross. Other trails, including the Pacific Crest Trail, lead through the adjacent national forests. The longer national park trails have campsites every three to four miles. Permits are required for overnight trips, either from the Park Service or Forest Service, depending on whose area you're hiking. Here are several of the many backcountry opportunities available in this vast wilderness region.

Big Beaver–Little Beaver Trail   *Access:* The trailhead is at Ross Dam, where there is a parking lot. The trail passes through the Ross Lake Resort on its way north along the lakeshore. You can also start at the northwestern trailhead, found on State Route 542, near its end at the Mount Baker Ski Area. This road leads from Deming and Interstate 5 (exit 255).

The Trail: The full length of this hike is 46 miles, from Ross Dam to Hannegan Campground, outside the national park boundary in the Mount Baker–Snoqualmie National Forest. It follows the courses of Big Beaver Creek, Brush Creek, and the Chilliwack River. The final part of the hike is along the Little Beaver Trail, which has an east-west course through the northern part of the park.

The Hike: Beginning by skirting the southern part of Ross Lake, leading along a hill above the lake, the trail meets Big Beaver Creek and starts climbing in a northwesterly direction. You'll see huge beaver dams that are thought to be at least 150 years old. There is an active beaver family, with dam, at 39-Mile Creek. This area has a fine stand of mature western red cedars. The trail offers a gentle climb, following the creek, with great views of the jagged Picket Range and Luna Cirque. The trail has a series of switchbacks while it climbs to Beaver Pass (el. 3,819 feet). The junction with Little Beaver Trail is found after a two-mile descent from the pass. Take the Little Beaver Trail, heading west (more or less), and climbing, as it curves over Whatcom Pass (el. 5,213 feet). Beyond the pass is another junction. Take the Hannegan/Chilliwack Trail to the left. You'll find Hannegan Campground about five miles into the national forest. The trail comes to an end at State Route 542—the road to Mount Baker Ski Area—five miles west of the campground.

Thunder Creek–Park Creek Trail   *Access:* One of the most popular longer hikes, this trail leads from the Colonial Creek Campground to the Stehekin Valley. Most hikers begin at the north end of the route on Highway 20. There's a ranger station near the campground with trail information.

The Trail: The 26-mile trail leads south, climbing and dropping several times, finally reaching its highest point (6,063 feet) at Park Creek Pass. It ends at Stehekin Valley Road, with access to several campgrounds and the rustic resorts north of Lake Chelan.

The Hike: The Thunder Creek Trail offers several fine views of notable mountain sights in the first few miles, including Snowfield Peak, Boston Glacier (sitting under Forbidden Peak), Buckner Mountain, and Boston Peak. The trail almost meets the toe of Boston Glacier. Park Creek Pass often has snow through July, and the path is marked by cairns. The trail descends to Stehekin River Road, providing access to Bridge Creek Campground, among several others.

Pacific Crest Trail *Access:* Several park and recreation area trails make up parts of the Pacific Crest Trail, which extends from Canada to Mexico, down the spine of the Cascades, and then south along the Sierra Nevada. The northern entry point is in Manning Provincial Park, northeast of the north shore of Ross Lake. The trail does not pass through the national park but stays to the east, in Okanogan National Forest, meeting Highway 20 near Rainy Pass.

The Trail: From north to south, the trail crosses the border from Manning Provincial Park and leads south to the west of Ross Lake, skirting Desolation Peak, then moving through the Pasayten Wilderness. The trail heads farther south, past Majestic Mountain, with two backcountry campgrounds available for an overnight stay, and connects with Highway 20 near Rainy Pass (west of Washington Pass). It then heads south into the Lake Chelan National Recreation Area with access to several campgrounds before heading farther west, following the Cascade ridges, through the Mount Baker–Snoqualmie National Forest. The northern portion of the trail, from Manning Provincial Park to the western edge of the Lake Chelan National Recreation Area, will involve a solid four-day hike.

The Hike: Our recommended hike involves the Bridge Creek Trail, a short portion of the Pacific Crest Trail, running between the North Cascades Highway and the upper Stehekin Valley. The hike shouldn't take longer than three or four hours, even if you dally. It begins near Rainy Pass, beside Highway 20, with the trail paralleling the highway for about two miles, then turning south and west to follow the flow of Bridge Creek. The trail provides access to several other trails, including Twisp Pass, Rainbow Lake, and McAlester.

The Walker Park Trail is farther to the south, leading north from the Bridge Creek Trail, following the North Fork of Bridge Creek to a vantage point between Mount Logan and Goode Mountain.

The main Bridge Creek (Pacific Crest) Trail continues southward through the forest, into the Lake Chelan National Recreation Area to Stehekin Valley Road and Bridge Creek Campground.

Mount Rainier National Park

There are a few mountains in the Western Hemisphere that appear to float high in the sky, seemingly unattached to the earth. When one first sees the great Denali, above the Alaskan tundra, it seems to be a huge white cloud. On closer inspection, it reveals itself as the top of a huge mountain, separated from its base—a gigantic fairy tale of a flying carpet made of ice and snow. Mount Rainier has the same floating effect, poised behind the cities of Seattle and Tacoma, sitting above the misty air that floats in from Puget Sound. The fifth tallest peak in the lower 48 states, Rainier doesn't show its immense size until you get close enough to sense where the slopes begin and to obtain a sense of scale. You're small, and the mountain's BIG. The peak is 14,411 feet above the nearby waters of the Pacific Ocean. The mountain stands alone, mounted on a green Northwest forest.

Glaciers hang from the upper levels for 9,000 feet. Below the glaciers, the perpetual snows and ice, are mountain meadows filled with subalpine wildflowers during the summer months. Water trickles from the toes of the glaciers and becomes small, and then rushing, streams. The streams transform for a time into clear alpine lakes, then head down the mountainsides, creating waterfalls and rapid cascades as they flow toward Puget Sound.

To see the mountain from above (flying in a helicopter or plane on a sunny day) is to see a gigantic, ragged star. The ice points out from the large, ice-filled crater in more than a dozen different directions, each glacier creating its own stream. The Wonderland Trail, a trip of 93 miles, runs completely around the mountain, just below the glacier line. This is one of the great hikes in the United States. It takes more than a week to complete. There are other long trails, in addition to a baker's dozen of shorter trails within the national park boundaries. Several roads lead through the lower portions of the park, with one (the road to Sunrise) taking you to higher elevations and supreme views at sunrise or any other time of day. The park is open year-round, with wildflower viewing in late spring and summer and cross-country skiing and snowshoeing in winter. It also offers experienced climbers a route to the summit, a journey attempted by some 8,000 people each year. For the rest of us, the park is a place to ponder the power of volcanoes, of perpetual snow and ice, and of the fertile Northwest environment, which provides just the right combination of rain, snow, and sun to create a perfect place for forests to grow and wildlife to thrive.

How to Get There

The Nisqually park entrance is 95 miles south of Seattle and 70 miles from Tacoma. From Seattle or Tacoma, take Interstate 5 to State Route 7, and then State Route 706. From Yakima, southeast of the mountain, take State Route 112 west to routes 123 or 410, and enter the park from the eastern gates (Stevens Canyon or White River). To reach the northwest gates (Carbon River or Mowich Lake), take State Route 410 and then State Route 169 to State Route 165.

The most popular and most accessible entrance from the Interstate 5 corridor is the southwest Nisqually gate. The park road leads to the Longmire Visitor Center and then climbs to the Paradise Visitor Center before leading west through Stevens Canyon. This same road continues to the southeast corner of the park (leaving the park to avoid crossing Backbone Ridge), reaching the Stevens Canyon entrance. Mather Memorial Parkway runs up the eastern side of the park, joining the three eastern entrances and providing access to the Sunrise Road. There is no road link between the northwestern Carbon River area and the rest of the park. From the Carbon River gate, transportation is by foot, along some of the most thrilling mountain trails in the Northwest.

Park Essentials

The park headquarters address is Mount Rainier National Park, Tahoma Woods, Star Route, Ashford, WA 98304; (360) 569-2211. The main visitor center, at Paradise, is usually open from mid-May to early October.

The park is open 24 hours a day, year-round. Use the Nisqually entrance during winter months. Other entrances are generally open from Memorial Day, except the White River entrance, which usually opens by mid-June. Fees are taken at the park gates. Ranger stations are located at Longmire, Paradise, at the Ohanapecosh Visitor Center, south of the Stevens Canyon entrance, at the White River entrance, at the Sunrise Visitor Center, and at the Carbon River entrance. Several backcountry ranger stations are open during summer.

Food and lodging are available at the National Park Inn, in Longmire near the Nisqually entrance. The Paradise Inn and cafeteria are open from late May to early October.

FIRE AND ICE

What has been created by fire has been ground away by ice. First there was the mountain, but as soon as it grew, glaciers formed and began to wear away at the rock. This seesaw of mountain building and glacial erosion has been going on for almost a million years. And the process continues today, although the several million people who live in the shadow of Rainier hardly consider the perils of living close to an active volcano, let alone several volcanoes located in western Washington. Rainier last erupted about 150 years ago, and in the meantime, snow has fallen on the crater, compacting and filling with ice, although several vents around the edge produce steam from water melting far below the mountain's crown. The heavy rains of the fall of 1995 caused scientists to wonder what effect the abundant water would have if enough of it seeped into the molten interior to build up a pressurized mass of steam.

Over those million years, Rainier has had thousands of lava flows, with molten rivers cascading down the slopes, filling river canyons and valleys. Deep deposits of fallen ash are found on the slopes, as is evidence of many mudfalls—the kind of alluvial flow that devastated the sides of Mount St. Helens less than two decades ago. The last eruption of any size on Mount Rainier occurred in the mid-1800s.

While fire and magma build the mountain, glaciers proceed to destroy it. There are 26 large glaciers on Mount Rainier above the 7,000-foot line. Most occupy places on deep crevices—U-shaped valleys of their own creation—and "flow" at an average rate of one foot per day. A few glaciers move much faster. In years past, the icefall at the toes of the faster-moving glaciers have created great ice caves. The few visitors to the mountain in the 19th century were able to see the huge Paradise Ice Caves, a phenomenon that melted away. The glaciers of Mount Rainier now cover an area of 38 square miles.

EARLY DAYS

Mount Rainier was a full-fledged volcano, regularly blowing its stack, when the first humans arrived in the Pacific Northwest about 12,000 years ago. By 1800, the Nisqually, Puyallup, Yakima, Cowlitz, and Klickitat all lived in the region, and all are said to have used the mountain as a summer hunting ground and a place to gather meadow berries, herbs, and roots.

The Native American name for the volcano was *Tahoma,* or *Takhoma,* a respectful term meaning "the Mountain." A vengeful god of the mountains was believed to have resided within Takhoma, blowing out smoke and ash, or sending down great walls of water when angered. Native Americans have always been more respectful of mountains, especially those with smoke and steam rising from their summits, than the more recently arrived European settlers.

Those settlers didn't arrive until 1833, when the Hudson's Bay Company established Fort Nisqually, an outpost of the company's headquarters, in what is now called Victoria, B.C. Before that, Spanish and English sea captains visited the Puget Sound area in the late 1700s, followed by Captain George Vancouver, who made note of the mountain in 1792 and named it for British Rear Admiral Peter Rainier. The admiral had to be content with hearing about the mountain. He never got a chance to visit the Pacific Northwest.

Most of the subsequent arrivals settled in the river valleys of Washington and northern Oregon. A few intrepid pioneers did settle on the mountain slopes, including James Longmire, who established a hot springs resort on the south side of the mountain. The springs now carry his name. Susan Longmire climbed to the summit at the age of 13 in 1891, following Fay Fuller who, a year earlier, was the first woman to reach the peak. People had been trying to climb Rainier since the mid-1800s, with reports of several successful ascents between 1850 and 1870.

A few local residents began a campaign to protect the mountain as a national park in the last decade of the 1800s. The National Geographic Society became involved, and Mount Rainier became America's fifth national park in 1899 with legislation signed by President William McKinley. Almost a century later, two million visitors come to the park each year.

PARK ATTRACTIONS

The same biotic zones define the type of flora and the birds, mammals, and other wildlife of Mount Rainier as are encountered in North Cascades National Park. From the transition zone at the bottom to the icy and rocky alpine zone, a steady change in vegetation and animal life occurs up the mountainside. Vine maples, salal, and Douglas fir give way to western white pine, salmonberry, and Pacific blackberry, which then give way to subalpine fir and meadows full of marsh marigolds, monkeyflowers, and Indian paintbrush.

Fifty mammals and more than 140 species of birds have been seen in the park. Golden eagles and hawks fly above the forests and meadows, while gray jays and Clark's nutcracker are the noisiest of the woodland birds. The white-tailed ptarmigan is found in the subalpine and alpine zones, while near the top you might encounter pika or whistling marmot families taking advantage of the summer sun.

Visitors usually plan their visit to the park as a series of drives. The most popular day trip takes tourists from the Nisqually gate to Paradise, a trip of only 18 miles but one that takes a half day or a full day if you really want to see all there is to see in this area of changing elevations and varied vegetation. The first few miles is through a Douglas fir forest peppered with western hemlock and western red cedar. From the Kautz Creek Bridge, about three miles from the entrance station, you can see the destruction brought on the landscape by mountain floods, this one caused when Kautz Glacier unleashed a flood of meltwater that carried volcanic debris, trees, and huge rocks down the streambed, burying the road with a pile of mud 28 feet high. The Longmire Museum (six miles from the park gate) is named for the pioneer settler who build the first hotel in the area, offering miracle cures from his hot springs. The Hiker Information Center provides information on trail and weather conditions.

Another drive of six miles leads to a spur road running to Ricksecker Point, with the Tatoosh Range in view. These Cascade mountains were created by volcanic action about 50 million years before Mount Rainier emerged from the valley floor. Back on the highway, you reach Narada Falls, where the Paradise River drops 168 feet; it's best seen from the viewing area below the bridge. Then, Paradise meadows come into view.

The Paradise Inn was built in 1917. Here also is the Henry M. Jackson Memorial Visitor Center: the best place to begin a stay in the park. Short and long trails lead from the visitor center area, including a hike to Paradise Glacier.

The second major excursion is the drive from Paradise to Sunrise, a distance of 50 miles, and a trip that should take a full day to thoroughly enjoy. This drive leads through some spectacular geology, including the Reflection Lakes, which have been carved out by glaciers. There's an outstanding view of Stevens Canyon from a vista point overlooking the gorge named for one of the first adventurers to successfully make the summit climb. You'll see several tributaries of Stevens Creek falling off the canyon rim. There's a picnic area near Box Canyon, with another viewing experience reached by walking a short trail to the rim of the 100-foot-deep canyon. Another 10 miles of driving leads to the Grove of the Patriarchs, an old-growth forest of western red cedar, Douglas fir, and western hemlock, located on an island in the Ohanapecosh River. The ages of many of these trees range between 500 and 1,000 years. Back on the highway, turn left onto State Route 123.

Mather Memorial Highway leads north through Cayuse Pass. You'll find the White River entrance, where you turn left onto the road to Sunrise. This is the subalpine zone, near the tree line, with stunted, gnarled, and twisted whitebark pine and subalpine fir. This is the vegetation known as krummholtz, or alpine timber. A visitor center at Sunrise provides information on the high trails from the site. Several short nature trails offer easy walks. Those who wish to do some ice walking and climbing can do it from here. Rangers should be consulted about proper equipment for this type of hike. Needless to say, a hike into the icy alpine zone into Glacier Basin and toward the summit from Sunrise is a spectacular experience.

Although no paved interior roads lead from Carbon River at the northwest corner of the park, a visit to this area can be richly rewarding. There are few people here, and the scenery is as good as at any other point in the park. An inland rain forest greets you at the park gate—enough reason in itself to visit the area. An unpaved road, suitable for most cars but better for vehicles with high clearance (pickups, four-wheel-drive), ends at a parking lot beside the Ipsut Creek Campground. There's a self-guiding trail through the rain forest at the park entrance, and then farther down the road is a seven-mile round-trip hike to the Carbon Glacier. Other longer trails fan out across the park, providing views of the Yellowstone Cliffs, where another hike takes you past Tolmie Peak and Castle Peak to mountain meadows beside Mowich Lake.

MOUNT RAINIER DAY-HIKES

Paradise is a popular place for taking short hikes. Paved wild-flower trails lead across mountain meadows with spectacular displays during most of the summer. As the season progresses, you'll see copious numbers of glacier lilies, lupine, and paint-brush, among many others. At various times, there will be car-pets of pink, white, yellow, or purple with monkeyflowers, painted cup, and Sitka valerian.

Skyline Trail   A five-mile loop through wildflower meadows, this features a climb to Panorama Point, passing a junction with the Golden Gate Trail, and then continuing to the Paradise Glacier Trail and Sluiskan Falls. The trail drops into Paradise Valley and makes a slight climb again to Myrtle Falls, returning to the Paradise Visitor Center.

Nisqually View Trail   This 1.2-mile hike leads to a great view of Nisqually Glacier. This trail runs to the lip of Nisqually Canyon where one can see close-up the effects of a moving river of ice.

Moraine Trail   Also leads to Nisqually Glacier for a different view—of the rocky moraine created by the moving ice. It leaves from the Jackson Visitor Center, and ends at the edge of the glacier. This is the trail to take to touch the glacier, after cross-ing the moraine.

Golden Gate Trail   Also leaving from the Jackson Visitor Center at Paradise, this four-mile loop covers some of the scenery along the Skyline Trail and leads to a wonderful wild-flower area in the Edith Creek Basin.

Paradise Glacier Trail   Also starts at Paradise, providing a six-mile round-trip walk to the glacier—another walk that offers a look at the recent effects of a moving glacier. The trip will take about five hours.

Lakes Trail   Starts at the Paradise Visitor Center and ends at the Reflection Lakes. This is a five-mile loop that takes about four hours. The trail leads through subalpine meadows to the beautiful small lakes, with tremendous views of the Tatoosh Range and Stevens Ridge.

Trail of the Shadows   From Longmire, this is a short nature trail, less than a mile long, that runs beside a meadow, passing the mineral springs discovered by James Longmire. This trail is self-guiding.

Sourdough Ridge Nature Trail   From Sunrise, this self-guiding trail leads for 1.5 miles to the Emmons Vista Trail, providing an additional half-mile walk to view Emmons Glacier. The Sourdough Ridge Trail has an easy climb through the subalpine zone. Emmons Glacier is Rainier's largest icefield.

Mount Fremont Lookout Trail   Also from Sunrise, the hike to the lookout starts from the visitor center, following Sourdough Ridge, climbing 1,200 feet through meadows and rocky terrain, to Frozen Lake. The trail intersects four trails at this point. The round-trip walk to the lookout is a distance of 5.5 miles, taking between three and four hours.

Other short trails leave from Stevens Canyon, the Nisqually park gate, and from the Carbon River park gate (a short, rainforest loop).

Mount Rainier Backcountry Hiking

Many trails, in all sections of the park, offer thrilling hikes with glacier views and lead to backcountry campsites. Two hikes grab the imagination of those willing to test their endurance and those with the time to pursue the ultimate in backpacking excitement.

Wonderland Trail   *Access:* The most popular trailhead is at Longmire, the location of the Longmire Museum, near the southwestern corner of the park. To get to the trailhead, drive into the park through the Nisqually gate and drive along the southern boundary, turning north for several miles to Longmire.

The Trail: Over the 93 miles of this trail, which circles Mount Rainier, the hiker will be visually and physically challenged: visually by the incredible beauty of every single mile of this odyssey; and physically by the ups, downs, and twisting route that moves from flat meadows to steep climbs many times over. Campsites are located 8 to 12 miles apart, providing a hike of about 10 days to two weeks. Most experienced hikers require close to two weeks to complete the walk, with enough time to regain muscle strength along the way, while leaving enough time to explore the beauty of the mountain. Most hikers do the trip in a clockwise direction.

The Hike: The availability of roads at Sunrise and Paradise make possible advance stocking of supplies at these locations. Sunrise is a particularly good place for stashing a cache of food.

Leaving Longmire, the trail climbs into forest, dropping into meadows and climbing again (and again), crossing the western slope of the volcano. The trail passes the toe of the Tahoma Glacier and leads onward to Mowich Lake, where there is a campsite and summer ranger station. The trail heads along the north slope on high, windy ground, beside a long stretch of Carbon Glacier, to Mystic Lake (5,800 feet), with another campground and a ranger station. The trail leads past Winthrop Glacier to Sunrise, where there is a campground plus a few creature comforts. White River (another campsite) is just beyond Sunrise. The trail really climbs past White River along the eastern slope to the high point on the trail (6,700 feet), with close-up views of waterfalls, more glaciers, lakes, and the Box Canyon of the Cowlitz River. The trail moves to lower levels to complete the trip to Longmire.

Climb to the Summit   *Access:* The summit trailhead is at Paradise (el. 5,400 feet). To get there, drive to the park and enter by the southwestern Nisqually gate, driving past Longmire to the Jackson Visitor Center at Paradise. All those attempting the climb must register with the park rangers before setting out. Those without much climbing experience should think about attending the snow- and ice-climbing school provided by the park. It's a one-day course.

The Climb: Eight thousand adventurous souls try the ascent to the summit each year, an 18-mile, two-day climb that tests the hiker's mettle in more ways than one. However, this is a climb that thousands of people are able to manage each year, and the thought of a rugged climb on snow and ice should not deter the otherwise determined. It's a test of mind and body that will be remembered as a peak life experience.

Camp Muir is located 4.5 miles from the trailhead. The trail first crosses the Paradise meadows and then climbs through subalpine terrain to reach rocky slopes, the remains of former lava flows. Crossing Pebble creek, the trail runs across snowfields, something to be concerned about if the weather is inclement. There are tent platforms at Camp Muir at an elevation of 10,000 feet. Climbing to Camp Muir without finishing the summit climb is quite rewarding. The terrain is not too difficult (not as strenuous as the rest of the climb), and the camp offers spectacular views of several mountains, including Mount Hood and Mount St. Helens.

The climb on the second day begins very early, before 2 A.M., with several climbers joined by a rope, using lights, as they climb toward the summit of the ice-filled cone. Returnees marvel at the sight of strings of lights snaking up the slope in the predawn morning.

The summit is 1,300 feet wide, filled with snow, with vents producing steam at the edge of the crater. Climbers usually return to Camp Muir by noon, avoiding the warmer afternoon period on the upper slope, which can bring melting snow and avalanches. After the muscle-straining effort to reach the summit, the afternoon descent to Paradise is a breeze.

Nearby Attractions

GIFFORD PINCHOT NATIONAL FOREST

Named for the founder of the Forest Service and sitting due south of Mount Rainier National Park, this evergreen forest offers many recreational areas north and south of Mount St. Helens. The forest area contains several glaciers and seven protected wilderness areas. Campgrounds, open between June and October, are located in every part of the forest. There are 900 campsites in all, beside fishing lakes, in prime climbing areas, and next to horse trails. There are also picnic areas and boat ramps. For information on forest facilities, contact the U.S.

Forest Service ranger station at Packwood, on State Route 12, 10 miles from the Mount Rainier National Park entrance.

Mount St. Helens National Volcanic Monument

Surrounded by the Gifford Pinchot National Forest, Mount St. Helens sits as a damaged stump of a mountain, its top third blown apart and away by the great eruption of May 1980. A road runs around the mountain, showing the devastation wrought by the mighty blast and the flow of rock, mud, water, trees, and other debris that descended down the Toutle River Valley and other slopes of the volcano. The Forest Service provides interpretation programs at several sites. Hiking trails offer close-up views of the devastation and subsequent repair work by nature. The recovery of wildlife on the mountain has been remarkable. Other attractions inside the monument include fishing, cycling, rock climbing (with permit), picnicking, and hunting. The visitor center is at Castle Rock, on State Route 504, about 80 miles south of Mount Rainier National Park, off Interstate 5 (exit 49). Winter snow closes most of the mountain roads.

BIRDS

Black-capped Chickadee
Parus atricapillus

This unafraid, plump little fellow lives in mountain forests, particularly in conifer groves, moving to warmer, lower levels in winter. You'll see it flitting about, picking up seeds, in both Mount Rainier and North Cascades National Parks. It has a gray back and buff-colored sides and is easily identified by its solid black cap; the chestnut-backed chickadee has a black cap, but rufous sides, and is slightly smaller than the black-capped. This chickadee's range extends from Alaska through Canada to the northern half of the U.S. Its voice is a clear *chick-a-dee-dee-dee.* Its song is a sharp whistle, *fee-be-e-eee,* or a descending *fee-bee.*

Brown Creeper
Certhia americana

Out of seven creepers in the world, this is the only one to be found in the western U.S., and it is in good supply in Pacific Northwest woodlands and conifer groves. A tree climber, similar to a nuthatch in its habits, it is small and slim, a mottled brown above and whitish below, with a long, stiff tail and a down-curved bill. It may be hard to see while sitting on a tree. This bird has very effective camouflage. It climbs trees in a spiral movement from the base. Its note is a single, high-pitched *seee.* Its song is a thin and piercing *see-tee-wee-too-wee.*

American Dipper
Cinclus mexicanus

Also called the water ouzel, this plump, slate-colored bird lives on fast-moving mountain creeks and rivers, which are numerous in the two national parks. Thus, there are a lot of dippers diving into the water and swimming underwater, often walking on the bottom. It feasts on small fish, insects, and aquatic invertebrates. It is a resident of Alaska and the rest of western North America, as far south as Panama. Its song is a clear, ringing succession of varied notes, rising and falling, similar to a mockingbird's. Its note is a loud *zeet.*

Golden Eagle
Aquila chrysaetos

Of the eagles, the golden is the most impressive flyer, soaring and gliding through the sky, with flat wingspread and only occasional beats. Its wingspread can be as wide as seven feet. They are easy to spot, as compared to other raptors in the sky, which are usually hawks. Golden eagles are found, in small numbers, in both North Cascades and Mount Rainier National Parks. The back of the golden eagle is about the same color as that of the bald eagle, and its head is the same brown color. It has a touch of gold on the back of the neck and a white tail with a broad brown terminal band. When flying, you may see a white flash at the base of the primary feathers.

It is a mountain bird in the Northwest, living in mountain forests as well as foothills. Its habitat also includes open plains.

Clark's Nutcracker
Nucifraga columbiana
A cousin of the jays and magpies, the curious nutcracker is shaped like a jay or small crow, with a light gray body and white patches on its black wings and dark tail. It looks somewhat like a gray jay, but the jay does not have the white tail patches. When flying, the patches are seen next to the "wing pits." The nutcracker is a noisy resident of subalpine conifer forests at the higher levels, close to the tree line. It is often seen mooching in mountain resort areas. Mount Rainier National Park is an excellent place to see this bird. Its voice is like that of a magpie: *aag-aag,* or *maag-maag.*

White-tailed Ptarmigan
Lagopus leucurus
This is the only ptarmigan found in the United States. It is also the only ptarmigan that wears a white tail in summer. It lives at the alpine and high subalpine levels, above the timberline, in both Mount Rainier and North Cascades National Parks. In winter it is pure white, and in summer, it bears the colors of its surroundings, with a brown color and a white belly, white wings and tail. This is a smaller bird than the more northerly rock ptarmigan. Its voice is often a cackle, or a soft cluck, and even softer hoots.

Red-breasted Sapsucker
Sphyrapicus ruber
A member of the woodpecker (Picidae) family, this Pacific Coast sapsucker is a colorful bird, with a fire-engine red head and breast. It has long, white wing patches and smaller white markings on its wings, belly, and tail. Its range is from Alaska to Baja California, in coastal regions. Its voice is a nasal *cheeeeeer.* Like woodpeckers and other sapsuckers, it also drums, with several rapid thumps, followed by slower, regular thumps. The red-headed woodpecker, a similar species, is found east of the Rocky Mountains.

MAMMALS

Black-tailed deer
Odocoileus hemionus
This is one of two variations of the mule deer. The regular mule deer, found to the south, has a tail with white above and just tipped with black. The black-tailed deer of the Pacific Northwest has a tail that is solid black or brownish above. It has long ears on a stocky body, which, in summer, is reddish brown or yellowish brown and grayish in winter. It has white throat patches and rump patch. The inside of its ears and legs are also white. The lower parts are tan to cream. The mule deer group has a range that extends to the Yukon territory, south through the western United States, as far east as Wisconsin, and as far south as west Texas. They live in a variety of habitats, including the edges of forests, in mountain terrain, and foothill woodlands.

Young does bear only one fawn. Older does usually produce twins. These deer eat almost anything they can find to graze on, including grass, herbs, berries, and even mushrooms. They are usually seen in evenings and early mornings, and when there are nights with bright moonlight, they are often seen during the daytime.

The black-tailed deer of Mount Rainier and North Cascades National Parks spend their summers on the high ranges in the Canadian and subalpine zones, retreating farther down the mountainsides for winter browsing. They are usually seen in small family groups: a doe with her fawn or with twin fawns and a pair of yearlings. The polygamous bucks are usually alone, ranging over a wider territory than a doe. They often herd into larger groups in winter—a process called "yarding up."

Pika (Cony)
Ochotonua princeps
The pika is a small alpine animal, about the same size as a large deer mouse (six to eight inches long), which lives on talus slopes, rocky banks, and hillsides covered with boulders. The pika lives on Cascade mountainsides above 8,000 feet. It has a brownish color, small, round ears, and no tail that you can see. One of the most interesting facets of the pika is its harvesting routine. In summer, it gathers green plants and carries them to boulders near its den. The greens are spread out in piles to dry in the sun, just as farmers dry their hay after cutting.

The pika gathers such plants as fireweed, sedges, dryad, stonecrop, and grasses, piling them as previously gathered plants dry out. The dry fodder is then stored in the den. It breeds in the spring, producing two to six blind babies in May and June. Sometimes, a second birth occurs in late summer.

Golden-mantled Ground Squirrel
Spermophilus lateralis
This common squirrel of the northern Cascades grows to a length of 12 inches. It looks like a large chipmunk, with a gray or buff back and a white belly. The head and shoulders are a copper color, giving it the "golden mantle." It has a white stripe, between black stripes, on each side. This squirrel lives in conifer forests and in mixed woodlands, all the way from the low forests to timberline. It is common to southern British Columbia and Alberta and through the Rocky Mountain states as well as the Cascade ranges, where a slight variation is called the Cascades golden-mantled ground squirrel. The female bears one litter each year of four to six young, born in early summer. It nests in burrows found near or under logs. The long, shallow burrows can reach a length of 100 feet.

Red Squirrel
Tamiasciurus hudsonicus
This conifer forest dweller is found across a wide swath of Canada and the U.S., including the Rocky Mountain and Great Lakes states.

It is a small squirrel—the smallest in this area. It is a rusty red above, lighter on the sides, with a whitish tint below. It feeds primarily on pine seeds, leaving piles of cone leavings all over the forest. It also eats acorns when living in oak woodlands. It is a voracious scavenger, eating birds' eggs and even young birds. Its home is a nest built in hollow trees and fallen logs, or as a grass and bark nest in the crotches of trees. It resides in conifer and mixed forests throughout Washington and Oregon.

TREES, SHRUBS, AND UNDERSTORY PLANTS

Pacific Blackberry
Rubus ursinus
This is the native blackberry of the Pacific coastal regions (other blackberries were introduced from Europe many years ago). It is called the dewberry and also trailing blackberry. A member of the raspberry family, it is a low-lying, trailing plant, with branches growing to a length of 15 or 16 feet or more. It bears small, slender prickles, with flowers produced during the second year. It is a deciduous plant, with alternate leaves. The flowers are white or pink. The dark fruit is delicious and enjoyed by today's residents of the Pacific Coast, as it was by earlier inhabitants who used this plant for food, brewing tea, curing hemorrhoids, mouth sores, cholera, fevers, and other ailments. West Coast Native Americans often dried the berries for winter eating.

The brambly plant is common in open forests in the transition and Canadian zones, and it does particularly well in disturbed soils.

Alaska Yellow Cedar
Chamaecyparis nootkatensis
This cedar has a narrow, pointed crown. The branches droop, with evergreen leaves that are opposite, in four rows. The leaf color is a bright yellowish green. The bark is grayish brown with long, narrow fissures. The bark becomes shredded with age. The tree's small cones are reddish brown, about a half-inch in diameter. This cedar grows along the Pacific Coast from Southeast Alaska through the Cascades and along the coast through western Oregon and just into California. It is found at altitudes of 2,000 to about 6,000 feet in the northern Cascades. The wood has a pleasant, resin odor. Native Americans used this tree for making canoe paddles and other crafted materials, including ceremonial masks. It is now used for boat construction and for making furniture.

Devil's Club
Oplopanax horridum
This prickly, rangey shrub has been a nemesis to almost anyone who tries to walk off the path through the understory of a northwest forest. Its long, meandering branches catch you unawares, tripping you, and then the final coup de grace comes with the sharp barbs piercing clothing and skin. After all, this plant has been designated *horridum.* Devil's club is found on the floors of almost all Northwest

coastal forests, including the western Cascade forests. It has large leaves, which are well suited for the dark understory ecosystem. Its thin, brown bark has been used by Native Americans as a pulverized, powdery deodorant. Northwest coast peoples believed that the plant had magical powers and made charms from the wood. It grows in swampy and boggy areas, and in deep shade. The plant is found from Alaska, along the coast and in the Cascade Range, and into Idaho and Montana. Its stings are also experienced in Michigan and Ontario.

Mountain Hemlock
Tsuga mertensiana

This is an endemic tree, found along the north Pacific Coast and the Cascades. Scattered groves are also found in the Rockies of northern Idaho and northeast Oregon. It is a species of the high mountains, growing from low altitudes, where it is a large tree (up to 100 feet tall), all the way up to the tree line, where it is seen as a dwarf shrub. It grows to an elevation of about 10,000 feet in the northern Cascades. It has a trunk which is tapered, and a cone-shaped crown. Its slender branches often droop, and the tiny timberline shrub version has prostrate branches—on the ground. It is an evergreen, with needles forming on the ends of the twigs. The bark is a dark brown or gray, and is thickly furrowed and ridged. The twigs are a light reddish brown, with very fine hairs. Cones grow to a length of about three inches. They are cylindrical,

and change from purple to brown as they mature. The cone scales are round, and each cone produces many seeds, with long wings.

Whitebark Pine
Pinus albicaulis

While this tree is found growing thickly in the northern Rocky Mountains (B.C., Alberta, Montana, and Idaho), it is found farther west in a very narrow line extending from B.C., through the western slope of the Cascades, and into northwestern Nevada. It is found in Mount Rainier and North Cascades national parks, at subalpine elevations of about 6,000 feet to the tree line. It is a tree with a short, twisted trunk, and an uneven crown. At timberline, it's a shrub. At lower levels, it can grow to about 20 feet. Its evergreen needles are found in bundles of five. They are short and stiff, on sturdy twigs. The cones are rounded or slightly conical, growing to a length of about 3.25 inches. It grows on rocky soils, usually on exposed slopes and ridges, sometimes with other species, and also in pure stands.

WILDFLOWERS

Western Wood Anemone
Anemone lyallis

This white-flowered plant is often seen with its cousin, the blue anemone (*A. oregana*). Both are found from northern Washington to central Oregon, and both are seen growing in the mountain meadows of both national parks in Washington. The western wood anemone grows in dry woods here and in the San Juan Islands. It has a tiny flower, about one-third inch (1 cm) across and with fernlike leaves. For some reason, it grows at sea level in the San Juans but is found at much higher elevations in the mountain parks. The anemones grow in open woods and brushy hills as well as on meadow slopes. They are both members of the buttercup family. The three-leafed windflower (*A. deltoida*) is also seen in the Cascades, but is rarely south of the Seattle area. It is a beautiful, white-flowered plant growing on creeping underground stems.

Avalanche Lily
Erythronium montanum
This plant with beautiful white flowers is found in subalpine and alpine meadows as well as in forests. It has a limited range, from British Columbia to northern Oregon. It is one of the first wildflowers to show after the snow melts, often seen as a wide, white carpet. The nodding flowers are at the end of stalks that grow from two basal leaves. The flowers are about 2.5 inches wide, with six petal-like segments that curve back, having a yellow band at the base. The stalks grow to a height of eight to ten inches.

Glacier Lily
Erythronium grandiflorum
Another plant that flowers early, often near melting snow, the glacier lily is found on subalpine locations in Mount Rainier National

Park. Its flowers, one to five at the top of a stalk, are a golden yellow. Each flower has six lance-shaped petal segments, one to two inches long, curving back like the blooms of the avalanche lily. The base leaves are four to eight inches long. The fruit is a fat capsule, with three sides. The stalks grow to a height of six to twelve inches.

Common Monkeyflower
Mimulus guttatus
Also called the yellow monkeyflower because of its yellow flowers, this plant grows in damp soils at elevations from the sea-level rain forest to the subalpine zone. It grows in various forms, from a thin, spindly appearance to a very bushy state. It is seen from March to September, depending on the elevation, growing to a height of three feet. There are many monkeyflowers; several have yellow corollas. This one has a long corolla, about 1.25 inches, with reddish spots near the opening. Two lobes of the upper lip are bent upward, with three lobes of the lower lip bent downward.

Spreading Phlox
Phlox diffusa
Also known as alpine phlox, this plant is a perennial wildflower that grows in a range from southern Vancouver Island and the B.C. mainland, through the Cascades to southern Oregon. It is also found in the Olympic Mountains, but not on the lowlands between the two ranges. Having taproots, this

plant has bright pink, lavender, or whitish flowers that form a mat, so that the base leaves are hidden. Five sepals are fused into a hairy tube with sharp lobes. Each flower grows singly at the end of stems and branches. The fruit is a three-seed capsule, one seed per chamber. It grows on rocky slopes, on scree, rocky outcrops, and open forest, from middle to high alpine elevations.

Tolmie Saxifrage
Tolmiea menziesii
We may better know this as the piggyback plant. It is a fascinating wildflower, related to other saxifrages, including the fringecup, except that this one forms buds near the bases of its leaves. The buds become little plants of their own, catching root. That's why it is also called "youth-on-age." The pinkish-brown or chocolate-colored flowers are borne in a spiky group at the top of a tall stem.

Trillium
Trillium ovatum
The trillium is probably the best-known wildflower in North America. It grows over much of the continent, in the forest understory, popping out of the ground from a perennial rhizome and dying back in the fall. The stem has a whorl of three broad leaves. Like most lilies, the trillium has three equal petals and three equal sepals. The whole plant is in delightful symmetry.

This plant has a fascinating relationship with ants. The seeds have an oily part, prized by ants who take away the seeds, consuming only the oily appendage, leaving the rest of the seed on the ground to germinate. Trilliums are found under rain forest trees, as well as in dryer (but still damp) conifer and mixed forests.

Sitka Valerian
Valeriana sitchensis
This perennial plant grows from a rhizome, or woody stem base, and it is found along the Pacific Coast from Alaska to the Cascade region at the California/Oregon border. Its flowers are white to pink, with a heavy scent. The bloom is tube-shaped, with five lobes. The stamens protrude from the tube, giving the top a fluffy look. The fruits are egg-shaped, topped with a feathery plume easily dispersed by winds. You'll find this valerian in the subalpine meadows, along stream banks, and in open subalpine forests. There are plenty of them in North Cascades National Park and at Paradise on Mount Rainier. The Sitka variety produces a strong, musky odor just after the first frost. Where it grows in profusion, the odor can be overpowering. The Tlingit name for this plant means "medicine that stinks." The plant was crushed for use as a pain reliever; valerian potions were available as a standard household remedy.

MOUNT RAINIER NATIONAL PARK

Unless you wish to stay inside the park, your choices for overnight accommodations are almost endless, with Seattle, Tacoma, Olympia, and Portland all less than a two-hour drive from the park entrance. Seattle and Tacoma are the closest cities to the western entrances. In the following listings, we include the lodges and developed campgrounds inside the park.

National Park Inn

Mount Rainier Guest Services
P.O. Box 108
Ashford, WA 98304
(360) 569-2275

This small inn is at Longmire at the 2,500-foot level, near the Nisqually entrance to the park at the southwestern corner. The overnight units all have private bath, and there is a restaurant. The inn is open year-round. **($$)**

Paradise Inn

Mount Rainier Guest Services
P.O. Box 108
Ashford, WA 98304
(360) 569-2275

This inn is at the 5,400-foot level, next to the Paradise Visitor Center and the subalpine meadows. A summer operation, it is larger than the National Park Inn, and it has a cafeteria-style restaurant. It is open from May through early October. **($$)**

Mount Rainier National Park Camping

There are five developed campgrounds, all with a 14-day limit. For information on all camping facilities, contact park headquarters at (360) 569-2211.

Sunshine Point Campground is open year-round. It is located near the Nisqually entrance at the southwestern corner of the park.

Other camping facilities include the following:

Longmire Campground, at 2,500 feet, is near the Longmire Museum and Visitor Center. There is a ranger station and trailhead nearby.

Ohanapecosh Campground is located in the southeastern corner of the park, on State Route 123, near the Ohanapecosh Visitor Center.

White River Campground is accessed by taking Highway 123 (from Packwood, to the south) and State Route 410 (Mather Memorial Highway) and turning west onto the road to Sunrise. You may also enter the park at the western gate on Highway 410, and turn west onto the Sunrise Road. Highway 410 also enters the western portion of the park from the north (Seattle). Take the parkway south to the Sunrise Road and turn right. There are rangers at the nearby Sunrise Visitor Center.

Ipsut Creek Campground is located in the northwestern corner of the park, a few miles from the Carbon River entrance. There is a summer ranger station at this location, with a visitor center at the park gate.

NORTH CASCADES NATIONAL PARK

While there are no overnight accommodations (motels, lodges) inside the formally designated units of the national park, you can find places to stay in the Ross Lake National Recreation area, which cuts a swath along Highway 20 through the middle of the park area. Additional places to stay are located near the south end of the park in the Lake Chelan National Recreation Area. For other accommodations in the Lake Chelan area, contact the Chelan Chamber of Commerce, P.O. Box 216, Chelan, WA 98116, or call (509) 682-3503.

Diablo Lake Resort
Rockport, WA 98283
(360) 386-4429 (seasonal)

In the Ross Lake National Recreation Area, this rustic resort operation has self-sufficient units with kitchens, on City Light's Diablo Lake, just off Highway 20 (North Cascades Highway). There is an on-site restaurant. **($ to $$)**

North Cascades Lodge
P.O. Box 1779
Chelan, WA 98116
(509) 682-4494

This longtime institution in the Stehekin Valley is within the Lake Chelan National Recreation Area, with short and long trails just out-

side the door. Access is by boat, ferry, seaplane, or by foot. This is a small, cozy, rustic lodge in a scenic setting. It is open year-round, with cross-country ski trails and snowshoeing in winter. **($ to $$)**

Ross Lake Resort
Rockport, WA 98283
(360) 386-4437 (seasonal)

You have to walk or take a boat to this unusual resort, located close to Ross Dam. The resort features cabins that float on the lake. The units are equipped with kitchens. It is open from June to late October. **($)**

Silver Bay Inn
P.O. Box 43
Stehekin, WA 98852
(509) 682-2212

This is a very small tourist operation. The cabins have kitchenettes. Breakfast is available at an extra charge. The inn offers an overnight and breakfast package. **($$)**

Stehekin Valley Ranch
P.O. Box 36
Stehekin, WA 98852
(509) 682-4677 (seasonal)

This is a truly rustic place to stay. It has tent-cabins with shared showers and meals for a package price. This is another seasonal operation, open June through September. **($)**

North Cascades National Park Camping
There are four campgrounds, plus a group campground, in the Ross Lake National Recreation Area, accessed by driving along Highway 20.

Goodell Creek Campground
is open year-round and is the

westernmost camping area in the Highway 20 corridor. There are tent and RV sites, but no hookups or showers.

Newhalem Campground is located at the company town and is open from mid-June through Labor Day. There is no limit on your stay at this or any of the other four campgrounds in the recreation area. A ranger station is nearby.

Colonial Creek Campground is farther west, next to the information center and ranger station. It is open from mid-spring to mid-fall, avoiding the snow.

Hozomeen Campground has remote campsites at the northeastern corner of the park area, on a trail that follows the eastern shore of Ross Lake. A road to the campground is accessed by driving through British Columbia, from the town of Hope, on an unpaved road. This is the only public boat launch location on Ross Lake.

Lake Chelan National Recreation Area has two public campgrounds:

Harlequin Campground, in the Stehekin Valley, is open after the snow leaves in mid-spring, and it closes in mid-fall. There are no fees, and the campground works on a first come, first served policy. Reservations are required to use the Harlequin Group Campground. Contact park headquarters at (360) 856-5700.

Purple Point Campground is also in the Stehekin Valley, with the luxury of nearby showers. There are only tent sites at this location. No fees are charged, and sites are taken on a first come, first registered basis.

The Southern Cascades

Eight thousand years ago a great volcano rose from the conifer forests of what is now southern Oregon. Like the other Cascade volcanoes, it rose to a height of more than 12,000 feet. Mount Mazama was covered with snow during much of the year and by glaciers year-round. It was a home for many birds and mammals. Hunters climbed its slopes for game, and food was gathered from the forests and mountain meadows in preparation for winter.

Mount Mazama was a link in the steady progression of volcanic mountains from north of the Canadian border to Northern California. Mount Mazama is not there now. It disappeared in a gigantic explosion of the earth about 5700 B.C., with an eruption—about three times the force of the 1980 Mount St. Helens blast—that not only tore the top off the mountain but sent virtually the entire mountain into the air. It is said that the eruption sent up from 12 to 25 cubic miles of volcanic solids from the core. Some of it, in the form of burning ash, flowed down the valley of the Rogue River. Artifacts of the period are still being found under the layer of ash.

With the interior of the mountain blasted over an area of more than 5,000 square miles, the rest of it collapsed into the empty core. It left a caldera 4,000 feet deep. Over the years, small creeks half-filled the caldera with water; today, we call this phenomenon Crater Lake. It is Oregon's only national park—a tribute to the supreme forces held within the earth we live on.

The fate of Mount Mazama tells us that all volcanoes are different. They may all be linked to the molten interior of the earth, but each mountain has its own way of reacting to these deep pressures. Some prefer to bubble and boil, venting steam and noxious gasses into the atmosphere. Others prefer a face lift, like Mount St. Helens, blowing their tops and remaking themselves in a different image. Others simply stay where they are, resting quietly, playing a waiting game until blowing themselves into smithereens in a single great act of self-destruction, and then folding back into themselves in a final withdrawal from existence.

But can we be sure that even that act of cataclysmic destruction is the end of Mount Mazama? No! Inside the crater of Mazama's caldera is an island, shaped like a medieval sorcerer's hat, called Wizard Island. This island is a little volcano itself, 760 feet high, with a perfect cone that people climb. Could the spirit of Mazama be down inside that little cone? Will the mountain build itself again? Will the chain of mountains be unbroken after a few million more years and the cottagers in the Rogue River Valley face another river of ash?

And what is Mount Shasta doing? Sitting just south of Crater Lake, this behemoth of a volcano, with four cones, has been sitting quietly since its last eruption in 1786. It has a habit of blowing its stack every 250 to 300 years.

Then there is Mount Lassen, contained in the eponymous national park. This volcano—last exploding in 1914 and 1915—is the replacement for another volcano called Mount Tehama. This area in Northern California has experienced eruptions for more than a million years. Lassen is not the only volcanic peak here; there are several others in the immediate area.

Lassen Peak is only about 11,000 years old, but it has been a hyperactive youngster and particularly obstreperous during the past 2,000 years. Its last big eruption was on May 22, 1915, three days after a smaller mudflow poured out of the summit onto a snowfield. On that day, a fierce blast propelled fire from the cone, devastating an area about three miles long by one mile wide. For the next two years, the mountain rumbled and sent steam and ash into the air. Then it calmed, waiting for the next time. But steam vents and boiling mud pots are seen on the side of Lassen Peak, signs that the mountain is young, active, and waiting for another chance to create havoc.

In the meantime, we and the government have created wonderful places to visit. We climb to the top, to be able to say we did it, largely oblivious to the molten lakes that lie below. Between eruptions, people build cities and towns near these sleeping rock-chimneys, largely oblivious to the powers of the natural process shaping the earth along the Rim of Fire. Thousands of years ago, gigantic sequoia lived in great groves throughout the southern Cascade region. Destroyed by volcanic eruptions, the sequoia disappeared.

Some geologists claim that like the Sierra Nevada area south of Mount Lassen, the Cascade region will be still and that glaciers will wear down the volcanic peaks until they look just like the Sierra, with only some volcanic outcroppings to remind us of an earlier day. After all, the Cascade Range extended far south, almost to Yosemite, about four million years ago.

These are questions to be answered by future generations. Pessimists are certain that the 250-year cycle of eruption will continue to repeat itself. As long as the earth's center is molten, lava will travel up the path of least resistance. In the meantime, some of us watch and wait, hoping our grandchildren won't move to Seattle or the Rogue River Valley or Mount Shasta City.

Crater Lake National Park

As a national park, Crater Lake is not very large. A drive of 33 miles will take you around the rim. The only long trail inside the park is the section of the Pacific Crest Trail that runs 33 miles from north to south, west of the lake. Three much shorter trails connect the Pacific Crest Trail to the rim. However, the size of the park and the lack of a tall mountain should not deter you from visiting this remarkable place.

First, there is the beauty of the lake, an almost round body of water that partially fills the caldera. It has extreme clarity, caused by its great depth and the lack of an outflow. While snowmelt and rainwater fill the lake to a constant level, only evaporation removes water. It is an isolated lake in perfect balance—a completely closed ecosystem.

Mount Mazama came and went in a very short period of geological time (less than half a million years). It took much more time to build the volcano than for it to obliterate itself, an event of extreme destruction that occurred 7,700 years ago, when ash from the volcano jetted more than 30 miles into the atmosphere, landing as far away as Canada. The top mile of the mountain folded into the core, making the crater, which slowly filled with rainwater and snowmelt. Since then, Mazama has been quiet, with only minor volcanic action creating the small cone of Wizard Island. What remains is a park area of incredible beauty.

HOW TO GET THERE

From Medford, on Interstate 5, take State Route 62 for 75 miles. After entering the park, the highway leads south of the lake to the Annie Springs entrance station. The park road then leads north to the park headquarters, Rim Village, and the Rim Drive.

From the south and Klamath Falls, take U.S. Highway 97 and State Route 62 to the park and the Annie Springs entrance station. The park boundary is 55 miles from Klamath Falls. From the northwest (Interstate 5 at Roseburg), take State Route 138 for 82 miles to the park boundary. The north park road is closed in winter.

PARK ESSENTIALS

Contact park headquarters at P.O. Box 7, Crater Lake, OR 97604; (503) 594-22111.

The Rim Village Visitor Center overlooks the lake from the south edge. It is located seven miles off State Route 62. The center is open daily from early June to the end of September.

Steel Center, located at the park headquarters south of Rim Village, is open daily throughout the year, except Christmas Day. An entrance fee is charged during the summer season only, when all facilities are open. However, the park remains open year-round, via the south entrance.

Park naturalist activities are offered throughout the summer season, with a two-hour narrated boat tour of the lake, including a stop at Wizard Island, where visitors may hike to the top of the cone. The tour leaves every hour on the hour, from 9 A.M. to 3 P.M., from the landing at the end of the Cleetwood Trail. Cross-country skiing and snowshoeing are popular winter activities in the south rim area.

Food and lodging are available inside the park. After being closed for almost a dozen years, the magnificent Crater Lake Lodge has been painstakingly reconstructed in its original form with modern conveniences added. Mazama Village Motor Inn has standard motel-style units. The nearest outside accommodations are available in Klamath and Chiloquin. Food is also available at the park cafeteria, deli, and fountain, located next to the Rim Village Gift Shop. For details and information on reservations, see page 175.

There are two campgrounds in the park: Mazama Campground and Lost Creek Campground (see page 175).

PARK ATTRACTIONS

Crater Lake is a summer place and also a winter place. The two seasons are very different from one another.

Summer is short. The lake, the deepest in the nation, glows with a translucent sheen, rimmed by rock with a few evergreen trees clinging to the slope. The soft green forests and flowery meadows are in sharp contrast to the rocky walls of the crater and the bare rock formations that poke above the rim. Wildflowers blanket the park meadows and forest floor for most of the summer. They are some of the 600 species of plants that have colonized the region since the volcano's ash covered the slopes for many miles around. The forest is primarily mountain hemlock and Shasta red fir, with stunted and twisted whitebark pine at the rim. Down from the rim, a more temperate forest of ponderosa pine and lodgepole pine is found.

Winter provides a stark, white environment. A year's snowfall on the rim can be as much as 50 feet, and because of the moderate Oregon climate, the lake hardly ever freezes over, using stored heat from its lower depths. The last time the lake developed a thin sheet of ice was in 1949. While snow falls in October and doesn't recede until May, the south park road is kept open for visitors, who come to look at the lake in this special time of year. Park rangers open a gate at 8 A.M. daily and close it at sunset. Snowmobilers can enter the park at the north gate and drive to a vista point overlooking the lake.

RIM DRIVE

The road circles the lake, offering more than 25 viewpoints overlooking the lake and geological formations. Heading clockwise (west) from the Rim Village parking lot, the road is often narrow and winds around sharp curves. The first few miles provide fine views of nearby mountains, including Hillman Peak to the far left of the rim, one of the remaining parts of Mount Mazama and the highest point on the rim. The Wizard Island overlook is at mile 4. There is a short trail south to a fire tower on "the Watchman." The Mount Theilsen Overlook provides a fine view, away from the crater, of other mountains and points of geological interest. Passing the road to the north entrance, Rim Drive continues, leading east to Steel Bay (mile 8.8), which commemorates William Gladstone Steel, who contributed much energy and money to creating the national park in 1902. He was also a leader in efforts to build Crater Lake Lodge.

Crestwood Trail, at mile 10.7, leads down the rim to the landing for the park's boat tour.

There is another view of the entire lake at Skell Head at mile 14.8. Mount Scott is the standout here. Another volcanic cone, it's the highest point in the park. There's a short spur road to Cloudcap, providing the park's highest vista point at 8,070 feet. Phantom Ship, the unusual island with a fanciful name, is located to the southwest. The vista point at Kerr Notch (mile 23.2) provides another view of Phantom Ship. Take the road to Pinnacles, leading south from Rim Drive, past the tent campground. The Pinnacles are spires of volcanic ash eroded into tall, weird forms.

The Castle Crest Wildflower Trail is found at mile 31.2. The Godfrey Glen Trail provides another short walk off the connector road to the Annie Springs entrance station. If you continue on Rim Drive, you'll shortly arrive back at the Rim Village starting point.

CRATER LAKE DAY-HIKES

Cleetwood Trail   At mile 10.7 along Rim Drive, this is a steep, one-mile descent with a strenuous one-mile climb back to the rim. The trail leads to the water's edge to the landing for the hourly boat tour, which includes a visit to Wizard Island.

Wizard Island Summit Trail   Offers a short climb, especially valuable to those who want to climb a mountain without spending too much time or effort. It begins at the island dock and leads through the hemlock and fir forest, rising to the subalpine wildflower level, and then to superb lake and rim views from the top. You'll find whitebark pines at the summit.

Annie Creek Trail   Begins behind the amphitheater at Mazama Campground and leads along a loop that is less than two miles long. It runs through wildflower meadows to the bottom of a canyon and ascends to the trailhead.

Mount Scott Trail   At mile 17 along Rim Drive. The one-way hike is 2.5 miles long, climbing to the highest point in the park. The peak has an elevation of 8,926 feet. It provides a view of the south shore of the lake and a vast panorama of most of southern Oregon. On a clear day, Mount Shasta is in full view across the California border. You should also be able to see, near the western edge of the park, an isolated bog of sphagnum moss, which has its own closed ecosystem, including four species of insect-eating plants: two sundews and two bladderworts. You'll also see the headwaters of the Rogue River at Boundary Springs.

Garfield Peak Trail   This hike starts behind Crater Lake Lodge and climbs to the peak's summit, a climb of about 1,700 feet. It offers views of Mount Shasta and park landmarks.

Larkspur

Castle Crest Trail Wildflower Trail A half-mile loop walk through a vividly colored meadow, leading up a nearby hillside. It begins with a short walk through the fir and hemlock forest, and then enters the meadows, which are ribbed with several streams, nurturing the water-loving plants including monkeyflower, lark-spur, violet, and corn lily. The hillside is dryer, with another set of plants, including paintbrushes, penstemon, phlox, and gilia.

BACKCOUNTRY HIKING

Pacific Crest Trail *Access:* To hike the entire Crater Lake National Park section of the trail, a 33-mile excursion of several days, you have to start outside the park. At the north, the trail crosses State Route 138 (the road from Bend and U.S. Highway 97) at a point east of the north entrance station on the park boundary. From the south, it is necessary to link up with the trail in the Winema National Forest. Contact the Forest Service for precise instructions on how to drive to the trail.

The Trail: From north to south, the trail enters the park and leads for 10 miles through a desert area with thick pumice and ash deposits. The trail crosses the north entrance road about two miles from the lake and heads east, past Red Cone, and in-tersects with the backcountry trail to Boundary Springs, the headwaters of the Rogue River.

From the junction, the Pacific Crest Trail heads south over a series of hills and through several creek valleys, linking with the Lightening Springs Trail, leading for another five miles to meet the trail from Rim Village. The main trail snakes south-ward to Annie Springs, crossing State Route 62 and continuing south. A spur trail leads west to Union Peak (el. 7,698). The main trail continues to meet two more spur trails: to Bald Top (el. 7,698) and another at Pumice Flat, which connects with the south entrance road. This connecting trail is about three miles long. The park boundary with the national forest is about 1.5 miles south of the junction with the two spur trails.

Three park spur trails connect Rim Drive with the Pacific Crest Trail. The Annie Springs Cutoff Trail (0.6 mile) leads from the Annie Springs entrance station area. Dutton Creek Trail is a 2.4-mile spur trail that leads from Rim Village. Lightning Springs Trail (four miles) leads from Rim Drive near the Watchman. There are two park locations where roads cross the

Pacific Crest route. In the south part of the park, the trail intersects State Route 62, west of the Annie Spring entrance station. The north entrance road also connects with the trail, north of the junction with Rim Drive. From here, you can hike in a counterclockwise direction, coming out at Annie Springs, or using one of the three spur trails to reach Rim Drive.

Nearby Attractions

KLAMATH BASIN NATIONAL WILDLIFE REFUGES

Located on both sides of the Oregon/California border, six refuges protect a wide range of animal habitat, including conifer forests, marshes, meadows, sagebrush, and juniper uplands, and open water. By visiting the area, you'll see the largest collection of wintering bald eagles in the lower 48 states.

The visitor center is located near Tulelake, a small town off California Route 139, about 100 miles south of Crater Lake National Park. For information, call (916) 667-2231.

Four of the refuges are in Oregon. Klamath Forest Refuge covers more than 16,000 acres west of U.S. 97, about 20 miles (as the crow flies) east of Crater Lake. It takes many more miles to get there via State Route 62 (southeast) and U.S. 97 (north to a sideroad, which leads to the refuge).

Upper Klamath Reserve is a marsh area on the northwest corner of Klamath Lake, reached from Crater Lake by taking State Route 62 (southeast) and turning west at Fort Klamath to take a sideroad west and then south. You can also reach the reserve by taking State Route 140 east from Grants Pass or northwest from Klamath Falls. Bear Valley Reserve is in the same area. This is a small preserve, protecting the large bald eagle population. It is closed from November through April, making it difficult to see the eagles while they are nesting. Lower Klamath Reserve straddles the Oregon/California border. This is the largest area, with some 51,000 acres. It can be reached from either U.S. 97 or State Route 39 (in California, it's State Route 139).

Two refuges are just south of the California border, both just southwest of California Route 139. Tule Lake Reserve has 38,908 acres of land and lake, and it's a prime place to see waterbirds. Stands of tule (bulrushes) surround the lake. Clear Lake Reserve is east of State Route 139 via sideroads with posted signs to the reserve. Clear Lake is closed in spring and summer.

LAVA BEDS NATIONAL MONUMENT

If you're not satisfied with the volcanic debris at Crater Lake, take a drive to Tulelake, California, to see a fine collection of lava-tube caves and cinder cones. It's quite a desolate sight, but it's also a valuable geological preserve. Native Americans have left their petroglyph markings on the soft rock of the monument. This is also a terrific bird-watching area, particularly in spring and fall. The facilities include a campground, hiking trails, and picnic area. The site is open year-round. The headquarters and information center is located 30 miles south of Tulelake and is 26 miles off California Route 139. It is 120 miles south of Crater Lake National Park.

Lassen Volcanic National Park

Until Mount St. Helens blew her top in 1980, the eruption of Lassen Peak in 1914 was the volcanic event of the century in the lower 48 states. The activity started in May of that year, with rumbling, steam ejection, and ash flying. There were more than 150 eruptions between then and early 1915. But the major event was in 1915, when the peak exploded. Lava sprang out of the crater, formed a year earlier. A 20-foot wall of ash, mud, and melted snow crashed down the mountain, snapping and ripping out trees and devastating the mountainside. Several days later, a tremendous mass of gas and ashes shot out of the cone, leaving a three-mile stretch of mountain slope in total destruction. The cloud of steam and ash climbed to 30,000 feet. The mountain then became quiet, with only a small eruption in 1921.

But the mountain has not been still. Its sides boil with water and steam erupting from vents. A geothermal area known as Bumpass Hell features a putrid sulfurous stink, boiling mud pots, fumaroles that rumble, and hot springs that hiss while disgorging hot water from deep in the earth. The god (or devil) within Mount Lassen is not happy and shows it every day.

Like Mazama, the volcano that disappeared when Crater Lake was formed, Lassen is only the latest in a line of volcanic mountains that has occupied this area in Northern California. The earlier, larger volcano was formed by lava flows as far back as 600,000 years ago, layer upon layer, until the mountain was 11,500 feet high and about 11 miles across. It was a hydra-headed mountain, with smaller volcanoes sprouting from its sides as the magma sought easier routes to the surface. These smaller volcanoes erupted, weakening Tehama and causing the big mountain to explode, leaving a caldera to be scoured by glaciers. Lassen Peak was one of the smaller side volcanoes, a youngster at 11,500 years of age.

How to Get There

Redding is a good-sized city located along Interstate 5, about 45 miles from the national park. From the city, take State Route 44 east to the Manzanita Lake entrance at the northwest corner of the park. A visitor center is at the park gate, with the Manzanita Lake Campground about two miles into the park

From the south and the city of Red Bluff (also on Interstate 5), take State Route 36 east to the town of Mineral, and head north on State Route 89 to reach the park's southwest entrance. Three other gates—Warner Valley, Butte Lake, and Juniper Lake—are accessed over unpaved roads. If your destination is the Drakesbad Guest Ranch (more about the ranch later), you will have to take a gravel road north from the town of Chester.

The main park road runs in a general north-south direction, with many switchbacks from the south entrance station through most of the accessible attractions to the Manzanita entrance.

Park Essentials

Park headquarters is in Mineral, CA 96063; (916) 595-4444.

Information centers are located near the southwest entrance station and at the Manzanita Lake entrance. Both have a selection of books on the area as well as hiking brochures and other park information. Both centers are open daily between June and late September. Information is available year-round at the park headquarters in Mineral, eight miles from the southwestern gate.

Food is available during summer months at the information center near the southwest gate. A little cafeteria-style cafe serves hot dogs and other lunch-type meals. The information center is on the ground floor, with the restaurant above.

Eight campgrounds are in the park; four of them are located along Lassen Park Road. The other four campgrounds are in more remote locations and can be accessed by gravel roads. The only overnight accommodations inside the park are at Drakesbad Guest Ranch. For details and reservation information, see "Where to Stay" on page 177.

Accommodations in motels and lodges are available in Mineral and along State Route 36, which leads from Redding to Chester. Several rustic lodges are located on nearby backroads. For a listing of all available resorts and inns, call the Chester Chamber of Commerce at (916) 258-2426. There is a line of rustic resorts and inns in the Hat Creek Valley, north of the northwest park entrance, on State Route 89. For information on these accommodations, contact the Burney Chamber of Commerce at (916) 335-2111. For accommodations at modern motels and hotels in Redding, call the Redding Chamber of Commerce at (916) 243-2541.

PARK ATTRACTIONS

I recommend that you try to start your tour of the park by entering at the southwest entrance, and begin your tour of geothermal wonders at the Sulphur Works. A paved trail and boardwalk lead you through what was once the magma heart of Mount Tehama, before it caved in on itself. This is the caldera, which still produces sulphur fumes, sputtering and boiling mudpots, fumaroles that steam and hiss, and boiling hot clay that burbles and gurgles while displaying pastel colors. This site is impressive enough (you really know the fury of the lord of the underground is still here), but this is just the start of what will be a trip through a kind of virtual hell.

Bumpass Hell is found by walking a trail from a parking lot, a little farther along the park road. The trailhead is marked by a large glacial erratic sitting next to the parking area. This is a three-mile (round-trip) hike. The site was named for K. V. Bumpass, a local promoter and mountain guide. In the 1860s, Bumpass poked his leg through the crust of a boiling mud pot. Returning from his painful adventure, he bragged, jokingly, about his descent into hell. And that is what it is today. Even while you're still approaching on the trail, the stench of sulphur hits you. A boardwalk leads beside furiously boiling mud pots, noisy hot springs, and fumaroles. Flakes of iron pyrite float in the hot pools, carried to the surface in the steam. The trail returns to the parking lot.

The road then climbs around Lassen Peak, passing the summit trailhead and arriving at the top point of the drive at Summit Lake. This is a beautiful, small alpine lake, where the Park Service has two campgrounds. Hiking trails lead to the east and west into Lassen backcountry, all connecting with the Pacific Crest Trail.

The road shortly arrives at the "Devastated Area," the site of the wreckage from the 1915 eruption that scoured the mountainside with a wall of hot ash and mud. It takes many years for vegetation to regenerate in this kind of damaged terrain, and for the sake of scientific research, the natural process has not been helped along by humans.

As the road continues ascending, it leads to several viewpoints that feature fine overlooks of shaggy peaks and canyons. Chaos Crags and Chaos Jumbles are two outstanding geological displays, created only by the forces of nature. They are the remains of a horizontal avalanche that ripped across the landscape about 300 years ago. The wall of rock dammed a creek, forming Manzanita Lake. The park road ends, and State Route 44 enters Lassen National Forest.

Lassen Day-Hikes

The following recommended day-hikes are in addition to the short trails mentioned previously. Most other trails inside the park, including the Lassen portion of the Pacific Crest Trail, are best suited for backcountry hikers. Two exceptions offer exciting hikes to almost anyone, even the hike to the summit.

Cinder Cone Nature Trail   Begins at the Butte Lake Campground in the northeastern section of the park. You get there by taking State Route 44 and then turning south onto the dirt road that leads into the park. The cone trail is a round-trip of five miles. The trip is mainly over a bed of loose cinders. It leads up the 755-foot mound of lava, surrounded by multicolored cinders. The cone is nearly symmetrical, and after reaching the top (6,907 feet), you'll see several craters where several recent eruptions have occurred—the most recent was in 1851.

Lassen Peak Trail This climb can take a half day to a full day, depending on your energy level. The hike from near the park road involves a five-mile round trip. The hike over gravel and ash begins at the 8,463-foot level, ending on the summit at 10,457 feet. This is high country, and the altitude—with its thin air—makes a difference when making the ascent. You are asked by park officials to wear a hat, carry a jacket, and bring water. The climb is prosaic, for those used to wildflower meadows and forest trails. The peak is dry and covered with volcanic rock and fine debris. There are few birds and animals, but the scenery is outstanding. On a clear, sunny day, Mount Shasta is visible to the north. Reminders of the 1915 lava flow are seen at the summit.

Boiling Springs Lake Nature Trail *Access:* This trail is in the park's Drakesbad area. To get there from the town of Chester, follow Feather River Drive west from town. There is a fork after two-thirds of a mile. Take the left fork and continue for another 5.5 miles to another junction, where you turn right. Just past the Warner Valley Campground, take the road to the left. This road is suitable for cars and short trailers.

The Trail: The trail provides an easy one- to two-hour walk (2.3 miles round trip), or more if you want to savor the many wildflowers along the route. This is a much lower, and warmer, part of the park than the high country along the main park road. The area is free of snow earlier in the spring, and wildflowers are more profuse from late June through mid-July. There is a picnic area at the start.

The Hike: Starting with a walk in a lodgepole pine forest, the trail crosses Hot Springs Creek, fed by the lake and several springs along its route. Alders and white fir grow along the creek, providing a habitat for birds. Wildflowers grow along the banks of this warm stream. The trail leads over a large bridge, across the creek. If you will need water, get it here. There is a small hot spring farther on, at milepost 8; it is not for drinking. The trail approaches the Drakesbad Guest Ranch. The right fork leads to the ranch, Devil's Kitchen (an area of fumaroles, mud pots, and hot springs), and Dream Lake. The left fork continues toward Boiling Springs Lake, climbing beside a stream bed, which in spring provides an overflow channel for the lake. The trail passes an enormous Jeffrey pine as the hike proceeds through a deep forest, with staghorn lichens growing on trees. A horse trail veers left. The trail to the lake goes right.

This trail is perfect for those who enjoy the smell of sulphur and the more "ugly" side of nature. This is an active hydrothermal area, with hydrogen sulfide rising to the surface through mud pots and boiling pools. The lake comes into view. It is always warmer than human body temperature: about 125°F in summer and about 110°F in winter. The hot pools beside its shore are much hotter—as hot as 200°F. The lake receives its heat largely by steam and gasses rising from underground vents. The circuit around the lake starts at milepost 24. Other interpretive posts around the lake mark points of interest, including geothermal sites such as fumaroles and mud pots. Mud pots are hot springs in which the water flows up through thick, usually boiling, mud, while fumaroles are holes through which hissing gasses and steam arrive at the surface under pressure.

The lake's only inlet stream is at the end of the lake. Curving back, the trail climbs to provide a good view of Terminal Geyser, with a steaming fumarole. A spur trail leads one mile to Little Willow Lake, which dries up during the summer. There is a good view of Lassen Peak from this height. Another spur trail leads from milepost 36 to a collection of mud pots. The main trail leads to milepost 16 and the return trip to the picnic area and your car.

LASSEN BACKCOUNTRY HIKING

Pacific Crest Trail   *Access:* Warner Valley Campground is the starting point for a south-to-north hike of the Lassen Park portion of the much longer trail. To get there, follow the driving directions from Chester detailed in the Boiling Springs Lake Nature Trail description above.

The Trail: Coming from the south, through Lassen National Forest, the trail enters the park to the east of Hot Springs Creek, near Terminal Geyser. The southern portion of the trail between the campground and Lower Twin Lake is the most popular section, offering a 7.2-mile hike that covers about half of the trail's distance within the park. Above Twin Lakes, the trail covers another 7.7 miles to Rainbow Lake, circling around Fairfield Peak and passing through a rough wilderness area before reaching Badger Flat (13.2 miles), the park boundary, (a total hike of 15.3 miles), and proceeding farther north into the Hat Creek Valley. The area north of Lower Twin Lake is for experienced and masochistic backpackers: It's a region of volcanic debris.

The Hike: The first portion of the hike leaves the northeast corner of the campground, crossing a small creek, and then climbing out of the fir, pine, and incense cedar forest, across lava flows, and back into a forested area of white fir and Jeffrey pine. There are wildflowers and even ferns along the fairly dry route. Another trail branches left, leading to Bench Lake, Kings Creek Falls, and Lassen Park Road. The Pacific Crest Trail continues to climb, crossing Flatiron Ridge, another lava flow, and then descends to a trail junction just before Corral Meadow. The spur trail follows Kings Creek. The main trail leads on, crossing two seasonal creeks and past an area with several campsites. A side trail leads 2.5 miles to Summit Lake, where there are additional campsites. The Pacific Crest Trail crosses Kings Creek (through the creek) and past another campsite. The creek in Grassy Swale drops swiftly to a pool.

The middle part of the hike has many mosquitoes in July, and it is best to do the portion through Grassy Swale at a good clip. However, there are many species of wildflowers in the area, and you may have to make the choice to slather yourself with repellent in order to enjoy the flower displays. The trail continues to climb through a red fir forest into another wildflower meadow, where the route goes around the meadow's south end and then fords of Grassy Swale Creek. There are several sunflower family members along the path, including California butterweed. You cross another wet meadow and a boggy area before continuing to Swan Lake and then Lower Twin Lake.

To reach the park road and Summit Lake (the most popular way to exit the area), walk along the east shore of Lower Twin Lake to a trail that descends to Summit Lake. At this point, you have to decide whether to proceed farther north on the Pacific Crest Trail or proceed west to Echo Lake and then to the park road at Summit Lake.

This part of the Pacific Crest Trail offers an unusual opportunity to see a wide range of wildflowers, in damp and dry conditions and at varied elevations, ranging from pine forest to subalpine.

Nearby Attractions

McArthur–Burney Falls Memorial State Park

Located off State Route 89, north of Lassen Volcanic National Park, this wonderful park is popular with Lassen visitors who visit to see the high falls, which get their water from springs, and then drop 129 feet to a pool below the cliff. For three-quarters of a mile above the falls, springs gush out at a combined rate of about 200 million gallons per day, providing the falls with an impressive year-round flow. Above the springs, Burney Creek is dry for most of the summer. A trail leads from the top of the falls along the creek and past the hot springs, reaching the usually dry creek bed. People come here to camp, fish on Lake Britton, and swim. Lake fishing (trout) is not reliable, but there is better fishing above the lake on the Pit River and along Hat Creek. The state park campground is open year-round, with cold-water showers, except during the summer months when the heaters are turned on. May is the best month for wildflowers.

The Burney Falls Nature Trail provides a one-mile walk from the park entrance station. Taking about a half-hour to walk, the trail leads past self-guiding information posts. The soft breccia of the rim is constantly being eroded and pushed back. Over the past two million years, the rim has moved about 1.25 miles, from Lake Britton to its present location. People in the future will see the falls only in the spring when snow is melting, while the springs bubble into a gorge. The short trail offers an outstanding look at the rock layers and plants, including California black oak and Oregon white oak, Douglas fir and white fir, and understory plants, including thimbleberry, Sierra current, and Pacific and creek dogwood. You'll also see green-leaf manzanita, a common shrub of this region. Incense cedar and ponderosa pine are also in good supply.

SOUTHERN CASCADE WILDFLOWERS

Lassen Volcanic National Park alone hosts nearly 700 species of vascular plants, including trees, shrubs, ferns, and herbs. Crater National Park has about 485 species. The rich mixture of plants (many of them wildflowers) is brought about by the differences in elevation in the southern Cascades. Lassen, in particular, is blessed because it lies at the conjunction of the Cascades and Sierra Nevada Range, with a mix of plants from both biotic regions. Lassen also shares some plants with the adjacent Great Basin region, bringing the desert plant community into the mountains. The volcanic activity and glaciation have scoured and scored the terrain, leaving creeks and many alpine lakes that provide water for nurturing wildlife. Meadows are wet well into summer, providing fertile growing places for myriad wildflowers. Even the harsher alpine zones in the two parks (and adjacent Mount Shasta) provide habitat for matted alpine wildflowers.

At the southern edge of the Cascade Range, elevations change from a low point of 3,000 feet (at Burney Falls) and about 6,000 feet on the lower southern portion of Lassen Volcanic National Park to over 10,000 feet (Lassen Peak) and even higher (over 14,000 feet) at the glacial peak of Mount Shasta. These extremes provide habitat for a range of biotic zones, from the ponderosa pine forest and the slightly higher sagebrush-juniper woodland, through the manzanita chaparral, to the Jeffrey pine, white fir, and lodgepole pine forests. The subalpine zone features mountain meadows rich with wildflowers, the red fir forest, and subalpine slopes. The alpine zone also has wildflowers, trees (mostly stunted and twisted), grasses, and sedges, all of which disappear at about 10,000 feet, leaving the higher terrain to the hardier lichens.

Because wildflowers are such an important part of the visitor's experience at both Crater Lake and Lassen, this section is devoted solely to these colorful herbaceous plants, including some of the smallest bellyflowers.

White Brodiaea
Brodiaea hyacintha
The several brodiaea species, also called fools' onions, bloom in the late spring and early summer, after their leaves have died down. This brodiaea (also known as *Triteleia hyacinthina*) is a perennial herb, with whitish flowers that sometimes have a light blue tinge and a blue-green midvein. The flowers are bell-shaped, with three petals and three sepals, so alike that the blooms appear to have six petals. The fruits are stalked capsules.

They grow on grassy meadows and other open areas at low elevations and on mountain meadows. It has no onion flavor or smell but looks somewhat like a hyacinth, making it easy to identify.

American Brooklime
Veronica beccabunga
(ssp. americana)
This perennial grows from shallow rhizomes and also roots from its trailing stems. It has erect stems, growing to about 24 inches. The lance-shaped leaves are opposite, with three to five pairs on the top of the flowering stem. The blue (lilac to violet) flowers are saucer-shaped, with two large spreading stamens. Fruits are round capsules. The brooklime grows in drying vernal pools or shallow water, in marshes, and along streams and springs. It is common at low to middle elevations. The name "brooklime" is from Europe, where it grows along stream banks where sticky mud "limes" (traps) birds.

Canadian Butterweed
Senecio pauperculus
This perennial herb has a short stem base with leafy stems. The basal leaves are quite thin and elliptical, with sharp teeth. The stem leaves are also toothed, or they may be lobed. The yellow flowers are disk-shaped. It is found in a small area near Haines and Skagway, Alaska, and along the Coast and Cascade Ranges from southeast Alaska to Crater Lake and Lassen. It is seen, in very small numbers, in isolated sites on Vancouver Island.

This wildflower grows in moist forest and meadowlands and along lakes, streams, and marshes in low to middle elevations.

Sticky Cinquefoil
Potentilla glandulosa
This member of the cinquefoil family grows in open forests and meadows at middle elevations and is found throughout the Cascade Range. Like other cinquefoils, it has hairy stems. This one, a perennial, is also covered with glands and is sticky to the touch. Its flowers are yellow. This is strictly a mountain plant and is not found below 6,000 feet. Other members of this large family are found along the Pacific Coast and all the way north to south-central Alaska.

Dirty Socks
Eriogonum pyrolifolium
Also named alpine buckwheat, this wildflower is a tufted, woody perennial, growing from a taproot. Each tuft has oval basal leaves and several flower stems that bear white or greenish-white to pinkish flowers. The flowers are hairy and glandular, with a foul smell (the dirty socks). It grows in dry, rocky scree and talus ridges, most common on pumice, which makes it a prime candidate to grow on the southern Cascade volcanoes.

Skyrocket (Gilia)
Ipomopsis aggregata
Also called scarlet gilia, this is a biennial plant, or a short-lived perennial, with a long, impressive cluster of bright red flowers, which

may also have orange or yellow tinges. It grows in dry, rocky land at high elevations. The red, trumpet-shaped flowers attract humming-birds. The gilia family is named for a 16th century Spanish botanist, Felipe Luis Gil. This is a particularly beautiful flower, having flecks of lighter colors over the red base.

Newberry's Knotweed
Polygonum newberryi
Like most wildflowers, this one has a second name, in this case fleece-flower. It is a perennial plant, with a thick root and branched crown. Several leafy stems emerge in spring with a deep red color. It bears numerous oblong to oval leaves. The flowers are greenish-white to pinkish. The plant is usu-ally covered with fine hairs, or fuzz, giving it its nickname. John Newberry was a naturalist and sur-geon who was on an 1858 Army ex-pedition looking for a railway route along the Cascades.

Menzies' Larkspur
Delphinium menziesii
Several varieties of larkspur grow in the Pacific Northwest, including tall larkspur (*D. glaucum*), which is found in the Olympic and Cascade Ranges, and Trollius-leafed larkspur (*D. trollifolium*), which grows along stream banks and in moist forests from southwestern Washington to California. Menzies' larkspur has distinctive purplish to deep blue flowers and a large spur that con-tains nectar. The flowers are alone or are formed in terminal clusters.

It grows to a height of about 20 inches (most in this region are much shorter). It grows in grassy pools, meadows, and grassy bluffs on the eastern side of the Olympic Mountains, throughout Oregon, and into Northern California.

Corn Lily
Veratrum ciride
This perennial herb is also known as Indian hellebore, or green false hellebore. Known by the Chinook as *skookum root* (meaning "strong and powerful"), this is probably the most poisonous and dangerous plant in the Pacific Northwest. However, it has been used (in small quantities) by the Nisga'a people as a toothache remedy and for curing colds. The Haida made the plant into a poultice for bruises and sprains.

Some species of the family are used to make a powdered form of garden insecticide called hellebore. It is best not to drink the water a hellebore grows in, to avoid stom-ach cramps.

The corn lily grows from a short rhizome with unbranched stems (often in clusters). The broad, often oblong leaves have "accordion" ribs with hairs beneath. The musky-smelling flowers are star-shaped and are pale-green with dark-green centers. There are many flowers on a stalk, in thin, branched terminal clusters, with drooping tas-sels. It grows on meadows, in bogs and wet thickets, and in some open forests. It is most abundant on cold, wet, subalpine meadows.

Gray's Lovage
Ligustichum grayi

This is strictly a southern Cascades wildflower, growing only in the range from the Canada/Washington border into Northern California. It is a hairless perennial, growing from a taproot. The leaves are mostly basal, divided into many toothed or cleft leaflets. The stems have a small number of smaller leaves. Flowers are white, grouped into 7 to 14 small, compact heads. Gray's lovage is similar to parsley-leafed lovage (*L. aplifolium*), which is found throughout Washington and Oregon and into California but can be identified by its well-developed stem leaves.

Large-leafed Lupine
Lupinus polyphyllus

This wildflower has been cultivated as a garden ornamental, and it stands out in a border, with its pastel flowers and large leaves. You'll see it in the wild throughout the Cascades, on the Olympic Peninsula, and on southern Vancouver Island. This plant grows from a branched, woody rhizome, sending up erect stems that are hollow at the base (and sometimes hollow higher). The flowers are blue to violet, like a sweet pea, growing in dense clusters to a length of 15 inches. The fruits are hairy pods. Like other lupines, this one grows best in disturbed sites, particularly after a fire, but it also grows in open habitats, including wet meadows, and beside streams at low to medium altitudes.

Yellow Monkeyflower
Mimulus guttatus

This plant is either an annual, growing from fibrous roots, or a perennial, from creeping stolons and rhizomes. It also roots from stem roots. The erect stems grow from 4 to 30 inches tall, with leaves in pairs. The lower leaves are stalked; the upper leaves grow from the stem. The yellow flowers are trumpet-shaped, with long stalks. The lower lip of the flower has one large or several small brownish-red or crimson spots. The flowers grow in terminal clusters. The fruit is a broad capsule, containing many seeds, formed as the sepals become fused and inflated. This plant and the dwarf monkeyflower (*M. tilingii*) grow along streams, near springs, along wet ledges, and in crevices. The dwarf variety is a short, creeping perennial; a subalpine and alpine species that bears large yellow flowers (looking too large for such a small plant).

Columbian Monkshood
Aconitum columbianum

This plant, with a leaf shaped like that of a geranium, is widely seen in the Washington and Oregon Cascades. It is a perennial herb, growing from a tuberous taproot. It has tall, single stems and leaves that are palmately divided, but not to the base, as is the mountain monkshood (*A. delphinifolium*) found in southeast Alaska and the Queen Charlotte Islands. The purple flowers of the Columbian monkshood are large, with hoods higher than they are wide. All parts of the plant are poisonous. The tubers contain a chemical that paralyzes the nerves—a poison particularly hard on cattle and other livestock.

Western Pasqueflower
Anemone occidentalis
Also called the western anemone, this hairy perennial grows a thick, short-branched stem from a taproot. It is usually about 15 inches tall, bearing tufted basal leaves, which are divided into two or three narrow segments. The large, white flowers are often tinged with blue, and they grow alone at the end of a stem. The flowers are often seen before the leaves unfold. The unusual fruit is a hairy achene with long, feathery styles, seen as a large hairy head. It grows from southwestern B.C. and the middle section of Vancouver Island (Strathcona Park), in the Cascades, and on the Olympic Peninsula. Its habitat is primarily subalpine and alpine meadows and also rocky slopes. You'll have to travel to above the 5,000-foot level to see this flower, also called moptop and tow-headed baby.

Davidson's Penstemon
Penstemon davidsonii
This low, shrubby perennial is seen as a dense mat of leaves and flowers growing on creeping stems. The thick, firm evergreen leaves are opposite, with some toothed. The color of the long, tubular flower varies from purple to lavender. The flower has a hairy throat and four stems that have two lips each, with dense, woolly anthers. The fruits are capsules, with narrow wings, about 3.5 inches long. It grows on rocky ledges and talus slopes in the subalpine and alpine zones. A similar family member, rock penstemon (*P. rupicola*), is also formed as a low, dense mat, but it has hairy leaves and pink to rose-purple flowers. It is also seen in the Washington and Oregon Cascades.

Meadow Penstemon
Penstemon oreocharis
You'll find this member of the figwort family (Scrophulariaceae) between 4,000 and 7,500 feet in the southern Cascades, particularly in Lassen Volcanic National Park. Like Davidson's, it has a tubular flower, magenta to purple. It grows in damp meadows, lasting into dry periods. The figworts make up a huge family of herbacious plants, all known as snapdragons, but including such common mountain residents as paintbrushes, foxgloves, louseworts, monkeyflowers, and brooklimes.

Yellow Montane Violet
Viola praemorsa
This is one of at least a half-dozen violets found in the Cascade Range, in all elevations except in the alpine zone. The yellow montane violet is not as its name suggests. It is a lowland flower, growing on meadows and dry grassy slopes. It is a perennial, growing from a short rhizome. It has erect, hairy, and egg-shaped or elongated ears. Look at the flowers to identify this violet. The flower petals are yellow. The

upper pair have brownish backs, the side pair are bearded, and the lowest petal has a spur.

In Lassen Volcanic National Park, you'll find the northern bog violet (*V. nephrophylla*), with blue to violet flowers and heart-shaped leaves, growing in wet, shady locations up to elevations of about 7,000 feet.

Gairdner's Yampah
Perideridia gairdneri
This is one of several members of the wild carrot family that are seen in the southern Cascades. It has a thick, tuberous root (the carrot), with thin leafy stems. The leaves are distributed along the stem, singly or opposite. It bears white or pinkish flowers, which are grouped in compact heads, with several heads growing from the tip of the stem. The fruits are almost round, wide, and with noticeable ribs. The roots of the yampah were eaten by native peoples from British Columbia to California and Nevada. It is also called wild caraway, because it smells and looks like the caraway plant (*Carum carvi*). Meredith Gairdner was a doctor (the Hudson's Bay Company surgeon) and an early plant specialist in this region. You'll also find Parish's yampah (*P. parishii*) in Lassen Park. This "carrot" has white flowers in similar clusters, about an inch wide. It is found in meadows up to the subalpine level.

BELLYFLOWERS

These are the almost invisible members of the wildflower world, very small because of the short growing season and dryer terrain. Bellyflowers are found growing on alluvial fans and other gravelly slopes, requiring the flower lover to get down and commune with them on their own level. A few minutes spent with bellyflowers brings feelings of wonder at their intense desire to survive, growing only an inch or two before bursting into bloom. The following flowers are found around the 6,000-foot level, and they are a real joy to experience in the area above Drakesbad in Lassen Volcanic National Park.

Torrey's Blue-eyed Mary
Collinsia torreyi
A dwarf member of the figwort family and a very small monkeyflower, this wildflower is widely known as Torrey's collinsia. Monkeyflowers are so-called because of flowers that seem to have a monkey-shaped face. It has two-lipped flowers. The upper lip is white or pale yellow, and the lower lip is a blue-violet. The plant grows in the southern Cascades, at elevations from the lowland levels up to the alpine zone (about 8,000 feet).

Dwarf Groundsmoke
Gayophytum humile
This is an annual of the Oregon and California Cascades, growing at low to middle elevations in dry, sandy locations. It is very low, with many branches. The alternate leaves are attached to the stalk under tiny, white to pinkish flowers. The plant gets its name because it is a seemingly fragile,

wispy herb and barely off the ground. *Gayophytum* was named for G. Gay, a 19th century French botanist and explorer of South America.

Torrey's Monkeyflower
Mimulus torreyi
Growing from one to six inches tall (usually one to two inches), this is another dwarf monkeyflower found on the slopes of Mount Lassen. It has pink flowers with yellow throats, and the characteristic monkey face. Like other members of the figwort family, this plant grows in dry sites, up to Lassen's 7,000-foot level. It is often seen with its cousin, Torrey's blue-eyed Mary.

Whisker Brush
Linanthus cilatus
A needle-shaped plant, the whisker brush is often less than one inch tall although it grows to a height of three to four inches. It is a member of the phlox family (Polemoniaceae), along with gilia, Jacob's ladder, and collomia. This diminutive plant has white to pink tubular flowers, with yellow throats. It is found around Mount Lassen, up to 8,000 feet, from the lowland elevations through the subalpine zone.

CRATER LAKE NATIONAL PARK

Crater Lake Lodge and Mazama Village Motor Inn
Off-Season:
P.O. Box 2704
White City, OR 97503
(541) 830-8700 or (541) 830-4053

Crater Lake Lodge, one of the finest of the old national park hotels, has been completely rebuilt, and it re-opened in 1995. It has comfortable rooms and dining facilities, and it is open from early June to mid-September. **($$ to $$$)**
　　Mazama Village Motor Inn has standard motel-style units and a restaurant adjacent to the Mazama Campground on Rim Drive. This motel-style facility is open from mid-May to early October. **($$)**

Crater Lake National Park Camping

Mazama Campground, the main camping facility in the park, is open from mid-June to mid-September, with sites for tents, trailers, and RVs. The campground, near the Annie Springs entrance station, has a store, showers, and laundry.

Lost Creek Campground, with sites for tents only, is open from early July to late August. It is accessed by a park road that leads south from Rim Drive past the campground to the Pinnacles.

CRATER LAKE VICINITY

Aspen Inn
52250 Highway 62
P.O. Box 437
Fort Klamath, OR 97626
(541) 381-2321

This small motel is located 20 miles southeast of the south entrance to Crater Lake National Park. It has standard units. **($)**

Crater Lake Resort
50711 Highway 62
P.O. Box 457
Fort Klamath, OR 97626
(541) 381-2349 (seasonal)

This operation is open May through September. It includes cabins, including some with kitchenettes, an RV park, trout pool, and swimming pool. **($)**

Diamond Lake Resort
Diamond Lake Recreation Area
Diamond, OR 97731
(541) 793-3333

This sizable resort has rooms, including some with kitchenettes, in a scenic area located about five miles from the north entrance to Crater Lake National Park, off Highway 138 (from Roseburg). You can also get there by taking Highway 230. To use this route, start in Medford or Klamath Falls by taking State Route 62, then turning north onto State Route 230. There is a restaurant. **($ to $$)**

Spring Creek Ranch Motel
H.C. 63, P.O. Box 440
Chiloquin, OR 97624
(541) 783-2775

Chiloquin is a tiny community situated southeast of Crater Lake National Park, a few miles southeast of Fort Klamath, which you reach by taking a sideroad from either U.S. 97 (from Klamath Falls) or State Route 62, which links Medford with the park and U.S. 97. This small motel has standard rooms and units with kitchenettes and the kind of very reasonable rates you would expect from a small motel in a tiny village. **($)**

Union Creek Resort
56484 Highway 62
Prospect, OR 97536
(541) 560-3565

All of the tourist accommodations near Crater Lake are small outfits, with rustic or semirustic cabins and rooms. This place has more cabins than most, including several with kitchenettes, and rooms with shared baths. The resort operates a restaurant. Prospect is located between Medford and Crater Lake, on State Route 62. **($ to $$)**

Crater Lake Vicinity Camping

The U.S. Forest Service has campgrounds surrounding Crater Lake National Park in its national forests.

Farewell Bend and **Union Creek Campgrounds** are located just off State Route 62, southwest of the park. Union Creek is found near the junction of State Route 62 and State Route 230. Farewell bend is located a few miles south of Union Creek.

There is a state park and a forest service campground off U.S. 97, southeast of the national park, just north of Chiloquin.

Collier State Park has a large campground, to the west of the highway, with water, RV hookups, showers, dump station, and hiking trails.

Williamson River Campground (Forest Service) is a small, more basic operation, with drinking water and hiking trails in the Klamath National Forest.

There are three Forest Service campgrounds at Diamond Lake, located about four miles due north of the park:

Thielsen View Campground (the farthest north of the three facilities) has drinking water, hiking trails and a boat ramp. This is a small facility.

Diamond Lake Campground is a huge operation, also on the lake, with upgraded services, including water, showers, dump station, hiking trails, and boat ramp.

Broken Arrow Campground, at the junction of State Routes 230 and 138, is another large campground, with water, showers, dump station, trails, and boat ramp.

For more information, write to the U.S. Forest Service, 800 Northeast Oregon Street #5, Suite 177, Portland, OR 97232. To obtain other information on USFS campgrounds, call (503) 872-2750.

LASSEN VOLCANIC NATIONAL PARK

Drakesbad Guest Ranch
c/o California Guest Services
Adobe Plaza
2150 Main Street, Suite 5
Red Bluff, CA 96080
(916) 529-1512

The only overnight accommodations inside the park are at Drakesbad Guest Ranch. The ranch is located in the south-central part of the park, with facilities including cabins, a hot spring pool, and trail riding. This is the place for an out-of-the-way experience; for hot springs fans, this place is a must. A lot of other people think so, too. Ranch accommodations are limited, and reservations must be made several years in advance for popular holiday periods. The ranch is located north of the town of Chester. Follow Feather River Drive west from town. There is a fork after two-thirds mile. Take the left fork and continue for another 5.5 miles to another junction, then turn right. There are signs pointing the way to Drakesbad. **($$ to $$$)**

Lassen Volcanic National Park Camping

Eight campgrounds in Lassen Volcanic National Park are operated by the National Park Service.

Southwest Campground is located near the information center, with tent camping only. **Summit Lake–North** and **Summit Lake–South** campgrounds are in high country, past Lassen Peak, with tent and RV sites and a 14-day limit. **Manzanita Lake Campground** has tent and RV sites, with showers, and also a 14-day limit. **Craggs Campground**, at the north end, is for overflow only. All are open from late May through September.

The other three campgrounds are in more remote locations and can be accessed by gravel roads. **Butte Lake Campground** is at the northeast corner of the park, via a gravel road from State Route 44. **Juniper Lake Campground** is in the southeastern section of the park, with a gravel backroad leading from Chester. The **Warner Valley Campground** is reached by taking another road from Chester (this is the same road that leads another mile farther to Drakesbad Guest Ranch).

LASSEN VICINITY

Black Forest Lodge
Route 5, P.O. Box 5000
Mill Creek, CA 96061
(916) 258-2941

Located on State Route 36, about halfway between Chester and the south gate to Lassen Volcanic National Park, this is a small inn with standard rooms and an apartment-style unit. The restaurant is well known for its German-style cooking. **($ to $$)**

Fire Mountain Lodge
Mill Creek, CA 96061
(916) 258-2938 (seasonal)

This little resort is on State Route 36, 1.8 miles northwest of the junction with State Route 32. It's a cabin operation, with meals served, a store, gas, and a trailer park. The resort is open during the summer tourist season. It's no more than a 20-minute drive to the southern park gate. **($ to $$)**

Hat Creek Resort
P.O. Box 15
Old Station, CA 96071
(916) 335-7121

This resort has been in the scenic country north of Lassen Volcanic National Park for more than 50 years. It is close to prime fishing lakes, including the Thousand Lakes Wilderness. Located on State Route 44/89, the resort is 12 miles east of the Manzanita Lake entrance to the national park, and it is almost precisely on the Pacific Crest Trail. The resort has cabins, a few motel rooms, and RV spaces with hookups. The facilities are limited in winter, with only the motel rooms and a cabin open. There is a restaurant and a bar, both within two minutes' drive, and both serve "down-home" meals. **($ to $$)**

Mineral Lodge
P.O. Box 160
Mineral, CA 96063
(916) 595-4422

This longtime tourist operation features rooms, a restaurant, pool, bar, store, gift shop, and ski shop. Some of the rooms have kitchenettes. It is the handiest full-resort operation with overnight accommodations for those traveling to and visiting

Lassen Volcanic National Park. It's located on State Route 36, a few miles from the southwestern park gate. **($ to $$)**

Lassen Vicinity Camping

Burney Falls Campground
The large developed campground, in McArthur–Burney Falls Memorial State Park, has sites suitable for tents, trailers, and RVs, with hot showers available from about late April through October 15. Cold showers can be taken the rest of the year. Reservations are available through Mistix at 800-444-7275. For park information, call (916) 335-2777.

Mount Lassen KOA Kampground
7749 KOA Road
Shingletown, CA 96088
(916) 474-3133

This is a small operation for KOA, but it has an adequate number of RV sites with full hookups and tent sites to satisfy most of the travelers who come through Shingletown to visit the Lassen Volcanic National Park area. The campground is located on State Route 44, 35 miles east of Redding and Interstate 5, and 10 miles from the south gate to Lassen Park. The operation also has showers, a laundry, grocery store, and souvenir shop. It is full every day during the summer season. Reserving a site is advised.

Volcano Country Campground
P.O. Box 55
Mineral, CA 96063

Located behind the post office in little Mineral, this private campground has RV sites with full hookups and sites for tenters, a dump station, laundry, and propane service.

FOREST SERVICE CAMPGROUNDS

The U.S. Forest Service operates campgrounds close to the north and south entrances of the Lassen Volcanic National Park and in the forest area near Drakesbad. Here are the campgrounds closest to the four park entrances.

Battle Creek Campground is a large facility, along State Route 36, south of Lassen Volcanic National Park and 1.2 miles west of the park headquarters in Mineral. It is just west of the Battle Creek Bridge.

Big Pine Campground, to the north of the park, is in the Hat Creek Valley. The medium-size campground is located a half-mile east of Highway 89, just a half-mile north of a vista point, and 1.6 miles south of the Hat Creek Resort at the community of Old Station.

Bogard Campground, located east of the national park, is two miles west of State Route 44, via Forest Road 31N26. This road joins Highway 44, 2.8 miles north of County Road A21.

Butte Creek Campground is a small facility, north of the Butte Creek entrance, near the northeastern corner of the park. This campground is reached by taking State Route 44 to a point 11 miles east

of the junction with State Route 89. Take Forest Road 32N21 for 2.4 miles.

Domingo Springs Campground is a medium-sized campground, south of the national park. Drive north from Chester via Feather River Drive. Take the left fork after two-thirds mile and drive west for another 7.75 miles.

High Bridge Campground is a small campground south of the park. Take Feather River Drive, driving north from Chester, and branch left after two-thirds mile. Drive another 4.9 miles and take the left fork after crossing the Warner Creek Bridge. The campground is only a short distance south of the bridge.

Rocky Knoll and **Silver Bowl Campgrounds** are close to each other, west of the national park and the Caribou Wilderness. Both are medium-size campgrounds located on Forest Road 110, which leads off County Road A21. To reach Silver Bowl, take Road 110 for 4.1 miles, branch left, and drive less than a half-mile to the campground. To reach Rocky Knoll, take Forest Road 110 for 5.1 miles.

Warner Creek Campground is a small facility in the lower Warner Valley, south of the park boundary, and on the same road leading to Drakesbad Guest Ranch. From the town of Chester, take Feather River Drive and take the left fork after two-thirds mile. Drive another 5.5 miles, take the right fork, and drive north 1.1 miles.

PART 3

Rain Forests

Each year, more than 140 inches of rain fall on the western slopes of the Olympic Range in western Washington state. At the same time, ocean weather patterns bring humid winds off the Pacific into the Olympic Mountains. These ocean breezes are often accompanied by fog. All of this moisture and the moderate ocean climate has created the right environment for three magnificent temperate rain forests, set into river valleys in the Olympics.

A few miles north, separated from the Olympic Peninsula by the Strait of Juan de Fuca, the west coast of Vancouver Island contains a series of rain forests, located along a 300-mile strip of Pacific shoreline. The spine of mountains separating the west and east coasts of the island have the same effect on the island environment as the Olympic Range has for the Olympic Peninsula. The west side is wild and wet. The east side, bordering the Strait of Juan de Fuca, is calm and relatively dry.

Another 300 miles to the north, the Alaska Panhandle contains the northernmost stands of temperate rain forest, again facing the Pacific Ocean, with a wind and rain backstop created by the Coast Mountains, trapping the abundant rains that move inland from the ocean.

We'll explore these three rain forest regions—each quite different from the other, and each with superb recreational opportunities. In addition, we'll look at nearby natural attractions, in the dryer parts of the three regions, including subalpine forests, hot springs, underground wonders, and probably the hemisphere's best chances to see forest and mountain wildlife.

We're probably more familiar with the concept of the tropical rain forest than we are the northern rain forest. In tropic regions, the rain falls consistently throughout the year, often daily. Daily temperatures in the tropics vary little from nighttime to daytime and from season to season, and the most common trees are broad-leaved evergreens. The understory comprises bamboos and tree ferns, with spreading and climbing tropical plants. The tropical rain forest canopy is of great importance. Most animal life resides in the hospitable canopy. When a tropical rain forest is cut down or otherwise destroyed, it takes a long time for regeneration and growth to occur. The soil is extremely damp, usually sopping, with nutrients leached away by the torrential rainfall.

Nature has conceived a much different scenario for life in a temperate rain forest. Abundant rain creates the right conditions for this special type of forest. Yet, in contrast to tropical conditions, rainfall tends to be more seasonal, with a long wet season during fall and winter months and a dryer summer where fog provides the dampness necessary for survival.

The trees of a temperate rain forest grow larger and higher than those of the tropics. This is the result of the Pacific Coast's moderate conditions, lacking extreme heat. The common trees are evergreen conifers: Sitka spruce and western hemlock, interspersed with western red cedar and Douglas fir. You'll also see broad-leaved deciduous trees, including bigleaf and vine maples, alder, amabilis fir, and (in some rain forests) cottonwoods growing in riparian habitats. Bigleaf maples are draped with mosses. The Sitka spruce is usually the climax tree, with ancient spruces growing to an extreme old age—as much as 700 years—after supplanting the earlier-growing Douglas fir and hemlock.

The temperate understory is composed of masses of sword and other evergreen ferns and shrubs including several huckleberries, salmonberry, and sorrel. Ferns also grow out of notches in the rain forest trees.

Maple branch with club moss

The wildlife of the Pacific Coast rain forests plays an important role in maintaining the forest environment. Roosevelt elk, found in all the northern rain forests, browse on the undergrowth, keeping it in check and promoting an open forest where conifer seeds may settle and generate new tree growth. Like the elk, animal life stays more on the ground of the temperate rain forest. This land is hospitable to black bears, deer, raccoons, river otters, and a host of other forest creatures. Resident and seasonal birds add to the wildlife mix. Above the rain forest, lowland and subalpine forests rise along the mountain slopes.

Olympic
National Park

The experience of walking into the Hoh for the first time must be like that of an infant's entry into the world. It is an alien environment, never before encountered—a staggering new world of immensely tall life forms reaching into the sky. Twisted, ancient tree limbs are clothed with thick mosses; ferns grow out of every available hole, crack, or chink in the trees and fallen logs. Moisture drops off the ferns, making circles on the bogwater below. Huge spruces are lined up in military order, precisely trained by their long-deceased nurse log. Bark is twisted and deeply furrowed. Trunks and branches are knurled. Ferns, salal, and a dozen other plants live in the floating understory.

Water drips continuously from the forest canopy, whether it's raining or not. Fog appears, tenuously at first; then, with a strong breeze picking up from the ocean, it moves through the forest to cover everything with an eerie, translucent cast. It is the ultimate in wetness and forest life.

This is the Hoh Rain Forest, the finest temperate rain forest in the world. The Hoh is one of three major rain forests contained in the western Olympic Mountain valleys.

In the mountains, forests, and coastal shores of the Olympic Peninsula exist a remarkable diversity in ecosystems, landscapes, plant life, and wild creatures—and more than a few contradictions. For instance, the mountains of the peninsula are no more than 8,000 feet above sea level, yet they are capped with more glaciers than most mountain ranges 50 percent higher. The west side of the Olympic Range receives an amazing amount of precipitation, with the top of Mount Olympus receiving about 220 inches (mostly snow). Yet about 30 miles to the east, the town of Sequim receives only 17 inches of rain a year and no snow. The four types of forest on the peninsula teem with plant and animal life, nurtured by the moderate climate that creates a wonderfully rich growing condition for plants.

Similar to the creation of Vancouver Island to the north, the Olympic Peninsula is the result of seamounts created long ago on the ocean floor. These undersea mountains were then shoved against the continent through the movement of the Pacific plate toward and under the North American plate, and part of the ocean floor and the seamounts were scraped and lifted above sea level. The huge dome deposited here was subsequently worn down by glaciers and streams into the sharp ridges and jagged peaks we see today. During later ice ages, huge glaciers moved beside the dome, carving out the Strait of Juan de Fuca and Puget Sound, leaving salt water on three sides of the mountain range.

On a hike from sea level into the mountains, the visitor passes through four separate biotic zones, each with its own forest life. The temperate rain forest is at the lowest level, not far from the Pacific shoreline, and it is characterized by the huge Sitka spruces and moss-covered bigleaf maples.

Above and beside the rain forest is the lowland forest, where western hemlock is the predominant tree; there are other trees, including grand firs and a few western hemlocks, but few Sitka spruces. Also in this system are red alder, bigleaf maple, Pacific dogwood, and black alder. Typical shrubs of the lowland are red elderberry, salmonberry, rhododendron, salal, and devil's club. Many varieties of fern thrive here, along with Oregon grape and the western (sanitized) version of skunk cabbage. This is a typical sea-level zone for this latitude, but the presence of rain forest conditions puts some of this lowland forest above its normal elevation. It is an area of much wildlife, from black bears and squirrels to many birds: kingfishers, jays, wrens, thrushes, and dippers are found along the streams.

When the red cedar begins to disappear, you know you're in the montane (Rocky Mountain) forest zone. Here, silver fir predominates with some western hemlock and Douglas fir growing where fires have cleared the land for a new forest. The undergrowth is not as thick as in the lower zones, but there are many shrubs and other plants, including vine maple, alder, devil's club, salal, and rhododendron.

The subalpine zone provides the transition between the montane and the treeless alpine zone. In the lower parts of the upper zone are the dwindling trees of the montane. At higher reaches are subalpine fir, mountain hemlock, and Alaska cedar; all are much smaller and shorter than the trees of the rain forest or the lowland forests. The trees are part of an ecosystem that includes glacial lakes, bogs, swamps, and meadows. Between the trees are low-growing shrubs: huckleberry, heather, willow, and slide alder. When the forest thins out, stands of stunted, misshapen trees are surrounded by alpine meadows, with masses of wildflowers in the spring and early summer. This, and the subalpine fir forest below, are zones of heavy snow. Above the wildflower blankets is rock and the ever-present glacial ice.

The three higher forest zones are found to the east, south, and north of the mountain peaks; only the rain forests are missing in these regions.

The National Park

Fifty-seven miles of Olympic coastline—almost the entire stretch of western coast on the peninsula—is within the national park boundaries. It was here that the first human inhabitants settled after their arrival from Asia over the Bering land bridge and down the coast. The Quileute were the first known people to live along the Olympic coast, although there was a predecessor group living here. The ocean provided much of the Quileute food, but they ventured into the forest to gather berries and to hunt for deer and elk. They made great canoes out of cedar trunks and used the same tree for lodge building. To the Quileute, the peaks of Mount Olympus were considered to be one large mountain and the home of their god the Thunderbird, creator of thunder and lightning.

The coastline is much like that of British Columbia, with rocky inlets and seastack rocks, miles of sand and cobble beaches, river mouths every few miles, and lakes with salt marshes offering habitat for many birds and animals. There are several reservations along the coast, including the Makah Reservation at the northwestern tip of the peninsula; the Ozette Reservation just north of Ozette Lake; the Quileute Reservation west of the town of Forks; the tiny Hoh Reservation at the mouth of the Hoh River; and the large Quinault Reservation southeast of Queets.

Native Americans were living in several villages along the Olympic coast when explorer Juan de Fuca stopped by. He is thought to be the first European to land on these shores. Later, in 1774, Juan Perez sailed along this coast, followed by British, Spanish, and American explorers, including Captain George Vancouver, a representative of the British Crown, and American Robert Gray. The first expedition into the Olympic interior was led by Lieutenant Joseph P. O'Neill in 1885. In 1889–1890, James Christie led a north-south expedition, taking five and a half months to complete the difficult crossing. Lieutenant O'Neill completed an easier east-west crossing in 1890, moving up and down river valleys.

Another key aspect of area history, the Roosevelt elk is at the high end of the animal chain. It is the coastal version of the western elk, differing from the Rocky Mountain elk (wapiti) in its antlers (more bunchy), rump (white), and its nature (more shy). This is the same species of elk that was almost decimated in the Redwood National Park area. Protecting the elk herds of the Olympic forests was a primary reason for the designation of much of the peninsula as a national forest reserve in 1909 by President Theodore Roosevelt. Legislation creating the national park was signed by President Franklin D. Roosevelt in 1938.

Today, more than 900 miles of hiking trails take visitors into virtually every valley, forest, and meadow as well as glaciers and several mountain peaks. A few of the trails are remnants of former logging roads. Most are trails constructed by the parks and forest services or hard-packed paths tramped out by hikers who have long known the Olympic Peninsula to be just about the finest hiking country in America.

Although hiking is the only way to see most of what the Olympic Mountains have to offer in scenery, geology, and wildlife, several accessible areas in the national park offer recreational opportunities to get a feel for the majesty of the mountains, woodlands, meadows, and rain forests.

How to Get There

The Olympic Peninsula lies west of Seattle and Puget Sound and northwest of the state capital of Olympia. It's possible to get to the peninsula from almost every direction by car, except from the north—you have to take a ferry from Victoria, B.C.

From the South and the Oregon Coast From Astoria, Oregon, cross the Columbia River on the Astoria Bridge (toll), and take either U.S. 101, which leads toward the Long Beach Peninsula, or take State Route 401 to join State Route 4 and Highway 101 (here, the Olympic Highway), arriving in Aberdeen. Highway 101 leads north and is the major highway route around the Olympic Peninsula. Should you wish to sample some more southern Washington shoreline along the way, take Highway 109 west from Aberdeen to Ocean City, Pacific Beach, and/or Moclips before heading east to join Highway 101.

From Portland, Oregon, and Vancouver, Washington There are two routes, both scenic, to get you to the southern part of the Olympic Peninsula from the Portland/Vancouver region. From Portland, take U.S. 30 northwest along the southern bank of the Columbia River to Astoria, cross the Columbia River Bridge, and take the suggested route described above.

Another route uses Interstate 5 north from Portland and Vancouver, exiting to Washington State Route 4 near Kelso. Route 4 leads west along the north bank of the Columbia River, past several quaint old communities including Skamokawa and Gray's River, meeting Highway 101 a few miles east of the Long Beach Peninsula and Willapa Bay. Then take the prescribed route north via Highway 101 to Quinault, Forks, and Port Angeles. The rain forests lie between Quinault and Forks.

From Olympia and Interstate 5 Take State Route 8 and U.S. 101 west from the city of Olympia. Highway 101 is the main route for the Olympic Peninsula, leading along the western shore of the Hood Canal to Hoodsport, Brinnon, Quilcene, and Port Angeles. Highway 101 continues in a counterclockwise direction, circling the Olympic Mountains.

From Seattle and Interstate 5 Highway lovers should drive south on Interstate 5 to Olympia and take Highway 101 to Port Angeles (see above). The more scenic and shorter way to reach

Port Angeles is to drive north from downtown Seattle on Interstate 5 and take the turnoff to Edmonds (just north of the Seattle city limits). A ferry will take you and your vehicle to Bainbridge Island. Following this short cruise, you'll drive northwest on State Route 104, to Poulsbo, joining Highway 101 north of Quilcene. Continue on Highway 101 to Sequim and Port Angeles.

From Victoria by Ferry   The Black Ball ferry company operates a car ferry, with several sailings per day, across the Strait of Juan de Fuca from the capital of British Columbia to Port Angeles. For information, call (360) 457-4491 (Port Angeles) or (604) 386-2202 (Victoria). The Victoria Express is a ferry for foot passengers only. It operates from May to October. For information, call 800-633-1589 (U.S. and Canada) or (604) 361-9144 (Victoria).

Our book *Pacific Coast Adventures* (Prima Publishing, 1995) provides a motorist's navigational guide to western Washington and the Olympic Peninsula, with strip maps and highway logs for the Olympic Peninsula Loop Drive.

Olympic National Park Attractions

Following are the major areas within the national park, beginning with Hurricane Ridge, near Port Angeles, and then working in a counterclockwise direction through the river valleys on the north and west sides of the park. The final areas covered are Dosewallips and Staircase, found on the eastern flank of the mountains, just west of the Hood Canal and accessed via Highway 101 and forest roads leading into the range.

PORT ANGELES MUSEUM AND HURRICANE RIDGE

The best way to begin a tour of the Olympic Peninsula is to visit the Olympic National Park Visitor Center and Pioneer Museum, located in downtown Port Angeles. You'll get not only an overview of park attractions and the history of the area but also a wealth of printed material to help you along your explorations. The shop stocks detailed topographic maps and has updated hiking trail information. Hurricane Ridge is less than a half-hour's drive from the museum. Take Race Street to reach both the visitor center and Hurricane Ridge.

In the 1930s, the Forest Service built a road to Hurricane Hill, a marvelous meadowland sitting high above Port Angeles, accessible until that time only by a trail from the Elwha Valley. The trail is still there, offering a wonderful climbing hike with great views, but most people save time by driving to the Hurricane Ridge site, now the most visited area in the national park. The 18-mile drive from Port Angeles to Hurricane Ridge is filled with scenic views as the road twists and turns up the mountain. Heart o' the Hills Campground is just inside park boundaries at an elevation of 1,807 feet, with 105 sites. The road continues, running beside Klahanie Ridge to climb to the Hurricane Ridge parking lot. Here, you'll find a ranger station, a snack bar, picnic area, and several trails both short and long. After the first snowfall or two, the cross-country ski center is opened, with skis and snowshoe rentals. Ski lifts are nearby.

This is an excellent place for those with wheelchairs to get a taste of the park. Most other locations (with a few notable exceptions) require a significant amount of hiking to scenic viewpoints.

HURRICANE RIDGE DAY-HIKES

Hurricane Hill Trail   Starts at the Hurricane Ridge parking area. The trail leads 1.5 miles to the top of the hill, providing views of the nearby mountain peaks, plus a look at Port Angeles and the Strait of Juan de Fuca to the north. This area of alpine meadows offers wildflower displays in early summer. The first half-mile is paved and suitable for wheelchairs.

Meadow Loop Trails   Multiple trails start near the Hurricane Ridge Visitor Center and offer walks through prime wildflower areas in a subalpine environment. Black-tailed deer are frequently seen, as are the unique Olympic marmots that sun themselves near the trail.

Heart of the Forest Trail   This begins at Loop E of the Heart o' the Hills Campground, offering a four-mile round-trip hike through a dense lowland forest.

ELWHA VALLEY

Because the Olympic Mountains are dome-shaped, rivers fan out in every direction from the central peaks. The Elwha River flows in an approximate south-to-north direction, with its mouth on the Strait of Juan de Fuca at Angeles Point. Its source is in the Elwha Snowfinger, between Mount Queets and Mount Barnes, flowing through the Elwha Basin and then turning north toward the strait. Along the way, it drops into narrow canyons, cascading through rapids and then forming deep, quiet pools. What used to be a fine salmon stream is now fished only for trout. Two dams were built before the national park was established, cutting off the salmon from their spawning waters. The Park Service is now preparing to have the dams removed, and after much future public consultation and planning, the salmon will return. The lake now held back by the Elwha Dam is called Lake Aldwell. The reservoir impounded by the Glines Canyon Dam is called Lake Mills.

The only access route into the valley is Elwha River Road. The road has its junction with Highway 101 at the Elwha River, 8.5 miles west of Port Angeles. The road provides access to the Elwha Campground, which sits at the base of the Elwha River Range. There's a park amphitheater near the campground, with regular summer interpretation sessions. The Elwha Ranger Station is located another mile along the road. Whiskey Bend Road branches to the left, just beyond the ranger station. The river road continues and crosses the Elwha, providing access to Altaire Campground. While the Elwha Campground has sites suitable for trailers and RVs (up to 21 feet), the Altaire Campground has sites that are better for tenting, although trailers are permitted.

The river road, now called Boulder Creek Road, then climbs to pass by the Glines Canyon Dam and continues above Lake Mills. There's a good view of the valley from Observation Point. The road follows Boulder Creek until it ends at a parking area near Olympic Hot Springs. There is a paved path to the Boulder Creek (walk-in) Campground.

Olympic Hot Springs was quite a popular resort in its day. The commercialization of the springs, discovered by Andrew Jacobson in 1892, began in the early 1900s when a trail was blazed. A Forest Service road was constructed in the 1930s. A resort attracted hot spring fans from far and wide. Now, only the seven pools remain.

ELWHA VALLEY DAY-HIKES

Cascade Rock Trail   Leads east from Elwha Campground to a high point with views of the small Elwha River Range. The trip involves a four-mile, round-trip walk.

Griff Creek Trail   Beginning behind the Elwha Ranger Station, this trails offers a round-trip hike of 5.6 miles. The trip out involves a steep climb with more than 30 switchbacks from the ranger station at 390 feet to the end at 3,300 feet. There is no water available along the route. Rising from river level, the trail passes through old-growth conifer forest, with some madrone (arbutus) trees and a thick understory of mosses, sword ferns, and Oregon grape. A short side trail leads left to a lookout hill, with views of the Elwha, the Highs Creek Valley, and Lake Mills. The trail levels (more or less) beside large moss-covered rock formations and again enters the forest. Crossing a ridge, the trail ends with a view of Griff Creek Valley, Unicorn Peak (to the left at 5,100 feet), and Griff Peak (el. 5,120 feet).

Krause Bottom Trail   Take this trail from its head at the end of Whiskey Bend Road, which leads south from the Elwha Campground. The trail follows a ridge above the Elwha River. The full trail involves a round trip of four miles. A spur trail (at 1.5 miles) leads to Krause Bottom and down to the river. The main trail continues for another half-mile to Humes Ranch, an old cabin built by homesteaders.

Madison Falls Trail   This short trail (0.2 mile round trip) is wheelchair-accessible. It follows Madison Creek after passing through a meadow and forested area, running through a narrow cleft to the falls, which cascade from a 100-foot-high cliff.

Olympic Hot Springs Trail   This is a short path leading from the west side of the parking area, at the end of Boulder Creek Road, to the seven hot pools. The round trip is one mile long. While the resort—built in the early years of the century—is gone, the pools remain, offering relaxation in a setting that is returning to a natural state.

Lake Crescent

Lying at the northern edge of the Olympics, this beautiful natural lake has an elevation of 579 feet and is almost nine miles long. The lake flows into the Lyre River, which empties into the Strait of Juan de Fuca, about five miles beyond its western end.

South of Lake Crescent, Aurora Ridge serves as the divide between the Lyre and Soleduck Valleys. Beyond the eastern end of the lake, Mount Storm King dominates the skyline, rising to an elevation of 4,580 feet.

While almost all of the Olympic parklands have been left in their wild state (without the kind of visitor facilities found in many popular national parks), Lake Crescent has facilities that, fortunately, blend into the lovely landscape. Lake Crescent Lodge is a historic building nestled amongst the hemlocks and firs, beside the lake. The operation offers rooms in the main lodge or in cottages with fireplaces. Nearby are two additional complexes: Marymere Motor Lodge and Storm King Motor Lodge, providing standard motel-style units, with the same woodsy, lakeside ambience. The lodge is a wonderful building, constructed before the national park was created. The fireplace cottages were built in 1937, at a time when President Franklin D. Roosevelt was touring the area, considering the idea of a national park. There's a huge stone fireplace in the lodge lobby. The dining room has a fine view of the lake. The food is mainly Northwestern cuisine, accompanied by an extensive wine list. The season extends from late April through October. The lodge provides box lunches for those wishing to take day-hikes or to pursue other activities in the area. Rowboats may be rented. The lake attracts anglers who go after the famous Beardslee trout. For information and reservations, call (360) 928-3211.

The lodge is just off Highway 101, west of the park ranger station. Piedmont Road leads along the north shore of the lake, from the junction with the Olympic Highway (101) 15.9 miles west of Port Angeles. It climbs through the forest and then drops to lake level and into the national park. It provides access to another (smaller) tourist operation, Log Cabin Resort. The origins of this rustic resort go back to 1895. The cabins were built in 1928 and have lake or mountain views. Each cabin has a private bathroom with a tub or shower. The camping log cabins are minimal facilities with two double beds. You can bring your own bedding or rent bedding from the management. There is no indoor plumbing in these cabins, which accommodate up to four people. There's a picnic table and campfire barrel outside each building.

The resort offers rooms in the lodge and the separate chalet. The chalet rooms include private bathrooms with showers, plus a kitchenette. Bring your own cookware. The lodge has rooms with queen beds and private bathrooms with showers. Trailer sites are also available, with restrooms, showers, and laundry. For information and reservations, call (206) 928-3245.

Boundary Creek Road branches to the left, crossing the Lyre River, entering the national forest, and ending at the parking area for the Spruce Railroad Trail. Piedmont Road continues to the right, crossing State Route 112 and ending at the shore of the Strait of Juan de Fuca at the village of Salt Creek (camping).

The paddle wheeler *Storm King* provides four 90-minute lake cruises each day from the last weekend in May to the end of October. Cruise tours depart (by bus) from the Storm King General Store on Highway 101. Departures are at 10 A.M., noon, 2 P.M., and 4 P.M., and is it necessary to be at the general store 30 minutes before departure time. For information, call (360) 452-4520.

DAY-HIKES NEAR LAKE CRESCENT

Marymere Falls Trail   A spectacular 90-foot waterfall one mile from Lake Crescent. A trail leads through the lush old-growth forest, with wheelchairs able to get to the three-quarter-mile point where there is the Barnes Creek Overlook. The trailhead is near the Storm King Ranger Station.

Mount Storm King Trail   This popular trail climbs about two-thirds of the way up the slope of Mount Storm King. To access the trail, park at the Storm King Ranger Station and take the Marymere Falls Trail. One-third mile from the trailhead, the mountain trail branches off, climbing through a Douglas fir forest. The trail then has a series of switchbacks with a succession of viewpoints, offering fine views of Lake Crescent, the Barnes Creek Valley, and Aurora Ridge. As the trail climbs the mountain, it runs along a steep hogback, with more overlooks. You will reach a sign warning that hikers should not proceed further.

Only experienced hikers should venture on the trail beyond this point. It becomes extremely steep, reaching an overlook with an even more stupendous view of the surrounding territory. Climbing to the peak, beyond the overlook, is an activity designed for only serious, talented climbers, and climbing gear is required as well as backcountry registration. The volcanic scree (crumbled rock) makes it a difficult task.

Spruce Railroad Trail   This is an easy trail, following the roadbed of the old Spruce Railroad along the north shore of Lake Crescent. The railroad was built during World War I, when spruce lumber was required for building airplanes. This trail can be hiked in both summer and winter. It is below the usual snow level, at an elevation of about 600 feet. The trailhead is located at the end of Boundary Creek Road (see above). The trail ascends from near the end of the lake, turning onto a former logging road before descending to the Spruce Railroad bed. It then hugs the shore, offering fine views of Mount Storm King and other peaks. Avoiding a collapsed tunnel, the trail crosses some cliffs, climbing around Devil's Point (more great views), crossing a cove on a bridge. The trail returns shortly to the railroad route, passing basalt cliffs and avoiding a second tunnel. Lake Crescent Lodge is seen on the other side of the lake, only a half-mile away. In its final moments, the trail leaves the railroad grade to descend to its end at North Shore Road. This is a four-mile, one-way hike.

Fairholm Campground Trail   Leads from the campground entrance, located at the western end of the lake off Highway 101. This nature trail takes a loop route and returns to a point 200 yards from the trailhead. The trail runs near the highway, but the thick Douglas fir forest muffles the traffic sounds. The length of the loop is 0.7 mile.

SOL DUC HOT SPRINGS

The Sol Duc River is one of the longest rivers on the peninsula, with its source high in the northwestern corner of the mountains. It runs below the mountains, from the north, winding through several valleys and joining the Bogachiel River to form the Quillayute before emptying into the Pacific near Forks. It has a tortured course, through several chasms with stretches of very white water and through lowland forests of Douglas fir and western hemlock. The river is also called Soleduck, and you'll see signs spelled either way.

Highway 101 and Soleduck River Road provide access to Sol Duc Hot Springs. The springs were long used by Native Americans who regarded these springs and the Olympic Hot Springs as the tears of two dragons who fought a battle on the nearby peaks. The duel is said to have ended with no victor and the dragons both wept in shame. These are the only two thermal springs in the national park. Michael Earles, a timber baron, bought the springs in 1910 and built a resort hotel. The hotel was destroyed by fire in 1916 and was not rebuilt. There is a small tourist operation at the hot springs, with food service.

Salmon

Soleduck River Road runs along the park boundary, around Aurora Ridge, then follows the river through an old-growth Douglas fir forest. Seven miles from Highway 101, the road provides views of the Salmon Cascades, the scene of a salmon run in spawning seasons. The road then leads to a campground, popular during the summer and fall months. The hot pools and campground are closed from October until spring returns. The Soleduck Trail is found at the end of the road, one mile beyond the campground.

Sol Duc Day-Hikes

Sol Duc Falls   The trail to the falls leads not quite a mile from the end of Soleduck River Road, a walk through a dense forest.

Mink Lake Trail   Begins at the Sol Duc Hot Springs resort and climbs 1,400 feet in about 2.5 miles, through the forest to the lake, which is stocked with eastern brook and lake trout. This is a lake in the final stages of life. A portion of it is choked with grasses and other vegetation. Birds, including loons, are plentiful in this marshy environment. The trail continues above Mink Lake, to the 4.3-mile mark where it intersects with the Bogachiel (backcountry) Trail, at Little Divide. There is a small meadow at this point, offering good views of nearby peaks and several varieties of summer wildflowers.

Ancient Groves Nature Trail Offers a half-mile loop through old-growth forest, connecting two roadside turnouts. For safety's sake, we suggest returning on the trail to your starting point rather than risk being in the path of traffic.

HOH RAIN FOREST

What was once a long glacier that flowed all the way from the Olympic peaks to the Pacific Ocean is now a long river valley, where the Hoh River tumbles to meet the ocean at the Hoh Reservation. It begins by receiving the outflow of the Hoh Glacier, gathering water from creeks and smaller rivers, with the milky water of five additional glaciers (White, Blue, Black, Ice River, and Hubert). The South Fork is the river's largest tributary.

The river and its tributaries run through what is considered the finest temperate rain forest in the world. The Hoh River Road provides access to the Hoh Valley and to all but one of the major attractions of the rain forest. The road parallels the river from Highway 101 to the Hoh Ranger Station and park information center. The road passes through ranchlands and second-growth forest at first, with little enclaves of rain forest in which you'll find the Willoughby Creek Campground and Minnie Peterson Campground and Picnic Area. Minnie Peterson ran pack trains into the mountains for many years. At the five-mile mark, the Peak 6 Adventure Store is a source of camping supplies, including raingear for the rain forest. Its main business is organizing hiking, climbing, and biking tours. Owned by the pioneer Peterson family, the shop is on the historic Peterson Ranch. The Westward Hoh Resort (5.5 miles) has a grocery store, gasoline, and a guided river trip service.

The road enters the national park, and here the rain forest really appears, with huge, tall spruces and firs and lacy vine maple underneath. You'll pass a giant Sitka spruce, named in honor of Preston Macy, the first superintendent of Olympic National Park. The tree is 270 feet tall and about 700 years old.

The road ends at the Hoh Ranger Station and information center, the point of entry for several short and long trails in the rain forest. The information center has a supply of maps and books in addition to interpretive sheets and other standard park literature.

The South Fork of the Hoh River is accessed by other roads: Honor Camp Road and Road 1000. The trailhead area, called the Bert Cole Forest, is outside the national park boundaries, on state land. Honor Camp Road joins Highway 101, seven miles south of the Hoh River Road intersection. Road 1000 leads from Honor Camp Road to the trailhead for the South Fork Trail. This is a narrow valley with steep walls, without access to the higher mountain slopes. However, it is a paradise for anglers who find lots of salmon and steelhead during the seasonal runs and a lush rain forest inside the national park boundary, with huge spruces, western hemlock, and a smaller number of Douglas fir. This is an excellent place to observe animal life.

The main Hoh Valley is much wider and leads to high elevations in the Bailey Range and beyond. The Hoh Trail is one of the park's three or four major backcountry trails and the main route to Mount Olympus.

The area close to the ranger station is a wonderland of dripping vegetation, with a variety of bird and animal life.

DAY-HIKES IN THE HOH RAIN FOREST

Hall of Mosses Nature Trail   This is one of two short trails near the ranger station and information center, a loop route crossing Taft Creek and climbing slightly to benchland with Douglas firs at first and then through a spruce-hemlock forest before reaching the Hall of Mosses. Here, the bigleaf maples are covered with moss in a cathedral-like setting. In addition to moss, the trees play host to ferns and selaginella. In the days before the park brought people to see this amazing sight, the tree trunks were covered with mosses to a thickness of six inches or more. Human visitors, not elk, have rubbed most of the moss off the lower parts of the trunks—the cost of allowing us into this once-pristine setting. The trail continues through the spruce forest, thick with vine maple, returning to the trailhead. The total loop is only three-quarters of a mile.

Spruce Nature Trail   This trail offers a 1.25-mile round-trip walk between the Hoh Trail and the river. Elk and deer are often seen close to the river, and the vegetation is a prime example of the thickest type of rain forest. There is also a paved mini-trail, suitable for wheelchairs.

Hoh Trail While hikers use this trail to access the Olympic high country, a short walk along the first section of the trail offers a wonderful trip through the rain forest. The trail begins at the ranger station, crossing Taft Creek, and runs through the forest on a level route through prime rain forest; the understory is covered with mosses, ferns, liverworts, and lichens, plus masses of vine maple, salmonberries, and red elder. Everything you could wish for in a forest is found here. The growth of new trees from the fallen logs of this forest is particularly profuse. In the first 1.5 miles, you'll pass through stands of alder and bigleaf maple and into a forest area where Douglas fir predominates. The path continues on the level bench to a viewpoint where Mount Tom can be seen (at 1.5 miles). If you wish to walk farther, the trail then descends to the Hoh River and climbs again to cross two rushing creeks until meeting the turnoff to the Mount Tom Trail. This point is at the 2.8-mile mark. Hiking this far and then returning to the ranger station provides a fine day-hike with little exertion.

QUEETS RAIN FOREST

The Queets River Valley widens from its narrow source as three major tributaries feed glacier melt and abundant rainwater into the main river. The river receives water from three glaciers: the Queets, and the Humes and Jeffers glaciers on Mount Olympus. The river is one of the largest on the Olympic Peninsula. This is a famed fishing river, revered for its salmon and steelhead and also for rainbow and cutthroat trout. This is a valley not widely visited by tourists, except for the lower fishing areas. There has been a deliberate attempt on the part of the Park Service to keep the upper parts of the valley as wild as possible. Therefore, the Queets Trail offers one of the best opportunities to experience a truly natural rain forest. Because of the lack of facilities, it has become a trail used mostly by backcountry hikers.

All of the existing trails and facilities are accessed by the Queets River Road, which joins Highway 101 seven miles east of the town of Queets. There was settlement in the valley as early as the 1890s. However, when the national park was created, the federal government forced the departure of the stump ranchers and other settlers from the valley.

The Queets Ranger Station is located 12.4 miles along the road. This station is open during the summer months. The Queets Campground is located beside the river at 13.4 miles, in a forest of Sitka spruce. The sites are suitable for tents, RVs, and trailers (with a limit of 21 feet). The road ends at the confluence of the Sams and Queets Rivers.

A Queets Valley Day-Hike

The Queets Campground Loop Trail is the only short trail in the Queets River area. The trailhead is located just west of the campground entrance, on the north side of the road. The trail wanders through forest and through old farm fields. After crossing the second meadow, you'll see the Queets Ranger Station. The trail then crosses the road and wanders through second-growth forest. Remaining stumps are seen, and you will probably hear the roar of logging trucks in the distance. Passing through a stand of alders covered with white lichen, the trail passes into a forest of spruce and into rain forest with thick vegetation, particularly salmonberry. The large formation atop the ridge is Klootchman Rock. The trail comes out at the end of Queets River Road—a hike of three miles.

Quinault Rain Forest

Draining most of the southwestern Olympics, the Quinault River also has two branches. The East Fork comes down from near Anderson Pass, tumbling down a long, narrow valley. Near the head of the East Fork valley stands the world's tallest western hemlock tree.

The East Fork joins the North Fork, and the combined river flows through the broad Quinault Valley into Lake Quinault. This is a lovely natural lake created by glacial action that formed the dam. The lake sits at 200 feet above sea level. Below the lake, the river flows through the Quinault Reservation and empties into the Pacific. The north shore of the lake is in the national park, while the south shore borders the national forest. The west shore lies in the Quinault Reservation.

The forest here is another fine rain forest. The lower area near the lake receives 140 inches of rain each year, while the upper parts get much more. The trees here are enormous, growing to world-record heights.

There are roads along both the north and south shores of Quinault Lake. North Shore Road departs from Highway 101, leading along the lake to the Park Service Quinault Ranger Station. The main access route to the rain forest attractions is South Shore Road. The road forms a Y at the west end. It is found just south of the Quinault River, 16 miles north of Humptulips and 27 miles southeast of Queets.

The Quinault Loop Trail and Willaby Creek Campground are located at the 1.8-mile mark on South Shore Road. The route continues along the lake, providing access to two private resorts and a ranger station in the community of Quinault. Falls Creek Campground is located just beyond the village. The road leads northeast through a harvested area to Cottonwood Campground (primitive), entering Olympic National Park at 12.1 miles. The rain forest appears as North Shore Road meets South Shore Road.

The road continues, climbing through the mossy rain forest, which includes stands of bigleaf maple as well as spruce and Douglas fir. Graves Creek Ranger Station is located at 18.8 miles. This summer-only station is the place to obtain back-country hiking and camping permits. Graves Creek Campground is located near the ranger station in the fir and maple forest. The road comes to an end just beyond the 19-mile mark, at the head of the Enchanted Valley Trail.

Most first-time visitors to the national park tend to visit the Hoh Rain Forest without exploring the beauties of this rain forest to the south. That's too bad, because this too is a magnificent example of the work of nature. Besides the lake, several Quinault trails lead through magnificent stands of huge trees, including bigleaf maples with a rich understory of mosses and selaginella. Campers will appreciate the quiet serenity of Graves Creek Campground, which is away from traffic noises and is located in a sublime setting.

South Shore Road provides access to two major resort operations: Lake Quinault Lodge and Rain Forest Resort Village. The historic lodge is one of those seemingly rustic park-style buildings constructed during the first half of the century, combining a natural ambience with comfortable accommodations in the national forest. There's a fine lobby with a stone fireplace, an excellent dining room focused on Northwestern cuisine, a swimming pool, and canoes to rent with nature trails nearby. For information and reservations, call (360) 288-2571 or 800-562-6672. Rain Forest Resort Village has an inn and cabins with fireplaces and kitchens. The village complex includes an RV park with full hookups. For information and reservations, call (360) 288-2535 or 800-255-6936.

Quinault Day-Hikes

Quinault Loop Trail Located in the national forest south of Lake Quinault, lying just above the lake. The trail is a continuous loop with several access points. A handy entry point is on South Shore Road near Falls Creek Campground. From here, the trail runs beside Falls Creek, past a bridge that leads to the campground and a picnic area, and then to several walk-in campsites (to the west). The trail then moves to the lakeshore, past Lake Quinault Lodge (another logical entry point). The vegetation in this area is thick and wild and includes salmonberry and thimbleberry, skunk cabbage, and hydrangea. Highlie Peak is in clear view across the lake. The trail turns away from the lake at Willaby Creek Campground, passing under the highway bridge crossing Willaby Gorge. Now you enter the rain forest, with an understory of sword and maidenhair ferns, huckleberry, devil's club, and salmonberry. You'll see cedars, along with the spruces and firs. Climbing to the junction with the Big Tree Grove Trail (also Quinault Rain Forest Trail), the route then drops through a second-growth (post-fire) stand of western hemlock, and back into the old-growth forest, getting more boggy as the trail proceeds along a boardwalk. The trail meets the Lodge Trail, crossing Falls Creek, and then crosses another creek with tumbling water, returning to the south shore parking lot. The total loop is four miles, and it is probably the best way to spend an hour or so while visiting the Quinault area, particularly if your time here is limited.

Big Tree Grove Nature Trail Also called the Quinault Rain Forest Trail. It begins on South Shore Road, just west of Willaby Creek. The route climbs through the Big Tree Grove, a fine stand of Douglas fir, about 500 years old. Ferns and oxtails cover the ground. Other trees in this forest include hemlock, western red cedar, and spruce. This is a short trail, less than 0.6 mile long, meant to be enjoyed slowly. There are benches placed along the pathway so that visitors may thoroughly enjoy the inspirational feelings of contemplating one's existence while sitting in a primeval rain forest. The trail ends at its junction with the Quinault Loop Trail. From there, you have the choice of retracing the walk or continuing along the loop trail to a point just east of the starting point, past Willaby Gorge.

Lodge Trail   A very short path starting across the road from Quinault Lodge, climbing through a young hemlock forest and then into an older growth of western red cedar and Sitka spruce with a few Douglas firs. The usual ferns and huckleberry are here, in addition to oxalis. Running above Falls Creek, the trail ends at the Quinault Loop Trail. Again, you have your choice of return routes to the lodge area.

Graves Campground Nature Trail   A circular route leading from and to Graves Creek Campground. Only a mile long, the path begins at the river. We suggest that you take a counter-clockwise direction, passing through bigleaf maples before crossing a gravel bar in what used to be a river channel. The forest is composed mostly of second-growth spruce and fir. The path then crosses river flats with rain forest, thick with bigleaf maples, before returning to the starting point through a stand of Douglas fir.

OLYMPIC SEASHORE

The Pacific Ocean is untamed as it crashes against the Olympic shore. Access to the coast is limited, except by taking long hikes. However, there are several access points where one may hike to and along the coast. One of the most scenic and rewarding areas is found in the Lake Ozette region, at the end of Lake Ozette Road. To get there, turn onto Highway 113, which meets Highway 101 (Olympic Highway) at the village of Sappho. After two miles, turn west (left) and drive along Highway 112, which leads to Clallam Bay and Seku. Turn left onto the Lake Ozette road. The Cape Alava Trail (the northern route) leads 3.3 miles to the coast. The southern route (Sand Point Trail) runs three miles to the beach. Both trails lead mostly along wooden boardwalks, through a wonderful wildlife area. For a 9.3-mile loop hike, walk along the beach between the two entry points. This is an area long occupied by Native Americans, with evidence of their habitation in Native American petroglyphs. You'll see Ozette Island and Cape Alava, the westernmost point in the contiguous 48 states.

To the south, State Route 110 leads to the ocean shore and the Native American community of La Push. A trail leads south from the end of the road, along the beaches and headlands, to Third Beach, Taylor's Point, and Scott's Bluff. It is possible to walk south, along the beaches, and along pieces of coastal trails across the more dangerous headlands. A handy and necessary guide to the coastal trails is the Parks Service packet "Strip of Wilderness," available at the ranger stations and visitor information centers. Hikes available include the 1.8-mile stretch from Cape Alava to Shi Shi Beach; the North Wilderness Coast Hike (from Ozette to Rialto Beach, via Cape Alava), a walk of 21 miles; and the South Coast Wilderness Hike, from the Third Beach trailhead to Oil City, a rugged journey of 17.3 miles. Backcountry permits are free and must be obtained from a ranger station before undertaking overnight backcountry trips.

Kalaloch Lodge is found near the southern end of the coastal strip, beside Highway 101. South Beach is at the extreme southwestern edge of the park. Short beach trails lead from Highway 101 to Ruby Beach (to the north), with six additional trails leading south to Beaches One and Two and South Beach. You'll find beaches with tide pools; beachcombing is particularly rewarding in this area. Clamming is permitted, in season and with a license. There's a park ranger station across the highway from the lodge. The lodge has overnight accommodations, a dining room, and coffee shop. For information and reservations, call (360) 962-2271.

DOSEWALLIPS

Located in the eastern Olympics, opposite the Hood Canal, the Dosewallips River has three tributaries, the North and South Forks and Silt Creek, which has its headwaters in the Eel Glacier on Mount Anderson. Several high mountains enclose the valley, including Anderson and the "Five Peaks": Wellesley, Sentinel, Lost, Fromme, and Claywood. This is a land of steep peaks and large meadows, including the spectacular Thousand Acre Meadow.

Highway 101 runs along the eastern slopes of the Olympics, providing access by Dosewallips River Road (Forest Road 2610).

The road cuts through the Olympic National Forest, through recently logged areas and second-growth forest. Approaching the nine-mile mark, the road enters virgin forest. Elkhorn Campground is situated in a large stand of Douglas firs beside the river. As the road climbs high above the river, it enters Olympic National Park, passing Dosewallips Falls. The road drops before reaching Dosewallips Campground (14.7 miles). Here are campsites and a picnic area located in a red cedar grove. The Dosewallips Ranger Station is located at the end of the road (14.9 miles).

Several lengthy trails have been constructed in the Dosewallips wilderness areas, including the Dosewallips Trail, which provides access to the Thousand Acre Meadow and beyond to a wildflower basin north of Sentinel Peak and up to Hayden Pass (15.4 miles). Hayden Pass offers one of the best views of the Olympic peaks.

A DOSEWALLIPS DAY-HIKE

Made by hikers over the years and ascending 3,250 feet over the two-mile length of the route, the Lake Constance Trail is a rather rough trail. So, while this is not a long trail, some time is required to climb to the lake. At the one-mile park, the trail does level out slightly. Half Acre Rock is a gigantic piece of basalt that tumbled down a cliff (or it may be a glacial erratic). Another formation, the Guillotine, is located here. The upper half of the trail is difficult, with fallen trees and brush on the route. Near the end, there is some rock scrambling to be done. The trail ends at Lake Constance, located in a bowl below Mount Constance. With an area of 11 acres, the lake is surrounded by subalpine forest. The lake is stocked with eastern brook trout.

Large numbers of mountain goats are found in the lake area. The goats are not natural denizens of the Olympics, but were imported before the park was established. They have thrived and grown to such an extent that a goat reduction program has been in force for many years. This has been a source of friction between the Park Service and goat lovers. You hear and see several species of birds, as well as the ever-present marmots. It is possible for experienced climbers to make the ascent of Mount

Constance from the lake. Due to overuse, the lake has become polluted, and camping is permitted by reservation only.

NORTH FORK SKOKOMISH AND STAIRCASE

The Skokomish River flows into the Hood Canal after tumbling down the southeastern Olympics, with two forks feeding the main river, which is seven miles long. The South Fork area is within national forest lands, accessed via South Fork Road. Lake Cushman is a glacier-made lake (made much larger with a power dam) on the North Fork, in the area usually explored by park visitors. The upper valley of the North Fork is inside national park boundaries. Above the lake, the river cascades down the mountainside, with large boulders making white water and quiet pools between the raging sections. The fork has many tributaries, most of them numbered during Lieutenant O'Neill's 1890 expedition. Thus, you'll see creeks identified as Four Stream, Six Stream, and Nine Stream. These were locations of O'Neill's stopping and camping places.

O'Neill named the section known as the Staircase. It comes from "the Devil's Staircase," coined for the route taken by O'Neill and company over Fisher's Bluff. The name refers to the steep root-covered path that expedition members had to take while descending the bluff. It later became simply known as the Staircase.

The main access road to this area is Jorstead Creek Road (Forest Road 24), which joins Highway 101 2.3 miles south of the town of Eldon. Along the initial part of the route are several visitor facilities, including Lilliwaup Camp and Picnic Area (6.9 miles), maintained by the state, and Big Creek Campground (nine miles). The road passes Cushman Falls. The trailhead for the Mount Rose Trail is at mile 11.5, and the road winds along the shore of Lake Cushman, meeting the Lightning Peak Road (mile 14). There is a picnic area beyond the intersection. Entering old-growth forest, the route also enters the national park, ending at the Staircase Ranger Station (15.2 miles).

NORTH FORK DAY-HIKES

Big Creek Nature Trail This national forest trail begins on Road 24, beyond the intersection with Hoodsport Road. The trail runs 1.3 miles on a loop route around the campground. Aside from one steep hill, the trail leads along a level grade with varied woods, including second-growth stands and an older forest with Douglas fir and western red cedar.

Shady Lane Nature Trail   You will find the start of this trail across a bridge from the Staircase Ranger Station. This is a three-mile round trip inside the national park, leading south to cross Elk Creek and moving toward Fisher's Bluff. Walkers encounter a tunnel, bored 20 feet into the mountain by prospectors. Then, the trail runs around the base of Fisher's Bluff, moving into stands of giant fir, cedar and hemlock, with an understory of vine maple. There is considerable scarring of the landscape by road builders who constructed a logging road in the 1950s. Many people leave the trail to walk down to the river, walking south to pass through the stand of large trees, and then returning to the trail. The route leaves the park area and enters second-growth forest, reaching a road with some vacation homes, leading to Road 2451. The nature trail continues on the opposite side of Road 2451 (at one mile) for another half-mile, here called the Dry Creek Trail. To return to the Staircase, retrace the route.

Staircase Rapids Trail   One of the most popular shorter trails in the eastern Olympics, providing a 3.5-mile (one-way) walk following the North Fork Skokomish and also offering the option of a two-mile loop walk. The trailhead is across the bridge from the Staircase Ranger Station. This is the same route taken by the O'Neill expedition in 1890, climbing beside the river to Four Stream. There's a huge western red cedar just off the trail before it reaches the banks of the Skokomish. A short spur trail leads to the Red Reef Pool. The main path ascends (with another spur to Dolly Varden Pool) through a forest beside Staircase Rapids (0.8 mile). The path then climbs Dead Horse Hill, a glacial moraine, where a path leads to the Rapids Bridge and a junction with the North Skokomish (backcountry) Trail. If you take the North Skokomish Trail back to the ranger station, you'll have a loop walk of two miles.

Staircase Rapids Trail descends to Beaver Flat, through a burn area, passing Copper View Camp before arriving at Four Stream. The trail crosses the creek where it forks. Taking the left fork is not advised. It comes to an end in the national forest. The right fork leads to a riverside camping area. For those who wish to get a taste of overnight backpacking, but don't have the experience or inclination for a major mountain hike, this trail and the woodsy campsites at the end offer an easy overnight experience.

Nearby Attractions

WILLAPA NATIONAL WILDLIFE REFUGE

Willapa Bay is a large estuary located south of the Olympic Peninsula, between the southwestern Washington mainland and the Long Beach Peninsula. The Naselle River flows into the bay near its southern end, and the northern part of the estuary is fed by the Willapa River. The land area of the wildlife refuge is made up of four separate parts: Long Island, in the southern part of the estuary; Leadbetter Point, at the north end of the Long Beach Peninsula; the Lewis unit, a series of freshwater marshes at the southern end of Willapa Bay; and the Riekkola Unit, where grasslands have been established behind saltwater dikes, also at the south end of the bay.

Long Island can be reached only by private boat, and there are several launching sites around the bay, including the refuge headquarters and information center, located on the eastern shore of the bay, on Highway 101. Another boat launch may be found at the Nahcotta Mooring Basin, on the Long Beach Peninsula. The 5,000-acre island is covered with a dense coastal forest, providing a home for black-tailed deer, black bears, Roosevelt elk, river otters, and many birds including bald eagles, pileated woodpeckers, grouse (blue and ruffed), plus many species of migrating birds that make stops here when traveling along the Pacific flyway. Tidal marshes on the east side of the island make shelter for herons, ducks, and shorebirds. The west side of the island is lined with eelgrass, which provides abundant spawning grounds for salmon, sea perch, and sole, as well as Pacific herring. As a result, the eelgrass areas attract black brant, Canada geese and many ducks. The bay is one of the most prolific shellfish areas on the coast, supporting oysters, clams and mussels.

Winter is the prime time for birding, with large flocks of migrating birds in attendance, including geese, brant, canvasbacks, mergansers, and cormorants, joined by loons, grebes, dunlins, plovers, and several species of sandpipers. You'll also see American wigeons, surf scoters, scaups, and buffleheads.

The 274-acre Cedar Grove is one of the last remaining examples of coastal old-growth forest. Growing at a fast rate and protected from fire by the damp environment, the western red cedar trees have large buttresses and sparse crowns that make the grove wind-resistant. By some kind of miracle, the grove has remained safe from clear-cutting, while practically all of the old-growth coastal forest in Washington and Oregon has been logged at least once during the last 150 years.

There are five primitive marine campsites on the island; three are on the west side, another is on Lewis Slough near the northeastern corner, and another is halfway along Sawlog Slough in the east-central part of the island. The trail to the ancient cedars is near the Smoky Hollow campsite, midway along the western shore, across the slough from the Sawlog campsite. Boats must be pulled ashore, above the high tide zone. There are no mooring facilities available for visitors.

A system of trails leads along the western side of the island, connecting with the loop trail leading to the Cedar Grove. The trails touch the shoreline at the southwestern end: near the Pinnacle Rock campsite; at the Smoky Hollow and Sandspit campsites, in the west-central area; at Paradise Point, in the east-central area; at the Sawlog Slough campsite; and at the extreme southeastern tip, across the narrows from the refuge headquarters on Highway 101. Detailed maps of the refuge are available at the information center. The best place to look for animals, including deer and elk, is High Point Meadow. Birds may be spotted in quantity at Sawlog Slough and the Smoky Hollow Marsh on the island's eastern shore.

While camping on the island is limited, Fort Canby State Park is nearby, near the town of Ilwaco, at the southern end of the Long Beach Peninsula. There is a state campground in the park. Other tenting and RV sites are available in several private peninsula campgrounds.

Clamming and crabbing is permitted, and visitors should consult the State Shellfish Lab at Nahcotta for maps and regulations. All oysters in Willapa Bay are private property. Oyster lovers should head for the oyster farms based in Nahcotta or visit a nearby seafood restaurant where the Willapa Bay oyster provides treasured feasts.

Some areas of the refuge are open to winter hunting during the prime migration period. However, firearms are prohibited on Long Island, and hunting takes place only in the mainland marshes.

DUNGENESS SPIT AND WILDLIFE RESERVE

Dungeness Spit, extending six miles into the Strait of Juan de Fuca, is the world's longest sand spit. The spit is visited by more than 200 species of birds, and the protected waters are home to the famous (and tasty) Dungeness crab (both natural and farmed).

This area is southeast of Port Angeles. The Dungeness Recreation Area and Dungeness Wildlife Refuge are located on a scenic drive that begins at Highway 101 and Sequim Avenue. Drive north and turn west onto Port Williams Road. The town of Port Williams is almost three miles from Highway 101. Here, you will find a boat launch and picnic tables at Marlyn Nelson Park. Take Sequim-Dungeness Way, past the historic Dungeness Schoolhouse (five miles) and across the river. Marine Drive begins at 5.7 miles. This route runs along the bluff, overlooking the strait, with good views of Vancouver Island, the San Juan Islands, and (on a good day) Mount Baker. There is another boat ramp on Oyster House Road.

At 6.5 miles, a county boat ramp is found on Cline Spit Road. Marine Drive ends at Cays Road. Take Cays Road for a mile and turn onto Lotzgesell Road. Then turn onto Voice of America Road to find the entrance to Dungeness Recreation Area. The Dungeness Wildlife Refuge is half a mile. Another half-mile of driving lands you at the parking lot for the trail to Dungeness Spit. The trail leads 5.5 miles to the tip of the spit, with the New Dungeness Lighthouse a half-mile before the end of the hike.

The return route on the loop drive uses Voice of America Road, Lotzgesell Road, and Kitchen-Dick Road to reach Highway 101. Sequim is almost five miles from the highway junction.

Because of the wide variety in coastal and mountain ecosystems, the Olympic Peninsula harbors an amazing range of wildlife. From prairie and oak savanna near Sequim on the Dungeness Spit as well as in the Lower Elwha area, through the rain forest, lowland, subalpine and alpine zones, there is much diversity in animal as well as plant life. At the upper levels, marmots join alpine birds on the treeless landscape. The conifer and mixed forests on the slopes at lower levels shelter songbirds including warblers and provide browsing areas for Roosevelt elk and deer. The rocky shoreline with salt marshes and tide pools provide habitats of a different sort for hundreds of marine species including shellfish, resident and transient shorebirds, and pelagic birds.

This is a naturalist's paradise, ready to be enjoyed in all four seasons. When there is deep snow on the mountain crests, the shore is usually snow-free, although rain falls in abundance during the fall and winter periods. Winter is prime time for observing migratory waterfowl attracted to the marshes and river estuaries. The freshwater lakes and rivers, with cattail marshes and bogs, are also habitat for birds and small mammals.

BIRDS

Common Loon
Gavia immer
Members of the loon family (Gaviidae) are large swimmers with long bodies and dagger-shaped bills. You'll see them floating offshore, just beyond the surf line, and in calmer bays. Loons live on lakes in conifer forests, on open lakes and inlets, and they summer on the far northern tundra. They are seldom on land except when nesting. When in flight, its large webbed feet stick straight out from the body, and its head and feet seem to sag beneath the body. The common loon is found across northern North America, as far south as northern Mexico, and also in Europe. It has a color change when breeding. In winter, it is dark above and whitish below, with a broken neck pattern. In summer, its head is much darker and it has a checkered back and a broken white necklace. The voice of the common loon combines wild yodeling with a seemingly crazy laugh; at night it's a loud *ha-oo-oo*. When flying it utters a sharp *kwuk*. This sound is rarely heard in winter.

Red-throated Loon
Gavia stellata
This loon has the same long, sharp bill, but this bill is upturned, unlike the bill of the common loon. In summer, it has a plain grayish back

that is speckled, a light gray head with a striped nape, and a reddish throat patch signifying the breeding period. In winter, it looks like other loons, with a slightly paler head and neck. It has the same *kwuk* sound while in flight, and in the northern summer it adopts the weird falsetto wailing sound also voiced by the common loon.

Red-Necked Grebe
Podiceps grisegena
This ducklike diver, like other grebes, has a tailless look, a thin neck, and lobed toes. When breeding, the red-necked grebe has its distinctive rufous (reddish) neck, as well as a distinctive white cheek and a yellow streak on its bill. Its winter plumage changes. The red neck becomes grayish, like its back, and the neck patch becomes a smaller white crescent. You can spot it in flight by its double wing patch. Its range is across northern North America and in Eurasia. It winters in southern North American regions and in North Africa. It inhabits lakes and ponds, and salt water during winter months.

Double-crested Cormorant
Phalacrocorax autitus
Trying to spot this cormorant by its crest may not be easy, because its crest is not very evident. It is more easily identified by its yellow throat pouch. Like other cormorants, it is a large black waterbird you will see flying over the Olympic (and most of the Pacific) shoreline, sometimes with other cormorants in a V formation, like geese. It stands on rocks and posts with its neck in an S-shape and often spreads its wings out to dry. It has a thin bill with a hooked tip. While swimming and floating on the water, the cormorant may be mistaken for a loon. The double-crested cormorant is often found inland as well as along the coast. It is found across North America, from coast to coast, wintering as far south as Belize. It lives on the coastlines, as well as on bays, lakes, and rivers. It nests on cliffs or in trees beside a lake.

Pelagic Cormorant
Phalacrocorax pelagicus
This bird is smaller than other cormorants, and it may be identified by its shaggy crests, one at the front of its head and the other at the back above the neck, along with a white patch on each flank (while breeding). It has an iridescent color, a small slender head, and a very slender bill. The narrow throat patch is a reddish color. This sea bird ranges from the Bering Sea to Japan and along the west coast of North America. It lives in bays and the large inland sounds, including the Gulf of Georgia and Puget Sound, as well as along the coast.

Black-footed Albatross
Diomedea nigripes
The albatross (family Diomedeidai) is a bird of the open ocean, ranging across the northern seas. This is one of three albatross species that nest north of the equator. The Laysan albatross (*D. immutabilis*) is also found along the Olympic

Peninsula shores. The black-footed albatross is large, with a wing span of seven feet. It has a dark gray, sootish color, long, slender wings, and it glides for long distances. The adult is identified by its distinctive shape and by the whitish patches on its tail, plus a white band above its beak. Below, it is dark, with white feathers toward the back of the belly. Young black-footed albatross are identified by their pink bill and pinkish feet. This pelagic bird has a very wide range, breeding on islands in the central and western Pacific, particularly the Hawaiian Islands. You may see it in the Olympic area during fall and winter months. Because of its long ocean journey, seeing an albatross is a thrilling encounter.

Sooty Shearwater
Puffinus griseus
This is also a bird of the open sea, gull-like in shape, which glides over the waves. The shearwater is a member of the Procelliaroiodae family, which includes fulmars and petrels. The sooty is often seen in huge flocks off the coast. At a distance it looks dark all over, but when closer has light, whitish lining on the underside of its wings. It is a summer visitor to the Olympic Peninsula, breeding in the Southern Hemisphere off southern Australia and New Zealand and South America. In summer, its range extends to the North Atlantic and the North Pacific, from the Bering Sea to Baja California. There are 61 shearwater species in the world, with eight commonly seen along the American West Coast.

Great Blue Heron
Ardea herodias
It's always a thrill to see this large grayish-blue bird dominating its marshy home, flying low with its great wings beating behind its pulled-in neck. This is a wading bird that feeds on frogs, fish, crawfish, and other water life, and it also catches land animals including mice and insects. When standing it is often four feet tall. The great blue has a black crest behind the eyes, a white head patch, and a yellow bill. Its range is from southern Canada to Mexico, wintering to northern South America. It lives in swamps, marshes, along tide flats and shorelines. It has a distinctive voice, a croaky *frahnk, frahnk, frahnk.*

American Bittern
Botaurus lentiginosus
A member of the family Threskiornithidae, along with ibises and spoonbills (including night herons), the bittern has a stocky, mottled brownish body, with a black stripe on the neck. When flying, the outer wing appears to be darker than the back. It has light greenish legs. When standing, the bill is pointed up. Wintering as far south as Panama, its summer range is from Canada to the Gulf states. Its habitats include marshy areas and lakes with reeds. The voice is a slow, deep *oong-ka' choonk,* repeated several times. When frightened, or flushed from the reeds, its note is a *kok-kok-kok.*

Harlequin Duck
Histrionicus histrionicus

This is one of the most greatly patterned ducks, with an overall dark color. The male has chestnut red sides and white patches and spots including a curving line on its head and a distinctive white patch on its wing. The female has three round white spots on the side of the head. The female has no wing patch. The harlequin has a wide range, from northeastern Asia, Alaska, and Canada to the western United States, Greenland, and Iceland. It lives in mountain streams during summer and on rocky waters along the coast during winter. Male and female have different sounds. The male squeaks and also has a *gwa gwa gwa*. The female's voice is *ek, ek, ek, ek*.

Osprey
Pandion haliaetus

This is the only western raptor that flies and hovers over the water, looking for fish to catch, then dives into the water for its food (although the bald eagle does pick up fish from the surface). The osprey plunges feet first into the water. It is blackish above, and white below. The head is mainly white, but it has a distinct black patch on its cheek. There is only one species of osprey in the world. It has a very wide range, but the osprey seen along the Olympic coast tends to arrive here in late April, spends the summer, then leaves around the end of August. A few stay in the park year-round. Its voice is a series of sharp whistles, *cheap,*

cheap, cheap, or *yewk, yewk.* When startled, it utters a loud, hurried *cheereek.*

Peregrine Falcon
Falco peregrinus

The North American falcons, like their cousin the crested caracara, are raptors that range across the continent. While the world has 52 species in the family Falconidae, only seven are found in the American and Canadian west, among them the merlin and the American kestrel. The rest are falcons. The peregrine is crow-sized, and like other falcons it has a narrow tail, pointed wings, and a fast wingbeat. It has a distinctive face pattern, with a white lower neck separated by a curving black crescent. Its barred and spotted chest is a light color, and its back is slate-gray. This falcon breeds on the islands of the Alaska and British Columbia coasts, a short distance (for a falcon) from the Olympic Peninsula. It lives in open countryside including cliffs, and it sometimes ventures into cities where it establishes itself on tall buildings. Its voice is a rapid *kek kek kek kek,* or (when nesting) a rapidly repeated *wu-chew.*

Ring-necked Pheasant
Phasianus colchicus

This ground bird breeds and lives year-round in Olympic National Park and is found in the woodland prairies. It tends to live in brushy areas, along the edges of marshes, and in farm fields. The bird is not native to the area (or to North

America, for that matter) but was introduced in past years before the park was established. A member of the family Phasianidae, like turkeys, grouse, partridges, and quail, this is the only pheasant found in the western U.S. regions. The male grows to a larger size than the female, to a length of 36 inches. The female is rarely larger than 25 inches. It is chicken-like with some distinguishing features, especially the long, pointed tail. It is a fast runner, and it flies with a noisy takeoff. The male is brightly colored with a reddish brown, mottled back, a white ring around the neck (sometimes), and an iridescent head that is blackish with scarlet wattles. During the courting season, the male makes a colorful display, fanning its tail much like a peacock. The female is plumper and plainer, with a shorter tail, although the tail is long and pointed. The flushing note is *kuk kuk kuk*. When courting, the male displays its tail and utters a sharp popping sound.

Blue Grouse
Dendragapus obscurus
The male grouse has a dark, sooty color. It can be identified by the broad lighter band at the tip of its tail. Above the eyes are orange or yellow combs, which become erect in courtship display. Coastal birds have yellow neck sacs, unlike the blue grouse of the Rockies, which have purple sacs. The females are brownish and mottled with black. Their bellies are pale. Its range is over all of western North America, living in mixed and deciduous

forests in the summer and in conifer forests in winter. This is one of a few animal species that moves to higher elevations for the winter months. During courtship, the male utters a series of five to seven hooting or booming notes.

California Quail
Calipepla californica
Growing only to a length of about 11 inches, this is a small, plump bird, with a black plume curving from the top point of its head. The male has a black face with white markings. The female is an overall duller, grayish-brown color but has the same curving plume. This quail lives in the west, from British Columbia to Baja California. It lives in coastal woodlands, mainly in scrub and on the edges of lower woodlands, in oak chaparral, and in farm fields. The California quail is a pure breed on the Olympic Peninsula. Farther south and inland in deserts, this species interbreeds with Gambel's quail. Its voice is a *kwa-kwer'-go,* or (yes) *chi-ca'-go.*

Virginia Rail
Rallus limicola
A member of the family Rallidae, along with coots and gallinules, the rails are marsh birds that are hen-like but much smaller in size, growing to a length of about nine inches. You will not see rails flying very often. They are reclusive and tend to hide, although they can frequently be heard. The Virginia rail has gray cheeks and black bars on its flanks. It is most easily identified by its cheeks and the long,

slightly down-curved bill. Its range extends from southern Canada to South America. Its habitats include fresh and stagnant marshes and salt marshes during winter months. It has several sounds, including a grunting noise, *wak-wak-wak-wak,* and *kidick, kidick, kidick.*

Western Screech Owl
Otus kennicottii
This owl is a common fixture throughout the Northwest and Southwest. On the northwestern coast, it is brown, unlike the lighter and grayer inland screech owl. This owl is frequently seen and heard in the rain forests and mixed forests of the Olympic Peninsula. It is a member of the Stringidae family, together with the barred, great gray, horned, and snowy owls. It lives from Canada to Central America, living in woodlands, in treed riparian areas, and swamps. It has a fairly light sound, usually eight hoots in two sets of four, *hoohoo-hoohoo,* or closer together, *hoohoohoohoaw.*

Northern Pygmy Owl
Glaucidium gnoma
Growing to a length of only 7.5 inches, this little brownish-red owl has black patches on each side of its hind neck, brown streaks on its belly and flanks, and bars on the tail. It has a spotted head, with a white chin and band around the bottom of the head. Unlike many other owls, it is seen flying during the daylight hours and also calling with its single *hoo,* whistled and re-peated. It also has a repeated song

with two or three notes: *too-too, too-too-too.*

Rufous Hummingbird
Selasphorus rufus
Only two hummingbirds, the small-est of all birds, visit the Olympic Peninsula. Anna's hummingbird, a common West Coast hummer, is a rarity in Olympic National Park. A few have been seen during the summer season. Much more com-mon is the rufous hummingbird, which begins arriving in March. Many more arrive in April and stay until July, when most leave for places farther south. A few stay for another month or two. The rufous is fairly easy to identify (aside from being just about the only humming-bird in the park). It is the only hummingbird species in which the male has a rufous back. The under-parts are a bright reddish-brown. Its throat is a bright orange-red. The female is not as brightly colored, having a green back, with a dull reddish-brown color on its sides and on the base of the tail. When flying it performs a fast, closed elipse, slowing as it climbs. While it breeds in the park, it flies to Mexico to spend the winter. In addition to feeding mainly on nectar, hum-mingbirds feed on small insects and spiders. There are 308 varieties in all.

Downy Woodpecker
Picoides pubescens
Looking much like the white-headed and hairy woodpeckers, the downy is distinguished by its black wings (without bars). It has a white

back and a very small bill. The downy woodpeckers that live in the moist climate of the Olympic Peninsula and Vancouver Island have underparts that are a light brownish-gray color, unlike the same bird in the Rockies, which has white underparts. It is a very hard worker, often heard before it is seen while pecking holes in Olympic trees. Its range extends to Canada and Alaska. Its habitats include forests and woodlands and in riverside groves of trees including willows, as well as in orchards and shade trees. Its note is a sharp pick, while its voice is a fast-paced series of descending notes, like a horse's whinny.

Red-shafted (Northern) Flicker
Colaptes autauts
Belonging to the same family as woodpeckers (Picidae), this is the only flicker found in the Pacific Northwest. In fact, the northern flicker has three subspecies, and only the red-shafted is found here. The other northern flickers are the gilded, found in the southwestern deserts, and the yellow-shafted, the northern and eastern version. The gilded and yellow-shafted both have a yellow wing color, while the flicker found along the Olympic coast is salmon pink with a reddish tail ending with black at the tip. The male has a red mustache—a black bar under each eye. Its range covers the western forests from Alaska through Nicaragua. It lives in open forests and low woodlands as well as in semi-open country in-

cluding farm fields. It is even found in towns.

Violet-Green Swallow
Tachycineta thalassina
A distinctive slim and graceful bird, it has long pointed wings, a short bill, and very small feet, like other swallows (family Hirundinidae). The violet-green has an iridescent blackish head and dark greenish-purple back, with a white band or patches that almost meet on the upper back. Its underparts are white. The white face almost encircles the eyes. It spends the summer, from April to September or October, in the Olympic area. It is found in subalpine regions, as well as in riparian habitats along the rivers and creeks, and in canyons and cliffs. It is also found in northwestern farmlands. Wintering as far south as central America, it breeds from Alaska to the mountains of northern Mexico. Its voice is a twitter and also a chipping sound or a rapid *chit-chit-chit, wheet, wheet.*

Red-winged Blackbird
Agelaius phoeniceus
Related to grackles, meadowlarks, and cowbirds, the male red-winged blackbird is black with bright red patches, or epaulettes, bordered with yellow at the front of its wings. The female is brownish with small black stripes below. Some have a very light pink tinge at the throat. These birds gather and fly in flocks. Living from Canada to the Caribbean Islands, this bird breeds in marshy areas including swamps and lives in meadows, fields, and in

riparian habitats. Its voice is a series of notes: a boisterous check and a loud *tee-eerr.* Its song is a gurgling *konk-la-ree* or *oh-ka-lay.*

MAMMALS

River Otter
Lutra canadensis
This freshwater mammal lives primarily along rivers, ponds, and lakes in forest areas. However, it does roam away from water, moving quite easily on land. Its den is often dug into river and creek banks, with above-water and underwater entrances. The nests are lined with grasses, reeds, leaves, and sticks. This dark brown otter also builds nests in tree root systems or in hollow logs. Babies are born in April or May, and then the mating period begins. Implantation is delayed. Newborns are blind and are weaned at four months, leaving the nest completely by eight months. The male is forced to leave the nest after the babies arrive, but is allowed back several months later to help take care of the young.

A fine swimmer, with a shape like a torpedo, it is active during the day, looking for fish—its main source of food. It also eats mice and ground-based invertebrates. You may be able to see its trail, about eight inches wide, and usually leading to the river or creek or between two bodies of water. Its tracks are about 3.75 inches wide, usually showing the heel pad and five claws. The otters' slides on riverbanks are usually eight inches wide. Slides on snow are about a foot wide.

Hoary Marmot
Marmota caligata
The Olympic marmot is the local variation of the marmot most often seen from Alaska and the Yukon and south to northern Idaho and Washington. The yellow-bellied marmot (*M. flaviventris*) is seen in nearby British Columbia, plus Alberta, eastern California, and throughout the Rocky Mountains.

The hoary marmot is the larger, growing to a length of about 32 inches. It is silver-gray above, with a whitish belly and a brown rump. It has black and light markings on the head and shoulders, and a whitish patch on the forehead around the eyes. The tail is bushy and reddish-brown. It has very small ears. Marmots are found in the alpine zone, usually on talus slopes. You'll often see them on warm summer days warming themselves on rocks. They build burrows, 9 to 15 inches wide, with mounds of dirt surrounding the entrance holes. Hibernating during winter, they emerge in the spring when mating takes place. The young (four or five) are born a month later. They grow extremely fat during the late summer and fall, feeding on grasses and other green plants. It has a sharp whistle, used as an alarm, giving the animal its nickname: "whistling" marmot or "whistler." The B.C. ski resort, Whistler, about 150 miles northeast of the Olympic Peninsula, is named for the hoary marmot's squeal.

Douglas Squirrel
Tamiasciurus douglasii
Another species named after the famed British biologist, the Douglas squirrel is found in all of the coniferous forests of the Olympic ranges, including the western rain forests. This squirrel has upper parts of reddish-gray or brownish-gray, and orange-gray underparts. The tail matches the back color, although the lower part is darker. Underneath, the tail is a rusty red color bordered by a black band. It has ear tufts in winter. It nests in conifers, building large, round homes (you'll see the remains of cones scattered under the nests). It mates in early spring, producing litters of four to six in May or June. An early spring may bring two sets of babies. The young remain together with parents for much of their first year. The range of the Douglas squirrel is from southwestern British Columbia through western Washington, Oregon, and Northern California. They are found in Redwood National Park.

Vagrant Shrew
Sorex vagrans
The Olympic Peninsula and southern Vancouver Island comprise the northern habitat for this small mammal. The full range is from southern B.C. to Northern California, Nevada, and south to Arizona and eastern New Mexico. It grows to a length of 4.75 inches. It is gray to brown above and grayish brown to red below. It has a long tail, which may have the back color or a lighter gradation. Seven out of the 11 shrews found in the western U.S. and Canada are found in Olympic National Park. These include dusky, marsh, Pacific, water, masked, and Trowbridge shrews. They are all hard-working, wandering creatures, living in mixed forests.

Little Brown Bat
Myotis lucifugus
This is the most common bat species in the Pacific Northwest. There are several species of the little brown bat, but only one (*M. l. alascensis*) inhabits the region. Dark brown in color, the span of its wings is about nine or ten inches. The slightly larger big brown bat (*Eptesicus fuscus*) is also a resident of western Washington and Oregon. Both bats feed on insects, leaving their caves at dusk to eat hundreds or thousands of insects each day. The big brown bat may be seen before dark. Most little brown bats migrate to southern homes for the winter months, although some do hibernate here.

Pacific Harbor Seal
Phoca vitulina
This seal grows to a length of from 4 to 5.7 feet and is usually a yellowish-gray or brownish color. It has dark spots above, but its underside can vary from dark brown to whitish or a spotted creamy shade. Harbor seals are gregarious creatures, gathering in small and large groups (as many as 500) and resting on rocky shores and beaches. When people approach, they give a bark of alarm and move swiftly into the water. You

may encounter harbor seals in rivers, moving with the high tides to feed on small fish and crustaceans. In deep water, it eats zooplankton as well as fish. Not quite at the top of its food chain, it is food for killer whales. Its range extends from Baja California, north to the Arctic Ocean, and down the Atlantic Coast to the Carolinas.

Pacific White-sided Dolphin
Lagenorhynchus obliquidens
Seen off the Olympic coast, this cetacean is thought to live up to 30 years. They live much shorter periods when in captivity. This dolphin has been seen in herds as large as several thousand. It grows to a length of 7.5 feet and has a cylindrical shape, with a head that tapers smoothly to a dark beak. It has a black back and white belly, with a white or gray stripe down each side, from the forehead and over the head, becoming a gray patch on the flank. There is a narrow, darker stripe between the mouth and flipper. The dorsal fin is crescent-shaped, dark to the front and light gray behind. It lives offshore, often close to the shore in areas where there are deep canyons next to the continental shelf. Its range is from the Aleutians, throughout the gulf of Alaska, and down the coast to Baja California.

FISH

Starry Flounder
Platichthys stellatus
Found from the Arctic Ocean off Alaska and along the Pacific Coast to central California, this fish grows to a length of three feet. It is not widely fished for commercial purposes and is not a prime sport fish. It is found in estuaries and bays where bottoms are soft and off the open coast to a depth of 150 fathoms, feeding on shellfish including crabs, shrimp, and clams, plus worms and small fish. It tolerates a mixture of salt and fresh water and is often found moving up large rivers, quite a distance from the ocean. It has a long snout, with a small mouth. Both of the diamond-shaped eyes are on its right or left side, which is a dark brown to black color. The blind side is white or creamy white.

Cutthroat Trout
Salmo darki
There are more than ten species of cutthroat trout, also called "native" trout. They vary in size and in color. The largest ever caught was reeled in on Nevada's Pyramid Lake, a monster of 41 pounds. However, this species is now extinct, and cutthroat of a smaller size (up to 15 inches) are caught on the Olympic Peninsula. A related species, the *crescenti,* is also found in the rivers and creeks of the Olympic Peninsula. Cutthroat are common sport fish from southern Alaska to Northern California and inland from southern British Columbia and Alberta to New Mexico. It is found in the waters of estuaries and coastal and alpine streams, as well as in lakes. It has an elongated, cylindrical body, with compressed sides. Its back is a dark

olive-green. The sides may vary from silver to olive to an orange-yellow color. Its belly is lighter. It has dark spots on the back, sides, and on its fins. The mouth extends beyond the eye.

AMPHIBIANS AND REPTILES

Olympic Salamander
Rhyacotriton olympicus
The Olympic salamander is not only found in its primary home, but along the Pacific Coast as far south as the northern coast redwoods area in California to Mendocino. This is smallest mole salamander, chocolate brown or a mottled olive-green above, with a yellowish-green or yellowish-orange belly. The belly is flecked with black. It has 14 or 15 grooves on its sides. It has distinctive eyes on its small head and a short tail. This amphibian lives in coastal forests, in cold year-round creeks, and in spring seeps. Breeding in the late spring and early summer, up to 14 eggs are laid. The larvae transform into salamanders when reaching a size of about 2.5 inches. Adult salamanders grow to 4.5 inches.

Long-toed Salamander
Ambystoma macrodactylum
A slender salamander, dark brown or black above, with a back stripe made up of bright yellow to tan blotches, this one has a dark brown or dark gray belly, a spotted head, and tubercles on its feet. A subspecies (*A. m. macrodactylum*) lives in all of the land habitats in Olympic National Park, from the alpine to coastal forest zones. In other regions, it lives at elevations up to 9,000 feet, making it a hardy little amphibian indeed. Depending on the elevation, it breeds in ponds between January and June. The eggs are laid on rushes near the water's surface or in clusters on the undersides of logs within the pond. The larvae transform from June to August or delay hatching until the following summer. The long-toed salamander is found in a contiguous area extending from the Alaska Panhandle through most of B.C. to northern Idaho and northwestern Montana and south through Oregon. Isolated groups are also found in Monterey and Santa Cruz counties on the central California coast. There are five subspecies in various parts of this range.

Northwestern Garter Snake
Thamnophis ardinoides
This is the most widely distributed snake in the Pacific Northwest region, found in all of the lowland areas and in mountains to an elevation of about 3,300 feet. On the Olympic Peninsula, this snake is found along with the common garter and western garter snakes. The rubber boa is infrequently seen on the peninsula. The northwestern garter snake is usually found in mixed woodlands or in brushy areas. It is not usually found close to the ocean. It relies on food from its home area: frogs, salamanders, earthworms, and the odd slug. Like other garter snakes, this species does not lay eggs but bears its

young in a live state. Babies appear in late summer and early fall. Growing to a length of about 23 inches, this snake varies widely in color. However, it usually has a dorsal stripe of red, yellow, orange, or cream. Lateral stripes are usually indistinct. The upper surface is normally brown or darker, with tinges of green or blue. The underside is a slate or olive-gray or yellowish. This snake is not considered to be a danger to humans when handled. It does exude a foul-smelling musk from its anal gland when it feels itself in danger.

Northern Rough-skinned Newt
Taricha granulosa
This water-breeding salamander is very much like the Olympic salamander, as it remains permanently aquatic because it fails to complete its metamorphosis from larvae to fully transformed amphibian. The newt's range extends from southern Alaska to the San Francisco Bay area. A close cousin (*T. g. mazamae*) is found only around Crater Lake, Oregon. They lay their eggs on submerged grasses or logs. The young develop legs in midsummer, when they are 1.5 inches long. Adults grow to a little less than seven inches. Newt migrations are amazing to watch because they travel in large numbers, heading to their breeding marshes and ponds in late fall. They stay there until after breeding season, with many staying on for the rest of the year. The female has bumps on its body when out of the water. After being immersed for a while, they develop a smooth skin. The newt's back is black or dark brown, and the belly is usually yellow or orange.

TREES AND FERNS

The rain forests and subalpine areas of Olympic National Park have at least eleven trees that hold national records for size. Most of these are found in the rain forests on the western slopes of the Olympic ranges. Several are reputed to be the largest of their species in the world. The world's largest Sitka spruce is found just outside the park boundary, in Olympic National Forest.

Grand Fir
Abies grandis
The national champ is found along the Duckabush River Trail, 7.5 miles from the trailhead. It is 251 feet tall and has a circumference of 229 inches. This tree is a true fir, unlike the Douglas fir, which is a spruce family member. The grand's needles are broader than those of the more common Douglas fir and are notched at the tips. The upper surface of the needle is a glassy green, while the lower surface has a green rib separating two whitish bands. Growing on the upper branches, the cones grow to about four inches long, staying attached long after the mature seeds have been shaken out. The tree has a distinctive shape, often like a cigar, with longer branches growing at the middle. The bark is gray and is not deeply cracked.

Subalpine Fir

Abies lasiocarpa

This is the most widely distributed true fir. It has a dense spire-like crown, with horizontal branches reaching almost to the ground. While the champion subalpine fir—near Cream Lake on the Hoh Range, with no trail access—is 125 feet tall, at higher levels it is very short, almost shrubby. The flat, dark green needles grow in rows of two, curving upward on the upper twigs. The needles have white lines above and below. The tree's bark is smooth and gray, with blisters formed of resin. When mature, the bark becomes scaly. It grows to the timberline in high subalpine mountain areas, often found with Engelmann spruce and other conifers. It is found from southeastern Alaska and the central Yukon to southern New Mexico, always in the mountains between 8,000 and 12,000 feet (in the south), almost to sea level in the far northern region. This tree has a distinctive rooting system. In snow-packed areas, the lower branches often lean to the ground, taking root and producing new shoots, which are browsed by deer and elk. A cousin, found in the mountains of Colorado and Arizona, is the corkbark or alpine fir (*A. l. arizonica*).

Vine Maple

Acer circinatum

This is the prominent understory shrub or small tree in the Olympic rain forests. It has a short trunk or several branches twisting from its base. The tree leans and sprawls in a vinelike fashion. Vine maples can grow to a height (or perhaps length) of 25 feet. While the trunk in the rain forests is usually smaller, it sometimes grows to a diameter of eight inches. The long, wide leaves are in opposite order. They are rounded, with 7 to 11 pointed, double-toothed lobes, bright green above and paler below, with tufts of hairs. The leaves turn in the fall, becoming orange and red. Its flowers are small (half an inch wide) purple sepals and white petals, clustered at the end of the twigs. The fruit are pairs of long-winged keys that are reddish at first, containing one seed. The keys fall in autumn. The vine maple is superbly suited to grow in rain forests. It prefers very moist soil, growing profusely along stream banks, and in wet conifer forests where it provides a wonderfully mysterious effect as it almost fills the understory with its wandering arms.

Licorice Fern

Polypodium glycyrrhiza

This is a small-to-medium evergreen fern, found in the Olympic rain forest and in the rain forests of British Columbia and southeastern Alaska. It is often seen growing from branches and trunks of deciduous trees, especially the bigleaf maple. It is not a parasite and does not take energy from the tree. It is epiphytic—taking nourishment from the air. The sori (groups of spore sacs) are oval to round, in one row on either side of the main vein on each leaf. The sori are not covered with an indusium (mem-brane), as are sori on other ferns. The licorice fern grows from a rhizome that has a distinctive licorice flavor. There are several other members of this family. All have leaves that are not too divided. Western polypody is a relative with a licorice-tasting rhizome. Some botanists consider it a hybrid, getting its good taste from *P. glycyrrhiza.*

Deer Fern
Blechnum spicant
A medium-size evergreen, the fern grows in tufts at the end of a short rhizome. There are two types of fronds. At the bottom, green, leathery, sterile leaves are pressed against the ground. The fertile leaves are upright, emerging from the center of the clump. They are deciduous, with narrow leaflets. The sori are continuously distributed near the leaf margin. An indusium protects the sori. The deer fern is found in moist and wet forests and also on stream banks and in boggy areas. It grows in lowland and high elevations to the subalpine. Native Americans used this fern as a medicine for skin sores, copying the deer that drub their antler stubs on the fern, and also ate the leaves as an appetite suppressant. It remains an important winter browse for elk and deer.

Common Wood Fern
Dryopteris austriaca
This evergreen fern is formed in a crown and is usually seen growing out of rotted logs and log debris. It looks much like the lady fern, a de-
ciduous fern that does not have a triangular blade. The outline of the wood fern blade is triangular, with the leaves growing to almost 20 inches. The leaflets are very small and a dark green color.

Running Club Moss
Lycopodium clavatum
This is called a fern ally, and this plant is a common sight in the Olympic forests. A trailing plant, also called running pine, it is an evergreen that produces its yellow reproductive shoots only in the summer. You'll see club moss on banks beside roads. It has short roots, with stems up to three feet long. Branches grow from the stems, with tiny leaves that taper to the tip. Some of the stems have short branches that produce shoots with scaled leaves and end in elongated cones. The cones consist of leaves that produce spores.

Oregon Selaginella
Selaginella oregana
This, too, is a variety of club moss. It is quite different from the running club moss in that it grows on deciduous trees, especially the bigleaf maples in the Olympic rain forests. The peninsula and the west coast of Vancouver Island are its most northerly habitat. The stems are loose and often sprawl over wet ground. The leaves are bright green, oval to triangular in shape, and somewhat overlapping. They are arranged in spirals and are grooved on the back and have tiny bristles on the tips. Small cones are found at the end of the branches. It

often grows in combination with mosses on the maple trees. Selaginella is the diminutive of *Selago,* the earlier name for *Lycopodium.* Another club moss that grows on the Olympic Peninsula is fir club moss (*Lycopodium selago*).

WILDFLOWERS

Oregon Oxalis
Oxalis oregana
Also called redwood sorrel, this perennial wildflower grows from scaly rhizomes, with stems that grow to a length of more than five inches. The leaves are cloverlike, with three heart-shaped, folded leaflets and narrow ends attached to the stalk. The flowers are white to pale pink, sometimes having light red veins. The flowers grow singly at the top of long stalks. The five-chambered fruit is oval (football) shaped, containing wrinkled seeds. This plant is common in Washington and Oregon. It grows in moist forest areas at the lower elevations. Two other sorrels or oxalis grow in the Pacific Northwest: Suksdorf's sorrel (*O. suksdorfii*) has yellow flowers and grows in forests and woodland clearings; trillium-leafed sorrel (*O. trillifolia*) has white or pink flowers on each stalk, growing on slightly higher territory than *O. oregana.*

Beadlilly
Clintonia uniflora
This is a creeping plant that likes lots of moist humus, particularly with a top layer of conifer needles. The pure white flowers, with white sepals, grow singly. The plant grows in large displays and is frequently seen in the woodlands and conifer forests of the Olympic Mountains, the Cascades, and the Coast ranges. The plant's leaves are also attractive, growing to about four inches long in groups of two to five. Blue berries follow the flowers. The berries seem to be dusted with a whitish sparkle, resembling beads.

Foam Flower
Tiarella trifoliata
A perennial growing from a short rhizome, the foam flower has medium brown leaves growing on long stalks, with three leaflets that have irregular lobes, and ragged teeth. The tiny and very delicate flowers are at the end of thin stalks. The flowers are arranged in clusters of varying numbers. Each plant produces a few fruit: capsules that split to form a shape resembling a sugar scoop. Inside the capsules are shiny black seeds. These delicate flowers may be seen on the floor of the rain forests and on stream banks. The plants grow at moderate elevations and sometimes at the subalpine level.

Buttercups
Ranunculus var.
Several buttercups grow in various settings in Olympic National Park. The subalpine buttercup (*R. eschscholtzii*) is found in mountain meadows, such as Hurricane Ridge, and on talus slopes, as well as along stream banks in the subalpine forest. Like the rest, it is a perennial, with basal kidney-shaped

leaves growing on thin stalks and yellow flowers with five petals. Another buttercup of the Olympic alpine zone is Cooley's buttercup (*R. cooleyae*).

The western buttercup (*R. occidentalis*) grows on grassy slopes and mountain meadows and in open or shaded forests from sea level to subalpine elevations. The leaves have long stalks, usually with three wedge-shaped divisions. The yellow flowers are about a half-inch in diameter, with several flowers at the end of long stalks. The rest of the plant is very compact. The little buttercup (*R. uncinatus*) is an annual or perennial, with single stems growing to 20 inches or more. The very small flowers give the plant its name. They have five petals, with a single yellow flower at the end of a stalk and several stalks clustered together above leafy bracts.

Cooley's Hedge Nettle
Stachys cooleyae
This perennial plant is another resident of the Hoh Rain Forest floor, and it is found along the Pacific Coast from the Queen Charlotte Islands and Vancouver Island to southwestern Washington. It has erect stems with few branches and leaves that are opposite and found along the stem from ground level to the tip. The long, hairy leaves are heart-shaped, with blunt teeth around the edges. The flowers are a deep reddish-purple. They are also hairy, with the sepals in a tube with five spiny lobes. The fruit consists of four nutlets. The hedge nettle not only grows in very damp areas, like rain forests, but also thrives on roadsides, in meadows, and open woods. They are usually found at lower elevations. The plant has been used by Native Americans for many years. The local Quileute put the leaves into a wooden tub with hot rocks, a sort of sauna devised as a cure for rheumatism. The Quinault sucked the nectar from the hedge nettle flowers. This is the only tribe known to have used the nectar for refreshment, although the Haida (Queen Charlotte Islands) chewed the stems to obtain the juice, which they swallowed.

Following are suggested accommodations for the Olympic Peninsula that provide easy access to Olympic National Park and recreation areas within the Olympic National Forest. Private campgrounds and RV parks are included, as are the developed campgrounds in Olympic National Park, which accommodate RVs and trailers as well as tenters. The private lodges and campgrounds that are concessions of the national park and forest, including accommodations on Lake Crescent and at Kalaloch, are shown under the park and forest heading. Other accommodations are found in Forks, Neah Bay, and Port Angeles.

FORKS

Bagby's Town Motel
1080 South Forks Avenue
Forks, WA 98331
(360) 374-6231 or 800-742-2429

This standard motel is located a half-mile south of downtown Forks, on Highway 101. It features complimentary morning coffee and has outdoor barbecue and picnic tables in a garden setting. Rooms with kitchen units are available. **($ to $$)**

Forks Motel
351 South Forks Avenue
(Highway 101)
P.O. Box 510
Forks, WA 98331
(360) 374-6243 or 800-544-3416

This large motel is in the downtown area of this lumber town, to the west of Olympic National Park. It has standard rooms, some rooms with kitchen units, and others with refrigerator and microwave oven. The motel has a heated pool. **($ to $$)**

Manitou Lodge
P.O. Box 953
Forks, WA 98331
(360) 374-6295

This bed and breakfast inn is located eight miles west of Forks, off Moran Road. It is in rain forest country, with a quiet setting. There is a Native American gift shop at the lodge. **($$)**

Miller Tree Inn
654 East Division Street
P.O. Box 953
Forks, WA 98331
(360) 374-6806

Located right in Forks, next to City Hall and near restaurants, this is a historic 1917 home on three acres. The ocean beaches are 12 miles to the west. The B & B home has two private full bathrooms, and two bathrooms are shared. There is a hot tub, and the management provides raingear for rain forest visitors—a nice touch! Children over six years are welcome, as are pets. **($ to $$)**

Misty Valley Inn
194894 Highway 101
Forks, WA 98331
(360) 374-9389

This bed and breakfast inn has just about everything you could want in comfort, and it is great for a romantic interlude. It's on the Olympic Highway, two miles north of Forks, with a fine view overlooking the Soleduck River Valley, in a rain forest setting. The rooms have queen-size brass beds, and the inn has a hot tub. A three-course breakfast is served in the dining room or on the outdoor terrace. **($$)**

Olympic Suites

800 Olympic Drive
Forks, WA 98331
(360) 374-5400 or 800-262-3433

A cut above most accommodations in Forks, this motor hotel has one- and two-bedroom suites, for about the same price you would pay for a standard motel. **($$)**

Pacific Inn Motel

352 Forks Avenue
P.O. Box 1997
Forks, WA 98331
(360) 374-9400 or 800-235-7344

This medium-size motel has rooms with queen beds (including non-smoking and handicapped-accessible rooms), and an on-site laundry. The Pacific Inn Family Restaurant is next door. **($ to $$)**

Rain Forest Hostel

169312 Highway 101
Forks, WA 98331
(360) 374-2270

This youth hostel is located 23 miles south of town, on the Olympic Highway. It has the same spartan amenities as other hostels, but overnight costs are what many traveling on a budget are looking for. **($)**

NEAH BAY

The Cape Motel and RV Park

Bayview Avenue
Neah Bay, WA 98357
(360) 645-2250

The community of Neah Bay is part of the Makah Reservation, located at the northwestern tip of the Olympic Peninsula. The Makah Cultural Center and Museum provides a historical and cultural focus for the community and for visitors. The beach is across the street from the motel, which features regular rooms and rooms with kitchenettes in addition to cabins. There's a boat and trailer storage area. **($ to $$)**

The motel operates a medium-size RV park and campground with hookups and a tenting area. There are restrooms with flush toilets and showers, as well as a laundry.

OLYMPIC NATIONAL PARK AND FOREST

Eagle's Rest

c/o Mari Reed, P.O. Box 159
Quinault, WA 98575
(360) 288-2633

This is a house sitting *inside* the national park, on the north side of Lake Quinault, with shake sides and roof, a front deck, and a wooden walkway to the water. If you want to rent a house with lake access and a quiet, forested ambience, this is what you need. It contains three bedrooms, sleeping eight. The house comes with a 17-foot fiberglass canoe, and it has its own boat launch. Fishing permits are required by the Quinault. **($$$)**

Kalaloch Lodge
157151 Highway 101
Forks, WA 98331
(360) 962-2271

Sitting on the oceanfront at the southwestern corner of the national park, the lodge is close to the rain forests and beach areas of the western part of the peninsula. There are a variety of accommodations, including rooms in the lodge, cabins on the bluff (fully contained), rooms in another building called Sea Crest House, and log cabins. Most of the units cost under or just over $100 per night, although several lodge rooms are much less expensive, and a few deluxe bluff cabins cost more. A park ranger station is across the highway. The restaurant has a wonderful ocean view, and there is a coffee shop. **($ to $$$)**

Lake Crescent Lodge
416 Lake Crescent Road
Port Angeles, WA 98363-8672
(360) 928-3211

The historic lodge sits beside a beautiful mountain lake, west of Port Angeles, with canoeing, nature trails, and longer hikes available in the area. The old country lodge has rooms and serves as the meeting area and dining room. The season runs from late April until the end of October. Rooms are available in the Roosevelt Fireplace Cottages, Storm King Motor Lodge (standard motel rooms on two stories), Marymere Motor Lodge (a one-story build-

ing), and Pyramid Mountain Lodge, a recently built two-story facility. There are also more comfortable cottages, with one and two bedrooms. Rowboats are available to rent. **($$ to $$$)**

Lake Quinault Lodge
345 South Shore Road
P.O. Box 7
Quinault, WA 98575
(360) 288-2571 or
800-562-6673 (Washington only)

This grand old lodge is perfectly situated beside Lake Quinault and close to the Quinault Rain Forest, south of Forks and north of Aberdeen. It is located on South Shore Road. National park lands are seen across the lake. There are rooms in the main lodge building, as well as fireplace rooms and newer lakeside rooms. The resort sits in the Olympic National Forest and is operated by ARA Leisure Services. There is an excellent dining room in the lodge. Trails start at the door, and there is a heated pool. Rental canoes are available. **($$ to $$$)**

Log Cabin Resort
3183 East Beach Road
Port Angeles, WA 98363
(360) 928-3325

This resort on the north side of Lake Crescent has been in operation for more than a hundred years, long before the area became a national park. There's an informal restaurant in the lodge building. The resort offers a variety of accommodations, including lakeside chalets, rooms in the lodge, rustic log cabins (private bathrooms with tub or shower), and camping log cabins (more rustic—bring your own bedding or rent some here, and no indoor plumbing). There are no telephones, radios, or TV sets in the rooms. **($$ to $$$)**

The resort also has RV sites with full hookups. To get there, drive on Highway 101 (18 miles west from Port Angeles) and turn onto East Beach Road. The resort is three miles from the junction. Write or phone ahead for room and RV site reservations.

Rain Forest Resort Village
516 South Shore Road
Lake Quinault, WA 98575
(360) 288-2535 or 800-255-6936

Located 3.5 miles from Highway 101 and complete with restaurant and lounge, rooms, cabins, and RV sites (with hookups), this resort on Lake Quinault also has a general store, gift shop, laundry, and guided winter fishing. You can stay in a fireplace cabin with whirlpool bath and kitchen, or a motel-style room. The resort is also close to several hiking trails leading into the Quinault Rain Forest. **($$ to $$$)**

Sol Duc Hot Springs Resort
P.O. Box 2169
Port Angeles, WA 98362
(360) 327-3583

What was originally a European-style hot spring spa with a hotel is now a more relaxed operation with single cabins, and duplex cabins with kitchens, plus a campground with tenting and RV sites. There's a bar, a poolside deli/restaurant, and a general store. The main attrac-

tion, of course, is the water from the springs, which flows into several pools with temperatures ranging from 98°F to 106°F. Massage service is available. There is a two-night minimum stay for holidays, and payment of a national park entrance fee is required (unless you have a handy Golden Eagle Pass). The resort is 12 miles off Highway 101, west of Port Angeles. **($$)**

Olympic National Park Camping
There are 16 developed campgrounds within the national park, in addition to numerous backcountry campsites. Most are open year-round, with only Altaire, Deer Park, Dosewallips, Graves Creek, and Sol Duc Campgrounds closed during winter months. A majority of the campgrounds accommodate trailers up to 21 feet long. Staircase Campground has a limit of 16 feet. Kalaloch is the largest of the campgrounds, and there are large campgrounds at Heart o' the Hills (near Hurricane Ridge), the Hoh Rain Forest, Fairholm, and Mora.

The July Creek Campground features walk-in sites. There is a fee charged at all but the Deer Park, Dosewallips, North Fork, Ozette, and Queets Campgrounds. For information on camping facilities, visit a ranger station or the National Park headquarters in Port Angeles.

PORT ANGELES

A Nice Touch Bed and Breakfast
1665 Black Diamond Road
Port Angeles, WA 98363
(360) 457-1938 or 800-605-6296

This inn in the country is two miles from downtown, is set on five acres, and features horseback riding. There's a fine view of the Strait of Juan de Fuca, a garden including a pond with waterfall, and rooms (some with whirlpool) with private baths. There are antique furnishings, and a full breakfast is served. Rental bikes are available. **($$$)**

Best Western Olympic Lodge
140 Del Guzzi Drive
Port Angeles, WA 98362
(360) 452-2993 or 800-528-1234

This motor hotel has large rooms with king beds plus microwaves and refrigerators. Facilities include a year-round heated pool, whirlpool, and a nearby golf course. There's a restaurant with lounge next door. **($$ to $$$)**

Domaine Madeleine B & B
146 Wildflower Lane
Port Angeles, WA 98362
(360) 457-4174

This delightful bed and breakfast home is on a waterfront estate, and each room has a fireplace, sundeck, private whirlpool, and antique furnishings. **($$$)**

Elwha Ranch Bed and Breakfast
905 Herrick Road
Port Angeles, WA 98363
(360) 457-6540

This bed and breakfast home is 10 miles west of town, overlooking the Elwha River and the national park. There are two suites, each with a bedroom, family room, and private bath. They serve a country breakfast. Children are welcome. **($$ to $$$)**

KOA Kampground
80 O'Brien Road and
Highway 101 East
Port Angeles, WA 98362
(360) 457-5916

Located seven miles east of Port Angeles and eight miles west of Sequim, this RV park has full hookups, camping cabins, tenting sites, a heated pool, and whirlpool.

Lyre River Park
592 West Lyre River Road
Port Angeles, WA 98362
(360) 928-3436

Outside of town, five miles west of the village of Joyce, this RV park is beside the Strait of Juan de Fuca and is reached via Route 112. This is a basic operation with RV facilities including full hookups, RV sites without hookups, tenting sites, restrooms, showers, laundry, and a small store with groceries, wood, and propane. There's a trout pond for children.

Portside Inn
1510 East Front Street
(Highway 101 at Alder)
Port Angeles, WA 98362
(360) 452-4015

This quite respectable standard motel has low rates, which are even lower during winter months. It's located near the waterfront and ferry landing. The motel has rooms with queen beds, a heated pool and whirlpool, and complimentary coffee. **($ to $$)**

Shadow Mountain Campground
232951 West Highway 101
Port Angeles, WA 98363
(360) 928-3043

Located just outside Olympic National Park, two miles east of Lake Crescent and 16 miles west of Port Angeles, the park has full hookups for RVs and trailers, tenting sites, plus a grocery store, deli, gasoline, and mini golf. There's a covered group picnic area.

Vancouver Island

The largest island along the Pacific Coast of the Americas, Vancouver is an amazing natural wonder. It is 483 kilometers (300 miles) long, with two contrasting ecosystems separated by a mountain range that climbs to an elevation of higher than 2,134 meters (7,000 feet). The eastern shore is tranquil and warm, with the sheltered water of the Strait of Georgia lying between the island and the British Columbia mainland. Near the southeast corner of the big island is the Gulf Islands archipelago. These bucolic islands are the Canadian counterpart to the San Juan Islands, which lie a few miles to the south. More islands (Texada, Quadra, and Cortes) are located farther north in the Strait of Georgia, further modifying the currents and the climate.

From the provincial capital city of Victoria to the storied fishing towns to the north—including Campbell River and the whale-watching village of Telegraph Cove—the eastern shore of Vancouver Island is lined with small, comfortable resorts focusing on fishing and golfing. Camping is available in several provincial parks, which have sand or pebble beaches facing the mainland.

Rather than concentrate on one natural place while exploring Vancouver Island, I suggest that you plan your vacation to visit several superb parks that, together, typify the west coast environment in all its glory.

First, at the northwest tip of the island is Cape Scott Provincial Park, with a prime rain forest; secluded beaches on deep inlets; the traces of old villages settled by Danish immigrants; and a marvelous opportunity to get close to wildlife, whether birds or mammals. This is a less-traveled wilderness area of growing renown. The shoreline of the park looks out across the Pacific with no land obstruction between the sand beaches and Japan. The interior of the park is a lush, dripping rain forest, crossed by hiking trails that lead to secluded beaches on deep fjords and across the top of the island to the rugged beaches of the north coast. The signs and sounds of wildlife are everywhere in this pristine area of old-growth and second-growth spruce, hemlock, and Douglas fir, with an undergrowth of huge ferns, salal, and salmonberry.

The second is Strathcona Provincial Park—lying in the center of the island, straddling the mountains, with astounding views of lakes, rivers, creeks, waterfalls, and superb hiking in dryer spruce/fir/hemlock forests. Trails cover both sides of the mountain divide as well as the depths of the vast mountain forest.

The third, and an absolute gem among the world's great parks, is Pacific Rim National Park. The western half of the island is the wild side: This park contains the world's largest group of moderate rain forests, fed by the Pacific mists and abundant rain. Deep bays and fjords indent the shoreline, from the southwestern tip at Port Renfrew to Cape Scott 300 miles to the northwest. The most impressive of these large inlets are named to commemorate the prominent cultures of the island: Clayquot, Nootka, Kyuquot, and Quatsino.

Getting to these special places is just about as enjoyable as your destination activity. Provincial highways lead up and down the mountain ridges and through long, deep valleys filled with dense conifer forests. Backroads, developed for the island's intense forestry industry, lead you through some untouched forest and the logged areas to protected lakes, rivers, and ocean bays. This is canoeing and kayaking country, where a visitor rarely sees another soul. Put a canoe onto an island lake as the sun sets, and you'll be alone with the loons.

A short stay in Victoria provides a fine counterpoint to a tour of the wilder places on the island. This small city, centered on its Inner Harbour, has been rated by the readers of *Condé Nast Traveler* magazine (November 1995) as one of the top 20 cities in the world to visit, while Vancouver Island was rated one of the top 20 islands. Two buildings dominate Inner

Harbour: the grand old Empress Hotel and the Provincial Parliament. The harbor area is wonderfully landscaped; the provincial history museum sits beside the parliament building.

Those interested in floral beauty should reserve at least a half day to see Butchart Gardens, located off Highway 17, north of Victoria on the Saanich Peninsula. This former quarry has been transformed into one of the finest show gardens on the continent. It's open daily, with a restaurant for lunch or dinner and special programmed activities on weekends and holidays. Also on the peninsula and close to the Swartz Bay ferry terminal is Sidney Spit Marine Park, with wilderness campsites on the islands and hiking trails along the beach.

On the Edge: Native Cultures

North coast tribes lived on both sides of the island long before the Spanish, Portuguese, or British explored the area. Comprised of several language groups, the tribes lived along the coast, fishing and hunting for their food, paddling long canoes along the wild Pacific and on the calm inland sea to the east.

In the coastal areas north of the Strait of Juan de Fuca, there were (and are) many tribes with several languages but with one culture. Every hundred miles of coastline housed a different tribe with regional languages that differed greatly, even within the linguistic region. However, all of the north coast tribes were driven by a single cultural focus. Social anthropologists have been struck by this dichotomy of isolated communities surrounded by water and mountainous forest but having a cultural basis so distinct that the members of north coast tribes differ from all others on the continent; the extent of the common cultural elements is remarkable.

In the thousands of years before Europeans came to try to settle the Vancouver Island coast, the mountains were virtually impenetrable. The standard mode of transportation was the canoe, as the tribes traded and communicated with each other by water travel—across the giant fjords, up the river valleys, and along the inland sea. The red cedar provided lumber for homes, logs for great cedar canoes, and wood for carving; the bark served to make harpoon lines.

The sea and its bounty shaped this unique culture. The tribes of the island's west coast are the only North American tribes to have hunted whales, using the meat and blubber for food and oil. Whale intestines were made into bags and bow-strings. Salmon were caught by nets between two canoes or in weirs and fish traps set in the rivers. Hooks and lines were used to catch halibut and cod. The smaller fish, herring and oula-chon, made runs to the beaches by the millions and were sim-ply raked. The oulachon (pronounced *ooo-la-kun*) is a fatty fish, similar in size to smelt, which is gathered and boiled for its oil. The oil was kept in bottles formed of dried kelp. While ancient Russians ate caviar from the Caspian Sea, the west coast tribes ate herring roe, which was dried and eaten with oil. Sea grass was cooked into a type of cake.

While the sea provided most of the food, Native Americans also hunted for meat in the nearby mountains, particularly for deer and elk but also black and grizzly bear, which were caught in huge traps.

Totem pole

The blanket is a common element shared by the coastal tribes. Blankets were fashioned from the skins of beaver, otter, marten, mink, and fur seal. Others were made of soft cedar bark and woven from dog's hair (they had dogs to help with the hunting), mountain goat wool, and feathers, or a combination of wool and feathers. The famous button blankets were donned for festivities. While always bare-legged, people wore shirts, petticoats, and cedar bark ponchos. In earlier days, before the advent of wool, women wore a cedar bark apron.

Baskets are another common theme among the tribes. The cedar canoe was another. Square wooden houses were built in all the northern coastal communities, from mid-Vancouver Island to the Alaska Panhandle. Only in the southern quarter of the island were houses built in the longhouse style of the Coast Salish people, the tribes that lived on the mainland in what are now the Vancouver and Seattle areas.

Three language groups lived on Vancouver Island. At the southeastern end of the island and along much of the eastern shore, influences from the mainland held sway, and the Coast Salish language was spoken. The Coast Salish are not considered to be a north coast tribe but are more closely associated with cultures to the south.

The *Nuu-chah-nulth* (Nootka) language (including variations) was the common native language from the northwestern tip of the Olympic Peninsula (Makah tribe) and along the west coast of Vancouver Island, almost but not quite to its northern tip. The gray whale was of great importance to the Nootka people of the west coast of the island, who hunted small numbers of whales for food and blubber, holding ceremonies after hauling a whale ashore.

The Kwakiutl occupied the northernmost and northeastern parts of the island, from Smith Sound, around Cape Scott, and down the northeastern side to the Campbell River/Quadra Island area. Kwakiutl and other language groups occupied the mainland and island communities farther north, including Bella Coola, Haida, and Tsmishian. Tlingit occupied most of the Alaska Panhandle.

The Kwakiutl, now as then, are dedicated to fishing and living by the sea. Some Kwakiutl live the traditional life in small reservation villages. Others live in or outside the villages and are engaged in commercial salmon fishing and in guiding sport anglers. Several reservations are located on the same islands occupied by one or more of the 15 bands, which were separated into 19 tribes. The museum on Quadra Island, just offshore from Campbell River, offers a fascinating glimpse into Kwakiutl life, in particular the unique north coast celebration of the potlatch.

During the potlatch period, the Kwakiutl tribes were highly stratified, ranked in comparison to other tribes in the group of tribes. Individuals within a tribe were ranked amongst each other. This system of social standing reached its zenith with the potlatch, a celebration involving public displays including dancing and the distribution of wealth from one group claiming hereditary privileges or rights compared to other groups. The more property and wealth distributed by the host, the higher the rank that could be claimed. Potlatches were common occurrences at major life events including birth, puberty, adoption, marriage, and death.

The host, with his family or a ranking group called a *numina,* invited other families to witness the claiming of status accomplished by the giving away of property. Hosts feasted the attendants with lavish spreads, presented ceremonial dances, and distributed gifts—first to the highest ranking tribal chiefs, and then down through the ranks, tribe by tribe. Not only did the host present gifts, others often gave property in order to bolster their own standing within the tribal groups.

The system of ranking and potlatch practices were extremely sophisticated. Meticulous attention was paid to the staging of the ceremonies, which included elaborate feasts, and dances were often staged with special lighting, smoke, and colorful costumes.

Potlatch excesses, including alcohol abuse, plus the authorities' view that the potlatch was an undemocratic and heathen observance, brought the government to ban the ceremony in 1884. Some coastal peoples continued the staging of surreptitious potlatches. Many leaders were heavily fined for holding the illegal ceremonies, and more than 100 years later, strong feelings are voiced on the banishment of this social mainstay of north coast culture and community development. The practice seems to have been an efficient way to develop a society's culture, including drama, music, dance, and the decorative arts. The potlatch system also preserved a remarkable social cohesion within the tribal groups, settling disputes and righting wrongs through the transfer of property.

The story of the potlatch, and its importance to Kwakiutl culture, provides the major focus of the historical museum in the Quadra Island village of Quathiaski, near the terminal for the short ferry run from Campbell River.

How to Get There

It's easy to reach Vancouver Island from the mainland, from either Canada or the United States. The extensive B.C. Ferries system connects the mainland with Vancouver Island, the Gulf Islands, and the islands lying to the north in the Strait of Georgia. The two major mainland departure points are located within a half-hour's drive of Vancouver: south of the city at Tsawwassen (ferries to Swartz Bay, near Victoria, and to Nanaimo, north of Victoria) and northwest of the Vancouver urban area at Horseshoe Bay (ferries to Nanaimo).

The ferries are spacious, car-carrying ships with cafeterias and dining rooms. Reservations are not taken for the 90-minute sailing between the mainland and Vancouver Island. Sailings are frequent: hourly during summer months and several times each day in winter. For information, call (604) 669-1211 (Vancouver) or (604) 386-3431 (Victoria). Ferries are available from several points in Washington state, all sailing to Victoria's Inner Harbour.

Port Angeles to Victoria   The Black Ball ferry company operates a car ferry with several sailings per day across the Strait of Juan de Fuca from this town on the Olympic Peninsula. For information, call (360) 457-4491 (Port Angeles) or (604) 386-2202 (Victoria).

The Victoria Express is a ferry for foot passengers only. It operates from May to October. For information, call (604) 361-9144 (Victoria) or 800-633-1589.

Seattle to Victoria   The Victoria Clipper is a large catamaran boat that transports foot passengers from the downtown Seattle harbor to the Inner Harbour in downtown Victoria. For information, call (206) 448-5000 or 800-888-2535 (Seattle), or (604) 382-8100 (Victoria). The Victoria Line transports foot passengers and vehicles from May to September. The ship provides an old-fashioned experience on a ship of a certain age. For information, call (206) 625-1880 or 800-668-1167 (Seattle), or (604) 480-5555 (Victoria).

Bellingham to Victoria   The Gray Line ferry takes foot passengers only across the Gulf of Georgia to Victoria, from this city between Seattle and the Canadian border, operating from June to October. For information, call (360) 738-8099 (Bellingham) or 800-443-4552 (U.S. and Canada).

Once on Vancouver Island, it's easy to find your way on the provincial highways. The route from the southern ferry terminal at Swartz Bay to Victoria is Highway 17. A single road runs the entire length of the island, from Victoria to Port Hardy. This highway (locally called the Island Highway) has two numbers. The southern portion, between Victoria and Nanaimo (113 kilometers or 70 miles), is part of the Trans-Canada Highway system and is designated Highway 1. The rest of the route (391 kilometers or 243 miles), between Nanaimo and Port Hardy, is Highway 19.

The southwest corner of the island is reached from Victoria by Highway 1 and Highway 14 (West Coast Road). The west coast communities of Tofino and Ucluelet and Pacific Rim National Park are reached by taking Highway 4 from Parksville, 147 kilometers (91 miles) north of Victoria. The only other suggested east-west provincial route is Highway 28, which leads west from Campbell River (at mid-island) through Strathcona Provincial Park to the resource town of Gold River.

While busses run to the major communities and attractions such as Pacific Rim National Park, along the Island Highway, and Highway 4, the vast majority of visitors to Vancouver Island use their cars and RVs to get around. For those interested in natural places and exploring wilderness, a vehicle is almost essential to reach the more remote areas covered here. Should you wish to fly to Seattle, Vancouver, or Victoria, rental cars are available in downtown Victoria through the usual agencies.

Pacific Rim National Park

One of Canada's newer national parks, Pacific Rim National Park offers some of the finest hiking challenges, boating, kayaking, and beach-walking on Earth. The three distinct sections of the park lie midway along Vancouver's wild west coast, close enough to each other to visit on the same vacation but varied enough to attract people who become entranced with one unit and stay for a few days, a week, or more. We will explore the three sections in depth here: the Long Beach Unit, the Broken Group Islands, and the West Coast Trail.

Canada is renowned for its national park system, which preserves an amazing range of scenery as well as animal and plant life. Canada was far ahead of most countries in identifying a need to preserve its most significant wilderness areas. From the designation of Banff National Park, the nation's first, Canada has steadily added new parks. The newest planned national park area on the west coast is the South Moresby Island Preserve, which will soon enchant visitors to the Queen Charlotte Islands off British Columbia's north coast.

PACIFIC RIM WILDLIFE

Situated along the Pacific flyway, the beaches offer an opportunity for exceptional bird-watching. Mergansers, mallards, and other ducks reside in the park year-round, along with bald eagles, great blue herons, Brandt's and pelagic cormorants, common loons, and many other waterbirds. Other seabirds are seasonal visitors, including the black turnstone, goldeneye and horned grebe (winter), and rufous hummingbirds, western flycatchers, orange-crowned and Townsend's warblers, and marbled murrelet (summer). Many transients stop in the park on their way, north and south.

Other wildlife includes bears, cougars, and smaller mammals of the nonthreatening kind, including bog animals. Gray whales migrate along the beaches, moving north from mid-February on their journey to the Bering Sea and the Arctic Ocean. In late December, the grays are seen heading south to their breeding grounds in the lagoons of Baja California. Whale-watching excursions are available in Tofino and Ucluelet. While most whales are transients, as many as 40 to 50 great gray whales stay along the Vancouver Island coast during the summer; a few regularly stay here year-round. The optimum time for whale-watching is from late February to early June.

The waters off the park have been designated the Pacific Rim National Preserve. The increase in gray whale numbers over the past 50 years followed the near decimation of the species. Vancouver Island had whaling stations, and as far back as the 18th century, commercial whalers, starting with the Russians, hunted the great gray along this part of the Pacific. But the height of the whaling industry was in the late 19th century. In only 18 years of whaling, the Pacific population of gray whales was almost annihilated. Today, the 18,000 or more eastern Pacific herd of whales proves the resilience of animal species. This is the largest population of gray whales remaining in the world. A small number of gray whales (180 total each year) are permitted to be caught, mainly in Alaska and Siberia.

The intertidal zone, particularly west of the headlands, provides a rich exhibit of seashells (mussels, finger limpets, barnacles), sea worms, anemones, hermit crabs, and several species of small fish, including tide pool sculpins. At low tide, the shoreline is crawling with life, in and out of the rocky pools. Purple shore crabs drag their bodies across the sand, leaving "tire" marks. Plants including the sea sac and sea palm are found at the water's edge.

Behind the beaches and headlands lies a remarkable procession of greenery zones. With a growing season of nine months and snow rarely falling, you will not see remarkable changes in the color of the vegetation as the annual cycle progresses. However, the shades of green are varied within the six plant zones in the park. Considering that the average width of the park is about one mile, this shows a remarkable diversity in plant life.

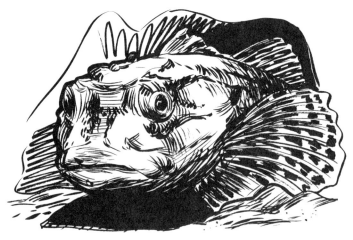

Buffalo sculpin

Just above the pounding waves is the spruce fringe, populated by stunted Sitka spruce—barely hanging on in the sandy soil and strong winds—with salal underneath. The fall berries of this thick, wiry groundcover provided a staple food for the local Nootka people, and they still are treasured by the park's hungry bears, although bears are infrequently seen along the shoreline. Behind the small, stunted Sitka spruce, taller stands of spruce grow, accompanied by the smaller Pacific crabapple.

Just in from the beaches are several fine bogs, irrigated by the 36 meters (118 inches) of rain that fall here each year. The bogs lie in lowland areas behind Long Beach. These are peat bogs, built up over hundreds of years, filled with spongy sphagnum moss. There are few trees in the boggy areas, although one tree, the shorepine (lodgepole pine) thrives in this stagnant, soaked environment. In such a wet area, this tree is exceptionally stunted, but it sometimes reaches to your shoulders. Labrador tea is a resident, exhibiting white flowers during June and July. You'll also see bog laurel, which has pink clusters of flowers in the spring.

Several streams bring water from the eastern hills, flowing across the beaches and into the ocean. Red alder is the primary tree in this streamside zone, flanked by willows in a shrub shape. The unusual small tree with groups of large oval leaves is the cascara. Under the alders, salmonberry and thimbleberry grow, with pink and white flowers respectively, followed by delicious berries. The salmonberry is rounded, varying in color from yellow to red. The red thimbleberry is shaped like a thimble, like its relatives the raspberry and blackberry. It has large maple-shaped leaves.

Inland, along the hills, is the typical Vancouver Island cedar/ hemlock forest. The western red cedar has long been used in this region for many purposes. Spruce is also found among the other conifers. There is so much rain here that the trunks of many of these trees are covered with moss.

Closer to the beaches are prime examples of the climax rain forest, old-growth trees including the amabilis fir, a member of the balsam family and considered to be a true fir. It is seen with the western yew, a smaller tree with thin bark, usually covered with moss. The understory is typical for the temperate rain forest: mainly salal, with false azalea and huckleberry; all three are members of the heather family. Blueberry bushes also grow in this environment. You'll also see western white pine in smaller quantities within the park boundaries.

Much of the eastern property now included in the park was extensively logged before the park was created in the 1970s. While much of Vancouver Island is covered with Douglas fir, there are few specimens in the park. Too much rain is the cause. Instead, the logged areas have been replanted with Sitka spruce, red cedar, and western hemlock, the trees that were previously logged. There are clear-cut swaths still covered with fireweed, waiting for the new forest to grow.

LONG BEACH UNIT

The expansive string of beaches stretches 11 kilometers (seven miles) in a rarely broken strand of white sand between the villages of Ucluelet and Tofino. Along the beach are temporary islands, pockets of trees, and underbrush raised 20 or 30 feet above the sand floor, made into islands by the high tides and then becoming part of the beach as the ocean recedes. These "air islands" are the result of the constant scouring and washing away of the earth. Standing on the beach, you can only see to the horizon, beyond which lies thousands of miles of Pacific and—somewhere in the distance—the islands of Japan. Some days the horizon is not visible, for this is a truly wild coastline often buffeted by wind, rain, and high, pounding surf. Walking along Long Beach in the rain is one of the greatest pleasures offered a nature-lover anywhere, as is sitting in the hospitable shelter of the Wickaninnish Centre (a marine museum and restaurant), gazing at the storms which frequently roll in, casting huge piles of logs to the back of the beach and creating a surreal backdrop to the gently sloping sand landscape.

Other beaches flank the main beach. Florencia Bay, to the southeast, has a crescent-shaped beach, the site of many shipwrecks over the past 300 years. To the northwest—beyond Portland Point—is another isolated stretch of beach, accessible only by boat. Several stretches of beach are separated by rocky headlands, jutting out into the ocean.

Long Beach—to the north of the Wickaninnish Centre—is the most impressive of the Long Beach unit, where the huge piles of driftwood logs are stacked in disarray. Surfing is a popular activity on Long Beach, but my favorite, and less exhausting, pastime is strolling along the beaches looking for razor clams and oysters and watching the shorebirds that dance with the outgoing tides in their constant search for snacks. Along the headlands are tidal pools containing a wide variety of sea life including mussels, sea stars, limpets, hermit crabs, varieties of seaweed, and barnacles.

There is no entrance gate to the Long Beach Unit. Parking charges are levied when using the park. The best tactic is to purchase a day ticket from the machines to avoid being caught on an overtime hiking excursion. The day ticket may be used throughout the unit.

Long Beach Camping   Green Point Campground is the major developed vehicle campground, located halfway along Long Beach, with an amphitheater for interpretive programs and restrooms. Primitive walk-in sites are located at the north end of the beach, at the end of a 1-kilometer (0.6-mile) trail. Additional camping facilities are located outside of the park boundaries in private campgrounds near Tofino (to the northwest) and in Ucluelet (southeast).

The Ucluelet-Tofino Road, an extension of Provincial Highway 4, runs through the length of the Long Beach unit. There are several good viewpoints along the route, including Radar Hill, the site of an old World War II installation that provides an excellent view of the northwestern beaches, the ocean, and nearby mountains to the east.

Long Beach Park Trails   All trails in the Long Beach Unit provide day-hikes through the beachside lands, including short nature trails that lead through the rain forest and bog areas. Others lead from visitor facilities at Long Beach, to more remote beaches, past salmon streams, and through stands of Sitka spruce.

South Beach Trail   This short trail begins behind the Wickaninnish Centre building, the same starting point as for the Wickaninnish Trail.

From its start, the trail leads through a small Sitka spruce forest, with the trees shaped by the strong winds that whip this shoreline. Side trails run to the cobble beaches, with Lismer Beach in first order. A boardwalk then climbs across the headland toward South Beach. There are wonderful views of Wickaninnish Bay and Lismer Beach from this height, with the trailside vegetation including salal and salmonberry. After passing the Wickaninnish Trail turnoff, the trail continues to the right, with more boardwalk and stands of Sitka spruce and western hemlock. After arriving at the pebble beach, look to the right to view the storm surges through the double sea arch. The south end of South Beach provides some quieter water in a little finger inlet.

Wickaninnish Trail   The main trailhead is beside the Wickaninnish Centre building. Park in the parking lot, a little over a mile from the Tofino-Ucluelet Road (leaving enough cash in the parking machine to cover your walk, or the entire day). The eastern trailhead is at the Florencia Bay parking lot. To get there, take the park road that leads south, off the Wickaninnish Centre access road, about halfway from the Tofino-Ucluelet Road.

The one-way hike is 2.5 kilometers (0.9 mile) long, and runs from the Wickaninnish Centre parking lot (behind the building). Take the first part of the South Beach Trail and take the Wickaninnish Trail turnoff.

You may be able to see the old log corduroy surface on a small part of the route. It passes a sphagnum bog with a border of shorepine trees, some of which are hundreds of years old, but rarely taller than 9 or 10 feet.

Willowbrae Trail   Willowbrae Road connects with the Tofino-Ucluelet Road, 4.8 kilometers (2.6 miles) south of the Highway 4–Port Alberni junction. Drive down Willowbrae Road, approaching the park boundary, where you'll find a small parking lot. The first part of the trail is outside the park.

This short trail (1.4 kilometers or 0.8 mile) is another part of the original foot trail between the two villages. The route—commonly walked until 1942, when the highway was completed—was about 30 miles long, including 10 miles (16 kilometers) of beach. Stay on a straight course, and you'll continue through the forest to arrive soon at the southeast end of Florencia Bay.

Spruce Fringe Trail   The trailhead is at the western edge of the Comber's Beach parking lot. To get there, drive along the Tofino-Ucluelet Road, toward Tofino (north), and turn left onto the park access road. There is a nature exhibit beside the parking lot.

This is a fine loop trail from which to observe the Sitka spruce fringe environment, a mixture of beach edge, piles of logs, and lots of salal. The fringe extends only about 200 meters (600 feet) inland from the beach. Look for pockets of moss and lichen attracted to the tree bark.

Schooner Trail The northern trailhead is located on the Tofino-Ucluelet Road (Highway 4) north of Green Point Campground, heading west and then south to approach the northwestern end of Long Beach. Another short trail, the route leads through two forest zones before reaching the beach. The larger island, just off the beach (at the point) is Box Island. Follow the beach to the right of the trailhead—past the island—and you'll arrive at Schooner Cove.

Shoreline Bog Trail The trailhead is just off the entrance road to Wickaninnish Beach and the museum. Drive along this park road to a parking area located a short distance beyond the Florencia Bay turnoff.

This loop trail leads along boardwalks, for a walk of less than 0.8 kilometer (0.5 mile). This is a self-guiding trail with interpretive posts. Trail brochures are available at the trailhead.

Most of the trees are shorepine. Peat moss grows throughout the bog, separated by little hills or hummocks where you'll see hemlock, red cedar, and yellow cedar.

Rain Forest Trails Trailheads are located on the Tofino-Ucluelet Road, 6.4 kilometers (4 miles) northwest of the park information center. There's a parking lot at which signs direct you to the two trailheads.

Two trailheads are at the start of two separate loop walks. These are both self-guiding, with markers explaining the forest features. Each trail is 1 kilometer (0.6 mile) long.

While leading through the same old-growth rain forest, the interpretation is different on each trail. Loop A focuses on the forest cycle. Loop B interprets forest structure and inhabitants. You'll find tall western hemlock, red cedar, and amabilis fir. Moss gardens hang from tree crevices, making a base for many ferns and conifer seedlings. This is a great place for bird-watching, with kinglets, chickadees, and other songbirds in attendance.

Gold Mine Trail The trailhead is located on Highway 4 (Tofino-Ucluelet Road), 1 kilometer (0.6 mile) west of the park information center. Cutting across the park between the highway and Florencia Bay, the route, which is 1.5 kilometers (one mile) leads from the highway to the beach where gold mining took place during the early 1900s.

This is an area that definitely suffered at the hands of logging operations, which began here in the 1950s. The original miners' trail was widened for logging. This area was replanted with Douglas fir and Sitka spruce, not the original trees found here. However, the original red cedar, amabilis fir, and western hemlock have managed to regenerate.

BROKEN GROUP ISLANDS

Sitting at the verge where Barkley Sound meets the Pacific Ocean is a boater's paradise: the Broken Group Islands. This small, rocky archipelago provides a wide range of coastal scenes including sandy beaches, tide pools, caves, surge channels, and quiet anchorages in sheltered bays between the islands. The islands offer an overwhelming sense of peace and oneness with nature that is available in few other places. Part of the Pacific Rim National Park Reserve, the islands are uninhabited by humans, except for the campers who find their way to the archipelago during the summer months.

The islands lie south of the park's Long Beach Unit and Ucluelet. To the southeast is the small port village of Bamfield. To the east of the islands is Barkley Sound, a long inlet, and the town of Port Alberni. Boat trips to the Broken Group are available from all three communities. They are also accessible by motor and sailboats, from Bamfield or Ucluelet, although the waters can be rough enough to make canoeing and kayaking to the islands very risky. Better to take a larger commercial boat to the islands and launch your canoe in the more sheltered waters.

The quiet nature of the islands wasn't always so. The *Nuu-chah-nulth* lived on several islands before the arrival of Europeans in the region. Then, exploring mariners arrived on the islands, followed by miners, traders, and others who came to escape the stress of civilization. Hermits could really be hermits in this secluded archipelago. Habitation has been forbidden since the creation of the park, except on Nettle, Keith, and Effingham Islands. These reservations are closed to the public. Pets are not permitted on any of the islands.

With more than 100 islands, some no larger than large rocks poking out of the sea, the group is a haven for many species of marine life including sea lions, seals, whales, and porpoises.

The tide pools are filled with seashell creatures and other marine life.

The superabundant marine life found in the group is the result of a deep ocean trench lying just off Vancouver Island's continental shelf. Much like Monterey Bay, the Pacific trench generates huge upwellings of nutrients, creating a home for plankton, which in turn nurture the marine creatures. Birds too are a part of island life, nesting in the many caves and surge channels.

Camping is permitted on several islands, but only in eight designated campsites. The easier places to reach by boat are Gibralter, Dodd, and Willis Islands. Skilled boaters could succeed at getting ashore on Gilbert, Benson, and Clarke Islands. The ship *Lady Rose* sails daily from Port Alberni, landing on Gibraltar Island as well as at the town of Bamfield. Toquart Bay, accessible via a logging road, is also a gateway to the islands for private boats. The waters of Barkley Sound are studded with reefs, and morning fog often shrouds the islands. The islands are rugged, with few beaches or tidal flats, but there are sheltered inlets at Hand, Gibraltar, and Jacques Islands. For those with larger boats, protected anchorages are available in Effingham Bay and in the bay between Dodd, Willis, and Turtle Islands.

The Broken Group has recently become a mecca for divers. Several shipwrecks lie between the islands, although these wooden ships have become unstable over the past century or two. The marine life alone is reason enough to bring your diving gear.

Anyone wishing to explore the waters of the Broken Group should be sure to obtain Marine Chart 3670, available at marinas and outdoor supply stores in the nearby towns. The chart may also be purchased ($8 at last report) from the Canadian Hydrographic Service, 9860 West Saanich Road, Box 6000, Sidney, B.C. V8L 4B2. Tide tables should also be used. Use the tide table for Tofino, found in Volume 6, "Canadian Tide and Current Tables," usually obtained at the same places. Another handy reference is the "Small Craft Guide–Volume One," published by the Canadian Coast Guard.

Because of the fragility of the islands' surfaces, some park etiquette should be observed. Visitors are asked not to build fires or create new paths across the islands. Camp stoves are suggested. For health reasons, the harvesting and eating of shell-fish is not permitted, and visitors are warned not to eat clams, mussels, and oysters, which may be affected by red tide in Barkley Sound.

The growing interest in the islands, with a recent increase in summer visitors, has caused Parks Canada to consider the possibility of rationing visits. We suggest that you write for full information on the Broken Group to: Superintendent, Pacific Rim National Park Reserve, Box 280, Ucluelet, B.C. V0R 3A0, or call the year-round park information office at (604) 726-7721. The seasonal information center at Long Beach is open from mid-March to mid-October; call (604) 726-4212.

WEST COAST TRAIL

Regarded by outdoor sport authorities as one of the more challenging hiking trails in the world, Canada's West Coast Trail provides not only the physical obstacles expected on a 77-kilometer (48-mile) hike, but it also puts the hiker in the midst of spectacular coastal landscape on a primitive seafront striated with several deep inlets, narrow creek canyons, waterfalls tumbling to the ocean beaches, and—best of all—walking through and beside a primal west coast rainforest.

The path is so fraught with interruptions in the shoreline by canyons and other geological obstructions that five cable cars are used to cross the most difficult of them. In addition, there is extensive beach-walking and beach-camping, requiring a knowledge of tide movements and an intuitive sense of place.

It was established during the 1800s as a lifesaving trail. Because of the strong winds and high surf that pound this rugged part of Vancouver Island and because of the isolation of the area, a trail was necessary for shipwrecked mariners whose ships foundered off the coast. It served that purpose for more than a hundred years.

When Pacific Rim National Park was created in 1970, the strip of beach and forest surrounding the trail was included in the park. Work began on trail reconstruction for hikers during the 1970s and was completed for hiking in 1980. Most people take five or six days or longer to hike the full length of the trail. It provides a rugged experience, testing one's self-sufficiency. It is not a recommended experience for neophyte hikers. Experienced hikers will be challenged and overcome by the intense natural beauty as the trail skirts the ocean: crashing surf, majestic inlets, and a seemingly unending panorama of wildlife, old-growth and newer forests, craggy landscape, and pristine beaches, both sand and cobble.

This trail is so popular, particularly among overseas hikers who come here just to walk the trail, that there is a daily limit placed by Parks Canada on the number of people setting out on the hike. Reservations are made months in advance, and you're as likely to see and camp beside visitors from England, Germany, and Australia as you are to meet Americans and Canadians.

Access and Preparation   The northern trailhead is located at Pachena Bay, five kilometers (three miles) from the village of Bamfield, on Barkley Sound. The southern trailhead is across the San Juan River from Port Renfrew, near the southeastern tip of the island. Hikers arrive at Bamfield by car, via a 60-kilometer (37-mile) logging road from Port Alberni, or by taking the *MV Lady Rose*, an old but fascinating coastal freighter that sails from Port Alberni around Barkley Sound each day except Monday. For information on the ship's schedule, call 800-663-7192. Port Renfrew is reached by car from Victoria via Highway 14 or over logging roads from the resort community of Lake Cowichan. You may wish to use bus services to travel to and/or from the trailhead towns.

Two other boat rides must be taken to access the trail. A boat service at the southern approach is operated by Trailhead Charters, with four boats a day from the government dock in Port Renfrew. The recent cost was $10 per person. Another short boat ride is necessary to cross Nitinat Narrows ($5). Service is frequent, and the wait at the narrows offers pleasant rest.

There are trail information centers at each end. The southern information office is just outside Port Renfrew. The northern one is a short distance along the trail from the trailhead near Bamfield. Not only must hikers have reservations for entry to the trail, but they should be completely prepared for the hike, including obtaining a detailed trail guide, tide tables, and a supply of food and camping supplies sufficient for a 10-day experience. An essential piece of information is the West Coast Trail map, published by Parks Canada. It is available at park information centers, along with other books and maps including tide tables. An excellent, detailed guide is the Sierra Club book,

The West Coast Trail and Nitinat Lakes. This book is available in bookstores in Victoria and Vancouver.

Parks Canada has established an $85 per-person fee for the hike. That fee, and the $15 in necessary boat transportation costs, is all you need once you're at the trailhead. Only 26 people are permitted to enter the trail daily from each end. Up-to-date trail information should be obtained a day or two before your scheduled hike. Call the Port Renfrew information center at (604) 647-5434, or the Bamfield information center at (604) 728-3234. If you wish to hike the trail and do not have an advance reservation, calling either of these numbers will enable you to find out how many days' wait is needed if there isn't an immediate vacancy on the list. June and September days are usually underbooked, and most hikers can hike the trail without reservation. It does pay to check in advance to avoid days on which there are groups passing through the trailheads.

The Trail From which trailhead should you start the trip? This is the first decision to make. The most difficult terrain is at the southern end, near Port Renfrew. So it would make sense for the less-experienced hiker to begin from the Bamfield trailhead and use the first few days to gather strength and confidence. On the other hand, starting from Port Renfrew puts one immediately into marvelous scenery, and it serves well as a test for those who might not be able to survive the complete route.

Those people with limited time and no inclination to do the most difficult parts will often walk from the northern trailhead to Nitinat Narrows and then retrace their steps to Bamfield.

Our description of the trail, which follows, begins at Port Renfrew, choosing the rigorous route. Should you wish to start with a milder walk for three or four days, the Parks Canada trail map will help you translate the reverse route.

The Hike The journey begins, not with walking, but with a short $10 boat ride to the trailhead. The first 4.8 kilometers (3 miles) of trail leads to Thrasher Cove, skirting Pandora Peak by following the hillside, and across Logjam Creek. A short distance past the creek is the real start of the trail, as the trail descends toward the beach. There's a tall ladder taking you down to Thrasher Cove, across the inlet from Port Renfrew. The beach is a natural overnight camping spot for those who start fairly late in the day.

Low tide is best for traveling the next stretch (along the shoreline), instead of climbing the 101 ladder rungs. The trail moves inland for this portion until it meets the sea beyond Owen Point. The seaside walk along the rocky ledges and some beach is a scenic delight. The trail, now heading north, enters a mixed spruce/fir/hemlock forest before entering the rainforest—a rich ecosystem with a boggy floor covered with skunk cabbage. This is not just a trail wandering up and down and through the woods. There are boardwalks, ladders, bridges, and a campsite in the forest. The first cable car is encountered at Camper Bay. The five cable cars are hand-operated devices. There's another campsite at the mouth of Camper Creek, five miles from the trailhead. This is a good place to stay if you have left Port Renfrew in the morning.

The next part of the route is the reason some people start at the other end. The trail wanders up and down through the wet forest, with tree roots lying over the trail. The next cable car crosses Cullite Creek, after descending on ladders. There's another ladder to climb, on the western side of the creek. The trail proceeds through the forest, including a boardwalk section, leading across a bog, with beautiful ferns on each side.

The trail descends from the bog to Logan Creek, with a campsite on the beach at the west side of the creek mouth. From here, at the lowest tides, it's possible to walk along the shoreline, across the mouth of Adrenaline Creek (waterfall), to Walbran Creek. The much safer inland trail runs above the shore on a moderate route. Logan Creek is crossed on an exciting suspension bridge, with a narrow board path and steel mesh sides. The views are spectacular. Once again, the rain forest and its bogs make for some fairly heavy slogging, and frequent rests are called for.

From Walbran Creek, the trail leads along the beach for 18 miles. Much of the walk can be done along the rock shelf, taking less energy than walking on the beach, but high tides necessitate taking the beach route.

The next major point of reference is the Carmanah Lighthouse (20 miles from the southern trailhead), seen after the trail crosses Bonilla and Carmanagh Creeks and passes the seastacks off Bonilla Point. The scenery here is awesome. Another waterfall cascades to the sea at Bonilla Creek. The forest on both sides of Carmanah Creek is Carmanah Pacific

Provincial Park, an area protected following years of angry disputes between logging companies and B.C. preservationists. The outstanding feature of the park is the Carmanah Giant, a huge Sitka spruce—312 feet high and Canada's tallest tree. The interior of the park is reached from the north, on a forest road.

West of the lighthouse is Swing Beach, an area of tide pools containing hundreds of intertidal species. The rocks here are resting places for Steller's and California sea lions. The trail leads along a cliff, and when you reach the beach at Dare Point, you'll be at the halfway point of the hike. Campsites are frequent in this area. Clo-oose, south of Nitinat Narrows, is in what was Nitinat country—a settlement for hardy Europeans that included a trading post. There was a fish packing plant at what is now called Cannery Bay, but it closed in the 1920s. The community of Clo-oose declined, and all but a few homeowners were gone by the early 1960s. The trail leads inland beside the narrows. A $5 boat ride takes you across the inlet, with 20 miles of trail remaining. There is often a logjam of hikers waiting to get across the narrows. The native boat operation shuttles back and forth, and hikers have the opportunity to rest at the dock and discuss the adventure with other hikers while waiting.

There is camping on the beach, beyond the narrows. More sheltered campsites (including wooded spots and caves) are available along the trail, slightly inland at Tsusiat Point.

Hole-in-the-Wall is a sea arch. It's possible to walk (or run) through the arch when the ocean is at low tide.

Perhaps the most beautiful sight along the route is Tsusiat Falls, where the water drops in a silken shimmer (for four stories) to the beach. This is a favorite camping spot. The trail crosses the river above the falls, but anyone walking the route *must* walk down to the beach to see this splendid scene. *Tsusiat* is the local word for "where the water always runs down." The trail is on a boardwalk and then on a cliff approaching the Klanawa River. This is an absolutely beautiful and wide stream, which is crossed in a cable car. To the west are the Valencia Bluffs, the scene of a seafaring disaster that saw the steamer *Valencia* go aground in 1906, with more than 125 lives lost. While the wreckage of the *Valencia* is not seen today, another famous disaster, that of the *Janet Cowan,* can be seen near the mouth of Billy Goat Creek, which plunges to the sea in a waterfall. The falls are said to look like the beard of a billy goat.

The final cable car on the route is taken across the Darling River. To the west is Pachina Point and the Pachina Lighthouse. In 1907, following the sinking of the *Valencia,* a wagon road was built from Bamfield to Pachina Point, and the lighthouse was constructed. The trail runs along this old road for the rest of the trip—a relaxing jaunt after what has been crossed.

Crossing Clonard Creek, the trail comes to an end. Trails lead to Pachena Beach, a camping spot for tired hikers finishing the journey and for people about to set out the next morning. Bamfield is a few miles away, with lodgings, dining, and other welcome amenities.

Some Final Advice   The West Coast Trail may be walked in five or six days, but you'll see very little but the oncoming path. At least eight days are necessary to begin to appreciate the natural environment of the coast, and 10 days is far better to capture the complete experience. A major reason to budget for a few extra days is the fickle weather along the island's west coast. Dense fog blankets the shoreline and, even during the warmest summer months, the chill can cause discomfort or even hypothermia if hot soup or cocoa is not used to warm the insides.

While the great majority of hikers are able to walk the trail without injury, people do slip and fall while negotiating the route, which includes ladders and boardwalks. Bones are broken and fingers are sprained. Others, without sufficient hiking experience, fail to make the grade and have to stop. Hikers who are seriously hurt have to be transported from the trail on an average of one person every other day. Some are taken by helicopter, and others are shipped by boat. Hikers are expected to stop to assist fallen comrades. The parks people ask that injured hikers attempt to reach (from north to south) Pachena Light Station, Tsocowis Creek, Nitinat Narrows, Carmanah Light Station, Logan Creek, Cullite Cove, Camper Bay, or Thrasher Cove. Other hikers can take messages to the nearest ranger.

Pets are not allowed, and hikers should be aware that the resident wildlife includes bears. The black bear is best encountered by standing up straight while looking at the animal, and backing up slowly to get out of its path. Bears (and cougars) are most active around the trail at dawn and dusk. It's always a good idea to set up camp well before dusk, and to strike camp after dawn (another reason to take a few extra days to do the trek. Shellfish should not be eaten, because of red tide dangers.

After all these cautions, I should stress that most hikers negotiate the trail with only natural encounters, without injury or wild animal scares. The secret is in taking the time necessary to make the hike a successful and safe trip.

Taking sufficient food is an absolute must. Don't expect to live, or even survive, off the salmon or halibut you'll catch along the route. There are plenty of fish in the sea, but beach fishing is rarely successful, and fishing the several rivers is not much better. Take lots of dried and prepared freeze-dried food, plus a good supply of drink mixes (coffee, tea, cocoa, soup) and all the other usual hiking supplies including toilet paper, a small camp stove if possible, and the lightest tent and gear possible. It all has to go on your back. Golf carts are not permitted!

The proper observance of normal hiking rules will get you through the trip. The walk will be life-changing, an experience you'll remember forever. Good hiking!

Strathcona Provincial Park

This large park, mainly forested, lies across the middle of Vancouver Island like a cummerbund. The first park area in the province, Strathcona saw its share of mining operations, and then logging, during the 19th and early 20th centuries. It doesn't quite touch either coast, yet it is reached within 15-minute drives from the shores of Georgia Strait and the Island Highway, and from the Pacific coast resource town of Gold River. With more than a half-million acres (210,000 hectares), this is a very impressive spread of mountains, lakes, rivers, and creeks.

There are two major accessible areas within the park, with the rest reached by backcountry trails. Buttle Lake, in the park's midsection, offers camping, nature trails, backcountry trailheads, and water recreation. Forbidden Plateau, to the south, is a high area of meadows and lakes, with swimming, nature study, fishing, and backcountry hiking, plus a ski area.

In both easy-to-reach areas, you'll be impressed by the variety of wildflowers (heather, phlox, Indian paintbrush, and violets, among many others) and wildlife, including Roosevelt (western) elk, coast black-tailed deer, and more than 150 bird species. While bears, cougars, and wolves live in the park, they are rarely seen, except on backpacking expeditions deep into the forests.

The dominant geological feature in the park is the Golden Hinde, Vancouver Island's highest peak, at an elevation of 2,200 meters (7,218 feet).

HOW TO GET THERE

Forbidden Plateau is accessed from the town of Courtenay and the Island Highway (Highway 19) by taking Forbidden Plateau Road, which leads west for 12 miles, ending at the ski area.

The Buttle Lake area is reached by driving to the town of Campbell River (north of Courtenay), via Highway 19, and then turning west onto Highway 29. The road follows the route of the Campbell River, coming to a fork at the north end of Buttle Lake. Highway 29 is the right fork, continuing west through the park to reach Muchalat Inlet on Nootka Sound and the town of Gold River. The left fork runs down the east side of Buttle Lake, past several picnic areas, to a campground and a dozen trails, many of which lead to backcountry campsites.

PARK GEOLOGY

Three hundred and eighty million years ago, there was no Vancouver Island. Instead, the great sea covered the region, lapping against the land mass far to the east. Then, three periods of volcanic eruption built a new land mass, called Wrangellia, emerging from under the ocean as a series of mountain ranges stretching from southern Vancouver Island through the present Queen Charlotte Islands, and continuing far north through southeastern Alaska to the Yukon.

Today, the noticeable parts of this region, the Wrangellian terrane, consists of a line of islands and mountain ranges that are among the most scenic regions of western North America. The region is awash with deep inlets, primal rivers, and high waterfalls, with green conifer forests.

The islands were created during the Devonian Period, over a span of more than 200 million years. The rocks from these ancient volcanoes are found in layers about 2,000 meters (6,500 feet) deep, composed of basalt, andesite, and some rhyolite. A result of the first volcanic eruptions, ending 360 million years ago, is seen as the upper layer in Strathcona Park. The Flower Ridge

Formation is composed primarily of basalt and volcanic tuff, containing deposits of fine quartz crystals. This rock structure is seen on ridges beside Buttle Lake and along road cuts on the hill at the south end of Buttle Lake and also on the trail to Myra Falls.

A second series of Triassic Period eruptions (ending 230 million years ago) flowed over the ocean floor through fault lines, resulting in a large, shallow submarine plateau. These basalt flows, about 6,500 meters (21,000 feet) thick, have formed the most common rock layer in the park. The lowest of three rock formations from this period has not only formed reddish-brown dome-shaped peaks but also appears as pillow-shaped lava rock. Above the pillows is a layer of breccia, broken rock consisting of lava fragments and shattered pillows not readily apparent when traveling on the park roads. The huge layer left by the basalt flow can be seen along the Crest Mountain Trail, on Forbidden Plateau—on the trail to Mount Albert Edward—and in the Beg Den Conservancy, north of the Gold River Road.

The final volcanic period occurred to about 180 million years ago, explosive times during the Jurassic Period, when deposits of andesite and rhyolite breccias formed other islands. There is some evidence of this rock outside the park, but the major effect of this period was to create the long crescent of islands stretching from this area north along the Pacific Rim.

Then came the ice ages, from one million to ten thousand years ago, bringing glaciers that scoured the mountains after covering the islands several times, grinding down the mountains to jagged peaks and creating large U-shaped valleys. The climate began warming about 13,000 years ago, with the ice receding until only a few glaciers exist today, including the Cliffe and Comox Glaciers. During this period, the glacier-fed streams were created, with large deposits of sand, mud, and gravel deposited in the valleys.

One of the outcomes of all this volcanic activity has been the creation of huge deposits of valuable minerals in the area of the park. Surrounded by parkland, the huge Strathcona Westmin area is the site of the Myra Falls mine, the latest in a series of copper/lead/zinc mines that have operated in this area since 1917. The HWW Mine was opened in 1985. The mining operation is subject to park supervision, creating a situation where the Parks Canada specifies and monitors environmental protection procedures. Mine tours are a popular attraction for park visitors, and the area includes several prime hiking trails.

Paleontologists are fascinated by the fossils found in the park, the most common being crinoids, relatives of sea cucumbers and starfish. These are found as doughnut-shaped fragments in the Buttle Lake limestone, particularly at Marble Meadows. Other apparent fossilized animals (called moss animals) are bryozoans, formed of branching or fanlike growths.

If you're interested in geology and the history of the rock of the region, ask the park rangers for the superb map and guide titled "Geological Guide to Strathcona Provincial Park." If only other parks, including the Grand Canyon, had a geological guide this comprehensive and handy.

PARK WILDLIFE

The island's isolation from the mainland forests has not only prohibited several major mainland species of animals from populating the island but has resulted in a difference between some island and mainland species. Grizzly bears, foxes, coyotes, porcupines, and chipmunks are not seen on Vancouver Island. On the other hand, the park has a thriving population of black-tailed deer and Roosevelt elk. These, plus the wolf and marmot, bear differing characteristics from their mainland cousins. Like the wolves, the resident cougars are seldom seen. Black bears and their signals are not often seen, except in heavily wooded areas— through scat sightings and very scattered personal appearances.

With no coastal boundaries, the bird population is restricted mainly to songbirds and jays. Gray and Steller's jays are here in good numbers, with the loudest voices. Also seen frequently are the band-tailed pigeon, kinglet, winter wren, red-breasted nuthatch, and the chestnut-backed chickadee. There is a scanty supply of white-tailed ptarmigan.

The coastal forest spreads throughout most of the park, containing western red cedar, Douglas fir, grand fir, western hemlock, and amabilis (balsam) fir. This is the typical Vancouver Island mountain forest. Below the solid conifer range is the subalpine zone with creeping juniper, mountain hemlock, and subalpine fir. The Forbidden Plateau is a fine place to experience the subalpine ecosystem. This area is also blessed with a supreme exhibit of wildflowers including Indian paintbrush, heather, lupine, violets, and monkeyflowers, as well as moss campion and phlox. Some of the park forests have been subject to logging. Most areas have been reforested with conifers, although some areas apparent on hikes on Forbidden Plateau and the Buttle Lake area have been left to successfully reseed and develop without replanting.

STRATHCONA ATTRACTIONS

Buttle Lake Area   One of two areas in the park where you'll find visitor facilities, the area centered on Buttle Lake offers hiking trails, water recreation, camping, and scenic wonders. The main access route from the east and west is Provincial Highway 28, which leads from Campbell River (on the east coast) to the town of Gold River (on Machalat Inlet, a long spur of water extending from Nootka Sound). A paved park road leads south from Highway 28 along the eastern shore of Buttle Lake, leading to camping areas on the south end of the lake, as well as to Myra Creek and the Westmin mining operation. Along this route are a number of steep streams and waterfalls. The most impressive of these is Myra Falls, found on the west side of Buttle Lake near the south end. Rising above the western shore of the lake are several prominent peaks, including Mount McBride, Marble Peak, Mount Phillips, and Mount Myra. The Golden Hinde, the highest peak on Vancouver Island, dominates the area around Buttle Lake.

Just beyond the Buttle Lake road turnoff, on Highway 28, is the Buttle Lake Campground—a scenic site with developed campsites. The highway crosses a narrows at this point. For those with boats or canoes, four marine campgrounds are located on the west shore of the lake, each with a few tenting sites. Titus Campground and Wolf River Campground are located on either side of the mouth of Wolf River. These are the more northern marine campsites. Farther to the south are Marble Rock and Phillips Creek Campgrounds.

Four picnic areas are located at scenic points along the road on the eastern shore. There's a short nature trail at the Lupin Falls picnic area, with other short trails at the Karst Creek and Ralph River turnoffs.

Myra Falls is found inside the Strathcona-Westmin area, after the road curves around the south end of Buttle Lake. A primitive campsite is at the end of the Phillips Ridge Trail, reached from the parking lot of Westmin Resources. Other trails accessed within the Westmin area include the Upper Myra Falls Trail (a second waterfall on this creek), Tennant Lake Trail, and trails that lead along Thelwood Creek (to Bedwell Lake) and Price Creek (to Crown Lake).

For those with but a short time to spend in the park, the Lady Falls trail offers a 10-minute walk up a hillside to a viewing platform, offering a superb view of the falls that seems to pour out of the rocks, dropping to a pool on the floor of a chasm. Conifers (mostly twisted cedars) cling for dear life to the sides of the canyon walls.

There are no indoor accommodations inside the park boundaries. Just outside the park, on the route from Campbell River, is Strathcona Park Lodge. This is both a lodge for overnight guests and an outdoor education center. Sitting on Upper Campbell Lake, the lodge offers accommodations packages for adults and family groups. It has become a favorite place for honeymooners who enjoy the quiet environment and the availability of canoeing and other outdoor recreation, plus food in a buffet, family-style setting. Rooms range from a penthouse to standard lodge rooms and several cabins that offer lake views and privacy. A minimum stay (of two or three nights, depending on the season) is required for cabin and large-group facilities. Motor boat, sailboat, canoe, and kayak rentals are available, with private instruction at an additional cost. The lodge's Family Adventure package (in August) includes five nights with food and outdoor activities including a canoe excursion, orienteering, rock climbing, evening social and campfire, and optional overnight camping with cookout.

Forbidden Plateau   The plateau forms an eastern finger extending from the eastern edge of the park. This area of 50,600 acres is reached by taking Forbidden Plateau Road, off Highway 19 from the town of Courtenay. While its name may seem cause for concern, it is a welcoming place today. The area received its name from a legend that evil spirits controlled the plateau, consuming women and children who went to the area. This is truly a wonderful area of subalpine landscape, filled with wildflowers in the spring, with small fishing lakes and meadows that offer views of the high, rugged peaks, glaciers, and forests. To the east are the farming areas of the Comox Valley and the waters of the Strait of Georgia.

Campsites, most with tent pads, are located at Lake Helen MacKenzie, Kwai, Circlet, and McKenzie-Douglas Lakes. Campfires are prohibited. Campers should pack camp stoves.

On the way into the park is the Wood Mountain Ski Area, a facility with lodges and dining facilities. By taking a northern spur road before entering the plateau parkland, you'll drive to the Mount Washington Ski Area, featuring the island's highest ski terrain and its longest runs. The water in the lakes with campgrounds is suitable for drinking with one caution: Water should be boiled before drinking. Campers should be aware that black bears may be in the vicinity of these camping areas. Pack sack hangers are provided at the designated campgrounds.

Della Falls   The highest waterfall on the island, and one of the highest in Canada with a drop of 400 meters (1,444 feet), Della Falls is in the southern end of the park. The falls must be reached from the north end of Great Central Lake, outside the park boundary. A hiking trail leads to the falls. Ark Resort, a commercial operation with tenting and RV sites, serves visitors with boat rides up the lake and also offers guided hikes to the falls. You may rent a canoe or power boat for the trip to the Delta Falls trailhead. A boat ramp and moorage for your own boat are available. For information and rates, call (604) 723-2657. Reservations require a deposit. The resort is at the south end of Great Central Lake, reached by driving west on Highway 6 from Parksville.

Strathcona Day-Hikes

Lady Falls Trail   Ten minutes' walk from the trailhead beside Highway 28. Lady Falls seems to flow out of a huge rock outcropping, and then it plunges some 200 feet to a pool, creating a constant mist. A viewing platform is located across the chasm. This is a pleasant and easy walk from the highway, up an incline through a mixed forest. The trailhead is found west of the Buttle Lake Campground as the highway proceeds toward Gold River.

Lupin Falls Loop Trail   Located eight kilometers (five miles) south of the Buttle Lake Parkway turnoff, this trail is found across the parkway from a picnic area. It leads through a forest of large trees and open spaces, with a fine display of shrubs and wildflowers on the forest floor. The complete walk to the falls and return will take about 20 minutes.

Auger Point Loop Trail   This short trail shows the effects of forest fires and offers a good look at a forest in a state of regeneration. It takes no longer than five minutes to walk this interpretive route, found a little more than midway down the Buttle Lake Parkway, south of the junction with Highway 28. There's a picnic area at Auger Point.

Karst Creek Loop Trail   This leads from the Buttle Lake Parkway, south of the Auger Point picnic area and trail. There is another picnic area, with swimming and a boat ramp, near the Karst Creek trailhead. The hike will take you through a fascinating piece of limestone geology, including waterfalls, sinkholes, and creeks that disappear into the ground. The loop trail climbs into the limestone area and then descends to the valley floor for the return to the day-use area. You should budget about an hour for this 2-kilometer (1.2-mile) trail.

Shepherd Creek Loop Trail   Only 2 kilometers (1.2 miles) long, the trail wonders through untouched forest on an easy, level route. The Ralph River Campground is located near the south end of Buttle Lake, on the east side, between the Buttle Lake Parkway and the lake.

Myra Falls Trail   One of two falls on Myra Creek, the lower falls are reached from a parking area near the south end of Buttle Lake. The hike, less than one kilometer (one mile) round trip, leads up a fairly steep hill, offering several views of the falls.

Upper Myra Falls Trail   This hike leads from the Westmin Resources parking lot at the west end of the mining operation and is 3 kilometers (1.9 miles) long. This is an easy, level route (165-foot elevation change), running through old-growth forest, to a lookout.

Phillips Ridge Trail   A four-hour hike from the Westmin Resources parking lot leads to pleasant meadows and Arnica Lake. The return trip covers about 6 kilometers (3.7 miles), with an elevation change of about 600 meters (2,000 feet). There's a primitive campground at the end of the trail, beside the lake. Less than a mile from the trailhead is a small waterfall and rest area.

Mount Becher Trail   One of several trails in the Forbidden Plateau area, this hike takes about two hours and about 4.5 kilometers (2.8 miles) of walking. The trail begins at the Forbidden Plateau parking lot, climbing to provide great views of the Comox Valley and Georgia Strait. The elevation change is about 480 meters (1,900 feet).

Douglas–McKenzie Lakes Trail   Covering nine kilometers (six miles) in about three hours, this route also begins at the Forbidden Plateau parking lot and follows the main Plateau Trail. Near the two lakes, a spur trail leads north, first passing Douglas Lake and then running along the west shore of McKenzie Lake. There is good fishing available at both lakes.

Kwai Lake Trail   This longer route takes about six hours over a trip of 15 kilometers (9.3 miles). There is some climbing involved, with an elevation change of 400 meters (1,300 feet). The trail begins at the Forbidden Plateau parking lot, taking the same main Plateau Trail, past the Douglas and McKenzie Lakes turnoff, and on to Kwai Lake. Those who wish to spend some time in this lake country may like to use Myra Lake as a base for extended hiking and climbing.

Paradise Meadows Loop Trail   Accessed from the parking lot of the ski facilities at Mount Washington, this short loop trail offers a walk of 45 minutes to an hour through a prime meadow. The wildflowers are spectacular in spring. The trail departs from Nordic Lodge. Longer trails are also available from this trailhead, including walks across Forbidden Plateau to the Myra Lake area. To get to Mount Washington, take Forbidden Plateau Road from Courtenay and turn right (north) onto the spur road to the ski area.

STRATHCONA BACKCOUNTRY HIKES

The following are two of the more popular longer hikes in the park. It would be possible to spend a month or more hiking all of the backcountry trails that lead into and across the park. Several of the trails (not described in this book) are accessible only by four-wheel-drive vehicles. These include the Comox

Glacier Trail and the Gem Lake Trail. A valuable reference tool for these and other central and north island hiking routes is the book *Hiking Trails III,* published by the Vancouver Island Trails Information Society, available at bookstores in the area.

Della Falls Trail *Access:* One of the great hikes of Vancouver Island, this adventure begins with a boat ride from the south end of Great Central Lake. At the end is Della Falls, the highest waterfall in Canada, with a drop of 1,200 meters (3,936 feet). To get there, drive west from Parksville on Provincial Highway 4 toward Port Alberni. Turn north (right), near Sproat Lake Provincial Park Campground, onto Great Central Lake Road, and drive nine kilometers (six miles) to the Ark Resort. This is a campground with boat ramp and other services, including boat rides up the lake to the Della Falls trailhead. The boat trip is about 35 kilometers (20 miles). The trailhead is near a small cabin. For boat and canoe rentals and information on the resort's boat service, call (604) 723-2657, or write Ark Resort, RR #3, Site 306, C-1, Great Central Lake, B.C. V9Y 7L7. Float plane rides to the trailhead are available from Walt Air Services at (604) 338-0771.

The Trail: The trail to the falls is 16 kilometers (10 miles) long, and a walk of six to eight hours (one way). If you're canoeing up the lake, you should add two days to the trip. Originally a trapping trail, the route was later used for logging and mining in the area. The first half of the walk is an easy, fairly level route, using the old logging road. It then becomes slightly more difficult (after crossing Drinkwater Creek on a suspension bridge) and then somewhat strenuous after the second suspension bridge. The views of the high, delicate falls are worth the expense of energy. The elevation change is about 520 meters (1,800 feet). Camping is permitted at Margaret Creek and at the second Drinkwater Creek suspension bridge. There are designated campsites at the end of the trail, with toilet and bear food cache.

This trail should be hikcd only after the late-spring sun has dried out the area. Flooding can make creek crossings impossible. Snow is found in June at the upper levels. Bears are common throughout the area, and secure food storage is necessary when camping. Fires are permitted but discouraged. Overnighters are urged to carry small camp stoves.

The Hike: The first 7 kilometers (4.3 miles) is easy, on a flat road bed through a mixed forest to Margaret Creek. There's a suspension bridge over the creek, and then the road climbs through old-growth forest. A bridge crosses Drinkwater Creek at 11 kilometers (6.8 miles), and the trail becomes more rough until reaching another suspension bridge at 12.5 kilometers (7.8 miles). The trail crosses a rock slide beside the creek and climbs to meet the Love Lake Trail at 15 kilometers (9.3 miles). The falls are found 1 kilometer (0.6 mile) beyond the Love Lake Trail junction after a hike through more old-growth forest. The trail is regarded as suitable for intermediate hikers.

There are wonderful views of Della Falls at several places along the trail. You may wish to hike the Love Lake Trail to catch the best views of the falls, along with other spectacular scenery including views of the "Nine Peaks" and Della Lake. The length of the Love Lake Trail (from the junction) is 5 kilometers (3.1 miles). The lake viewpoint is at 4 kilometers (2.5 miles). The Della Falls viewpoint is less than a mile from the junction. Other falls are seen along the main Della Lake Trail: Beauty Falls at 13.5 kilometers (8.3 miles) and Love Falls at 14 kilometers (8.7 miles).

There is one final "trail" (the Cliff Route) just before reaching Della Falls. The path leads to the left, over a bridge, to Della Lake. This is not an easy route, and it entails scrambling and crawling.

Bedwell Lake Trail   *Access:* From Campbell River, take Highway 28 west (toward Gold River). At 33 kilometers (20.5 miles), the highway meets the Buttle Lake Parkway before crossing the narrows. Take the parkway south, beside Buttle Lake, until reaching the south end of the lake. Turn left onto Jim Mitchell Road after crossing the Thelwood Creek Bridge. Drive another 6.8 kilometers (4.2 miles) to the trailhead. The gravel backroad can be rough and is not ploughed during winter.

The Trail: While shown here as a backcountry hike, it is possible to accomplish this as a long day-hike. The recommended trail (the earlier part of a longer trail system), is 7 kilometers (4.3 miles) long, taking from three to four hours. Baby Bedwell Lake is at about 5.5 kilometers (3.4 miles). There's an elevation change of 600 meters (2,000 feet). A toilet and information shelter are at the trailhead, and you'll find designated campsites at

Baby Bedwell Lake (10 tent platforms, with toilet and bear food cache) and at Bedwell Lake (10 tent platforms, water access, toilet, and bear cache). The trail provides access to additional routes.

The Hike: The trail begins along the valley floor, crossing through old-growth forest and passing cascading creeks before climbing steeply for almost four kilometers (three miles). After climbing 800 meters (2,600 feet), the trail enters the subalpine zone with views of the surrounding countryside. At 4.5 kilometers (2.8 miles), the route runs across a plateau, passing beside Baby Bedwell Lake and then the larger lake. The views are impressive, The second campground is found at the south end of Bedwell Lake. This is considered an intermediate trail.

The longer Bedwell River Trail is found at the end of the lake trail. Camping is not permitted outside the designated campgrounds, because of the fragile subalpine ecosystem. Fires are not permitted. There are no fish in the lakes.

If this trail isn't long enough to suit your needs, you can hike from Bedwell Lake to Cream Lake—a distance of 4.8 kilometers (3 miles) lasting between two and three hours. There are views of Della Falls before the trail reaches Cream Lake. This is for advanced hikers (class 4). You may continue farther, on the Price Creek Trail, which provides a steep descent to the Price Creek Valley. The eventual end of this trail, 8.8 kilometers (5.3 miles) from Cream Lake, is the Price Creek trailhead, near the Thelwood Creek Bridge. Camping is permitted at Cream Lake, although it is discouraged.

STRATHCONA PARK CAMPING

Developed campgrounds are found in the Buttle Lake area. The Buttle Lake Campground (off Highway 28) has 85 sites, suitable for RVs, trailers, and tents. Water, toilets, and firewood are available. This is a scenic site, overlooking the lake at its north end. The other camping area is the Ralph River Campground, also suitable for RVs and tents, with 76 units, toilets, drinking water, and firewood. This campground is located closer to the south end of Buttle Lake, accessed by the Buttle Lake Parkway.

There are many backcountry campsites on the park trails, some located next to subalpine lakes. Generally, backcountry hikers are permitted to camp 1 kilometer (0.6 mile) from main roads or in some areas at designated sites.

There are four marine camping areas on the western shore of Buttle Lake, and another on Rainbow Island near the eastern shore of Buttle Lake, just south of the narrows and immediately south of a boat ramp and picnic area. This area is directly across the lake from the Buttle Lake Campground.

Cape Scott Provincial Park

The northwestern tip of Vancouver Island is a wonderfully wild place, with wide sand beaches along the northern stretch; long ocean inlets on the western, Pacific side; and one of the world's finest temperate rain forests in the southern portion of the park. This is a wilderness of spectacular proportions, in an area so far from the beaten track that it takes a two-hour drive along logging roads to reach the park's edge. From the park boundary, it takes a hike of 24 kilometers (15 miles) to reach the northern beaches (although you can hire a boat from nearby Port Hardy to deliver you to the northern shoreline).

The Quatsino Rain Forest is bordered by San Josef Bay, a deep inlet at the southern edge of the park, Sea Otter Cove to the west, and the San Josef River, which offers canoeing and boating through the rain forest to the white sandy beaches of the bay. Three northern bights (Experiment, Nels, and Nissen) are large bays that stretch along the coastline made up of long sand beaches.

It was in this region that several early pioneer communities were established, including the Cape Scott Settlement. The settlers were Danish immigrants who homesteaded and established farms in a landscape scoured by high winds and much rain. San Josef was another settlement, with a store, church, and post office at the south end of the present-day park area. The settlers arrived in the late 1890s. By 1910, the Cape Scott Settlement had disappeared, as the settlers' extreme isolation from the outside world made it impossible to get their farm produce to consumers in the south island areas. There were no road links to the outside, and coastal steamer service had given up on the Cape Scott area. Some settlers moved to San Josef, then this community was disbanded when most moved 10 miles inland to the village of Holberg or completely out of the area.

Another settlement wave took place in the early 1910s, with people arriving from Washington state as well as the Canadian prairies and eastern provinces. There were 1,000 new settlers in 1913. World War I decimated the communities in 1917, and the landscape was again deserted.

Before the immigrants left the area, a wagon road had been constructed from the San Josef River to Cape Scott. This old road now provides a bed for the long trail across the park—between the rain forest and the beaches.

Before the settlers arrived, Cape Scott and the surrounding area had been occupied by three groups: the Tlatlasikwala, the Nakumglisala, and the Yutlinuk. The Yutlinuk, who lived on the Scott Islands, died out by the early 1800s. The other tribes amalgamated in the 1850s and moved to Hope Island, where they remained until 1954. With only 32 remaining, they moved to Quatsino Sound to join the Koskimo people. Known today as the Nahwitti, they occupy six reservations, two of which lie within Cape Scott Park.

In the end, it was the climate that caused the settlers to abandon their dreams. The weather at the top of Vancouver Island is fierce. Storms roll in off the Pacific, making winter landings difficult if not impossible. However, this same weather nurtured the rain forest and created the wild landscape that now attracts visitors from around the world. This is a place for lovers of wilderness who are prepared to spend several days or a week to fully explore the wonders of the wildest of the Vancouver Island coasts. However, it is possible to have an enjoyable one-day trip to the rain forest and the beaches of San Josef Bay.

Although not quite as drippy as the Hoh Rain Forest in Olympic National Park, the Quatsino is very wet. It receives between 150 and 200 inches of rain each year, providing ample water to flood the extensive bog areas that are crossed by a combination of bridges and boardwalks. As with the Hoh, the Quatsino has huge old-growth (and second-growth) trees, dense undergrowth of salal, ferns, and other bog plants, and rich odors.

Hot to Get There

Port Hardy, a fishing port where the Inland Passage ferry leaves for the B.C. north coast and Prince Rupert, is the largest community on what is called the north island. The town is reached by driving north from Victoria and Nanaimo on the Island Highway (19). Port Hardy is at the end of the paved highway.

There are other roads, all used by the logging industry, and one leads to the old village of Holberg and the southeastern edge of Cape Scott Provincial Park. The route between Port Hardy and the main park trailhead follows 67 kilometers (40 miles) of logging roads. The road to Holberg (NE 60) is taken from its junction with Highway 19, 4.8 kilometers (3 miles) before Part Hardy. The Holberg office of Western Forest products has an up-to-date forest recreation map, which is extremely helpful for navigating the logging roads of the area and also finding the location of forest campgrounds. From Holberg, follow the San Josef main logging road to the trailhead. A campground, provided by the forest company, is found just before reaching the trailhead parking area. Signs along the way provide directions to Cape Scott Provincial Park.

Two other logging roads lead to scenic areas and visitor facilities. The South Main Road runs south from the western end of Holberg to the port town of Winter Harbour. There's a forest campsite at the end of the road. The Ronning Main (found halfway between Holberg and the Cape Scott trailhead) leads south toward Raft Cove.

BEAR RULES

I had a late-afternoon experience, in early October, while walking the San Josef Bay Trail. The hike proved to be an object lesson in encountering, or not encountering, wildlife. Trying to cram too much activity into a day, we drove from Port Hardy to the Cape Scott trailhead in mid-afternoon, arriving at the park boundary about 4 P.M. The sun was still up but waning. The walk to San Josef Bay took about 45 minutes, and a visit to the beach took up another half-hour. Along the way we had observed several accumulations of bear scat but had paid no attention.

Now, at dusk, we had barely started along the trail to return to the car, when my companion stopped, lightly touched my arm, and whispered, "There's a bear ahead." The big black bear was no more than 12 feet away in the gathering darkness and was moving at a lumbering pace—toward us. Forgetting all that

I had learned about bear etiquette, I shouted something loud (ostensibly to scare the bear off), and we headed as fast as we could back toward the beach. After several hundred yards we stopped and headed into the nearby brush, hoping the bear had wandered off the trail. It hadn't. There it was, ambling down the trail as if it owned it. It continued along the trail and over a wooden bridge and boardwalk. Not wanting to spend the night in the park avoiding bears, we decided to take to the water and headed through the brush to the slough running beside the rain forest. Stumbling over fallen logs, walking through deep mud, ducking under more logs, we worked our way through the shallow slough for about a quarter-mile, while hearing what sounded like a bear thrashing above us in the forest.

We returned to the trail, after slogging along the slough, finding fresh mounds of bear scat before arriving at the trailhead. We managed to make the return hike in less than half the time it took us to do it on the way out—adrenaline surging and hearts pumping. Bears are largely nocturnal, a fact I had not considered before starting out too late in the day. I'll go back to walk the same trail sometime, but I'll do it while the sun is shining and when the bear is resting and not patrolling his trail.

Excitement aside, it was a handsome bear—much better looking than any seen in a zoo—fat and filled with salal berries and just about ready for a long winter's nap. I later talked to a park ranger who laughed at my adventure and said that the bear does own the trail and is seen often during evening hours. Almost always, it's enough to slowly back off the trail to permit the bear to pass. Bear rules!

CAPE SCOTT PARK TRAILS

Two trails lead from the main trailhead at the end of the San Josef main forest road. Both trails offer good day trips to and from San Josef Bay and Eric Lake. These hikes should involve little backpacking, although you may wish to pack a picnic lunch. There are no facilities (except privies) inside the park. Both trails begin by leading through the Quatsino Rain Forest. The Cape Scott Trail runs beyond the rain forest, across meadows and forest lands to the northern beaches and Cape Scott.

Cape Scott Trail *Access:* From Port Hardy, drive 4.8 kilometers (3 miles) along Highway 19 and turn left onto Road NE 60, the route to Holberg. From Holberg, continue on the San Josef Main (the logging road) to its end at the trailhead. There is a campground turnoff before reaching the trailhead. You'll find an information board at the end of the parking lot offering updated bulletins on trail and park conditions. Toilets are located at the end of a short spur trail, off the main trail, just inside the park.

The Trail: The Cape Scott Trail is 23.6 kilometers (14.7 miles) long. It begins with a walk through the rain forest. The trail will be muddy in spots, particularly during the first hour's walk through the rain forest to Eric Lake (3 kilometers or 1.9 miles). For those who begin the hike later than noon, the gravel bar at the mouth of the creek provides a good camping place. There is superior fishing and swimming in the lake. The trail continues north to end at Fisherman Bay and Nissen Bight at the northeastern corner of the park. Camping and water are available to the east, along Nissen Bight. Along the way is the turnoff (left) to Hansen Lagoon, Nels Bight, Guise Bay, and Cape Scott. More campsites are found after the crossing of Fisherman River, on Nels Bight, and on the narrows between Experiment Bight and Guise Bay.

The Hike: After the first hour of walking through the rain forest, you'll find facilities at Eric Lake, including fresh water, a toilet, and a food cache. The remains of the old community hall are found at the southern end of the lake.

The trail leads beside St. Mary's Creek, and another walk of 6.3 kilometers (4 miles) beyond the Eric Lake campsite takes you to the Fisherman River crossing (a two- to three-hour walk). There's a log bridge spanning the river. The trail continues to the north, beside St. Mary's Creek, passing a second camping area.

If your destination is Fisherman Bay or Nissen Bight (straight ahead), you may wish to spend a little time along the turnoff to Hansen Lagoon. Along this trail is what is left of the original Cape Scott Settlement, including a fallen toolshed, a rusted Caterpillar tractor, and an old wooden cart. Take the spur trail due west to reach the lagoon (actually the extension of a long sea inlet, Hansen Bay). Just past the old settlement, the main trail leads north and then west toward the end of the lagoon and on to Nels Bight, Guise Bay, and Cape Scott.

The trail to Nissen Bight continues north through boggy country with cedar and hemlock groves before reaching the ocean at Fisherman Bay (a small bay with gravel beach and wooden shipwrecks) and Nissen Bight with a small sandy beach. Reaching the ocean at this point takes about six hours of easy walking (16.4 kilometers or 10.5 miles). Between Eric Lake and Nissen Bight, and north of the Fisherman River Bridge, is the ruins of the old Donaldson farm and youth crew center.

Back at the Hansen Lagoon turnoff, the main trail leads west, through the old Cape Scott Settlement. A side trail continues west to the edge of the lagoon. The main trail turns north and then curves to the west. From the main trailhead, Experiment Bight is 18.9 kilometers (11.7 miles), Guise Bay is 20.7 kilometers (12.9 miles), and Cape Scott, at the end of the trail, is 23.6 kilometers (14.7 miles).

Camping is available at Nels Bight and the spit between Experiment Bight (north) and Guise Bay (to the south). There's a ranger cabin on Nels Bight, operated during summer months, in addition to toilets and fresh water (which should be boiled). The superior camping area is at Nels Bight, with piped water and food caches. Water is limited at Guise Bay. There are several buildings in ruins at Guise Bay, as well as an old plank road, built in 1942 to carry materials between the buildings of a World War II radar station. The driftwood fence (or what is left of it) was part of the Jensen family's attempts, in 1910, to turn the sand dunes into pasture.

Experiment Bight has several interesting features. You'll see an old midden, the remains of a former fishing camp, at the west end of the bight.

The second plank road, found between Guise Bay and Cape Scott, was used to transport goods to the lighthouse. The short walk (2 kilometers or 1.2 miles) between Guise Bay and the lighthouse takes you through heavy vegetation. Approaching the end of the trail, a spur path leads to a gravel beach with seven seastacks. The main trail ends at the lighthouse, built in 1960. A boardwalk leads to the northwest tip of Vancouver Island. Drinking water is not available at the lighthouse.

Hiking from the trailhead to the trail's end at Cape Scott takes approximately eight hours, a walk of 23.6 kilometers (14.7 miles).

San Joseph Bay Trail   *Access:* Use the same main trailhead as for the Cape Scott Trail (above). There is a junction along the main trail, with the left fork leading to San Josef Bay.

The Trail: This is an easy hike, almost in the class of a short nature trail, leading for 2.5 kilometers (1.6 miles) to the sand beach on the bay. You should be aware that bears (one in particular, which thinks it owns the path) are sometimes seen at close range on this trail. Their scat is even more apparent on the trail. As with all other wilderness trails, do your hiking while the sun is shining, to avoid bear confrontations. Camping on the beach is permitted.

The Hike: Along the way, you'll pass through the Quatsino Rain Forest, with its tall trees, lush undergrowth, and bogs. The trail is surfaced with gravel. There are several bridges and boardwalks over the boggy areas (which is most of the region traveled on this trail). You can also canoe down the San Josef River from the campsite maintained by Western Forest Products, near the trailhead. The hike from the trailhead to the beach takes about three-quarters of an hour.

CAPE SCOTT CAMPING

There are two campgrounds within easy reach of the trailhead, for those who wish to camp with their vehicles and take day trips into the park. These campgrounds are operated by Western Forest Products, the logging company licensed for this area. Another campground is available at Winter Harbour, reached by road from Holberg.

Inside the park, the camping areas can only be described as primitive. Camping at the north end of the park is along the beaches. There are pit toilets on Nissen Bight, Nels Bight, and Guise Bay. There are camping areas with pit toilets on the east shore of Eric Lake, and along the Cape Scott Trail, north of the Fisherman River crossing. Cabins may be used at this site.

At the south end of the park, camping is permitted on San Josef Bay, and at Lowrie Bay. Fresh water (to be boiled) is available at both locations.

Other Vancouver Island Attractions

Except for Victoria and a dozen smaller communities, Vancouver Island is almost totally a natural wonderland, whether you enjoy some creature comforts with your almost-natural landscape or want to get completely away from any sign of civilization.

The following attractions combine the enjoyment of nature with camping or staying at unique inns or rustic resorts.

RAFT COVE PROVINCIAL PARK

For a wild and windy experience, you would find it hard to improve on this small park, located on the Pacific Ocean just south of Cape Scott Park. The surf is almost always very high, and the hike into the park is not for the fainthearted. The park was accessible only from the water until a logging road was recently constructed to a point near the park. This is the Ronning Main, which begins west of the village of Holberg, running south from its junction with the San Josef Main. The new trail is far shorter and much less irritating than the older trail, which joined the Ronning Main east of the new trailhead. For a detailed forest recreation map, stop at the logging company office in Holberg.

The new trail to the cove is 1.2 kilometers (0.75 mile) long. It begins at the end of the Ronning Main (marked by orange ribbons) and leads through a tangled coastal forest filled with cedar, salal, salmonberry, huckleberry, and skunk cabbage. It comes out to the ocean at the north end of the cove. Camping on the beach is a fine summer experience, and you'll probably be the only one there. An old deserted cabin is located on the south side of the Macjack River. It used to belong to trapper Willie Hecht and has bunk beds, a stove, and table. It is usable but has animal guests. Hecht and his family were first here in 1913.

The river is easily crossed at low tide. Low tide periods offer pleasant walks along the shore, with several rock islands to the south. It is possible to walk around Cammerell Point, and there is a trail across the point marked with blue ribbons. Fresh water is available near the cabin from the stream emptying into the south side of the Macjack.

Staying on the beach for a day or two brings even the most harried individuals to a peaceful state. The park is little known and attracts few visitors. From the beach, you can watch fishing boats on the open sea and the occasional oceangoing ship passing by. The park climate can be wild, yet its very wildness and privacy provide an experience available only in a few special places. If you really want to get away from it all, this is it!

TELEGRAPH COVE AND ROBSON BIGHT

Robson Bight, a bay southeast of Port Hardy, is probably the world's best location to observe killer whales. Johnstone Strait, at the northeastern corner of Vancouver Island, is the prime area for orcas from mid-June to October. Robson Bight, on the south side of Johnstone Strait, is an ecological preserve set aside to protect the whales. The bight features a long stretch of shallow, gravelly water, which the orcas enter to rub their bellies on the smooth gravel. Several whale pods can be seen in the area.

Camping is permitted at Telegraph Cove (see below), Kaikash Creek, and at Boat Bay and Growler Cove, which are both located on West Cracroft Island. Boat Bay and Growler Cove offer whale-watching from the shore. The reserve is 5 kilometers (3.7 miles) by water from Telegraph Cove. Landing or boating in the reserve waters are prohibited.

During summer months, Stubbs Island Charters operates four- to five-hour whale-watching excursions from the old pioneer fishing port of Telegraph Cove. The cruises depart at 9 A.M. and return in the early afternoon. From July to mid-September, an additional cruise leaves the dock at 3 P.M., ending between 7 and 8 P.M. Snacks are available on-board, and meals can be purchased with an advance reservation.

Two hours' drive north of Campbell River, and a half-hour from Port Hardy, Telegraph Cove is a little village set in time, located at the northern entrance to Johnstone Strait. Looking very much like the typical west coast fishing ports of the early 1900s, including several Alaskan fishing ports, this historic community—now a resort—has houses and other buildings set atop pilings. You can stay in one of the original houses or reserve a rustic-looking but modern cottage set on the hill above the pier. There is a campground with hookups for trailers and RVs, plus tenting sites, showers, and washroom facilities. Overnight rates for indoor accommodations are reduced between the beginning of October and the end of April. All rental units are self-contained with kitchen, dishes, cutlery, and linens. There is no such thing as television at Telegraph Cove.

You may launch your own boat for your own explorations, either to cruise the quiet interisland waters or to fish for steelhead in a North Island river. Charter fishing (for salmon, ling cod, halibut, and red snapper) is available. For information and overnight reservations, call (604) 928-3131 (summer) or (604) 284-3426 (winter). Write Telegraph Cove Resorts Ltd., Telegraph Cove, B.C. V0N 3J0.

UPANA CAVES

Most of us have sampled underground caves in national parks or in commercial cave attractions (I think of Ruby Falls in Chattanooga as the ultimate commercialized cave). The Upana Caves are different!

The caves are located in the Vancouver Island outback, reached by a logging road from the town of Gold River near Strathcona Provincial Park in the mid-island area. These are natural, ungimmicked caves, offering an unspoiled look at the wonders of nature, including an underground stream that disappears from view only to emerge from the ground, outside, a hundred feet away.

The driving time from Gold River to the caves parking lot is 25 minutes. The road distance is 17 kilometers (10.6 miles). To get there, take the Head Bay Forest Road from Gold River and turn onto Branch Road H-27 to reach the parking area (with toilet). The access trail begins to the north of the parking area.

A short trail leads from the parking area to five caves set in an old-growth forest. The Upana River flows through the area, doing its disappearing act. From the start, the trail leads along the river, through an old-growth forest of western hemlock, white pine, and yellow cedar. Some of these trees are more than 200 years old. Leaving the river, the trail veers north into a young forest replanted in 1981 with amabilis fir, hemlock, and cedar. The first underground experience comes at Insect Cave, a haven for crickets, spiders, and other insects.

The Keyhole is a large limestone tube that serves as the entrance to the Main Cave. This is a large cave with several passages. The main underground route follows the Upana River siphon, in which the river follows the underground course for 30 meters (98 feet) before reappearing in another cave (to be seen later). Exiting at the Keyhole, the trail then leads to Tunnel Cave, a longer tunnel where limestone was dissolved, creating the tube. Now outside, there is a vista point providing a water-fall view, and then a side trail leads to Corner Cave. Just before entering Resurgence Cave, the trail passes the Canyon Viewpoint, from where one can see the Upana River reappear below the cave entrance. The steps into Resurgence Cave lead to a viewpoint for a look at a mass of smooth, white marble.

The Upana Caves are five out of more than a thousand found on Vancouver Island. All were all formed by the action of water (mainly from the Upana River), which combined with carbon dioxide to create carbonic acid. The acid ate away at the soft limestone, creating the passages. The combined length of the caves is almost 1,500 feet, and there are 15 known entrances to the cave system.

As these are basically unprettified caves, without pipe organs, majestic angel choirs, or floodlighting, visitors should bring a good supply of light so that the adventure may be enjoyable and safe. Strong flashlights or battery-operated camping lights are ideal. You'll also need a warm jacket; the caves are at a constant temperature of 7°C (45°F). It is suggested that visitors wear a hard hat (bicycle helmet if you have one) and sturdy boots with rubber soles. Some may wish to get on their hands and knees. And please, don't disturb the crickets, spiders, salamanders, and other life forms found in the caves.

The Upana Caves offer a fine opportunity to see caverns in a natural state and explore side passages like a true spelunker without the physical risks inherent in most natural caves.

BIRDS

Black Brant
Branta bernicla

This black-necked goose is closer in size to a duck than to the much larger Canada goose. It is white beneath the tail and usually has a white belly. A distinguishing feature is a small band or fleck of white on the front of the neck. Aside from this small patch of white, the entire fore part of the brant is black. The white underparts are visible while the goose is flying or floating on the water. Its range is along the coasts of North America and also in northern Eurasia. During summer months, it lives on the far northern tundra, and in winters in pockets from southern British Columbia to California and South America. Its voice is a deep *kr-r-r-ruck,* or *krrr-onk.* A large group of brants arrives in April and settles for a while in Parksville, on Vancouver Island's east coast. A three-day arts and crafts festival is held each April to celebrate the migration of the geese.

Common Merganser
Mergus merganser

The three mergansers found along the northern Pacific Coast are all members of the Mergini family. They are diving fish ducks, with slender bodies and narrow, spike-like bills. The male common merganser has a slender, whitish body, black back, and a green-black head. Its feet and bill are red. The female is rusty-headed with a crest at the back of the head, and a grayish back with a large, white wing patch and red feet. The male makes a low, staccato croak. The female's voice is a throaty *karr.* Other members of the family found along the coasts of Vancouver Island are the hooded and red-breasted mergansers.

Surf Scoter
Melanitta perspicillata

Sometimes called the "skunk duck," this is another member of the Mergini family. Scoters are plump, black ducks often seen floating a hundred yards or more off the shore behind the crashing surf. They also live on coastal inlets and salt bays. The male is black with one or two white patches on the front and back of the head (crown and nape). The bill has patches of orange, white, and black. The female is a brownish color, with two whitish spots on the side of the head. These spots are usually difficult to see. Surf scoters summer in northern Canada and Alaska, and they winter farther south along the Atlantic and Pacific coasts.

Common Goldeneye
Bucephala clangula

This duck is seen throughout Vancouver Island, along the coasts and in salt bays as well as inland on rivers and wooded lakes. The male has distinctive markings, particularly a large, round white spot in front of the eye. It has a black back, white bottom and a large, glossy-green head. When flying, the wings show large, white patches. It can be heard while flying; the beating of its wings makes a singing sound. The female is gray, with a dark brown head and white collar band. The wings show large, square, white patches. Both male and female have yellow eyes. Its range is from B.C. to the Arctic regions (summer), to the Gulf Coast and Eurasia (winter). The female's voice is a distinct quack. The breeding male makes a harsh double note, something like *pee-ick.*

Horned Grebe
Podiceps auritus
All grebes are ducklike, diving birds with no apparent tail and thin necks. Their bills are pointed. All grebes except the pied-bill have white wing patches. The male is dark (almost black) above, and white below. It has a black cap that comes to eye level. Like many shorebirds, the males change color for breeding season, showing golden ear tufts and a rusty or chestnut-colored neck. The female is always dark-colored with the head cap and white underparts. The feet of grebes are lobed. You'll find this bird on ponds, lakes, and along the coastline.

Black Turnstone
Arenaria melanocephala
Spotted by its black and white geometric coloring when flying, this is a short-legged black shorebird with a black head and chest and white belly. Its legs are dark. In spring, it has a round white spot in front of the eye. It has distinct white harlequin markings on its back and on each wing, as does its more colorful and orange-legged cousin, the ruddy turnstone. The black turnstone breeds in Alaska and then winters along the Pacific Coast as far south as Mexico. It is a coastal bird, living along rocky shores, in bays, and (during breeding season) on the tundra of the Arctic coast. Its voice is a high-pitched rattle (*tuk-a-tuk,* or *cut-a-cut*) similar to but higher than the song of the ruddy turnstone. Both turnstones also voice a single *kewk.*

Golden-crowned Kinglet
Regulus satrapa
This tiny resident lives year-round in the Vancouver Island forests. The ruby-crowned kinglet is a summer resident. The male wears a bright yellow crown patch, while the female's crown patch is orange with a thin yellow border. Male and female have a whitish stripe over the eyebrow. Other than their colorful heads, the kinglets are a dull olive-gray color. They often give an upward flick to their wings. This kinglet is found from southern Alaska to Guatemala. It prefers to live in conifer forests in winter, and thus is quite satisfied with the fir and spruce forests of the island. Its voice is a high, piping *see-see-see.* Its song is a series of high, reedy notes ascending in pitch and then dropping down to a chattering sound.

Pacific Slope Flycatcher
Empidonax difficilis
One of two flycatchers found in the western regions (the other is the cordilleran), this flycatcher shares the common markings of all the empids: two pale wing bars and a light ring around the eye. The Pacific slope flycatcher has an olive-brown head, back, and tail, a yellow throat, and yellow underparts. When sitting, it regularly flicks its tail and wings. It is a summer resident of Vancouver Island, flying as far south as Honduras to winter. This flycatcher's voice is a *tseep,* slurred upwards.

Orange-crowned Warbler
Vermivora celata
Several warblers live and breed in Pacific Rim National Park, including Townsend's, Wilson's, and the orange-crowned. The latter is a summer resident of the island, flying to Guatemala for the winter months. It is a drab, olive-green color above with a more yellowish green color below. It has very faint breast streaks and, unlike other warblers, does not have wing bars. It is somewhat misnamed, for its "orange" crown is rarely seen. The bird turns gray in the fall. Its song is a trill, without much passion, sometimes changing pitch and becoming weaker at the end. Townsend's warbler is much easier to spot. It has a distinctive black cheek patch with yellow border, yellow underparts, and a yellowish breast with black stripes. Wilson's warbler has a round, black cap (male), while the female only shows a trace of a cap. Wilson's is a golden color, with a yellow stripe above the eye.

Marbled Murrelet
Brachyramphus marmoratus
The object of much ecological discussion (and fighting) in these parts, the marbled murrelet is a ducklike shorebird that nests and breeds slightly inland, high in the canopy area on mossy conifer trees. The rain forests of Vancouver Island are perfect breeding areas for these rare birds. Their breeding habits have been responsible for the stopping of logging in several important Pacific Northwest forests, including the Carmanah Park area south of Pacific Rim National Park. They live during summer months in the national park as well. It is a small, chunky bird, rather dark above and whitish below. Its summer plumage is dark brown, heavily flecked or "marbled" on its underparts. Its voice is a *kee,* or a higher *keer, keer.*

Gray Jay
Perisoreus canadensis
This large, fluffy bird is the same size as the more familiar Steller's jay, or the scrub jay of the oak woodlands. It looks quite different, having no head crest (unlike Steller's), nor a blue color. It is a gray bird, with a black patch across the back of the head and a white forehead. It is whitish below. Immature gray jays are a darker color, with a whitish bar or "whisker" across the cheek. Loggers and trappers have long called this bird the "whiskey jack." Like other jays, its voice dominates the scene.

It offers a fairly subtle *wheee-ahh,* but also has other, more boisterous, notes. It is found primarily in spruce/fir forests, and can be seen and heard throughout the wooded areas of Vancouver Island.

Winter Wren
Troglodytes troglodytes
Wrens are very small, very busy birds, brown in color, with slightly curved bills. The tails are usually cocked. The winter wren is one of the smallest of the family, growing to about four inches. It is a dark, gray-brown color, with a barred belly, a light eyebrow, and a stubby tail. It is seen close to the ground, where it perches, bobbing its head. It is truly a songbird. Its song is a series of high, tinkling warbles and trills. Its double note is *kip-kip,* or *chip, chip.*

FISH

Sockeye Salmon
Oncorhynchus nerka
While prized for eating, the sockeye is much shorter than the chinook, growing to a length of about 33 inches. It is the prime commercial fish of British Columbia and is found from the Bering Strait to the Sacramento River in Northern California. Its body is elongated, and its sides are compressed. In salt water, it is tinged with greenish blue above and is silvery below, with fine black speckles on the back. When it reenters fresh water to spawn, its fins and back change to a bright red, its head is a pale green, and it is pale below. Females

in fresh water often have green and yellow blotches, even changing to a scarlet color. It has a large mouth and its snout is bluntly pointed, with fleshy lips.

Vancouver Island has several notable salmon streams, containing gravel beds in which female sockeye and other salmon lay their eggs. The sockeye spawn in lake tributaries with the young spending one to three years in fresh water before departing for the open ocean. They usually return in their third or fourth year to begin a new cycle of life and then expire.

Chinook Salmon
Oncorhynchus tshawytsha
Growing to a length of four feet, ten inches, the chinook or "king" salmon is the great sporting fish of Vancouver Island and along the whole northern Pacific Coast. Anglers come from around the world to stay in fishing camps at Campbell River and other coastal towns. This elongated fish is greenish blue to black above (in salt water) and silvery below. It becomes very dark after reaching fresh water. The gums at the base of the teeth are black, and it has an adipose fin. It is found from Bering Strait to Southern California and spawns in large rivers, as far south as the Sacramento River. The spawning runs are mainly in the spring and fall, with the red eggs deposited in gravel on the river bottoms. The chinook's food includes herring and other smaller fish, including anchovies and rockfish, as well as crustaceans.

Yellowtail
Seriola lalandei
British Columbia is the northern-most habitat of the yellowtail, and its presence here depends on the temperature of the water in any year. It ranges south to Chile. It is found around islands, in kelp beds, and around more southerly reefs. It is elongated with compressed sides, olive-brown above, with yellow stripes along the sides. The fins are also yellowish. This is a very large fish, growing to five feet, and is much prized as a sport fish. The yellowtail feeds on much the same diet as salmon: smaller fish including sardines and mackerels, but also squid and crabs.

Buffalo Sculpin
Enophrys bison
There are numerous members of the sculpin family (Cottidae), found in tide pools and around reefs, piers, and wrecks. In all, 111 species of sculpin are found on the continent. These fish are all quite small (growing to a length of 3 to 15 inches), although the buffalo is the largest sculpin found along the shores of Vancouver Island. It is elongated and tapered, almost round around the middle, a mottled dark green or brown above, with whitish blotches. Its large head has a rounded snout and a long, sharp spine in front of the gill cover. It has heavy, bony plates on the side. Sculpins are not suitable for eating by humans. This and the other sculpins swim around piers and wrecks and over shallow reefs.

They eat shrimp, crabs, and small, young fish.

MAMMALS

Columbian Black-tailed Deer
Ododoileus hermionus columbianus
This is the common deer of Vancouver Island, and most of the Pacific coastal regions. Like the Roosevelt elk, a member of the same family and also found on the island, the black-tailed deer has two hooves on each foot. The deer on the island are somewhat smaller than those on the mainland, with a maximum weight of less than 200 pounds (more likely about 100 pounds). The deer's chest is brown, and the belly and throat patch are white. The whole tail is black. Fawns are a lighter brown with some white spots and have the black tail in a slightly lighter shade. Males bear two antlers, each of which has two forks. They are shed in the spring, with the new antlers growing during summer and fall. Deer are herbivores, eating tender shoots and leaves from shrubs and trees. They have a life span of about 10 years.

Black Bear
Ursus americanus
Bears are numerous in the forests of Vancouver Island, and their often-used trails are frequently seen when walking along backcountry trails. When provided a human-made trail, the black bear will use it as if he or she owns it. The black bear of Vancouver Island grows to a

height of six feet. Its footprints are about four inches long and five inches wide, showing five toes on fore and hind feet. The stride is about one foot long. Other signs of local bears include trees scarred with tooth marks, four or five feet up the trunk. You may see bear hair clinging to tree bark. The tree is used for back rubs.

As an omnivorous mammal, bears feed on whatever is available, including small mammals, insects, roots, small plants, and the plentiful berries (salal, salmonberry, and huckleberry) that arrive in late summer. It is usually found at lower elevations, below 7,000 feet in wooded and mountain areas. It is usually nocturnal but may be seen at any time of day. Bears are seen alone, except during the mating season (June and early July). They do congregate at garbage dumps. Though technically classed as an omnivore, it rarely attacks humans, except when sorely harassed. The best thing to do during a bear encounter is to back off, calmly and quietly getting out of its way. The bear is probably more interested in eating berries than in eating you.

Sea Otter
Enhydra lutris
This mammal lives, breeds, raises its young, and feeds totally at sea. It stays in the water except to spend brief times on shore, and only during storms. Floating on its back, it fishes (for mussels, fish, sea urchins, and crabs) with its tail, using it as a tool to scoop up its

floating lunch and dinner. It also dives for food, hunting sea urchins and abalone, and staying underwater for as long as four or five minutes. After catching shellfish, it uses a small rock to break the shell. The sea otter is far advanced as a user of tools, more so than any other mammal except humans. It uses strands of kelp as a tool, wrapping itself for protection in a kelp bed before sleeping. The sea otter is a survivor. It was plentiful along the Pacific Coast until the arrival of Europeans, who hunted the otter for its thick pelt. By 1911, when an international protection treaty was signed, it was almost extinct. The sea otter has recovered, with still "endangered" herds in California and much larger populations from British Columbia to Alaska and the Aleutian Islands.

Killer Whale
Orcinus orca
The amazing orca is the best-loved "killer" of the Pacific Coast. A member of the dolphin and porpoise family, rather than being closely related to the larger whales, the orca lives in family groups (pods). The black and white mammal is seen and enjoyed by whale-watchers in the inland waters of Johnstone Strait and farther south in the Strait of Georgia. Its Pacific range is from the equator to the northern Chukchi Sea. It is an efficient killing and eating machine, catching a wide variety of sea creatures: fish (including the plentiful salmon), squid, sea birds, sea turtles, seals, and even baleen whales,

which they attack and wound but often do not eat.

These mammals are black with large areas of white, with some tan or yellow on the undersides. There's a white patch above and behind the eye. Its broad head is rounded, with a large mouth and large teeth. The paddle-shaped flippers are rounded. The crescent-shaped dorsal fin is tall and usually straight, although some are curved forward. This is usually regarded as a sign of stress. Curved dorsal fins are common for orcas in captivity.

The male orca is more energetic and more ferocious than the female. There are few records of unprovoked attacks on humans, but people are urged to be wary of close encounters with male orcas.

INVERTEBRATES AND CRUSTACEANS

Blue-handed Hermit Crab
Pagurus samuelis
This small crab and the related little hairy hermit crab (*P. hirsutiusculus*) are found on rocky shores along Vancouver Island and along the Pacific Coast from Alaska to Baja California. About 0.75 inch long, it can be seen in tide pools and on rocks in the intertidal zone, between the mid- and low-tide lines. The blue-handed hermit finds its home in snail shells, preferring the shell of the black turban snail. The crab is pear-shaped, olive-brown in color, with bright blue bands near the tips of the walking legs. The tips of the pincers are a bright blue. The little hairy hermit crab has a grayish-tan color and has hairy legs with white bands and white pincer tips.

Pacific Rock Crab
Cancer antennarius
This crab provides a natural follow-up to the hermit crabs, for the Pacific rock crab hunts and eats the smaller hermits, inserting its pincers into the snail shells that are the hermit crabs' homes. It then chips away the shell until the hermit crab is trapped. The rock crab grows to a length of 2.75 inches and is up to 4.5 inches wide. It is fan-shaped, with a bluish-red upper side and a lighter, cream-colored underside with red spots. The tips of its fingers are black. It has an oval carapace. The pincers are short and stout and bend downward at the tips. Its walking legs are also short. This crab lives on rocky shores and gravel bottoms and in kelp beds throughout the intertidal zone, to water 130 feet deep.

Giant Sea Star
Pisaster giganteus
One of a dozen stars that inhabit the British Columbia coastal waters, the giant sea star is the largest and most easily spotted. It has a radius of 12 inches. It comes in several colors: red, purple, tan, or brown, with blue rings around the base of the spines. It has thick arms and large spines. British Columbia is the northern edge of this sea star's range, and it is found to the south as far as Baja California. It is found

on rocky shores and in shallow water on rock bottoms below and near the low-tide line.

Other sea stars found in B.C. waters include the broad six-rayed (black, green, brown or red, about two inches); Trochel's (orange to brown to blue-gray, to eight inches with five slim, tapering arms); and ocre (10 inches, yellow, orange, brown, red, or purple, with five stout tapering arms).

Blue Mussel
Mytilus edulis
This is the most common mussel along the Pacific Coast, and it is probably the mussel you last ate in a restaurant. While it is seen in abundance along the Vancouver Island coast, eating it is not recommended because of the danger of red tide poisoning. It is found firmly attached to rocks and submerged wood, in protected waters, and in the intertidal zone near the low-tide line. This mussel is also found along the Atlantic Coast. Growing to a length of four inches, it has a long, fan-shaped shell with a rounded hind end. The outside of the shell is purplish gray. The interior is a bluish-white. The oval muscle near the hind end is bluish-gray to bluish-black. There are four to seven sharp teeth at the front end. Other mussels found on Vancouver Island include the northern horse, fan-shaped horse, and the California.

Finger Limpet
Collisella digitalis
This intertidal creature is commonly seen on vertical sides of rock pools, where there is wave action near the high-tide line. It is found from Alaska to Baja California. The name refers to the coarse ribs that look somewhat like several fingers. Growing to a length of 1.4 inches, its shell is a dark gray with a greenish tinge and irregular white spots or streaks, with radiating ribs. The interior of the shell is a bluish white, with a large, dark brown patch in the center, and a wavy border dotted with white or bluish-white spots. You'll see this interesting shellfish among periwinkles, barnacles, and algae on which it feeds.

TREES AND SHRUBS

Coast Douglas Fir
Pseudotsuga menziesii
The major timber species in British Columbia, the Douglas fir is a large tree with a narrow, pointed crown that has drooping branches. It grows to heights of 80 to 200 feet, with a trunk diameter of from two to five feet and often much larger in the wet rain forests where gigantic trees are produced. It is an evergreen, with the flattened needles spreading in two rows, yellow-green or blue-green, on short twisted stalks. The bark is reddish-brown and very thick and twisted, resembling cork (similar to the bark of sequoias). The cones are long and egg-shaped, light brown with many thin cone-scales and paired seeds with long wings. The range of this tree is from the central British

Columbia coast to central California. The Rocky Mountain Douglas fir is found east of the coastal regions and south to southeastern Arizona and Texas.

Amabilis (Balsam) Fir
Abies amabilis
David Douglas, the famous Scottish botanist (for whom the Douglas fir was named) discovered this species and gave it the Latin word for "lovely." Also called the Pacific silver fir, this large tree has a conical, sharply pointed crown of short branches that curve down. Its foliage is fernlike. Growing to heights of 80 to 150 feet, this evergreen's needles are in two rows, curving upward on the twigs. Needles are flat, shiny dark green, silvery underneath, and grooved on top. The bark is smooth, a light gray color, growing to a scaly state and reddish brown when mature. The cones grow to a length of six inches. They are long and cylindrical with fine hairs and long-winged seeds.

Western Hemlock
Tsuga heterophylla
Growing abundantly in association with cedars, spruces, and firs on Vancouver Island, this is the largest of the hemlocks, reaching a height of 150 feet in damper forests. It has a long, slender trunk, with a cone-shaped crown of short, slender branches that sometimes droop. The evergreen needles are short and rounded at the tip, shiny green above, with two whitish bands. The needles often have tiny teeth underneath. The thick bark of the

western hemlock is reddish brown or grayish brown, with fine hairs. The twigs are a yellowish brown with fine hairs. Its cones grow to about one inch long and are brown and elliptical, without stalks. They have many rounded scales with long-winged seeds in groups of two.

Western Red Cedar
Thuja plicata
This member of the cypress family is abundant throughout the B.C. coastal areas, growing to a height of more than 200 feet. It has drooping branches, with fleshy, scalelike evergreen leaves, set in alternative pairs. The leaf color is a lighter green than most of the other conifers with which it grows, including firs and hemlocks. Its bark is reddish-brown and is so thin that it tears off in strips. The cones have only a few scales and are about a half-inch long. When new, the cones point upward. After the seeds have matured and fallen out, the cones droop toward the ground.

Shorepine
Pinus contorta (var. *contorta*)
This is the coastal variety of the lodgepole pine, a major lumber tree of the British Columbia interior. Along the coast, it is found mainly on rocky shores or in salt marshes, where it grows very slowly in a very stunted form, often no more than four or five feet high. In more satisfactory environments at higher elevations, the lodgepole pine grows to a height of 80 feet. A good place in which to see the shorepine is the bog in Pacific Rim

National Park. It has a spreading crown, and its yellow-green needles are bundled in pairs. The bark is thick and light brown, furrowed in scalelike plates. The cones (growing to two inches) are egg-shaped and stalkless. The shiny, yellowish-brown cones point backwards and stay on the tree for years. The lodgepole name (for the taller version) comes from the use of these trees as poles for teepees or tents.

Labrador Tea
Ledum glandulosum
This Labrador tea (there are several) is a short shrub, a member of the heather family, found in wet, mountainous areas. You'll see it as one of the primary plants in the bogs of Vancouver Island, including the bog in Pacific Rim National Park. It bears white flowers with five petals, set in round clusters at the ends of the branches. The oval leaves are from one-half to two inches long, with whitish hairs on the underside. In bogs, it is stunted, growing to a height of from two to three feet.

Another Labrador tea (*L. groenlandicum*) growing in the same region has rust-colored hairs on the underside of the leaf. This is a taller shrub, also growing in less boggy areas, to a height of about seven feet.

Salal
Gualtheria shallon
A common shrub on the floor of a rain forest, the salal has long, shiny, oval leaves, two to four inches long, with tiny teeth along the edges. The flowers are pale and pink, urn-shaped, and hang in racemes, long flower clusters on which individual flowers bloom on a lengthy stalk. The corolla is hairy, with five pointed lobes. The salal plant bears many dark purple berries, which are loved by bears and have been eaten by humans for hundreds of years. The plant grows to a height of four feet. It is found in conifer forests, particularly in moist woodlands. It is particularly thick on the floor of the Quatsino Rain Forest at the northern end of Vancouver Island. It grows from British Columbia to central California

Red Huckleberry
Vaccinium parvifolium
This is one of three huckleberry plants that grow widely in the Pacific Northwest. You'll see it in both Pacific Rim National Park and in Cape Scott Provincial Park, both on the west coast of the island. Unlike other huckleberry shrubs, this one's berries are red instead of blue or black. It grows to a height of four to six feet. The short leaves (less than an inch long) are oval, thin, and bright green. The angled stems have a distinctive green color. It has small, hanging, vase-shaped flowers, which are greenish with a pink tinge. You will rarely see the red huckleberry growing outside of a rain forest or a damp woodland. It grows out of rotted logs and decaying stumps, often beside hiking trails.

There is an evergreen huckleberry (*V. ovatum*), which has round, thick leaves. The flowers are pink and bell-shaped. It bears shiny, black (and fairly sour) berries in the fall. The berries of both huckleberries are eaten by humans and bears.

Salmonberry
Rubus spectabilis

One of three common raspberries in the Pacific coastal region, the salmonberry plant is a tall shrub, sometimes growing to a height of about 10 feet. The divided leaves are formed as three dark green leaflets. The unique flowers are magenta or light purple, almost an inch across. The berries when ripe are a yellow-orange color or even reddish, and they are longer than they are wide. The berries are good tasting, not very sweet, and quite juicy. People of the coast have used salmonberries as food, and B.C. people often make it into delicious jam or jelly. This plant tends to grow in damper areas: along the banks of creeks and rivers, at the bottom of stream canyons, at the edges of rain forests, in marshes, and in wetlands next to lakes.

Sword Fern
Polystichum munitum

One of several evergreen ferns found in the damp forests of the B.C. coast, the sword fern roots itself in soil as well as in rotted logs and old stumps. It is seen in great numbers throughout the coastal regions, particularly in the rain forests. Its serrated leaves grow to a length of 30 inches, forming a crown. The spore sacs grow on the undersides of the larger leaflets, in close clusters (sori), covered by a shield (indusium). New leaves appear each spring, pushing the older leaves toward the plant's base. The licorice fern (*Polypodium vulgare*) and the common wood fern (*Dryopteris austriaca*) are other often-seen ferns in the Vancouver Island forests. The licorice fern does not grow in soil but clings to rotten logs and mossy tree trunks. Its leaves are added in the fall. The common wood fern, with darker green foliage, grows almost exclusively out of fallen logs or the totally rotted remains of logs.

Skunk Cabbage
Lysichitum americanum

A member of the arum or calla lilly family, the skunk cabbage is the only member of this family native to the Pacific Northwest. If you get close to the plant, you'll detect a mild skunky smell. Its eastern cousin (*Symplocarpus foetidus*) has a much more disagreeable odor. You'll see masses of the western variety on the floor of rain forests and in bogs. The spathes that enclose the tall flower stalks are similar to leaves. The actual leaves often reach a length of three feet in truly damp environments.

WILDFLOWERS

Starflower
Trientalis latifolia

The starflower is a member of the primrose family, but it does not resemble the everyday primrose you have as a bedding plant. It grows from a tuber on a thin stem that reaches a height of about three or four inches. The stem is crowned with a cluster of leaves and sev-eral flowers that are vari-ous shades of pink. The leaves are oval, coming to a point at the end. The number of petals on each star-shaped flower is highly variable, from five to nine.

Tufted Phlox

Phlox caespitosa
This is a low, somewhat woody plant with tufts of slim, dagger-like leaves. It bears tubular flowers that may be mauve, pink, or white. Each flower has five narrow lobes, joined with a flat, colorless mem-brane. The leaves are opposite, growing to a length of a half-inch. The tufted phlox grows in south-ern British Columbia, as well as in Washington, northeast Oregon, northern Idaho, and Montana. It thrives in dry, piney woods.

The skunkweed (*Navarretia squarrosa*), common to the coastal areas, is also a member of the phlox family. Growing to a height of about five inches, the basal leaves are divided into many lobes, with the leaves high on the stem, branching twice. Each lobe is tipped with spines. It has bright blue flowers and emits a fairly strong skunk-like odor.

Indian Paintbrush

Castilleja hispada
Several members of the figwort family are found in southern British Columbia, including the monkeyflower (*Mimulus alsinoides*) and Blue-eyed Mary (*Collinsia parvi-flora*). The Indian paintbrushes (there are several) are parasitic plants, attached to other plants under the ground. The distinctive but small flowers have a two-lipped corolla, similar to snapdragons. The more conspicuous bracts are divided into three or more lobes, and in hispada, the bracts are bright red or orange-red. It has hairy stems and leaves. Another common paintbrush (*C. miniata*) has bracts that are rarely lobed. Both varie-ties of paintbrush are found in Strathcona Provincial Park.

The listings below are in the towns close to the three major park areas. Listings for Victoria are included for those catching ferries to and from the mainland. Almost all of the following places to stay have reduced rates in the off-season, which is any time except June through September.

ALERT BAY

A former canning port and still a busy fishing village, Alert Bay is a 40-minute ferry ride from Port McNeill at the northeast corner of Vancouver Island. The town, located on Cormorant Island, is the home of the Kwakwaka'wakw band and has long been a Kwakiutl community.

Bayside Inn Motel
81 Fir Street
P.O. Box 492
Alert Bay, B.C. V0N 1A0
(604) 974-5857

This standard motel overlooks Broughton Strait and the harbor. Facilities include single and double rooms with showers, restaurant, and pub. Fishing charters and whale-watching tours can be arranged. **($)**

Ocean View Cabins
390 Poplar Street
Alert Bay, B.C. V0N 1A0
(604) 974-5457

A group of cottages, one mile from the harbor and ferry terminal. These are self-contained cabins with kitchens, queen beds, and TVs. **($ to $$)**

Oceanview Camping and Trailer Park
Alder Road
P.O. Box 28
Alert Bay, B.C. V0N 1A0
(604) 974-5213

A campground and RV park, this operation is located on a hill overlooking Johnstone Strait, with full hookups, flush toilets and showers, barbecues, picnic tables, and dump station. Nearby are a free boat launch, stores, the ferry dock, and nature trails. Daily and weekly rates.

CAMPBELL RIVER

Anchor Inn
261 Island Highway
Campbell River, B.C. V9W 2B3
(604) 286-1131 or 800-663-7227

This oceanfront motor hotel has a fine view of the channel, and guest rooms have balconies, some with kitchens. Other facilities include an indoor pool, whirlpool, dining room, lounge, and sushi bar. Pets allowed. **($$)**

Coast Discovery Inn
975 Shoppers Row
Campbell River, B.C. V9W 2C5
(604) 287-7155 or 800-663-1144

There are standard rooms and suites in this modern high-rise hotel, adjacent to the town's shopping plaza. Facilities include twin, queen, and king units, Jacuzzi suites, restaurant, pub, beer and wine store, and health club. Pets allowed. **($$ to $$$)**

Elk Falls Provincial Park Campground
(604) 286-0642

This campground is located on Highway 28, west of Campbell River and on the way to Strathcona Provincial Park on the Quinsam River. Campground facilities include waterfront locations, flush toilets, dump station, nature trails, and waterfalls.

Haig-Brown House
2250 Campbell River Road
Campbell River, B.C. V9W 4N7
(604) 286-6646

This bed and breakfast inn is the historic (1920) former home of the celebrated naturalist and writer Roderick Haig-Brown. The house is located on two acres of riverfront property with gardens and orchards. The rooms have fireplaces and cable TV, private and shared baths. There is a lounge and a library, and a full country breakfast is served. **($$)**

Holiday Shores RV Park
3001 Spit Road
Campbell River, B.C. V9W 5B1
(604) 286-6142

Open May to October, this large park is three miles from downtown, with full hookups, laundry, showers, and boat launch. Fishing guides are available.

Painter's Lodge and Fishing Resort
1625 MacDonald Road
P.O. Box 460
Campbell River, B.C. V9W 5C1
(604) 286-1102 or 800-663-7090

This is the classic B.C. fishing resort, a very classy place with a fine dining room and wonderful views of the channel. All rooms have private bath, and the resort features include a heated pool, lounge, pub, tennis courts, a fitness center, boats, and fishing guides. There's a golf course close at hand. **($$$)**

Thunderbird RV Park and Campground
2600 Spit Road
Campbell River, B.C. V9W 5W8
(604) 286-3344

Open from May through September, this RV park has full hookups, flush toilets, showers, laundry, and dump station.

COMOX

Evergreen Resort Motel
1950 Comox Avenue
Comox, B.C. V9M 3M7
(604) 339-3012

This older motel is in a treed setting in downtown Comox. Facilities include one- and two-bedroom cottages, rooms with balconies and full kitchens, sauna, whirlpool, barbecue area, laundry, and playground. Close to restaurants, pubs, and harbor. **($ to $$)**

Port Augusta Resort Motel

2082 Comox Avenue
Comox, B.C. V9M 1P8
(604) 339-2277 or 800-663-2141

This recently remodeled motel has one- and two-bedroom units (some with kitchens), a restaurant, lounge, and pool. It's close to downtown Comox, on the main road into town. **($ to $$)**

Seaview Tent and Trailer Park

685 Lazo Road c/o RR#1
Comox, B.C. V9N 5N1
(604) 339-3946

Facilities include full hookups, firepits, flush toilets, laundry, showers, and store. A boat launch and beach are nearby. Pets are allowed, on leash.

COURTENAY

Beach House Bed and Breakfast

2614 South Island Highway
RR#6, Site 668, Comp 28
Courtenay, B.C. V9N 8H9
(604) 338-8990

This B & B home overlooks Comox Harbour, one mile south of Courtenay on Highway 19. There are several units, with single and double beds, private and shared baths. A full rustic breakfast is served. **($)**

Coast Westerly Hotel

1590 Cliffe Avenue
Courtenay, B.C. V9N 2K4
(604) 338-7741 or 800-668-7797

Part of the regional Coast chain of modern hotels, this hotel in downtown Courtenay has some with bal-conies overlooking the Courtenay River. Features include sauna, exercise room, whirlpool, heated indoor pool, coffee shop, dining room, pub, and beer and wine store. **($$ to $$$)**

Greystone Manor

4014 Haas Road
RR#6, Site 684, Comp 2
Courtenay, B.C. V9N 8H9
(604) 338-1422

To get to this B & B home, drive one mile north of the traffic light in Royston, turn right onto Hilton Road, and then left on Haas Road. This is a heritage home set on a waterfront property with flower gardens, overlooking Comox Bay with a view of the Coast Mountains. There is a sitting room with fireplace. Full breakfast is served. Children over 12 are welcome; nonsmoking. **($ to $$)**

Maple Pool Campsite

4685 Headquarters Road
P.O. Box 3543
Courtenay, B.C. V9N 6Z8
(604) 338-9386

This campground has 50 sites, with full and partial hookups, overlooking the Tsolum River a short distance off Highway 19. Some sites are pull-throughs. There are flush toilets, a dump station, and showers.

Travelodge Courteney

2605 South Island Highway
Courtenay, B.C. V9N 2L8
(604) 334-4491

If all you require is an overnight sleeping place, this quite new motel should fill the bill, with standard rooms and larger units with kitchenettes, laundry, pool, with restaurants and shopping nearby. **($ to $$)**

GOLD RIVER

Located west of Strathcona Provincial Park and near the Upana Caves, Gold River is a small mill town in a scenic setting on the Gold River (a steelhead stream) and Nootka Sound.

Country Comfort B&B

409 Donner Drive
Gold River, B.C. V0P 1G0
(604) 283-2587

Two rooms with double beds, shared bath, sitting room with TV, kitchenette. **($)**

Gold River Chalet

390 Nimpkish Drive
P.O. Box 10
Gold River, B.C. V0P 1G0
(604) 283-2244

This standard motel features a coffee shop, dining room, lounge, pub, and heated outdoor pool.
($ to $$)

Peppercorn Trail Motel and RV Park

Muchalat Drive
P.O. Box 23
Gold River, B.C. V0P 1G0
(604) 283-2443

There are several motel units, some with kitchen plus 60 RV sites with full hookups. Guided fishing and mountain hiking tours can be arranged. **($)**

The Plum Tree B&B

454 Chamiss Crescent
Gold River, B.C. V0P 1G0
(604) 283-7147

Three rooms with double or two single beds, continental breakfast. **($$)**

Ridgeview Motel

395 Donner Court
P.O. Box 335
Gold River, B.C. V0P 1G0
(604) 283-2277

There are several units in this motel, including some with kitchenettes, plus a honeymoon suite and executive suite—both with whirlpool bath. There's a pub serving lunches and full dinners. **($)**

PARKSVILLE/QUALICUM BEACH

Parksville is the junction point for driving trips to the west coast and Pacific Rim National Park. It is a small, cozy resort town, with a high senior population and a long gravel beach on the eastern side of the island. Qualicum Beach is located six miles north of Parksville and is a similar type of community. In fact, the two towns pretty much run together, in one continuous strip of resorts, beaches, and restaurants.

French Creek Campground

1025 Lee Road
Parksville, B.C. V9P 2E1
(604) 248-3998

This is a basic campground without hookups in a parklike setting. There are flush toilets, showers, an oceanfront restaurant and pub, store, with a boat ramp and moorage next door. There are 40 campsites.

Holiday Inn Express Motel
424 West Island Highway
Parksville, B.C. V9P 1K8
(604) 248-2232 or 800-661-3110

For those who like their accommodations simple but risk-free, this modern cookie-cutter motel (with some extras) is conveniently located on Highway 19 in Parksville. From the south, the entrance is off Molliet Street. There are standard rooms and suites, free breakfast, indoor pool, whirlpool, with shopping and restaurants a block away. The motels in this chain are a cut above the really low-priced budget motels. **($$ to $$$)**

Maclure House Inn
1015 East Island Highway, Unit 11
Parksville, B.C. V9P 2E4
(604) 248-3470

This Tudor-style building is located in the Beach Acres Resort, overlooking the strait and Mistaken Island. There are four units, with twin and queen beds, private baths, a pool, whirlpool, tennis, sauna, and breakfast is served. There's an adjacent restaurant. Rathtrevor Provincial Park is nearby. **($$ to $$$)**

Park Sands Beach Resort
105 East Island Highway
P.O. Box 179
Parksville, B.C. V9P 2G4
(604) 248-3171

Located in downtown Parksville, this seaside resort has cottages, a campground, and RV park. There are six cottages booked on a weekly basis. **($$)**
The RV park has 99 sites, with full and partial hookups, showers, and playground, with a community park and playground nearby.

Qualicum College Inn
427 College Road
P.O. Box 99
Qualicum Beach, B.C. V9K 2G4
(604) 752-9262

This is an excellent place to stay, having more ambience than just about any other motor hotel in the area. Built as an exclusive boys' school, it is a historic landmark overlooking the Strait of Georgia, with rooms and suites (some with fireplaces), landscaped grounds, a restaurant, lounge, pub, pool, and whirlpool. The rooms are modern and large. The inn periodically stages murder mystery weekends. **($$ to $$$)**

Tigh-Na-Mara Resort Hotel
1095 East Island Highway
Parksville, B.C. V9P 2E5
(604) 248-2072 or 800-663-7373

This fine resort operation features log cottages, lodge rooms, and ocean-view condo units, set in a forest beside the strait on Rathtrevor Beach. Some rooms have fireplaces, kitchens, and whirlpools. Other facilities include tennis courts, steam and exercise rooms, dining room, lounge, playgrounds, and boat rentals. **($$ to $$$)**

PORT ALBERNI

The Barklay
4277 Stamp Avenue
Port Alberni, B.C. V9Y 7X8
(604) 724-7171

This hotel has air-conditioned units including suites, with double and queen beds. There is a restaurant, pub, outdoor pool, sauna, whirlpool, marina, fishing charters, and tennis. **($$)**

China Creek Marina and Campground
Bamfield Road
P.O. Box 575
Port Alberni, B.C. V9Y 7M9
(604) 723-9812

Open from May 1 to October 1, the marina is 15 kilometers (nine miles) southwest of Port Alberni, with open and wooded sites on Alberni Inlet. Facilities include a full-service marina with boat rentals, propane, and fishing charters. There are 260 sites for tents, trailers and RVs, with full and partial hookups, coffee shop, laundry, showers, store, playground, tackle shop, and freezer (important for anglers).

Coast Hospitality Inn
3835 Redford Street
Port Alberni, B.C. V9Y 3S2
(604) 723-8111 or 800-663-1144

This hotel features coffee and tea service, beer and wine store, restaurant, and pub. Fishing charters can be arranged. **($$$)**

Grey Heron Bed and Breakfast
8285 Dickson Drive
RR #3, Site 323, Comp 21
Port Alberni, B.C. V9Y 7L7

Located near Sproat Lake, about 10 miles east of Port Alberni, this home has a room with queen bed, coffeemaker, and cable TV. There's an outdoor hot tub, swimming at the nearby beach, and a complimentary canoe. **($$)**

Timberlodge Inn and Campground
2404 Alberni and Highway 4
Port Alberni, B.C. V9Y 7L6
(604) 723-9415

The inn has 22 rooms, some with kitchen. Breakfast is included in room rate. There is a restaurant (closed for dinner November 1 to March 1), lounge, and heated indoor pool. **($$)**

The campground has 24 sites with full or partial hookups, showers, laundry, picnic tables, and firepits.

Water's Edge B & B Sproat Lake
9606 Stirling Arm Crescent
Site 340, Comp 9
Port Alberni, B.C. V9Y 7L7

Pete and Kathy Sevigny operate this family home in the country, with the beach outside. There are three units: two with shared bath and one with private bath. There are queen, double, and twin beds. A gourmet breakfast is served. The home is 10 miles southeast of Port Alberni. **($$)**

PORT HARDY

Kay's Bed and Breakfast
7605 Carnarvon Road
P.O. Box 257
Port Hardy, B.C. V0N 2P0
(604) 949-6776

This home with an ocean view has four units including self-contained suites, with private and shared baths. **($)**

North Shore Inn

7370 Market Street
P.O. Box 88
Port Hardy, B.C. V0N 2P0
(604) 949-8500

This hotel in downtown Port Hardy offers rooms with great views of the ocean, balconies, double and twin beds. Five-day fishing packages are available. There's a superior dining room with lounge. **($$)**

Pioneer Inn

4965 Byng Road
P.O. Box 699
Port Hardy, B.C. V0N 2PO
(604) 949-7271

This is a motel and RV park in a wooded setting in the country across from the Quatse River. The inn is a large, rustic building with 36 large two-room units with kitchens, in-room coffee, a restaurant and coffee shop, laundry, and playground. **($ to $$)**

 The campground has 20 sites with full hookups.

Quatse River Campground

5050 Hardy Bay Road
P.O. Box 1409
Port Hardy, B.C. V0N 2P0
(604) 949-2395

The campground is five miles from the ferry dock in downtown Port Hardy, with power and water sites, tenting sites, flush toilets, showers, laundry, dump station, firepits, and ferry pickup. There are 61 sites.

PORT MCNEILL

A fishing and lumber town, Port McNeill is a half-hour's drive south of Port Hardy and 199 kilometers (124 miles) north of Campbell River. It is a handy stopping place for exploring the "north island." A ferry departs from here for Alert Bay.

Broughton Strait Campsite

Mine Road
P.O. Box 729
Port McNeill, B.C. V0N 2R0

With 226 sites, this campground is three blocks from the ferry terminal and has full hookups, flush toilets, showers, dump station, a barbecue area, firepits, and firewood. A boat launch is two blocks from the campground.

Broughton Strait Resort

(campground)
P.O. Box 245
Port McNeill, B.C. V0N 2R0
(604) 949-1164

This campground and RV park has 104 sites and is located off Highway 19 north of Port McNeill. It sits on the Cluxewe River estuary, with grassy and shaded sites including pull-throughs, full and partial hookups, beach sites, laundry, showers, flush toilets, and playground.

Dalewood Inn

1702 Broughton Boulevard
P.O. Box 280
Port McNeill, B.C. V0N 2R0
(604) 956-3304

This motel has 36 units and is located close to the public wharf and ferry landing. A restaurant serves up a seafood smorgasbord during June, July, and August. **($$)**

Haida-Way Motor Inn
1817 Campbell Way
P.O. Box 399
Port McNeill, B.C. V0N 2R0
(604) 956-3373

With 66 units, including housekeeping facilities, this motel has rooms with balconies, one suite, dining room, coffee shop, lounge, pub, and a beer and wine store next door. **($$)**

STRATHCONA PROVINCIAL PARK

Strathcona Park Lodge
Highway 28
P.O. Box 2160
Campbell River, B.C. V9W 5C9
(604) 286-8206 or (604) 286-3122

Although it is located just outside the park boundary, this fascinating outdoor education center and lodge is closely associated with the park. It is located 28 miles southwest of Campbell River on Upper Campbell Lake. The lodge has waterfront cabins, rooms with balconies and private baths in three-story chalets, hostel-style rooms, and waterfront campsites. Buffet meals are served. The lodge operates a full outdoor adventure program from daily water and mountain activities to extended wilderness hikes and sea kayak trips. Motor boats, sailboats, canoes, and kayaks are rented. Instruction is available. The lodge has special weekend, week-long, and extended program packages, as well as a "Honeymoon Interlude Package." **($ to $$)**

TELEGRAPH COVE

Telegraph Cove Resort and Campground
Telegraph Cove, B.C. V0N 3J0
(604) 928-3131 (summer)
(604) 284-3426 (winter)

Telegraph Cove is a historic fishing port located at the head of Johnstone Strait on the northeastern edge of Vancouver Island. Original homes and other buildings on the harbor have been preserved and serve as overnight accommodations. Modern cottages are also available. The main attraction is fishing and the popular whale-watching expeditions to view the killer whales of Johnstone Strait. The campground is suitable for RVs and trailers, with hookups, showers, flush toilets, and marina.

TOFINO

Bella Pacifica Resort and Campground
This is a campground for tenters and RVs, two miles south of Tofino, on Mackenzie Beach. There are oceanfront and wooded campsites, full and partial hookups, cable TV, flush toilets, showers, laundry, ice, firepits, and firewood. Pacific Rim National Park is a few minutes' drive south. There are 160 sites.

Best Western Tin Wis Resort
1119 Pacific Rim Highway
P.O. Box 389
Tofino, B.C. V0R 2Z0
(604) 725-4445

What used to be a seaside lodge with barely livable accommodations is now a modern resort operation with a glassed-in restaurant facing the Templar Channel, landscaped grounds, rooms with double and queen beds, and access to the ocean beach. **($$ to $$$)**

Chesterman Beach Bed and Breakfast

1345 Chesterman Beach Road
P.O. Box 72
Tofino, B.C. V0R 2Z0
(604) 725-3726

This is an oceanfront B & B operation with two rooms and a separate cottage. The rooms have single and double beds and private baths. There's also a sauna, and the sandy beach is at the door, with hiking trails nearby. **($$ to $$$)**

Weigh West Marine Resort

634 Campbell Street
P.O. Box 69
Tofino, B.C. V0R 2Z0
(604) 725-2224 or 800-665-8922

This is a fancy name for a motel at the Tofino fishing port, with standard rooms and one-bedroom housekeeping units. The dining room is open from March through October. There's also a marine pub, and the action on the fishing piers is fascinating. Downtown Tofino is a 10-minute walk away. Fishing charters and sightseeing boat tours can be arranged. **($$ to $$$)**

UCLUELET

Burley's Bed and Breakfast

1078 Helen Road
P.O. Box 550
Ucluelet, B.C. V0R 3A0
(604) 726-4444

This B & B home has a great waterfront setting on Ucluelet Inlet, with six units, twin, double, queen, king and waterbeds, shared baths, a lounge with fireplace, and continental breakfast. Other facilities include a recreation room with pool table, rowboat, and canoe. **($ to $$)**

Canadian Princess Resort

Peninsula Road
P.O. Box 939
Ucluelet, B.C. V0R 3A0
(604) 726-7771 or 800-663-7090

This resort operation is open from March 1 through September 30 and includes a historic steamship permanently moored in Ucluelet Harbour. You can stay in a stateroom on board or ashore in superior motel-style rooms, some with fireplaces. There is a dining room with lounges, and fishing packages can be arranged. For such an unusual resort, prices are quite reasonable. **($ to $$$)**

Island West Fishing Resort

140 Bay Street
P.O. Box 32
Ucluelet, B.C. V0R 3A0
(604) 726-7515

Right in the midst of the fishing docks, this lodge with campground is at the foot of Bay Street. The motel section has standard rooms. **($ to $$)**

The RV park has partial hookups, showers, flush toilets, laundry, dump station, freezer, ice, a boat launch, bait and tackle shop, and a private marina. Guided salmon and halibut fishing can be arranged. There's a marine pub with libations and pub food on-site.

Pacific Rim Motel
1755 Peninsula Road
P.O. Box 172
Ucluelet, B.C. V0R 3A0
(604) 726-7728

This is a standard, concrete-block motel on Ucluelet's main street, close to shopping and the fishing harbor. There are standard and housekeeping units, some with views of the harbor. Restaurants and the grocery store are nearby. **($ to $$)**

VICTORIA

Captain's Palace Inn
309 Belleville Street
Victoria, B.C. V8V 1X2
(604) 388-9191

This bed and breakfast operation has three historic mansions, on the Inner Harbour across the street from the Port Angeles (Black Ball) ferry terminal. Rooms have private baths. There is morning coffee service, and full breakfast in the dining room is included. **($$ to $$$)**

The Empress
721 Government Street
Victoria, B.C. V8W 1W5
(604) 384-8111 or 800-441-1414

This fine hotel on the Inner Harbour was built by the Canadian Pacific Railway and is one of the grand old railway hotels of Canada, and a tourist attraction on its own. It has been recently renovated from top to bottom. There are rooms and suites, with indoor pool, whirlpool, several dining rooms, lounges, health club, and a magnificent lobby where afternoon tea is served. The hotel is across the street from the Royal B.C. Museum and the Parliament buildings, close to downtown shops and restaurants. Small pets are allowed. **($$$ to $$$++)**

Fort Victoria RV Park
340 Island Highway 1A
Victoria, B.C. V9B 1H1
(604) 479-8112

This RV park with 300 sites is located four miles north of the city center, with full hookups, cable TV, laundry, dump station, showers, flush toilets, and playground, with shopping nearby.

Grand Pacific Hotel
450 Quebec Street
Victoria, B.C. V8V 1W5
(604) 386-0450 or 800-424-6423

This modern high-rise hotel is a Clarion operation, with rooms and suites, dining room, lounge, pool, sauna, whirlpool, fitness center, and underground parking. It's adjacent to the Inner Harbour and Parliament buildings. There are 145 units. **($$$)**

James Bay Inn
270 Government Street
Victoria, B.C. V8V 2L2
(604) 384-7151 or 800-836-2649

This old, historic hotel is a mainstay of the downtown Victoria area and is located near the Parliament Building and Beacon Hill Park. As an older hotel, some rooms have shared bath but rates are the most reasonable in the Inner Harbour area. A pub and restaurant are also in the building. **($ to $$)**

Oak Bay Beach Hotel

1175 Beach Drive
Victoria, B.C. V8S 2N2
(604) 598-4556

Why go to Victoria and stay in a standard motel? There are plenty of motels, but this fine old Tudor hotel is a standout. Located on a quiet bay, with fine views, the rooms have antique furnishings. The dining room is renowned for its scenic setting and fine food. There's a tiny English pub and gardens to walk in. The hotel is located on Victoria's Marine Scenic Drive. **($$$ to $$$ + +)**

Stay 'N Save Motor Inn

3233 Maple Street
Victoria, B.C. V8X 4Y9
(604) 475-7500 or
800-663-0298 (Vancouver)

This is a standard motor hotel for those who prefer quick get-aways and standard facilities. This motel does have some extras, including suites and queen and king beds. Some rooms have kitchen units. There's a family restaurant and laundry on-site. A large shopping mall is nearby. **($$)**

Southeast Alaska

Forests, glaciers, and islands are the major markers of the 540-mile stretch of forest and water called southeast Alaska, or just "the Southeast." The region is about the same size as all of New England, and it contains the Alexander Archipelago, one of the most impressive island chains in the world. Aside from a thin coastal strip—the western slope of the Coast Mountains—this part of Alaska is made up of islands.

An aquatic highway surrounds the islands, and ferry transportation through the Inside Passage is an important factor in the commercial life of the region. Using the ferry system is the only way for a visitor to see the area in all its splendor. Travel by air is also an option, and a visit to southeast Alaska is not complete without at least a short air tour of the coastal waters and forests. From outside the state, the area is serviced by Alaska Airlines. Within the region are a host of small air operators that fly from island to island and offer tourists sightseeing flights and seaplane excursions to the important wilderness attractions.

Often called the Alaska Panhandle, the narrow strip of mainland is joined to the northern part of the state by a piece of land only 11 miles wide. The Coast Mountains provide a boundary wall for the Panhandle, rising to a height of almost 20,000 feet and creating spectacular scenes from sea level. From Glacier Bay to the huge Tongass National Forest—stretching from the wooded islands and up the mountain slopes to the

Canadian boundary—this is a region of unparalleled natural wonder: the world's largest collection of tidewater glaciers; dense, damp forests covering islands and mountainsides; major rivers—including the mighty Stikine; and silty glacial streams flowing to the Inside Passage.

Southeast Alaska presents a wide range of ecosystems within four major biotic zones. You'll experience all of the zones, from the thick rain forests of the Tongass National Forest at sea level to alpine muskeg in Glacier Bay National Park. You'll also walk the gamut by hiking the Chilcoot Trail, which ascends from the Lynn Canal to the alpine zone in the high country above Skagway—in a little more than 15 miles. The moderate, sea-level zone has the hemlock spruce forest common to most of the mainland areas north of Vancouver, B.C. But here, much of the land is boggy, with large displays of skunk cabbage, groupings of water-loving huckleberries, and fast-growing underbrush.

Muskegs are an altogether fascinating phenomenon of the region; they are quite common as the result of combining much rain with poor soil drainage. Over time, dips and depressions in the ground hold water, which nurtures peat or sphagnum moss, creating bogs that can be as deep as 30 or 40 feet. Many of the muskeg bogs sit in depressions scooped out by glaciers in times past. The continuing cycle of creation is seen here over a relatively short period of time (a few hundred years). A dip in the ground is carved by a glacier, and the bottom is lined with fine glacial till, much like a free-form swimming pool is lined with hard gunnite. The depression fills with stagnant water.

Bog plants grow over a hundred years or more, not only providing a moss foundation, but other plants—Labrador tea, blueberry, skunk cabbage, salal, marsh marigold, bog rosemary, shorepine, and others—place their roots in the moss. All of this growth builds a mat, which then compacts and provides the conditions for a new forest to generate. This cycle of bog development and forest generation goes on along the length of the Alaska Panhandle but particularly in the heavy rainfall areas such as Tongass National Forest.

There is muskeg in the alpine areas of Glacier Bay National Park and again in the high country above Skagway. But here, just across the Canadian border, in the colder and dryer rain shadow on the eastern side of the Coast Range is also permafrost, which provides the cement that keeps water at the surface. The muskeg becomes alpine tundra.

Early Days

Two of the four groups that first inhabited Alaska and the neighboring northern Canadian territories settled in the Southeast. Aleuts stopped in the Aleutian Islands. The Athabascans settled in the Alaskan interior, with some migrating south to become the ancestors of the Apache and Navajo peoples. The Inuit (Eskimo) people came much later, settling along the Arctic coast. The Tlingit and Haida came to the continent, as did the others from Siberia over the Bering Land Bridge. All but the Inuit came from Asia as long ago as 20,000 to 40,000 years. The Haida and Tlingit, collectively known as the Koluschan, traveled along the coast and settled on the islands of the Alexander Archipelago, on the mainland of the southeast coast and in the southern Yukon. The Haida also occupied the Queen Charlotte Islands (to the south in Canadian waters), and these islands became the Haida tribal homeland. While the Queen Charlotte Islands are the cultural center of the Haida, there are Haida living today in the southern part of southeast Alaska.

The two southeastern tribes fashioned a rich and complex society, filled with cultural observances including the potlatch. They took slaves and lived within a strict clan structure. The peak of their artwork resulted in the famed totem poles and distinctive architecture, as well as finely decorated blankets and baskets made of cedar bark and spruce roots. A visit to the Southeast is incomplete without an adventure into the Native American history and culture of the area.

Aside from Native American habitation, the region has been occupied by three nations. First, Russian fur explorers traveled through the Aleutians, moving down the coast to the Panhandle. Vitus Bering, a Danish captain sailing under the flag of Russia's Peter the Great, first touched what is now Alaska in 1741. Coming from the south, English, French, and Spanish explorers made trips through the Inside Passage. After Gregor Shelikof established Russia's first permanent settlement on Kodiak Island (in northwestern Alaska), other Russian fur trade managers, called governors, maintained settlements along the Inside

Passage for more than 60 years. Alexander Baranof established the city of Sitka on Baranof Island in 1799, warring with the Tlingit people (who sacked and burned Baranof's fort in 1802). After it was rebuilt, Sitka became an important community, called the "Paris of the Pacific." Five to six hundred Russians lived here, importing a thousand Hawaiians to do menial work. Admiral Baron Ferdinand von Wrangell replaced Baranof as governor.

Sitka was a long distance from Russia. Transportation was difficult, and the little colony became a drain on the national finances. Russia gave way to the British along the Inside Passage. In 1867, Russia sold northern Alaska to the United States for $7.2 million. Not only was the purchase of Alaska unpopular in the rest of the United States, but Canadians protested the ceding of the Panhandle to the United States by the British government.

While fur-bearing creatures, particularly the sea otter, were almost decimated during the Russian period, the communities of southeast Alaska existed on a fishing economy until the U.S. Forest Service began opening the forests to logging activity during World War II. As the once-abundant salmon were reduced in numbers by overfishing, logging companies established sawmills and paper factories.

Today, fishing and lumbering remain as the prime staples of the Southeast economy. But tourism has become an important factor in the Inside Passage. And it is no wonder. All along the Inside Passage are little towns that are reminders of the Russian era. In Sitka, and other places, you'll find Russian churches and graveyards that tell the story of that short but important period of outreach by emperors Peter and Paul. Native American culture is represented in the wonderful artwork and dancing to be experienced. Villages may be visited, and all of the Panhandle communities feature museums telling the long history of Native Americans in the region.

How to Get There

There are few highways in southeast Alaska, and those that are here run only a few miles from a handful of towns and the city of Juneau. Water provides the real highway, with ferries plying the Inside Passage from island to island and small town to small town. You can also use your own boat for the journey or use a combination of ferries, your own boat, and/or local boat charters to fully experience the natural beauty of the region.

The main ferry route from the outside to southeast Alaska begins in Bellingham, Washington, where the car ferries travel north several hundred miles, past forested islands and mainland mountains, to the major Panhandle towns. The ferry from Bellingham that has overnight accommodations and food service does not stop in Canada. The southeastern Alaska service of the Alaska Marine Highway system does stop in Prince Rupert, B.C., just south of the Alaska boundary, with car ferries servicing the mainline cities of the Panhandle, starting with Ketchikan and ending at Haines and Skagway. From May to September, a smaller ferry runs a commuter route from Ketchikan to Hollis, Metlakatla, and Hyder. You can actually drive to the small border village of Hyder from the interior of B.C., just as you can drive to Skagway and Haines from the Alaska Highway. All other southeastern Alaska towns are accessible only by water or air.

For information on all ferries in the southeastern system of the Alaska Marine Highway, call (907) 465-3941 or 800-642-0066, or write Alaska Marine Highway, P.O. Box 25535, Juneau, AK 99802-5535.

You can also take a car ferry from Vancouver Island to Prince Rupert, where you can change to the Alaska Marine Highway. The B.C. Ferries ship *Queen of the North* sails from Port Hardy on the northern tip of Vancouver Island, departing at 7:30 A.M. and arriving in Prince Rupert at 10:30 P.M. The ferry's summer season runs from late May to late September, with positioning cruises between Tsawwassen (near Vancouver) to Port Hardy at the beginning and end of the season. For information and reservations, call (604) 669-1211 (Vancouver) or (604) 386-3431.

Southeast Communities

The major natural places visited in this chapter are Glacier Bay National Park and Misty Fjords National Monument. However, there are many other places of interest to the visitor, among them the islands and towns of southeast Alaska, including the state capital, Juneau, and the historic Klondike gold rush towns of Skagway and Haines. Only 69,000 people live in this vast area. Each community has only a few thousand people, who live in an area of unspoiled splendor. We'll work our way through the Inside Passage from south to north.

METLAKATLA

The southernmost Alaska town, Metlakatla sits on Annette Island, located just north of the British Columbia city of Prince Rupert. The island was settled in 1887 by William Duncan, a Scottish-born lay minister who came here with several hundred Tsimshian from B.C. after a confrontation with church authorities. Reservation status was granted by Congress to the entire island. Duncan built a sawmill and canning factory, giving the island a strong economic base. Many of the residents are commercial fishermen. Visitors are welcomed, and those who plan to stay for more than a short visit should obtain a permit from the Metlakatla Community. For information, contact the city clerk at (907) 886-4441.

KETCHIKAN

Located on Revillagigedo Island, this town is 90 miles north of Prince Rupert, located on Tongass Narrows. The first salmon cannery was established here in 1889, one year after the discovery of gold in the area. Silver and copper mining sustained the community, along with the salmon canning industry. A dozen canneries were in operation by the 1930s. Today, only four remain. A sawmill and paper mill (a few miles outside of town) now employ many of the residents. Cruise ships and many casual visitors come to Ketchikan to savor the unique flavor of the town. It is a linear community, built for more than three miles along the waterfront, with buildings in the business section sitting on pilings, linked by boardwalks. Many homes are perched on wooded cliffs. There are several motels, bed and breakfast homes, and a summer youth hostel set up in the Methodist church. Campers will enjoy the four public campgrounds and one private camping resort north of Ketchikan on the Tongass Highway and Ward Lake Road. The Tongass Historical Museum, Saxman Totem Park, and the Totem Heritage Center offer a glimpse into Native American and pioneer settlement and the amazing artists of the region. For information, call the Ketchikan Visitors Bureau at (907) 225-6166 or 800-770-2200.

Ketchikan is also the gateway to Misty Fjords National Monument, a superb wilderness area of deep inlets, mountains, and rain forests (see below).

PRINCE OF WALES ISLAND

About 15 miles west of Ketchikan, this is the third-largest U.S. island, after Hawaii's Big Island and Kodiak Island. The heavily forested island has several small communities, including Craig (the largest), Thorne Bay, Klawock, and Hydaburg. These and the smaller communities are connected by road from the ferry landing near Hollis. Kasann is a small Haida village, not connected by road, at the head of Kasann Bay on the eastern side of the island. There are several world-class spawning streams on the island, including the Klawock River (trout, steelhead, and salmon), the Thorne River (Dolly Varden and trout), and the Sarkar for salmon, steelhead, and trout. There are four public campgrounds on the island. Boat ramps are available, and saltwater fishing charters take serious ocean anglers out for halibut and salmon.

There are motels and bed and breakfast homes, plus 20 Forest Service cabins accessible by boat, plane, or foot. For information, call the Prince of Wales Chamber of Commerce at (907) 826-3870.

WRANGELL

This fishing port, on the northeastern tip of Wrangell Island, is 85 miles north of Ketchikan. The town is 2.5 miles south of the Stikine River delta on Zimovia Strait. The nearest sizable community is Petersburg. Wrangell began its life in 1834 as a Russian fort, built to counter efforts by the Hudson's Bay Company to establish fur trading in the area. It became part of the Hudson's Bay Company empire in 1840, when Russia abandoned the region. The U.S. flag was flown for the first time in 1867. The mighty Stikine River is a prime attraction for anglers and hunters. In addition to tourism, Wrangell is supported by a Japanese-owned paper mill. There is still a considerable fishing industry, centering on salmon. The town has motels and restaurants, as well as bed and breakfast inns and rustic lodges. The City Park, on Zimovia Highway, accommodates campers. For information on the town and its attractions, contact the Chamber of Commerce at (907) 874-3770. During summer months, information is available at the Wrangell Visitor Center (Brueger Street and Outer Drive), and at the Wrangell Museum at 122 Second Street.

PETERSBURG

Located at the north end of Wrangell Narrows, on the northwest tip of Mitkof Island, Petersburg sits midway between Ketchikan and Juneau. A fishing port, the town boasts the largest halibut fleet in Alaska. Shrimp, crab, herring, and salmon are also important sea products for the local residents. The community was named not for Peter the Great, but for Peter Buschmann, who found the townsite for a sawmill and canning operation, in 1897. The cannery existed under several owners and is still in operation as Pacific Fisheries. LeConte Glacier, 25 miles northeast of Petersburg, is America's southernmost tidewater glacier. The glacier is continually calving, sending ice from its face into LeConte Bay. Visitors may experience this amazing scene, augmented by the presence of porpoises, seals, and whales, by taking a helicopter ride or chartering a boat.

The Forest Service (Tongass National Forest) offers backcountry cabins, hiking trails, and canoe routes. The Forest Office Service is located in the Federal Building; call (907) 772-3871. For information on local events and attractions, call the Chamber of Commerce at (907) 772-3646.

SITKA

This is the gem of southeast Alaska communities, located on the west side of Baranof Island, 185 miles north of Ketchikan and 95 miles southwest of Juneau. The town reflects both its former importance as the Russian capital of Alaska and its present life as a fishing and lumber town. It is a charming, scenic community that sits on the steep ocean shore, across the water from many small islands. Mount Edgecumbe—a dormant volcano—dominates the scene. The first place to visit is St. Michael's Cathedral, the religious and cultural focus of the Russian days, from 1844. It was destroyed by fire in January 1966 and was rebuilt as an exact replica. The cathedral still serves as a place of worship for 100 Russian Orthodox families. The Chamber of Commerce office and information center is located in the Centennial Building, which also sees Russian dance performances and music festivals and is the site of the

Isabel Miller Museum, which features permanent exhibits on Sitka history. Sitka National Historic Park is a living monument to the Tlingit peoples and the Russian settlement. The park has two sites: the Russian Bishop's House, on Lincoln Street near Crescent Harbor, and the Fort Site, at the end of Lincoln Street, where a Tlingit fort was burned to the ground by Russians following the 1804 Battle of Sitka. This site is the location of the Southeast Alaska Indian Cultural Center.

Old Sitka is a National Historic Site, on Halibut Point Road. This is the location of the original Russian settlement, then called Fort Archangel Michael, and burned down by Tlingits in 1802. Those Russians who weren't killed in the attack and fire fled from the area, returning to establish the "new" Sitka in 1804.

There are many other historical attractions in Sitka, and a visit of several days is necessary to take in the history of this wonderful town and nearby outdoor attractions. Hiking trails are available, including a short walk off Sawmill Creek Road, on Blue Lake Road, to Blue Lake (rainbow trout, from May to September), the Harbor Mountain Ridge Trail, and Mount Verstovia Trail. For information, contact the Sitka Convention and Visitors Bureau at (907) 747-5940.

SMALLER COMMUNITIES

Hoonah, Tenakee Springs, and Pelican are villages on Chicagohof Island. All are served by ferry and by private air carriers. Tenakee Hot Springs is a major attraction for fans of soaking. The spring water ranges from 96°F to 108°F, and a bathhouse is located on the waterfront with posted times for men and women. This facility, built in 1940, is maintained through contributions from local residents and visitors. The community has become a popular retirement center, with summer homes lining Tenakee Avenue.

Pelican is located on the eastern shore of Lisianski Inlet, on the island's northwest coast. Pelican Seafoods is the processor of a variety of seafood from salmon and halibut to crab, sea urchin, and sea cucumber. Like Ketchikan, Pelican is on pilings, built over the water with boardwalk streets. Visitors—who can stay in a lodge, B & B home, or above a bar and grill—come to hike, fish, and watch birds and whales.

Hoonah is on the northeast shore of the island, due west of the entrance to Glacier Bay. This is a fishing community of more than 900, occupied by the Tlingit for thousands of years. Halibut and salmon are the main catches and are processed at the Excursion Inlet Packing Company. Many families depend on subsistence hunting and fishing. The Tlingit provide guide services for hunters and anglers. There is extensive logging of the northern section of Chicagohof Island, with forest roads leading to recreation sites.

Kake, located on the northwest coast of Kupreanof Island, is a village of the Kake tribe of the Tlingit. After a stormy relationship with Europeans and Americans, the tribe settled here in the last decade of the 19th century. There is a cannery, and logging adds to the local economy. This is a fine salmon fishing area, and chinook of record size have been taken from the waters around Kake.

Angoon has a population of more than 600 and is located on the west coast of Admiralty Island on Chatham Strait. This is another longtime Tlingit settlement and the only town on this large island. All but the northern end of the island was declared a national monument in 1980. The monument is managed jointly by the U.S. Forest Service and the Native American community. The scenery is spectacular, with many small islands and reefs in Mitchell Bay and with quiet waters perfect for kayaking. The other major area in the monument is Admiralty Lakes Recreational Area. Wildlife to be seen include many bald eagles, brown bear, and Sitka black-tailed deer. Twelve USFS cabins are available for rental by visitors, through the Forest Service office in Angoon. For monument information, call (907) 788-3166, and for local attractions and accommodations, call (907) 788-3653.

JUNEAU

The state capital is a mainland community, sitting beside Gastineau Channel opposite Douglas Island. Even though Juneau is at the northern end of the Panhandle, the climate is moderate and damp. An average yearly snowfall of 103 inches falls, and usually melts, during the winter months. This was originally a gold rush town, founded in 1880 by Joe Juneau and Dick Harris, a pair of rugged prospectors who found gold in a stream they named Gold Creek. The creek now runs through the downtown area. The discovery turned out to be one of the largest quartz gold lodes in the world. Miners flocked immediately to

Harrisburg (its name during that first year), and the hard rock mines eventually produced about $150 million in gold. Juneau became the territorial capital in 1906.

Government buildings now dominate the city skyline. Squeezed between the channel and Mount Juneau, the community climbs the mountainside. There is a residential suburb on Douglas Island, linked to the downtown area by the Juneau-Douglas Bridge. A downtown development is a major sign of Native American commercial activity following the passing of the Alaska Native Claims Settlement Act in 1971. Sealaska Plaza is a modern commercial center developed by Sealaska Corp., one of 13 regional Alaskan Native American corporations.

Juneau has a good selection of hotels and motels, plus a few bed and breakfast inns. It must be the influence (financial and otherwise) of the government's being here, but there are more than 60 restaurants—including a fine microbrewery—serving a wide variety of cuisines and excellent local beer. The Juneau International Hostel is located at 614 Harris Street, near the Capitol building. This is a major cruise ship port, with almost all of the cruises to Alaska stopping in the city for a short stay. Visitor services have developed near the ferry terminal. The Log Cabin Information Center, at 134 Third Street, services visitors' needs year-round; you can call (907) 586-2201 or (907) 586-2284.

The most popular attraction for tourists is a drive to Mendenhall Glacier, located 13 miles from downtown Juneau, via Glacier Highway (Egan Drive) and Mendenhall Glacier Spur Road. A trail leads from the large parking lot to the edge of the lake. The visitor center is open from Memorial Day week through September. Three trails lead from the visitor center area, including a half-mile, self-guiding nature trail. Other trails are Nugget Creek and East Glacier. Guided hikes with Forest Service rangers are available in summer.

The Mount Roberts Trail leads from the top of Starr Hill, via Sixth Street, to the summit at 3,819 feet. There's a fine view of the area available from an observation point, about two miles (20 minutes) along the trail. Marine Park is a picnic area and summer concert venue, located at the foot of Seward Street.

For an appreciation of the historical and environmental qualities that make Alaska so special, visit the Alaska State Museum, located at 395 Whittier Street, off Egan Drive. Exhibit rooms present displays on Alaska's Russian and American history, the mining period, Alaskan wildlife (including the Bald Eagle Nesting Tree), and art history. Tours are conducted during summer months.

SKAGWAY AND HAINES

Haines and Skagway are the only communities of the Inside Passage accessible by highway routes. You can take your car or RV to the other cities and towns, but you have to float there on a ferry. While the two northern towns are also accessed by the Alaska Marine Highway system (ferries), you can drive to Skagway over the Klondike Highway (2), which links the old Gold Rush town to the Alaska Highway. Haines, at the end of Lynn Canal, is also reached from the Alaska Highway, deep inside the Yukon Territory, by taking the paved Haines Highway for 151.6 miles and four hours of spectacular scenery in the St. Elias Mountains. What was originally a Chilkat trail was co-opted by the enterprising Jack Dalton as the Dalton Toll Trail, operated by Dalton during the Klondike Gold Rush.

Haines is 80 air miles from Juneau and 13 miles from Skagway. Yet, by taking highway routes, Haines and Skagway are 360 miles apart. John Muir played a part in establishing Haines. He was brought here by his friend, the Presbyterian missionary S. Hall Young. They intended to construct a Christian village for missionary purposes. The mission, named Chilkoot, was established by 1881. Just south of Haines is what used to be called Fort Chilkoot, founded as a U.S. Army post (Fort William H. Seward) in 1904. The post folded in 1946 and was sold to local businesspeople. The two communities merged in 1970, and Fort Seward was designated a National Historic Site. Some local people continue to call it Port Chilkoot. I can vividly remember attending a memorable Strawberry Festival in Haines in the 1960s—a celebration that was held in the early summer for many years. The festival later metamorphosed into the Southeast Alaska State Fair.

This town is geared for visitors. The Hälsingland Hotel is one of the major buildings on the parade square at the former Fort Seward. Other motels and inns cater to summer tourists. Public campgrounds include Portage Cove, Chilkat State Park, and Chilkoot Lake (eight miles from Haines). The Chilkat Dancers perform several times each week during the summer period. Walking tours of Fort Seward are offered. The Sheldon Museum and Cultural Center presents the history of the Chilkat Valley and the culture of the Tlingit people. The state fair is held each August. There are guided float trips with Chilkat guides, nature tours, two daily water taxi trips between Haines and Skagway, even one- to three-hour bicycle tours through the Bald Eagle Preserve in the Chilkat Valley. The preserve is a fascinating place to visit, whether you ride a bicycle or not. The Haines Rodeo brings together northern cowpokes and rodeo riders in early July. Dalton City, a commercial gold rush town, is housed in Disney's White Fang movie set. There are excellent restaurants, and several serve fresh seafood.

The visitor center—on Second and Willard Streets—is an excellent source of free brochures and other information on all of Alaska and the Yukon. It's open June through August. For information at any time of year, call (907) 766-2234 or 800-458-3579.

Skagway, another prime tourist destination, is a living reminder of the Klondike Gold Rush. This little town, at the north end of Taiya Inlet on the Lynn Canal, is devoted to conserving and presenting memories of the stampede of miners—most of whom came through this frontier community on their way to dreamed-of riches. In its early days, particularly during 1898 and 1899, Skagway was one of the roughest and rowdiest towns in the American West, bossed by the notorious crook and conman "Soapy" Smith. It had been founded a year earlier by Captain William Moore and his son Bernard.

A narrow gauge railway, the White Pass and Yukon Route, was built over the mountains between Skagway and Whitehorse, Yukon. Nearby Dyea, a temporary tent town established at the foot of the Chilkoot Pass, came and went, but Skagway survived, mainly because of the railway, which operated as a freight line until 1982, after mines in the Yukon played out. However, the railway was revived in the 1980s as a summer passenger line, and it currently offers round-trip excursions to the White Pass summit, to Fraser, and the shores of Lake Bennett. The train also picks up hikers who have climbed the famed Chilkoot Trail for the return trip to Skagway from the trail's end at Bennett Lake.

Most of downtown Skagway has been designated Klondike Gold Rush National Historic Park. It includes six blocks of the business district, the 17-mile Chilkoot Trail corridor, and a mile-wide corridor that includes the White Pass Trail, another historic gold rush route where hundreds of horses died while struggling to carry prospectors and their supplies over this nearly impossible (and impassable) route to Dawson City. Operated by the National Park Service, the historic park offers ranger-led walking tours in summer, plus films in the visitor center.

The 33-mile Chilkoot Trail begins a few miles from Skagway, on Dyea Road, climbing to Chilkoot Pass at an elevation of 3,739 feet. The hike traces the exact route used by the gold seekers bound for Dawson City and the gold fields of the Klondike. While the trail provides a steep climb, it provides great scenery and historic sites and artifacts. A particularly touching site is the Dyea Slide Cemetery, at the foot of the trail, where more than 100 Chilkoot Trail travelers perished in a snowslide on April 3, 1898.

Skagway is a prime stopping point for Alaska cruise ships, and many visitors travel by car from the Alaska Highway. It has modern and more meaningful accommodations, including the historic Golden North Hotel (1898) and the Skagway Inn Bed and Breakfast (1897). For information on the town, its attractions, accommodations, and saloons (there are several), call the Skagway Convention and Visitors Bureau at (907) 983-2854; for information on the Chilkoot Trail and other historic park activities, call (907) 983-2046.

Glacier Bay National Park

What was a solid river of ice only 200 years ago has become a dramatic bay, almost surrounded by the most impressive collection of icefields in North America. For some reason, or reasons, the gigantic layer of moving ice, formed over thousands of years, began to recede. However, for today's visitor, the creation of the bay is a godsend. At 65 miles long and up to 15 miles wide, the bay offers access to myriad scenes of unspeakable beauty. To the west is the huge Brady Icefield: a series of glaciers flowing from the peaks of Mount Cooper, Mount Abbe, Mount Bertha, Mount Salisbury, Mount Fairweather, and Mount Quincy Adams—all mountains of the Fairweather Range. To the east of Muir Inlet, a long arm off Glacier Bay, is a constellation of glaciers: Casement, MacBride, Riggs, and Muir. Farther west and north are the Fairweather and Sea Otter Glaciers.

This is extremely thick ice! Mount Fairweather is 15,350 feet above sea level. Quincy Adam's peak has an elevation of 13,650 feet. By cruise ship, kayak, or by your feet along an iceside path, the spirit of Glacier Bay brings a sense of power (nature's, not your own) and feelings of smallness (yours, not nature's). Eagles cruise the chilled air over the icefields, while whales cruise the waters of Glacier Bay and Muir Inlet, creating an unforgettable natural spectacle.

Native Americans first came to Glacier Bay when the region was recovering from a period of glaciation, around 9,000 years ago. These were primitive peoples who used stone tools, including scrapers and choppers. Later, a Tlingit group known as the Hoonah lived on the lands surrounding Glacier Bay. The Hoonah were seminomadic, moving with the changing ice conditions. Some of their temporary communities are now buried under glacial ice. They camped at Lituya Bay, on the outer coast, on the Beardslee Islands, and also at Cape Spencer and Dundas Bay. The Tlingit named the bay *Sit'ee ti geiyi,* which means "the bay in place of the glacier." This name remains today (although bowdlerized) as Sitakaday Narrows, the entrance to Glacier Bay.

Captain James Cook visited the bay, and Captain George Vancouver, who sailed with Cook, returned with his own ship in 1786. Muir visited the glaciers in 1879. Mining operations moved into the area after Joe Juneau's find near the present state capital, and gold was discovered near Reid Inlet in 1924. It took until 1976 for environmentalists to successfully lobby for the closing of mining in federal park lands in 1976. Glacier Bay had been designated a national monument since 1925, and became a fully fledged national park in 1980.

Glacier Bay began to collect its year-round coating of ice some 20 million years ago. A long period of uplift had created the mountain ranges of the region, creating two major faults. This has long been a seismic-sensitive zone, as part of the rift between the Pacific and mainland plates. A major earthquake in 1958 loosened a huge wall of rock off Mount Fairweather, bringing 1.3 million cubic feet of ice and rock into the head of Lituya Bay, generating a huge wall of water that flipped icebergs high onto the mountains. Fishing boats were flung many miles into the ocean. The quake registered as eight on the Richter scale.

There are 14 major glaciers; Brady is the largest, covering 188 square miles. How can such ice be created and maintained in a moderate climate, where the rain falls as often as it snows? What Glacier Bay proves is that nature doesn't need cold temperatures to create year-round rivers of ice. The weather systems, including serious storms roaring in from the Pacific, collide with the mountains of the Coast Range, creating great differences in temperature between the bay level and the high ice cap, which is as much as 7,000 feet above the waterline. While it may be raining at sea level at the outer edges of the icefields, sea level at the north end of Glacier Bay is usually much cooler, as much as 20°F cooler.

GLACIER BAY LOGISTICS

The main entrance point to the national park is Bartlett Cove, 100 miles from Juneau. There is no road to the park, and visitors get themselves to Bartlett Cove by boat and to nearby Gustavus by air. Those in private boats or kayaks should consult rangers at park headquarters on how best to see the park attractions. Permits are required for motorized pleasure boats between June 1 and August 31. For reservations, write no more than two months in advance to National Park Service, Gustavus, AK 99826-0140. For information, call (907) 697-2627 (May 1 to Labor Day).

Glacier Bay Lodge provides the only indoor accommodations inside the park, at Bartlett Cove. The lodge offers guided tours of the park in addition to overnight visits and meals. There is also a developed campground at Bartlett Cove; backcountry camping is available throughout the park.

Gasoline and diesel fuel may be purchased at Bartlett Cove, where anchorage is also available. Gustavus has a small boat harbor and a public dock. Sandy Cove, 20 miles from Bartlett Cove, is another popular mooring place. The small community of Gustavus is located at the mouth of the Salmon River, 48 miles northwest of Juneau and just around the point from the mouth of Glacier Bay. It is connected by road to the park headquarters at Bartlett Cove. Many visitors stay at one of the lodges and inns in this town of 400, and go to the park through a local tour service. For those without their own boat, this is the way to enjoy the experience most thoroughly. It really pays to have your visit conducted by an experienced local guide. Glacier Bay Lodge and several Gustavus lodges organize their own guiding services or put you in touch with tour companies. One call—to book your accommodations—can also take care of organizing your stay in the park.

The closest port of call for the state ferry system is Hoonah Bay. You can catch a local flight from there to Gustavus. In addition, Glacier Bay is serviced daily by Alaska Airlines from Juneau and by air charter services to Gustavus Airport from Juneau, Sitka, Haines, and Skagway. Bus service to Glacier Bay Lodge is available for those on the Alaska Airlines jet flights, and taxi service is also available. Some of the Gustavus lodges have their own shuttle services. For details on accommodations, see page 337.

PARK WILDLIFE

For a park nearly covered by ice, Glacier Bay has an amazing range of plant life in its four biotic zones. At the top, above 2,500 feet, is alpine tundra. This is an area of open rock, interspersed with grasses, willow, heath, and the dwarf version of blueberry. Next to the glaciers are the moraines, which have horsetail, lichen, mosses, fireweed, willow, cottonwood, and soapberry. You'll also find the Sitka alder along the gravelly moraines. Where there is fresh water, there is wet tundra, giving life to Sitka alder, willow, and low-spreading plants such as sedges and cottongrass. The park forest is a typical Panhandle conifer forest of western hemlock and Sitka spruce, found on the southern, western, and eastern boundaries. Along streams are alder and cottonwood, the common riparian trees of the Pacific Northwest. The forest understory includes blueberry, devil's club, mosses, and several ferns.

Each zone in the park has its own families of birds and mammals. In the forest are black bears, wolves, coyotes, red squirrels, martens, and porcupines. Forest birds include bald eagles, ravens, blue grouse, hermit thrushes, chestnut-backed chickadees, and fox sparrows, very much the same as found in the forests of Vancouver Island. Mountain goats are found at higher levels, including the icefields in summer. There is plenty of animal life on the alpine tundra, including black and grizzly bears, goats, marmots, wolverines, and tiny voles. Birds of the alpine zone include ptarmigan, water pipit, raven, and junco.

The bay and inlets are home to a wide range of pelagic and shorebirds. Flying in from the ocean are kittiwakes, pelagic cor-

Bald eagle

morants, Arctic terns, jaegers, and tufted puffins. Gulls, scoters, and several ducks are found along the shorelines. Marbled murrelets breed in the old-growth forest. Common redpolls and snow buntings are sighted near the glaciers, while yellow warblers and gray-cheeked thrushes live in the streamside habitats. Nesting areas in the park are closed to people during the crucial weeks during May, June, and July. Seal breeding areas within the park are also closed, and kayakers are asked not to get too close to icebergs with female seals and pups on them.

It is amazing that in this chilly, icy place, there is an abundance of wildlife. The natural spectacle of the park is best seen from a boat, whether it's your own pleasure boat, a cruise ship, or a smaller tour boat operated by several local guiding companies. Apart from a small area around Bartlett Cove, the park is not a hiking place. While backcountry campsites are available, the trails necessary to make an easy trek are not. Open glacial terrain is suitable for exploration, but inveterate hikers should be aware that hiking in the park requires a great deal of scrambling over ice and rock. Tour boats will drop you off on their trips around the bay and will pick you up at a predetermined time. There may be a slight extra charge for this service. Some planning and knowledge of the dropoff points is necessary to have a safe and enjoyable time. Checking in advance with the boat tour operators is worthwhile, and you are encouraged not to go on a solo land and ice journey.

For those who know how and have the courage, kayaking is one of the most enjoyable ways to get the full glacier experience. Kayaks may be rented from Glacier Bay Sea Kayaks in Gustavus (Box 26, Gustavus, AK 99826); call (907) 697-2257. The company, which operates Glacier Bay Lodge, has a variety of packages including a two- to five-night cruise on the *Wilderness Explorer,* a small ship that has kayaks and Zodiacs on board for close-up explorations. They also offer day cruises to the glaciers, including a cruise with an on-board naturalist. For information and reservations, call 800-451-5952, or write Glacier Bay Cruises and Tours, 520 Pike Street, Suite 1400, Seattle, WA 98101.

DAY-HIKES FROM BARTLETT COVE

Beach and Nature Trail   Park rangers provide a daily one-mile round-trip walk along the cove's beach and through the forest along the shore. If you miss the guided walk, do it yourself, with directions available at the visitor center or lodge. It is possible (with some attention to tide tables) to walk the seven miles around the point to the town of Gustavus. Doing this hike at high tide forces one into the adjacent forest.

Bartlett River Trail   This half-day hike can be expanded into a full day's activity by simply stopping from time to time to enjoy the spectacular scenery and taking picnic supplies with you. Starting at Glacier Bay Lodge, the trail ends at the river's estuary. This is a four-mile round-trip walk. The trail leads along a tidal lagoon and through the forest. The river hosts a salmon run in late summer. Along the way (particularly in the forest sections), you'll hear and probably see red squirrels and many birds. Great blue herons and other waterbirds are found along the estuary, while bald eagles fly overhead. Across the estuary are the Beardslee Islands. To the west, across Sitakaday Narrows, is land that was buried by the ice sheet around 1750.

Misty Fjords and Admiralty Island

The magnificent wilderness of Misty Fjords National Monument is made up of deep fjords, steep mountains rising from the sea, wonderful rain forests, rivers and creeks with waterfalls, and—at the higher reaches—alpine lake country. You cannot get there by road, but you can by boat or by air taxi. Ketchikan is the gateway to this beautiful region, situated at the southern end of the Alaska Panhandle. Yes, it is often "misty" in this panorama of inlets and mountains. However, the often rainy weather is interspersed with dry periods, however short, making it possible to have an enjoyable exploration.

This is part of the enormous Tongass National Forest, a land area of 16.9 million acres, covering 90 percent of southeast Alaska. "Tongass" is the Tlingit clan name for the Native Americans who lived at the southern edge of the forest. The area was set aside by President Theodore Roosevelt, in 1902, as the Alexander Archipelago Forest Reserve. Five years later, the reserve was included in the national forest system. It is now the largest national forest in the nation. It stretches along the coast for 500 miles, from Prince of Wales Island to Malaspina Glacier. It reaches east to the large icefields, which lie across the Alaska/B.C. boundary. Fourteen protected wilderness areas lie within the national forest, the largest of which is Misty Fjords, 2.1 million acres located 22 miles east of Ketchikan.

There are no developed trails in Misty Fjords, and recreational activity is restricted to boat use or flying to remote campsites. There are several Forest Service cabins in the monument, available through the office in Ketchikan. For information and cabin reservations, contact the Monument Manager, Misty Fjords National Monument, Tongass National Forest, 3031 Tongass Avenue, Ketchikan, AK 99901, or call (907) 225-2148.

It is impossible to put into words how incredibly beautiful this part of the world is—rain or shine. Anywhere else in the United States, Misty Fjords would be considered a national treasure, civilized with grand lodges à la the Grand Canyon, steam trains running through along the steep mountain slopes, backpacking trips to the glaciers, and magazine articles extolling the virtues of a natural fjord-side vacation. But maybe it's better this way. If you really want to see primeval beauty, you have to go out of your way—own or rent a boat, charter a seaplane flight to a remote cabin, then stay with nature for a day, or three, where no one else will be seen, in an area of primitive grandeur.

Other wilderness preserves in this area are Admiralty Island, slightly more than a million acres and the home of black and brown bears. The Pack Bear Refuge is a popular place to see the bears while retaining some sense of safety. In July and August, the bears are out for the annual salmon run. Alaska Discovery, a local guiding outfitter, has guided trips on the island; call (907) 586-1911.

The island is 100 miles long and nearly 30 miles wide. Compared to many of the other islands, which have been extensively logged, Admiralty Island has remained largely untouched. Its extensive coastline (some 700 miles) includes many inlets and bays, with tidal flats and rock pools holding a great range of intertidal life. This is one of the finest places along the Pacific Coast for canoeing, with a chain of lakes running from the village of Angoon to Mole Harbor, with several forest cabins available for overnight stays. Several quiet inlets also offer prime canoeing.

Old-growth trees—Sitka spruce and hemlock—provide the canopy for a rich understory of salal, skunk cabbage, mosses, ferns, dwarf dogwood, and more. Sitka black-tailed deer roam the island. Along the coast, you'll see sea lions and humpback whales. There are bald eagles everywhere, particularly in Seymour Canal. The main reason for the existing old-growth forest is the administration of the island by the Forest Service since 1909. As a national monument, the island has been subject to some logging and mining. Some areas have been logged under federal agreements with the Native American residents of the island, with some clear-cut sections logged by the Native American corporation Shee-Atika, and others logged before the 1970s by commercial contractors. Conservationists lobbied (and sued) during the 1970s to stop commercial logging on the island, and the areas not assigned to Native American cutting are managed by the Forest Service as a wilderness.

Chilkoot Trail

This part of Alaska provides some of the best terrain for backcountry hiking and camping. There are trails leading from virtually every town along the coast and on the islands. Aside from the Chilkoot Trail at Skagway, most of the trails offer shorter hikes than many backcountry hikers are used to. So, in this region, most people who would otherwise camp at a wilderness site hike the trails and head back to town for an overnight stay. For the ultimate backcountry experience in the region, head for Skagway to tackle the Chilkoot Trail and the beginning of the long journey to the 1898 Dawson City gold fields.

ACCESS

To reach the head of the trail from Skagway, find your way by your car, or someone else's, or walk eight miles to the northwest to the site of Dyea, the gold rush camp. The trailhead is just before the Taiya River bridge. A ranger station is open daily during the summer months. One advantage of staying in Skagway before you make the hike is a free ride to the trailhead offered by several local B & B inns and hotels. Taxis are also available from town.

THE TRAIL

This is an international trail, crossing the Canadian border at Chilkoot Pass. Topographical maps for U.S. and Canadian sections are sold in Skagway stores. While there are warming cabins along the trail, there are no overnight cabins. The miners of 1898 didn't have them either, and retracing the historic route, and doing it as the trekkers of '98 did it, is much of the excitement of walking the trail. The complete trail is 33 miles long, from Dyea to Lake Bennett where the gold seekers built rafts and boats for the long Yukon River trip to Dawson City. The trip can be broken down into four days of hiking, with the steepest climb during the third day. The narrow-gauge excursion train turns around at Bennett, providing a return ride to Skagway. There is a campground near the ranger station and trailhead.

THE HIKE

From the trailhead at Dyea to Canyon City is a distance of 7.8 miles and a hike that takes between three and four hours. The route begins with a climb of almost 300 feet, and then it drops down to Taiga River level through a brushy area. After a mile, the trail joins an old logging road for three more miles of fairly easy walking. The route passes the site of an old sawmill (mile 3) and then reaches the first campground along the trail, at mile 4.9. Irene Glacier lies across the river. The trail ascends from river level, crossing several hills before descending to Canyon City. The campground here has a warming shelter with stove.

The remains of the old city are found a half-mile north of the campground.

The second section of the trail runs 5.2 miles, from Canyon City to Sheep Camp, taking about four hours. This is a fairly soft hike, stretching muscles in preparation for the more strenuous climb to the pass on the third day. From the Canyon City Campground, the trail leads north, passing the spur trail to the old Canyon City site, and then climbs as it winds around the canyon. There's a fine view of Mount Hoffman as the trail levels out, then descends at the one-mile point, passing several telegraph poles remaining from 1898. The trail continues to descend as it reaches Pleasant Camp (mile 10.5), again joining the Taiga River. It's another 2.5 miles to Sheep Camp, crossing a suspension bridge and reaching the ranger station and campground. Sheep Camp was once a community of 8,000 souls, with facilities that included several saloons, general stores, hotels, and restaurants. It was a place where, during that awful winter of '98, the journeyers stopped to store their supplies. All Klondike gold seekers were required to carry a year's worth of supplies across the Canadian border. Rangers are stationed at Sheep Camp during the summer months.

The hike from Sheep Camp to Deep Lake is a 10-mile journey, taking 8 to 10 hours. Because of the steep climb, this section takes a full day to hike, with an elevation change of 2,500 feet. This climb is performed during the first 3.5 miles, past the tree line, starting with a half-mile climb over what the miners called "Long Hill." Here is an old powerhouse that serviced a temporary tram. The Scales, another old tramway ruin, is 3.5 miles from Sheep Camp.

Then comes the ascent to Chilkoot Pass, a steady climb of a half-mile. The slope is 45 degrees, over loose rock, to the 3,535-foot summit. There can be some confusion over which route to take up to the summit. Take the left path, marked by an old tramway cable. Once at the top, you cross the Canadian border, then descend to cross a field of snow while keeping to the right. Below is Crater Lake, and after descending about 300 feet, you come to Stone Crib and two emergency shelters, a haven during bad weather.

The trail continues along the east side of the lake, crossing several streams to follow the route of another old wagon road that ran to Lindeman City. The trail descends through the tundra, passing a little waterfall (mile 20) before reaching Happy Camp. This small campground is four miles past the summit. The trail climbs to pass around Long Lake and then drops to cross a bridge. Deep Lake Campground is at mile 23. Lindeman City (with shelters) is a three-mile hike down the trail.

The final section, 10 miles (six to eight hours) from Deep Lake to Bennett, runs along the west side of Deep Lake, descending to Lindeman City. You're now in a conifer forest (fir and lodgepole pine), passing an old cemetery on a hill from which are great views of the mountains. Lindeman Lake is one of the departure points for the Klondike. In the spring of 1898, some 10,000 gold seekers stopped here to build boats and rafts for the remaining float (600 miles) to Dawson. There's a campground, with a Canadian ranger station and two warming huts, at the Lindeman City site. Bennett is seven miles from the bridge over Moose Creek, at the far side of Lindeman City. Another campground appears after a walk through the woods at Dan Johnson Lake. Then Bare Loon Lake appears, with another camping site. Beyond the campground is a junction, with the right fork leading to the White Pass and Yukon Railroad line—a 30-minute walk. From the tracks, it's another five miles to the site called Log Cabin, a point on the Klondike Highway for pickup by a bus or maybe a friend. The left fork leads to Bennett, following the lakeshore for another four miles. This was once a bustling railway town. The station is still here. In Bennett, you can take the trail to Fraser and Skagway.

Clearing with customs before leaving Skagway is essential. You can phone the Fraser Customs Office at (403) 821-4111, or register at the National Park Visitor Center in downtown Skagway. Hikers taking the route from Bennett to Skagway must register with U.S. Customs in Skagway; their telephone number is (907) 983-2725. Or, register in the office after the hike. The U.S. Customs office is located on Dyea Road, two miles from the southern trailhead.

This trail offers one of the few historical treks in the Northwest, an exciting piece of travel through time, reliving the famous journey of the Klondike stampeders of 1898. For anyone with "gold fever," this is the hike of a lifetime.

BIRDS

Brandt's Cormorant
Phalacrocorax pencillatus
About the same size as the double-crested cormorant, this water bird has a dark blue throat pouch when breeding. It is darker at other times. It has a buff-colored band across the throat, behind the pouch. The young Brandt's has a buffy breast with a lighter "Y" just below the breast. It lives along the coast and on the ocean, often nesting in sea cliffs. Its range is just about all of the Pacific Coast of North America.

Bald Eagle
Haliaeetus leucocephalus
Found widely along the southeast Alaska coast, this is probably the most widely and easily recognized bird in the Northwest. It has that great head of white feathers, the strong, yellow bill, a brown back and wings, and a pure white tail. Immature bald eagles have a darkish head and tail and a dark bill. Its range is from Alaska to the southern United States, along the Pacific Coast and spreading across southern British Columbia and into the Rocky Mountain states. It lives on coasts, by rivers and lakes, and in open country. Its voice is a hard cackle, *kleek, kik, ik, ik, ik*, or a low creak, *kak-kak-kak*.

Black-tailed Godwit
Limosa limosa
While regarded as an Asian "stray," this shorebird is sometimes spotted as far from its usual home as the Southeast coast. It is (like other godwits) a long-billed shorebird, standing on slender, graceful legs. It has a white rump, distinctive black tail, and white wing stripe. The underlining of the wings are white. The bill is quite straight, unlike most godwits, including the much more numerous marbled godwits, which have upturned bills. Sighting this rare visitor always brings a thrill. It is usually found in Eurasia, migrating to the outer Aleutians.

Parasitic Jaeger
Stercorarius parasiticus
The term "parasitic" perfectly de-scribes all jaegers. Jaegers and skuas are dark-colored, hawk-like seabirds that prey on other waterbirds, partic-ularly terns and gulls, forcing them to disgorge their food. Doing this at sea, they also eat lemmings while flying over land, or eggs, or young birds. This one is the size of a falcon, and like other jaegers has two longer central tail feathers that show as a projection. It has a darkish brown back, with a darker—almost black—tail, and has a white wing flash, like other jaegers. Its range circles the Arctic. Living along the ocean, in-cluding coastal bays, and in tundra in summer, this bird winters at sea

from the southern U.S. to Tierra del Fuego.

Black-legged Kittiwake
Rissa tridactyla
A year-round resident of the entire mainland Alaskan coastline, the kittiwake is a small, oceangoing gull. It is identified by its black legs and also by the black wing tips. Like the red-legged kittiwake, it has an unmarked yellow bill. Its summer range is throughout the entire Northern Hemisphere—along coasts—and it winters on both coasts of the U.S., Japan, and the Mediterranean region. It is usually seen flying over water and is rarely on beaches. When nesting, its voice is a *kitti-waak,* or a loud *kaka-week.*

Yellow-billed Loon
Gavia adamsii
At first glance, it looks like the common loon (*G. immer*), but its bill is a light yellow or straw color. The bill is upturned, another distinguishing feature. Its checkered markings are less clear than those of the common loon. In winter, it has a pale neck with a dark round neck patch. In summer, this loon resides on tundra lakes, moving to warmer coastal regions in winter. Its summer range is from the Arctic (Canada and Russia) to northwestern Canada and Alaska.

Rock Ptarmigan
Lagopus mutus
Three ptarmigans are found in the northwest portion of North America, and all three reside in southeast Alaska as well as throughout the northern part of the state. Other species are the willow ptarmigan (*L. lagopus*) and white-tailed ptarmigan (*L. leucurus*). The rock and willow ptarmigans have a similar look, brown or gray, with white wings and white belly in summer. The rock ptarmigan is grayer and finely barred. Its bill is smaller. The rock lives in barren, hilly areas, above the timberline, often in muskeg (southeast Alaska), and Arctic tundra (farther north). It lives at lower levels in winter, and this is usually when you'll spot the rock ptarmigan along the coast, below its more barren summer home at alpine levels.

Horned Puffin
Fratercula corniculata
A member of the auk family (Alcidae), the horned puffin is found in Glacier Bay National Park. Its range is along both sides of the North Pacific. It is a seabird, nesting in colonies on sea cliffs. Auks are a northern counterpart to penguins, except that these birds can fly, and do. They flap their small wings at a very fast rate. They are excellent anglers, making swift dives to catch their seafood dinner. The horned puffin has bright orange feet, white underparts, and a wide black collar. It has a large triangular bill that is yellow with a red tip. Immature puffins have duskier cheeks, much like the wintering adult.

Short-tailed Shearwater
Puffinus tenuirostris
Unlike its sooty cousin, also found along the northern Pacific Coast,

the short-tailed shearwater is smaller (about 13 inches long), and has bluish-gray wing linings. This bird of the open sea has a short tail, a short bill, and very fast wingbeats. It sometimes has a whitish throat. Its breeding range is far away, on islands off the south coast of Australia. In the late fall and early winter, it is seen along the North American coast, as far south as Baja California. You'll see the shearwaters gliding over the ocean, with wings extended to an almost straight form. Their tails are smaller than the tails of gulls, although they do look somewhat like gulls.

Northern Shrike
Lanius excubitor
Two shrikes are seen in the western half of North America, the logger-head (*L. ludovicianus*) and the northern. They are similar in appearance, with black wings and tails with white markings, and a black mask. While the loggerhead has a pale gray breast, the northern shrike has a faint barring on a lighter breast. It also has a lower bill that is paler. This bird is seen in scrubby countryside with trees and posts, which it uses for lookouts. These are songbirds, but they act like hawks, preying on small birds, mice, lizards, and insects. In southeast Alaska, they are mostly found in areas of muskeg, in a similar setting to that of the pine siskin.

Pine Siskin
Carduelis pinus
This small, dark brown, streaked finch is a muskeg dweller in Glacier Bay National Park and in other parts of the Alaska Panhandle. It is the size of a goldfinch, with a sharp, pointed bill and a noticeably notched tail. Its habitats include conifer and mixed forests and woodlands including those damp areas populated by alders. It winters in central Mexico and spends its summers in the U.S.—including southeast Alaska—and southern Canada. Its call is a coarse *chlee-ip,* a *shreeeeee,* and also a lighter *tit-ee-tit.*

Fox Sparrow
Passerella iliaca
Spending summers in Alaska and Canada, the fox sparrow is also observed in the mountains of the American West. It winters in the southern states. Resembling a song sparrow, but larger, the fox sparrow has a rust-colored tail and rump, with heavy triangular spots on its breast. The northwest version of this bird has a dusky (gray-ish-brown) head, back, and breast. They have a clear, musical song, including whistles that slide up and down the scale, in addition to a series of short, clear notes.

FISH

Dolly Varden
Salvelinus malma
This treasured sport fish is a trout-like char, a cousin of the Arctic char (*S. alpinus*) and is also related to the brook trout (*S. fontinalis*). It is a cold-water fish, like the salmon (another member of the Salmonidae family). The sea-run Dolly Varden

is dark blue above, with silvery sides and silvery to whitish on the belly. It has cream spots on the sides. In mountainous northern streams the spots are a bright orange or red. The leading edge of the ventral and anal fins are white. Its range is from Oregon, north along the Pacific Coast to the Bering Sea, and to the Korean coast. It is found in streams that run into the ocean along the southeast Alaska coast.

Pacific Halibut
Hippoglossus stenolepis
After spending many years eating halibut as my preferred fish for fish and chips, I was amazed upon my first viewing of the actual whole fish, to see that it was a flatfish, looking like a giant, flying tailed bath mat, five or more feet long, with its two eyes together, on one side. The female is larger than the male, often soaring in weight to more than 400 pounds. The male, if lucky, weighs 40 pounds. The females have prodigious breeding habits. A small female will lay more than two million eggs—at a time. The halibut's range is from the Bering Sea to Southern California. They are at their finest, and largest, along the Alaska coast. Charter outfits in Ketchikan, Juneau, and elsewhere will take you out for a halibut excursion. It is closely related to flounders, soles, and sand dabs.

Copper Rockfish
Sebastes caurinus
One of a range of rockfish and scorpionfish that live along the northern Pacific Coast, the copper is a target of anglers in southeast Alaska, as are the China and quillback rockfish. The bocaccio (*S. paucispinis*) is another found in this region. There are 69 family members in all. They live in a wide variety of environments including kelp beds, shallow tide pools, and out in the open ocean, swimming around in large schools. While looking quite ugly to the human eye, the copper and other rockfish have fascinating features, with brilliant colors and markings: stripes, spots, even quills or spines, which provide names for many of them. The copper rockfish has a wide, white stripe that runs along much of the body, separated from the white belly by a speckled brown stripe. It ranges from the Kenai Peninsula, farther north in Alaska, to Baja California. While the copper is a sport fish that is eaten, the China rockfish is reported to be even better tasting.

Steelhead
Salmo gairdneri
The sea-run version of the rainbow trout, the steelhead is one of two sea-run trout, the other being the cutthroat (*S. clarki*). This native American trout grows to a length of almost four feet and to 40 pounds, although most steelhead caught in southeast Alaska weigh in at under 10 pounds. As a fish that likes racing water, it is a prized sport fish along the rushing rivers and streams of the Southeast coast, including the Stikine. Rainbows and steelheads have small black spots

on the back and most fins. The head is short, and the inside of the mouth is whitish. Unlike the local salmon, the steelhead survives the breeding season, swimming out to sea to live another day, or year. It is found north, to the Bering Sea, and in Japan.

INVERTEBRATES AND CRUSTACEANS

Giant Acorn Barnacle
Balanus nubilis
Found from Alaska to Southern California, this is one of two barnacles that are widespread in southeast Alaska. The other is the thatched barnacle (*Semibalanus cariosus*). The giant acorn is a shellfish that attaches itself to rocks, hard-shelled animals, and pilings, from the low-tide line to ocean waters as deep as 300 feet. This is a large barnacle that grows to almost 4.5 inches wide and 3.5 inches high. Flat on top, it has a conical shape and a whitish color. The sides are made up of two plates that overlap. There are two plates at the top, with space between. One pair of top plates has a long, upward projection. The thatched barnacle is smaller, usually about two inches wide and two inches high, also cone-shaped, and rough all over. It is seen on rocks above the low-tide line.

Hairy Chiton
Mopalia ciliata
Also called the hairy mopalia, this shellfish is found from the Aleutian Islands to Baja California.

One to two inches long, it has an oval shell, grayish green or a light brown. The shell is usually mottled, with whitish blotches in the center. It has a leathery, bristled girdle, with a notch at the rear. This chiton lives in coves and under rocks in the intertidal zone. It is seen on rocks at low tide. It eats animal and plant material including sponges, algae, and diatoms. The larvae come out of egg envelopes, swimming about a week before metamorphosis.

Black Katy Chiton
Katharina tunicata
Named after Lady Katharine Douglas, who sent specimens to England in 1815, this is a long, oval chiton, growing to a length of about three inches, much smaller than the giant Pacific chiton (also found in southeast Alaska) that grows to a huge 15 inches. The black Katy has a black girdle, a wide black or brown band that is leathery and covers at least half of the valves, which are a greenish brown. It is commonly found on exposed rocks, as it grows in the intertidal zone, to just below the low-tide line.

Frilled Dogwinkle
Nucella lamellosa
Also called the dogwhelk, this common dogwinkle is one of the environmental workers of the northern Pacific Coast, limiting the spread of mussels and acorn barnacles, drilling holes in the shells of its target food supply. It is found on rocks, particularly in crevices or other sheltered areas just above and

below the low-tide line. Growing from 1 to 3.25 inches high, with a conical spire, its canal is quite long, narrowly open, and curved. It has an oval aperture, which has a yellowish tint. The shell's spire whorls have two spiral cords, crossed by ridges with hollow spines. The body whorl also has spiral cords and spines. The shell's outer lip is flared, with three rounded teeth. This is one of a variety of whelks native to the Alaska coastline.

Sitka Periwinkle
Littorina sitkana
A small seashell, brown with white spiral bands, its thick, round body whorl is as tall as its spire. The entire shell can grow to almost one inch high, and as wide. The aperture is usually a light brown. This is one of several periwinkles found along the coast of southeast Alaska. It lives on rocks and in weedy areas along the low-tide line, ranging from this part of Alaska to Oregon. It lays its eggs in a large gooey mass on rocks, and algae. You'll see the egg masses in sheltered, shady places where they have less chance to dry out, rather than on exposed, sunny rocks.

Agassiz's Peanut Worm
Phascolosoma agassizii
A very common ocean worm, it grows to a length of 4.75 inches. It is a half-inch wide—a slender ribbon of a worm with no appendages, and brown in color, ranging from light to dark. It sometimes has purple or dark brown spots. Its trunk is a cylinder, tapered to a blunt point

at the rear covered with papillae. Its mouth is surrounded by a ring of small tentacles. It lives from Alaska to Baja California, under rocks, in the roots of sea grass, in sand, as well as in mussel beds. You may see these worms on pilings above the low-tide line. Their larvae feed on plankton.

Red Sea Cucumber
Cucumaria miniata
This sea creature grows to a length of 10 inches and is about one inch wide. It gets its name from its cucumber shape. It is a deep (brick) red, orange, pink, or purple. It is round and is tapered at the rear. It has 10 branched tentacles, which are retractable. Its feet are in five rows, two above and three below. Living from Alaska to Baja California, the animal is shaped so that as it positions itself in crevices, its front end (with tentacles) and rear end both are in the path of moving water. It is found near the low-tide line, in tide pools, and under rocks.

Green Sea Urchin
Strongylocentrotus droebachiensis
This is a very common creature along the Pacific Coast, from Alaska to northern Washington, and along the Atlantic Coast as well. Growing to more than 3 inches wide and 1.5 inches high, it is oval-shaped and spiny. The skeleton is brownish-green. Its green spines may have a light gray tinge, or in rare occurrences a reddish-green color. The tube feet are brown. These urchins

grow in kelp beds and on rocky shores, from the low-tide line to a water depth of more than a half-mile. The red sea urchin (*S. fransiscanus*) is also found in Alaska. This is the sea urchin that is harvested in great numbers in California to satisfy the demands of sushi lovers, who eat sea urchin eggs on sushi. It is also considered a tasty treat by other sea creatures.

MAMMALS

Brown Bear
Ursus arctos
While the black bear may be sometimes black and sometimes brown, there is no mistaking the Alaska brown bear. This is the bear you see on television programs snatching salmon from the Katmai River, far to the north of the Southeast region. It is the same species as the grizzly. While it thrives in large numbers farther north, there are brown bears in Glacier Bay National Park and along the mainland strip, to Skagway and Haines. These are huge animals, with males growing to a weight of a half-ton (before hibernating in the fall), and mature females of six to eight years weighing up to 650 pounds. Even with this weight, the brown bear is agile and a fast runner. The grizzly and the Alaska brown (*U. a. middendorffi*) are yellowish-brown to almost black, usually with white-tipped hairs. It has a hump over the shoulders, and its face is concave. These bears hibernate for a period in winter, in dens near lakes on the higher mountains. The brown bear is omnivorous, eating just about anything from marine animal remains on beaches (including seals) to berries on the hills. They eat grasses, roots, deer, and other animals.

Mountain Goat
Oreamnos americanus
The shaggy white goats, often seen climbing on seemingly impossible ledges and mountainsides, are actually rock antelope, and this partially explains their surefootedness. They have an amazing ability to stay upright on icy glacier slopes. Their natural range is as far west as the Kenai Peninsula, with a transplanted colony living on Kodiak Island. They are found at the high alpine levels of Glacier Bay National Park during the summer months, coming down to lower elevations during the heavy snows of winter.

Porcupine
Erethizon dorsatum
This chunky mammal is best known for the protective quills on its rump and tail. It also has guard hairs on the front of the body. Its hair is yellow. It has unique feet, with a series of raised, fleshy knobs, and curved claws. It has four toes on its forefeet and five toes on its hindfeet. You rarely hear a porcupine except during mating season in October and November, when it presents a selection of grunts, groans, and squeaking sounds. Mating is a careful matter, with the female required to feel relaxed enough to keep her quills

down. After seven months, a single baby is born in late spring. You'll know that porcupines are in your vicinity when you see patches of bark stripped from tree trunks and branches, with tooth marks and signs of gnawing. Their tracks are easy to spot, particularly the pebbled look from the raised foot knobs. The claw marks are far ahead of the main footmark. In southeast Alaska, porcupines live in conifer forests and stands of mixed woodland. Their range extends into tundra regions, almost to the Arctic coast, and to southwestern Alaska.

Steller Sea Lion
Eumetopias jubatus
Larger than any bear, the male Steller sea lion grows to a length of 10.5 feet. The female is smaller, at a maximum length of about seven feet. This is the largest-eared seal. The bull seal is a buff color above, and reddish-brown below. The females (cows) are brown overall, and more cylindrical in shape than the fat bulls. Their faces are like those of the otter. Stellers inhabit rocky shores of the Pacific Coast from southern Alaska and the Aleutian and Pribilof Islands to the Channel Islands off the coast of California. These heavy creatures spend much time basking on rocks, staying in the water during bad weather. They are voracious eaters of fish, including rockfish and blackfish, and on more rare occasions, salmon and squid. They tend to feed at night, within a few miles of the shoreline, venturing out as far as 10 to 15 miles.

TREES, SHRUBS, AND GROUND COVERS

Dwarf Birch
Betula glandulosa
Also called bog birch, this shrub has stiff, leathery leaves—about the size of a quarter—and twigs that have fine hairs on a rumpled stem. Seen along the Chilkoot Trail, in the higher regions around Skagway, this plant grows to a height of one to six feet. It is found only in damp places, usually in wet meadows and boggy areas. The leaves turn copper in autumn. The bark is smooth and dark brown. The alternating leaves are rounded at the tip, with rounded teeth. They are dark green above and paler beneath. The male and female flowers are found on the same plant. The male flowers are formed in drooping catkins, about one inch long. The female flowers are arranged in straight, upright catkins, less than an inch long. The fruit is an oval nutlet with a narrow wing. The shrub is found from Alaska south to Northern California and east to the Rocky Mountains, and along the East Coast in New England and Newfoundland.

Alaskan Blueberry
Vaccinium alaskaense
We begin a short guide to good eating along your favorite Southeast trail. This erect or spreading shrub grows to a height of about six feet. When mature, the bark is grayish. The younger bark is a

yellowish-green. The shrub flowers in the early spring, bearing pinkish-green to bronze blooms, round to urn-shaped, appearing with or after the leaves. The fruit is the bluish-black berry, looking like other blueberries. It, too, is edible. This is one of the most dominant shrubs in southeast Alaska, growing beside oval-leafed blueberry (*V. ovalifolium*), a slightly smaller but erect shrub. To tell the difference, turn the leaf over and look for whiskers along the midvein. If the whiskers are there, it's an Alaskan blueberry. Native Americans—and current wilderness gourmands—prefer the taste of the oval-leafed variety.

Dwarf Blueberry
Vaccinium caespitosum

A low-spreading, matted shrub, the dwarf blueberry produces a very sweet and quite edible berry. It is found at low elevations, in boggy areas, and in the subalpine regions on moist, rocky ridges and even higher in alpine tundra. The shrub grows to a height of about one foot. It has rounded, often hairy twigs, that are a yellowish-green to red in color. The alternate leaves are oblong, with teeth. They are green on both sides, with noticeable veins underneath. Native peoples along the coast encouraged the growth of the dwarf blueberry and the higher-growing species by undertaking controlled burns. The berries are available for picking and munching from late July until September.

Dwarf Dogwood
Cornus canadensis

Often called bunchberry, this low, trailing dogwood has a woody base, with very tiny hairs on the erect stems. It grows in moist forests along the coast, including coniferous and mixed woodlands, in bogs, on meadows, and at the subalpine level. It is often seen growing out of rotting logs and stumps in seaside forests. It bears small greenish-white, or yellowish, or purplish flowers. The fruit is berrylike, bright red, fleshy and pulpy, with a sweet taste. The bunchberry has an unusual mechanism for propagation. When mature, the flower petals suddenly spring open, flinging pollen into the air.

Old Man's Beard (Lichen)
Usnea hirta

This is one of several similar-looking lichens of the Fruticose lichens found along the Pacific Northwest coast. A lichen is a double plant combining a fungus and an alga. They seem to have a symbiotic relationship, which permits them to grow on inhospitable surfaces, including bare rock, at high altitudes. There are two other lichen families in the region: Foliose (found on the bark of deciduous and coniferous trees); and Crustose (mostly growing on the bark of alders and willows). Old man's beard and the other Fruticose lichens form grayish beard-like growths, especially on the branches of deciduous shrubs. They have many branches, all of which have a white central core.

They infrequently have fruiting bodies, tiny bumps that break away from the main plant and generate new growths.

WILDFLOWERS

Yellow Dryas
Dryas drummondii
Known in some regions as the yellow mountain avens, the yellow dryas is a low, creeping evergreen shrub with trailing, woody stems that root as they spread. The alternate and quite leathery leaves are oval to oblong, dark green above and covered with dark hairs below. The flowers are pale yellow, arranged singly on leafless stems. You'll see the flowers nodding as you pass. The fruits have a golden-yellow plume, each winding around other plumes, creating a tangled, fluffy mass. The seeds are carried off by winds. The yellow dryas grows on rocky slopes, and next to the glaciers in Glacier Bay National Park. It also grows from wooded lowlands to alpine tundra. When visiting the Haines/Skagway/Glacier Bay region, you will be able to see this flower and the related entire-leafed mountain avens (*D. integrifolia*) displayed in large masses. This shrub has white flowers. Yellow dryas is often used in domestic rock gardens.

Fireweed
Epilobium angustifolium
The evening primrose family (Onagraceae) includes more than a few plants in the Pacific Northwest region, including the epiboleums, or willowherbs. The best known is the fireweed, which is often the predominant plant in a post-fire area. It is also a lovely roadside companion on the Haines and Klondike Highways, linking Haines and Skagway to the Alaska Highway. It is the territorial flower of the Yukon. It grows from roots that are like rhizomes. The leafy stem is topped with many rose-to-purple flowers, with more than 15 flowers in each long cluster. The fruits are capsules, like pods, which break open to disgorge hundreds of fluffy white seeds that are then carried by wind. Fireweed, like the more southerly lupine, likes distressed areas in which to grow. It is most abundant on the coastal regions, rather than in the interior forests of southeast Alaska. The plant has been used by Native Americans for twine making (the stem fibers) and for fishing nets, and the fluffy seed fibers were used with wool for making blankets. Fireweed tea is a drink with plenty of vitamin C. Fireweed honey, a subtly sweet nectar, is too tasty to be adequately described here. The honey is available along the Pacific Coast, including towns in southeast Alaska and Vancouver Island.

Alaska Saxifrage
Saxifragia ferruginea
The saxifrage family includes a set of perennial herbs found in

great numbers in western North America, with several regional species. Many of the species are ornamental, including coral bells, the plants known as saxifrages, bergenia, and piggyback plant. All members of the family have leafless flower stems, with some having a few small leaves or bracts. The Alaska saxifrage is a short, erect plant with hairy, flowering stems that reach to a height of more than a foot. The wedge-shaped leaves are in a cluster at ground level. Each has 5 to 15 teeth. The flowers are white to purplish. The petals are stalked, the upper three usually larger with two yellow spots. You'll find several flowers in open clusters. The fruit is a capsule. This saxifrage grows in moist environments, along streams, and in open habitats from sea level to alpine elevations.

ADMIRALTY ISLAND

Pybus Point Lodge
c/o 1873 Simmons Road
Juneau, AK 99801
(907) 790-4866

This small lodge offers exciting salmon fishing and nature viewing in Admiralty Island National Monument. There are lodge rooms and private cabins. This wilderness lodge provides a different kind of overnight experience, away from civilization and close to superb canoeing. **($$ to $$$)**

GLACIER BAY NATIONAL PARK

Glacier Bay Lodge
c/o Glacier Bay Tours
and Cruises
520 Pike Street
Seattle, WA 98101
800-451-5952

To reserve a room in this lodge, located inside the national park, contact a travel agent or call the lodge's toll-free number. You may also book whatever sightseeing tours you wish to take while at Glacier Bay. The lodge has comfortable, although quite standard rooms, in addition to a dining room with a fine view, and a national park interpretation center on the mezzanine. Reservations are essential. **($$ to $$$)**

GUSTAVUS

Annie Mae Lodge
P.O. Box 80
Gustavus, AK 99826
(907) 697-2346

There's something about Gustavus and Glacier Bay that promotes eating and down-home cooking. The Annie Mae also has a restaurant with fresh seafood, garden vegetables, and berries straight from the bramble (in season). In addition to comfortable rooms, the lodge (like the others) arranges glacier and whale watching tours. **($$)**

Glacier Bay Country Inn
P.O. Box 5
Gustavus, AK 98826
(907) 697-2288

This is also a seasonal operation, with another noted dining room. Food specialties include fresh home-baked bread, seafood entrees, and vegetables from the inn's garden. Rooms have private baths. **($$ to $$$)**

Gustavus Inn
P.O. Box 60
Gustavus, AK 99826
(907) 697-2254 (summer)
(913) 649-5220 (winter)

This family-operated place has been here since 1965. Located in the town of Gustavus, 10 miles from the Glacier Bay Park headquarters, you can take a bus to the park or ride a bicycle provided by the inn. The family-style dining room has a well-deserved reputation for great food. **($$)**

HAINES

Bear Creek Camp and Hostel

P.O. Box 1158
Haines, AK 99827
(907) 766-2259

The youth hostel and campground are seasonal operations, open from June to September.

Captain's Choice Motel

P.O. Box 392
Haines, AK 99827
(907) 766-3111 or 800-247-7153 or 800-478-2345 (Alaska and Canada)

This highway motel is open year-round, with rooms and suites, in-room coffee, a good view of Lynn Canal, and a downtown Haines location, close to stores, bars, and restaurants. It's four miles from the ferry terminal. **($ to $$)**

Eagle Camper RV Park

P.O. Box 28
Haines, AK 99827
(907) 766-2335

Located at 751 Union Street, this campground has hookups for RVs and trailers, plus tenting sites, laundry, barbecues, showers, and propane. It is located a few blocks from downtown Haines, on 3.5 acres of grass and trees.

Fort Seward Lodge

P.O. Box 307
Haines, AK 99827
(907) 766-2009 or 800-478-7772

This smaller hotel (open year-round) is in historic Fort Seward. It has a dining room, specializing in locally caught seafood, with steaks and a salad bar also part of the eating action. In past years the lodge has had an all-you-can-eat crab dinner. Kitchenettes are available. **($ to $$)**

Haines Hitch-up RV Park

P.O. Box 383
Haines, AK 99827
(907) 766-2882

On a five-acre site, this campground is located a half-mile west of Main Street, offering pull-through sites, full hookups, grassy spaces for tents, a laundry, showers, gift shop, and propane.

Hälsingland Hotel

P.O. Box 1589
Haines, AK 99827
(907) 766-2000 or 800-542-6363 or 800-478-2525 (Yukon and B.C.)

Victorian buildings—once used as officers' quarters in the former Fort Seward, just south of downtown Haines—now have rooms with private baths, facing the historic parade square. There's a wine bar and cocktail lounge, and seafood is a standby in the hotel's restaurant. **($ to $$)**

Port Chilkoot Camper Park

P.O. Box 1589
Haines, AK 99827
(907) 766-2755 or 800-542-6363 or 800-478-2525 (Yukon and B.C.)

This campground is at Fort Seward, within walking distance of the historic area's restaurants, lounges, and shops. It offers full and partial hookups, tenting sites in a wooded setting, showers, and laundry.

Summer Inn
Bed & Breakfast
117 Second Avenue North
P.O. Box 1198
Haines, AK 99827
(907) 766-2970

This inn, open year-round, is owned by the Summer family. It is a historic home, built around 1900 by a certain Mr. Tim Vogel, whose somewhat tarnished life story you can hear from the Summers. Located in downtown Haines, the house provides views of Lynn Canal. A full breakfast is served. **($$)**

JUNEAU

Alaskan Hotel
167 South Franklin Street
Juneau, AK 99801
800-327-9347

More properly called the Alaskan Hotel and Bar, this old building is on the National Register of Historic Places. Established in 1913, the hotel has a period saloon with an antique oak bar. The rooms include some with kitchenettes and whirlpools. **($ to $$)**

Auke Village Campground and Mendenhall Lake Campground
c/o USFS
8465 Old Dairy Road
Juneau, AK 99801
(907) 586-8800

Both campgrounds are operated by the U.S. Forest Service. Auke Village Campground is located at mile 15.8 of the Glacier Highway, and it is open from mid-May until late September, with picnic tables, water, pit toilets, and one flush toilet.

Mendenhall Lake Campground is on the west side of Mendenhall Lake. Some campsites have a view of the glacier. The campground accommodates trailers up to 22 feet. This is also a summer operation, with picnic tables, pit toilets, and dump station.

Baranof Hotel
127 North Franklin Street
Juneau, AK 99801
(907) 586-2660 or 800-544-0970

This downtown hotel, like the Westmark Juneau Hotel (51 West Egan Drive) is operated by Westmark Hotels, the large Alaska and Yukon chain. It is handy to downtown offices, including nearby government buildings, although accommodations and food are more expensive than in many of the smaller hotels and motels in Juneau. **($$$)**

Breakwater Inn
1711 Glacier Avenue
Juneau, AK 99801
(907) 586-6303 or 800-544-2250

Overlooking the Aurora Boat Harbor, this small hotel has standard rooms, plus some with kitchenettes. One has a whirlpool bath. There is a dining room and lounge. **($$)**

Driftwood Lodge
435 West Willoughby Avenue
Juneau, AK 99801-1727
(907) 586-2280 or 800-544-2239

This downtown motel has housekeeping units, reasonable rates, in-room coffee, and pets are allowed. There is an adjoining restaurant.

Larger rooms can accommodate up to eight persons. **($$)**

Inn at the Waterfront
455 South Franklin Street
Juneau, AK 99801
(907) 586-2050

One of the oldest hotels in Alaska, this B & B operation serves a continental breakfast. There are suites, and the rates are about the lowest in town. A dining room and lounge are on-site. **($)**

Juneau International Hostel
614 Harris Street
Juneau, AK 99801
(907) 586-9559

This hostel is open year-round, offering accommodations for singles and family groups, showers, cooking facilities, and laundry. Check-in time in summer is 5 P.M. to 11 P.M., and 5 P.M. to 10:30 P.M. the rest of the year. **($)**

Pearson's Pond B & B Inn
4541 Sawa Circle
Juneau, AK 99801
(907) 789-3772

This deluxe bed and breakfast home, near the glacier, offers suites, an outdoor whirlpool, bicycles, self-serve breakfast, kitchen, and a fitness facility. There is a two-night minimum stay in summer. **($$ to $$$)**

Silverbow Inn
120 Second Street
Juneau, AK 99801-1215
(907) 586-4146

This historic inn (1890) has a fine restaurant and a limited number of rooms—all with private baths. Breakfast comes from the in-house bakery. The inn is located in downtown Juneau. **($$)**

KETCHIKAN

Best Western Landing Hotel
3434 Tongass Avenue
P.O. Box 6814
Ketchikan, AK 99901
(907) 225-5166

Conveniently located across from the ferry terminal, near the airport, this operation has rooms and mini-suites, a restaurant, and lounge. It is open year-round. **($$ to $$$)**

Clover Pass Resort
P.O. Box 7322
Ketchikan, AK 99901
(907) 247-2234

Located at mile 15 on North Tongass Highway, the resort offers lodge rooms and cabins on the waterfront, plus sites for RVs and campers. It is open from April through October. **($$)**

Ingersoll Hotel
303 Mission Street
Ketchikan, AK 99901
(907) 225-2124 or 800-478-2124 (Alaska only)

Ketchikan accommodations are on the basic side, and the Ingersoll Hotel is no exception. This hotel has been on the waterfront, in the downtown area, for a long time, offering standard rooms, close to shops and restaurants. **($$)**

Ketchikan Youth Hostel
First United Methodist Church
Grand and Main Streets
P.O. Box 8515
Ketchikan, AK 99901
(907) 225-3780

This is a summer operation, using
the local Methodist church as a
place for very basic accommodations. **($)**

Westmark Cape Fox Lodge
800 Venitia Way
Ketchikan, AK 99901-6561
(907) 225-8001 or 800-544-0970 or
800-999-2570 (Canada)

This is the exception to the norm:
a deluxe Northwest-style lodge,
perched on a high point overlooking Tongass Narrows and the town,
with luxurious rooms and suites.
There's a restaurant and lounge,
gift shop, and a scenic tram ride
that descends 130 feet to the
downtown, waterfront area. The
restaurant specializes in fresh
seafood. **($$$)**

PETERSBURG

Leconte RV Park
304 South Fourth Street
P.O. Box 1534
Petersburg, AK 99833
(907) 772-4680

This campground, with facilities
for RVs, trailers, and tenters, is lo-
cated at Fourth Street and Haugen
Drive, one mile from the ferry ter-
minal. It's within walking distance
of downtown. There are hookups,
showers, and a laundry.

Scandia House
P.O. Box 689
Petersburg, AK 99833
(907) 772-4281 or 800-722-5006

Located downtown, close to the
waterfront, this is a historic inn,
renovated several years ago, with
comfortable rooms (some shared
baths) and free continental break-
fast. Skiff rentals are available, as
are rental cars. **($ to $$)**

Tides Inn
307 North First Street
P.O. Box 1048
Petersburg, AK 99833
(907) 772-4288

This two-story motel is located at
First and Dolphin Streets, in the
downtown area. Aside from the
standard rooms, the motel offers
free continental breakfast. **($$)**

PRINCE OF WALES ISLAND

Bucareli Bay Bed & Breakfast
206 Cedar Street
P.O. Box 473
Craig, AK 99921
(907) 826-2951

This small B & B inn is located in
the town of Craig. The hosts are
Bill and Betty Abel. The Craig Clay
Works, a studio and shop selling
sturdy handcrafted pottery, is lo-
cated at the same address.

Columbine Inn
P.O. Box 155
Klawock, AK 99925
(907) 755-2287

This bed and breakfast home, on Klawock Bay, offers straight rooms or rooms with kitchenettes. Fishing charters are available, as is a whirlpool. **($$)**

Fireweed Lodge

Hollis Highway, mile 7
P.O. Box 116
Klawock, AK 99925
(907) 755-2930

A typical southeast Alaska fishing lodge, this one has comfortable rooms and an informal dining room serving filling meals. Rental cars are available, and fine canoeing waters are nearby. **($$ to $$$)**

Log Cabin RV Park & Resort

P.O. Box 54
Klawock, AK 99925
800-544-2205

This informal resort operation on Saltwater Beach has cabins **($$)** and campsites with full hookups. It also offers skiffs and boats with outboard motors, free mooring, fish freezing and smoking, and fishing packages.

Wales Resort

P.O. Box 9835
Ketchikan, AK 99901
800-531-9843

Located on the north shore of Prince of Wales Island, this fishing resort is in a wilderness setting. Fishing is taken seriously here, as is eating in the dining room. This is a thoroughly modern operation with guided fishing packages using cabin cruisers. **($$ to $$$)**

SITKA

Alaska Ocean View Bed and Breakfast

1101 Edgecumb Drive
Sitka, AK 99835
(907) 747-8310

This is a cozy B & B home that serves a full breakfast and offers rooms with private baths and a whirlpool on the patio. It is a non-smoking facility. **($$)**

Helga's Bed and Breakfast

2827 Halibut Point Road
P.O. Box 1885
Sitka, AK 99835
(907) 747-5497

This small B & B operation is located on the beach, with a fine view of the sound. **($$)**

Potlatch House

713 Katlian Street
Sitka, AK 99835
(907) 747-8611 or 800-354-6017

This modest motel has rooms and suites, with daily and weekly rates, and laundry facilities. There is a restaurant, and some rooms have good views. **($$)**

Sitka Youth Hostel

303 Kimsham Street
P.O. Box 2645
Sitka, AK 99835
(907) 747-8356 or (907) 747-8775

The hostel is one of several in southeast Alaska, offering basic accommodations, particularly helpful for young people and older folks traveling on a budget and not needing cozy rooms. There are no kitchen facilities in this hostel, which is open from June 1 to August 31. **($)**

Westmark Shee Atiká
330 Seward Street
P.O. Box 318
Sitka, AK 99835
(907) 747-6241 or 800-544-0970

Close to the historic area and the boat harbor, the hotel has comfortable rooms and suites, and a very good restaurant, however pricey. There's also a lounge, and the hotel has room service, a luxury not available in most Panhandle places. **($$ to $$$)**

SKAGWAY

Golden North Hotel
P.O. Box 343
Skagway, AK 99840
(907) 983-2451 or (907) 983-2294

This is the oldest operating hotel in Alaska, a remnant of the Klondike Gold Rush, built in 1898. The rooms are wonderfully furnished in period antiques, and the hotel has a dining room and saloon. If you're a history buff and prefer staying in historic places, this hotel is a must! It's open year-round, and reservations are recommended. **($ to $$)**

Skagway Inn
P.O. Box 500
Skagway, AK 99840
(907) 983-2289 or 800-478-2290
(Alaska only)

Another historic place, it was built in 1897 but not operated continuously as a hotel. This bed and breakfast

inn is at Seventh Street and Broadway, close to downtown, with Victorian decor, substantial breakfast, and helpful advice from innkeepers Sioux and Don Plummer on what to do and see in Skagway. **($$)**

Skagway RV and Camping Parks
P.O. Box 324
Skagway, AK 99840
(907) 983-2768

These two campgrounds in Skagway are parts of the same operation. Pullen Creek RV Park is next to the Alaska State Ferry dock and the city's Pullen Creek Park, a short walk from the Klondike National Historic Park office and the downtown area. It has electrical and water hookups, showers, and a dump station. Hanousek Park, located on Broadway, is also within walking distance of downtown, with electrical and water hookups, wooded RV and tenting sites, showers, fire pits, and dump station.

Wind Valley Lodge
P.O. Box 354
Skagway, AK 99840
(907) 983-2236

All rooms in this modern motel have private baths. There are non-smoking rooms and a guest laundry, with the Siding 21 Restaurant located next door and open from 6 A.M. **($ to $$)**

WRANGELL

Harding's Old Sourdough Lodge
P.O. Box 1062
Wrangell, AK 99929
(907) 874-3613

This is an unusual bed and breakfast operation, open year-round. The dining room, with home-style meals, brings memories of the old-fashioned boarding house. Breakfast and lunch have a standard price. The low-slung lodge has rooms with private bath that are furnished with either a king bed or twin beds. There's a cocktail lounge, sauna, steam bath, whirlpool, and laundry. The management arranges fishing charters as well as other kinds of activity including eagle watching excursions and photography outings. **($ to $$)**

Stikine Inn
P.O. Box 990
Wrangell, AK 99929
(907) 874-3388

This large and nondescript building looks more like a factory than a hotel, but it is the largest hotel in town, offering rooms with baths, TV, phones, and the Dock Side Restaurant, one block from the ferry terminal. **($ to $$)**

The Ultimate Outdoors

The American Northwest's supreme wilderness region, Salmon River Country covers a vast area comprising ten national forests, three Rocky Mountain ranges, four pristine protected wilderness areas, six tributaries of the Salmon, and the finest recreational river in the United States. All of these could vie for second place.

This is the section of the Rocky Mountains that belongs to the Northwest: a region of deep river valleys, a gorge (cut by the Snake River) known as Hell's Canyon, the strangely winding river—running both south and north—that was called the River of No Return by Lewis and Clark, who failed to reach its mouth and opted, instead, to discover the Columbia River for a less discouraging trip to the Pacific.

The Rockies are a mystifying set of mountains. They are not just one range of tightly joined peaks running down the "spine" of the continent. They are a widespread set of ranges with different characteristics, rising in the east as a seemingly solid wall but changing in the west to become a series of separate ranges divided by rivers flowing west and emptying into the Columbia basin. Even though their shapes and geological makeup are vastly different, one characteristic defines the Rockies: their age. As a relatively new set of mountains, all of the Rockies were created about 100 million years ago, during an event called the Laramide Orogeny. It was a period of uplift, followed by erosion, volcanic eruptions, more uplifting, and the most recent ice age (about two million years ago), which built glaciers that brought more erosion and valley sculpting. In some places, the uplifting continues to this day.

The Salmon River drains an impressive part of the interior Northwest. The Payette, Boise, Selway, Lochsa, and the Clearwater all drain into the Salmon, bringing water from the Rocky Mountain ranges in Montana and Idaho. This region of the Rockies is composed of igneous rock and is named the Idaho Batholith. It is this hard rock that gives the Sawtooths and the Bitterroots their jagged peaks, exposed when erosion took away the overlying sediment, leaving the rock revealed as a series of rugged, knife-sharp edges.

With all of this wilderness majesty and federally owned forest lands covering more than 21 million acres, there is no designated national park in this section of the Rockies. There are three significant federal monuments. Nez Perce National Historic Park is a series of more than 30 sites that commemorate the culture and turmoil of the Nez Perce as they battled the U.S. Army, along a 300-mile trail that the Nez Perce used as an escape route. The end of the trail, in northern Montana, was

Lynx

the site of their final defeat by the Army. Big Hole National Battlefield commemorates one of the largest victories of the Nez Perce over the Army troops, as the tribe fled toward Montana and their never-realized refuge in Canada.

Craters of the Moon National Monument, at the foot of the Sawtooth Mountains in southern Idaho, is a formerly significant volcanic region and a natural place of a different kind: stark and darkly mysterious, with plenty of lava rock and gritty craters but little granite in sight.

The western Rockies were home to the Nez Perce and Shoshone, and both lived by and obtained food and water from the river and its tributaries. There are campsites and the remains of old villages, with rock paintings throughout the region. They paddled canoes down the rivers but stayed away from the infamous gorge of the Salmon, where Lewis and Clark were to meet their own Waterloo.

The two adventurers from Washington, D.C., were the first Europeans to visit the region. They had spent more than a year getting to the Continental Divide just east of this region. They had traveled up the Missouri and along the Gallatin, and as far up the Beaverhead River as was possible, in the company of French-Canadian guide Toussaint Charbonneau and his teenage Shoshone wife, Sacajawea. They cached their canoes, starting over Lemhi Pass on foot, hoping to find another river that would take them to the sea. Dropping into the Lemhi Valley, the explorers met a group of Shoshone led by Sacajawea's brother, Cameahwait. Lewis and Clark asked members of the tribe for advice on how to reach the ocean. Cameahwait advised not to take the Salmon River, because it was very dangerous. Not taking the good counsel seriously, Lewis and Clark set out to explore the Salmon, reaching the great gorge (not knowing that it stretched for more than 130 rapid miles). After a while, they realized that they could not navigate the Salmon and returned to the Shoshone village, persuading Cameahwait to sell them 29 horses (not enough). They set off on a trip along the route the Shoshone had first suggested, back over the Bitterroots, north to Lolo Pass, and west into Nez Perce country and the Columbia River.

After Lewis and Clark, the tribes faced an influx of fur trappers, then settlers traveling through the area on the Oregon Trail. Then, miners flooded into Salmon River Country in a gold rush after a find at Orofino and another at Elk City. The fringes of the prime wilderness areas are awash in detritus from the mining and settler era: a collection of ghost towns, rusted mining equipment including dredges, tailing piles, and bits and pieces left from the old stamp mills that processed the raw ore.

The logging industry became the driver of the central Idaho economy; an industry that continues, although muted severely by environmental concerns and government restrictions.

Salmon River Country

When Gifford Pinchot first conceived of the U.S. Forest Service to protect and manage forests and to use these resources wisely for the public good, he must have been thinking of the Nez Perce National Forest, or at least the incredible swath of territory and natural features it now encompasses. Sitting squarely across most of north-central Idaho, between Montana and Oregon, the forest is larger than several states, more than two million acres with all or parts of four major designated wilderness areas—more than a million acres of forests, valleys, and rivers, protected from commercial exploitation.

The Selway-Bitterroot Wilderness occupies much of the western flank of the Bitterroot Range. The Nez Perce Forest includes a small part of the Frank Church–River of No Return Wilderness, shared with the adjoining Payette and Salmon National Forests. The Gospel Hump Wilderness borders the north bank of the Salmon River, which is the summer scene of thousands of rafters floating down the river toward the town of Riggins. The Seven Devils Wilderness lies west of the Salmon, hard against the Snake River, as it cuts through the deep gorge known as Hell's Canyon. There are no roads inside these wilderness areas, although the phenomena called "cherry stems" allow the visitor to drive to many trailheads and other wilderness attractions. When the Nez Perce National Forest was created, private landowners were satisfied by drawing wilderness boundaries around their properties (the cherries), with thin access corridors to permit travel.

The Selway-Bitterroot, River of No Return, and Gospel Hump are backpackers' heaven. For those used to the dramatic peaks and rock walls of the more easterly Rocky Mountain terrain, the mountains of north-central Idaho are not as impressive. This, after all, is the western flank: the gentler, sloping area created by the upthrust of the eastern peaks. But the area is so huge and so filled with fine rivers, large creeks with high waterfalls, and verdant valleys, that it is eminently suited to backcountry travel—by foot, horse, or mule, as well as canoeing, kayaking, and rafting. Hikers even fly to their trailhead of choice, using one of several bush air services located in the small towns that border the forests.

The Nez Perce National Forest was the first of the western forests to pursue a new code of forest management in the 1980s. It was the first to severely reduce logging, especially the damaging clear-cut techniques that left huge scars in the landscape in the 1960s and 1970s. Degraded streams and clear-cut areas have been receiving restorative work. Millions of dollars have been spent on restoring fish habitat and fish stocks in the major rivers and spawning creeks. Most impressive of all is the new forest ethic pioneered by the Nez Perce rangers, led during the 1980s by Tom Kovalicky, who took over in 1980 and immediately set to restricting cattle grazing, making fisheries and wildlife management a top priority, and fostering the idea of pure wilderness so that rangers and work crews could not drive motorized vehicles and equipment into wilderness areas. For the past 10 years, mule teams have carried supplies over trails into the wilderness. By the time he retired in 1991, Kovalicky had imbued the staff, and their superiors in Washington, with such a strong wilderness ethic that his plan continues to be fulfilled.

The Nez Perce National Forest is only a part of the recreational landscape that sprawls over this part of Idaho and the nearby western Montana Bitterroot region. The Sawtooth Range lies north to south in this part of Idaho. Here, the Sawtooth National Recreation Area offers hiking, camping, fishing, and backroad driving. This area is filled with small, clear alpine lakes. The White Cloud Peaks are also part of the recreation area, partly in the Challis National Forest and partly in the Sawtooth National Forest. The Sawtooth Wilderness lies to the west of the national recreation area, providing more backpacking experiences.

The Salmon

To the first-time visitor, the course of the Salmon River can be confusing. Rivers usually flow in a more or less direct line, using the path of least resistance, toward a river that will take the water to one sea or another. In this case, we're on the west side of the Continental Divide. But the Salmon starts as small streams flowing generally north from central Idaho, near Sun Valley and Ketchum, and then moves in a northeasterly direction toward the Bitterroot Mountains. At the point (near the town of Salmon) where it comes against the Bitterroots, it changes direction and flows almost due west across the entire width of the state, through its famous canyon, until turning abruptly north again and emptying into the Snake River at Lewiston.

The watershed of the Salmon covers 14,000 square miles of central and eastern Idaho. Water pours into the Salmon from streams flowing from the Sawtooth, Lemhi, Clearwater, and Bitterroot Mountains. The length of the Salmon's run is 425 miles, beginning at 8,000 feet in the Sawtooths and ending at 905 feet when it joins the Snake.

The upper Salmon, in and near the Sawtooth National Recreation Area, is a small stream prized by anglers. In these early stages, as the river moves through the Sawtooth National Recreation Area, the river drops an average of 12 feet per mile. After bumping against the Bitterroots and flowing north, and then west, it picks up water (and pace) from the Lemhi River, and enters the great canyon. This is the part of the river that defeated Lewis and Clark and forced them to cross the Rockies again to find another river. Until the 1890s, only a few tried to conquer the canyon, and most of those few did not survive the trip. But flatboats did run the canyon's rapids toward the end of the century, operated by an adventurous pair, David Sanderland and Henry Guleke. They carried gold miners' supplies downriver on scows, which were then taken apart to provide wood for mining camp construction.

Hardy adventurers now run the most dangerous part of the river, starting at a campground 45 miles west of West Fork,

Idaho, near Salmon, ending the run 80 fast miles later, just above Riggins. At Riggins, the Salmon becomes peaceful, moving along a long, flat stretch of valley land, offering tube and raft trips for a host of people, including families, who stop on sandbars for picnics or for sunning. On a summer weekend, you'll see literally thousands of floaters lazily moving down the Salmon from Riggins.

The more adventurous trip through the canyon is available from late June, when the river is still raging with snowmelt. The summer permit season runs from June 20 through September 7, with applications accepted from December 1 to January 31, each year. After a lottery, dates are assigned and the lucky winners have until March 15 to confirm that they will do the trip. New openings are allotted on a first come, first served basis by telephone on the second Monday following March 15. For application forms and information on the canyon trip and the permit process, write North Fork District, Salmon National Forest, P.O. Box 180, North Fork, ID 83466, or call (208) 865-2383.

Gospel Hump Wilderness

The smallest and least-known of the three major wilderness areas in north-central Idaho, this protected part of the Nez Perce National Forest is nonetheless huge. It joins the Frank Church–River of No Return Wilderness at the western end of the Salmon River Gorge and stretches along the north side of the river for 20 miles, from the town of Riggins to the old Elk City Road. This road, State Route 14, leads along the west side of the wilderness area, providing access to several trailheads and forest roads, including one that leads to the river's edge. Other trails are found on the north and east sides.

Two forest road routes lead to great scenery and spectacular views, without a long hike. Forest Road 1614 leads 12 miles from the south end of Riggins, along the Salmon to the Spring Bar Campground. From there, Forest Road 444 leads along a cherry stem to a fine panorama at the Square Mountain Viewpoint.

Another forest route runs to the Salmon River from the Elk City Road. This route is suitable for four-wheel-drive vehicles or those with high clearance, such as pickups. Elk City is 50 miles from the Highway 14 junction with U.S. 95. The road continues, in an unpaved condition, to Dixie. Forest Road 222 runs south from Dixie to MacKay Bar. You may wish to visit Red River Hot Springs located in the area. This is a region rich in mining history. A notable gold rush occurred at Elk City, one of two in the area (the other was at Florence, now abandoned). Elk City managed to hold on to life and now has a population of about 400. Many backroads lead to old diggings, several of them accessed by driving to Dixie.

Sawtooth National Recreation Area

Administered by the Forest Service, the recreation area protects the headwaters of the Salmon River. The jagged peaks of the Sawtooth Range are to the east side of the river, as is the beautiful Sawtooth Valley, the home of the famed Sun Valley resort. East of the valley is another range, running north to south, from the eastbound Salmon west of Challis all the way south to the Snake River Plain. While this is one continuous line of connected peaks, it has become known by three names: the northernmost White Cloud Mountains; the Pioneer Mountains (in the Sun Valley/Ketchum area); and the Boulder Mountains, found east of Hailey. The southern Pioneers and the Boulders are not within the national recreation area, but they offer many fine opportunities for hiking and are included in the hike descriptions that follow.

The Sawtooth Wilderness, the heart of the rugged range, takes up more than 200,000 acres of the recreation area. This is an area of small mountain lakes and beautiful meadows, all framed by the pink granite of the Idaho Batholith. This is prime hiking country, where a hike of a few miles brings startling changes in terrain and scenery. Around every corner is a new lake or wildflower meadow. Entry to this area is mainly from the east and north sides, near Stanley. Most of the hiking is done after mid-July, after most of the snow has melted. The season ends in early September. A few roads lead from the west, via State Highway 75. This is the road that runs north from Shoshone on the Snake River Plain, passing through Ketchum and then entering the recreation area eight miles north of Ketchum and Sun Valley.

East of the Stanley Basin sit the White Cloud Mountains. Castle Peak, 11,815 feet high, dominates the scene. More than a hundred lakes sit atop the range, providing wonderful vistas and easy day-hikes. This is an area not under wilderness protection, thus permitting a variety of recreational uses, including mountain bikes and motorcycles. Visitors usually enter the White Clouds from the northeast (the Challis side of the range). Roads wander beside the East Fork of the Salmon, with trails along Little or Big Boulder creeks. You may also wish to enter the White Clouds from the north, via Slate Creek Road.

The Pioneer Mountains provide a spectacular backdrop for Ketchum and Sun Valley. Ketchum is the town; Sun Valley is the resort, on a sideroad leading east from Ketchum. This was the first mountain resort in the western Rockies, developed by railroad magnate Averill Harriman, who had visited Europe and thought that the U.S. and his railway company could benefit from an alpine ski resort. A ski area was created on Dollar Mountain and featured the world's first chairlift. A ranch in the scenic valley was purchased, and the Sun Valley Lodge was constructed.

Around the lodge, swimming pools, ice rinks, and gardens were installed. Originally a gambling center, Sun Valley concentrated on skiing after gambling was prohibited in the 1940s. Bald Mountain was opened to skiers and new lifts were built. Vacation mansions were built in the valley, while Ketchum grew to service tourists' needs. Ernest Hemingway was the area's most famous resident, and several memorials are in place, including his house north of the town and a bust and plaque on Sun Valley Road. The resort continues to thrive, with golfing during summer months and the obligatory showing, each evening, of the 1940s Sonia Henie/Glenn Miller movie *Sun Valley Serenade.*

DAY-HIKES

Alpine Creek Trail Located in the Sawtooths, at the southern end of the Sawtooth Wilderness, this trail is reached by driving north from Ketchum along Highway 75 for 40 miles to the Alturas Lake road. This is a paved road running through forest and meadowlands, leading to Alturas Lake. The pavement ends and after another 1.2 miles, you arrive at Alpine Creek. There is a parking area on the east side of the creek. The 2.5-mile trail climbs to a rocky vantage point above the canyon of Alpine Creek, with more views of the Sawtooth crags. The trail then leads through forest and an open area, where avalanches have washed out the trees, ending in a thick forest beside the creek. Above this point are several of the creek's tributaries and 45 lakes (small and large). You can continue farther, following a rough trail along the south side of the creek. This route ascends 900 feet, to the largest of the lakes.

Hyndman Creek Trail and North Fork Trail   The two trails depart from the same trailhead in the Pioneer Mountains, each offering an easy day-hike. The North Fork hike leads to a pioneer cabin three miles from the trailhead. The trail along the main creek is perfect for families, using an old logging road and passing several springs that have beaver dams and ponds (about a half-mile). It continues along the creek to a crossing at three miles, which is a natural place from which to return. You can extend the hike by continuing to the right (now off the roadway), climbing the side of a canyon to a basin below Hyndman Peak (el. 12,009 feet). You'll also see Old Hyndman Peak (el. 11,775 feet) and Cobb Peak (el. 11,650 feet).

It is possible to continue up the old roadbed from the creek crossing, through the forest to an elevation of about 8,700 feet, from which you get wonderful views of the nearby peaks. You'll find several campsites in this area.

Trail to Ibex Pass   The Boulder Mountains offer a one- or two-day hike, 13 miles north of Ketchum, in the Sawtooth National Recreation Area. The trail follows the North Fork of the Big Wood River. The trailhead is five miles from the headquarters of the recreation area, off Highway 75. Drive into the headquarters area and continue on the dirt road for 5.1 miles, up the North Fork Canyon. The trailhead is at the end of the road. Two early fords are easy to spot. The trail then continues through forest and many open areas (avalanche-cleared), to a junction with the West Pass Trail (two miles; see below) as a waterfall appears. To reach Ibex Pass, continue on a straight line, following the canyon and beginning the climb to the pass. The trail seems to come to an end at the edge of the canyon, but cairns mark the rocky route northwest to the pass at 10,250 feet. The last part requires some scrambling, passing the timberline and crossing a talus slope. You'll know when you reach the pass. The trail swiftly descends on the other side. Staying at the top, you'll get a magnificent view of Castle Peak (el. 11,820 feet) to the north.

You have an opportunity to hike the West Pass Trail, which leaves the North Fork–Big Wood River Trail when you see a waterfall plunging down a side canyon. The West Pass Trail crosses a meadow after you pass the waterfall scene. It climbs through the side canyon to West Pass, an elevation change of 2,900 feet. From the junction, the trail is about two miles long.

BACKCOUNTRY HIKING

Boulder Chain Lakes Trail   This 13-mile trail, with possible turnaround locations before then, leads through the supremely beautiful White Cloud Mountains to a series of lakes. The trail is popular with anglers who go for the rainbow trout. It is also a favorite with others who just want to enjoy the absolute beauty of the White Clouds.

Access: The trailhead is in the Sawtooth National Recreation Area, about 35 miles west of Challis. Drive to Challis and take State Route 93 south for a mile to the junction with State Route 75. Drive south along Highway 75 for 16 miles to East Fork of the Salmon Road. Drive 20 miles along this partially paved road until you see the Livingston Mine–Boulder Chain Lakes Trailhead.

The Trail: The trail climbs to a high alpine basin with views of Scree and the Shallow Lakes. Good camping is available at the lower Boulder Chain lakes. There is also earlier camping at Frog Lakes, the turnaround point for off-road vehicles, and even earlier via a one-mile spur trail to Little Redfish Lake.

The Hike: There is a steep climb during the first few miles, over Red Ridge, with heart-stopping views. Then the route drops to Frog Lake. The trail has switchbacks on the descent, passing springs and camping areas. Merriam Peak and Castle Peak appear at Frog Lake. The trail continues past the two small lakes, leading west and climbing a dry hill. Surprisingly, there is sagebrush all around, but more forest and lakes lie beyond. The trail forks, with the left trail leading to the Little Boulder Creek area. The main trail ascends between several lakes—a perfect setting for camping, relaxing, and fishing. The lakes are named for their elevations (for example, Lake 9,643).

The route continues climbing to the pass to Slickenslide Creek. The views of Castle Peak and Serrate Ridge are fantastic. The trail involves quite a bit of climbing, but the lakes and views make it all worthwhile.

Frank Church–River of No Return Wilderness

The largest designated wilderness area in the lower 48 states, with 2.36 million acres in six national forests, this vast wilderness was formally designated by the federal government only in 1980. Before that, this was an area of hot dispute between environmentalists, logging companies, and the Forest Service, which found itself in the middle of the fray. The disputes continue to this day.

This is an area the size of Yellowstone National Park. The Salmon River runs through it for more than 95 miles, including the canyon that gave the Salmon the name "River of No Return." The river flows on the side of the wilderness area between Stanley and Salmon, and then plunges through the middle of the protected area and the long canyon. This canyon, and the canyon of the Middle Fork (also within the wilderness), are more than 7,000 feet deep in places. When you realize that this is deeper than the Grand Canyon, you might wonder why there has been little interest in making at least some of this wondrous landscape a national park. Perhaps the idea of wilderness supersedes the notion of building roads to a tourist hotel on the brink of the canyon. Idaho is not Arizona, and many Idahoans like it the way it is.

To fully explore this area with its lack of on-the-spot visitor services, some planning and research are necessary. First, get all the material you can from the Forest Service. Four national forests share custody of the wilderness area. Write or call to obtain the two 50-meter contour maps (north and south), and trail leaflets. Contact one or more of the following offices:

- Payette National Forest: P.O. Box 1026, McCall, ID 83638; (208) 634-2255
- Salmon National Forest: Cobalt Ranger District, P.O. Box 729, Salmon, ID 83467; (208) 756-2240
- Challis National Forest: Middle Fork Ranger District, P.O. Box 750, Challis, ID 83226; (208) 879-4321

- Nez Perce National Forest: Red River Ranger District, Elk City, ID 83525; (208) 842-2255

Ralph Maughan and Jackie Johnson Maughan have written a fine book, *The Hiker's Guide to Idaho,* published by Falcon Press in 1995, in which they provide details of 100 hikes throughout the state.

There are myriad habitats within the wilderness area, including forests, open stands of ponderosa pine, Douglas fir groves, mid-level meadows, low river valleys, creek canyons, and dry canyons. Nearly 200 bird species are sighted here, and all of the mountain mammals reside in the wilderness, including lynx, bobcat, moose, mule deer, white-tailed deer, bighorn sheep, mountain goats, wolverines, and mountain lions. There also are black bear and elk.

Bald eagles, osprey, and falcons fly overhead. Anglers come from afar to try their luck against chinook salmon, steelhead, Arctic grayling, smallmouth bass, and trout.

Many trails lead through the wilderness, reached in two ways: by driving to the end of long dirt roads, sometimes for more than a hundred miles, or flying with one of the charter plane services available in Salmon, Challis, McCall, and Cascade, among other communities. Some trailheads have airstrips.

Moose

Knowledgeable hikers drive to one airstrip, take a hike, and charter a plane back to the car. Snow is found into July, with low altitude hiking beginning in mid-June. The high-level hiking and camping season runs from sometime in July until mid-September.

The more popular hiking areas include the Middle Fork of the Salmon, on the eastern side of the wilderness, and the Bighorn Crags, on the west side, with trailheads at the Crags Campground near Cobalt, a mining town.

BACKCOUNTRY TRAILS

The Frank Church–River of No Return Wilderness is backcountry and not a place for day-hikes. The Big Creek Trail leads from the Payette National Forest on a journey of 50 miles, after a drive of at least 160 miles to reach the trailhead. Several trails wind and climb through the Bighorn Crags, including the Crags Trail and the Clear Creek Trail. The Middle Fork Trail provides another major multi-day excursion. Here are two hikes to get you started.

Reflection Lake Trail *Access:* This trail has relatively easy access, with only a short drive from Challis or Stanley. To reach Bighorn Crags Campground from Salmon, take Williams Creek Road for 12.2 miles to the Panther Creek Road junction. Take Panther Creek Road until you get to Porphyry Creek, and turn right to reach the campground.

From Challis and Stanley, take U.S. Highway 93 northwest to the Morgan Creek junction. Turn left and take Morgan Creek Road for 19.6 miles, where its name changes to Panther Creek Road. Turn right on Porphyry Creek Road to drive to the campground.

The Trail: The round trip is 28 miles, through the Bighorn Crags to Reflection Lake (13 miles) and Buck Lake (14 miles). More lakes are located over a few more hills. This is the southern part of the Bighorn Crags. This is a less-traveled part of the area than the busy northern section. The trail is of moderate difficulty, climbing to an elevation of 9,000 feet and then dropping into the lake basin.

The Hike: The trailhead begins at the campground, on the same trail that leads to Ship Island Lake (another fine hike). You climb along a ridge to a junction with the Clear Creek and Waterfall trails (five miles). Moving through a lodgepole pine forest, the route descends for a half-mile to a small creek. There's a second junction beyond mile 7. The right path leads to Gentian and Birdbill lakes. Take the left path, leading toward Welcome Lake. Just before reaching this lake, another trail leads to Reflection Lake, climbing steeply over a series of switchbacks (to 9,000 feet) and then drops through the forest for three miles. You'll see a basin full of lakes (eight of them): Turquoise, Skyhigh, Echo, Reflection, Twin Cove, Buck, Doe, and Fawn. Look for bighorn sheep and elk. The trail crosses Skyhigh Creek (11 miles) and reaches Reflection Lake at mile 13. Another mile farther and you've reached Buck Lake. This is another place to take your fishing gear, for rainbow and cut-throat trout.

Big Creek to Salmon River Trail   *Access:* The trail is northeast of McCall, a small tourist town on the Payette River, which is a tributary of the Salmon. To reach the trailhead at Big Creek, take the road that starts at McCall and passes Ponderosa State Park. There are signs to the park. Continue on this road for 55 miles until you reach Yellow Pine. Take the road east, up the East Fork of the Salmon, for about three miles to the junction with Profile Gap–Big Creek Road. The road climbs to the pass and then descends to the trailhead, which is 12 miles beyond the pass.

The Trail: The hike leads 55 miles, from the Big Creek trailhead to Ramey Ridge and Lower Ramey Meadows. There are campsites along the way. The route follows the course of Moose Jaw Creek and then McCalla Creek. From Ramey Ridge, the trail crosses the Chamberlain Basin, a high plateau. The trail moves to follow Whimstick Creek for about a hundred yards, and then heads toward Grass Mountain (a scenic sidetrip), then down to Disappointment Creek, and then the Salmon River, which you cross (more about that later). The hike concludes with a walk through the Salmon River Canyon, 12 miles from the river crossing. The hike takes five days, ending at Corn Creek, a put-in point for river rafters. Hikers usually catch a ride to Salmon or have someone bring their car to Corn Creek.

The Hike: The trail first leads through a pine forest, climbing to Ramey Ridge and reaching an old cabin after five miles. There is water, from a spring, in the cabin. After 10 miles, the trail branches to the right, leading to the Rock Rabbit lookout, and another fork. Take the right fork to Lower Ramey Meadows.

Campsites are located in the trees. This is the usual first-night stopping place. Continuing the next morning, proceed down the trail, taking the left fork to follow McCalla Creek. There's a camping area at 22 miles (near the McCoy outfitter's cabin). The junction with the Whimstick Trail is another three miles. Take Whimstick for only a short distance, until a trail veers left. After another 2.25 miles, a short spur trail leads left to Grass Mountain, a viewpoint atop the 6,252-foot hill. Following the main trail, the route descends to Disappointment Creek, and less than a mile farther to a campsite, at the Hungry Creek Trail junction. It's another three miles to the Salmon River, where you'll have to hitch a ride across the stream with a cooperative river rafter (this is done all the time). The sandbar on the north bank is a perfect place to rest those tired muscles. The final jaunt through the canyon follows a good path, eight miles long.

BIRDS

Mountain Bluebird
Sialia currucoides

Growing to a length of about eight inches, this colorful bird of the western forests has turquoise-blue upperparts, a light blue breast, and a white belly. The female is grayish-brown, with a light blue tint on the wings, rump, and tail. It lives in the forested mountains of western Canada, the western states from Washington to California, and east to Oklahoma. It is found in good numbers in the wilderness areas of Idaho and Montana. It lives in open areas where there are small stands or single coniferous trees. In Idaho, it nests at low elevations in pine woodlands. You may see this bluebird hovering over the ground, looking for insects, then dropping to catch its prey. Its voice is a quiet warble in the early morning. Its call is an unsubtle *phew, yior,* or *terr.*

Dark-eyed Junco
Junco hymalis

With five subspecies having variations in color and markings, the Oregon junco is the best known and most colorful, with a black hood, chestnut mantle, and white underparts with light brown sides. Another junco, called the slate-colored junco, has a slate-gray head, upper breast, upperparts, and flanks. The dark-eyed junco breeds in central and southern Idaho, including the Sawtooth Range, spending winters on the Pacific Coast. Another variation, the gray-headed, winters south to northern Mexico. In this area, it lives in conifer forests and in open woodlands. Its song is a rolling trill, on one pitch. Juncos communicate by giving their call: a *tchet,* or *tsick.*

Long-eared Owl
Asio otus

Best identified by its catlike voice, this owl is similar in appearance to the great horned owl, except it is smaller, growing only to about 16 inches and without a white throat. It is a mottled grayish-brown above with dark gray barring below. The ears also place this bird apart from other Rocky Mountain owls. Its dark ear tufts sit close together on top of its head. Its habitat includes conifer groves and mixed woods, and it is seen in the Mojave and other sagebrush deserts. Its voice is a repeated *hoooooo,* and its call resembles the sound of a cat.

MAMMALS

Snowshoe Hare
Lepus americanus

This hare is camouflaged by its changing fur, as the seasons change. In summer, the coat is dark brown, with a dark tail above and white below. In winter, it is as white as snow. But the colors also change to match the fall and spring landscape. When the snow starts to fall, creating a patchy scene, the hare has the same patchy appearance. In spring, the white coat is shed as the snow leaves, gradually changing to its summer browns. This hare has large hind feet, with extensive fur in winter, making it easy to move over the snow. And that's a good thing, because it needs to move fast when chased by a lynx (see below). You'll see its footprints in the snow, as deep as one inch. The snowshoe hare bears two or three litters each year, with an average of three babies in each litter.

Lynx
Felis lynx
Sometimes called the Canadian lynx, this cat is subtly different from the bobcat (*F. ruffus*). Slightly smaller, darker, and rougher-looking than its cousin, the lynx grows to a length of 41 inches. The female is smaller than the male. It is buff, or tawny, with black hairs mixed with the predominant buff hairs. Its underparts are a cinnamon color. Its short tail is tipped with black. The lynx has large feet with much fur. It has large, whitish ruffs on the cheeks. It lives deep in the Rocky Mountain forests, across Canada, and in the west, from Alaska to central Idaho and northern Montana. It usually prowls at night, resting under ledges while the sun is shining. It is a tree climber and a good swimmer, and its extremely large, furry feet act as snowshoes. Its prime prey is the snowshoe hare.

Moose
Alces alces
I have to admit it—the moose is my favorite northern animal. Should one love such an ungainly (many say ugly) Quasimodo kind of beast? After all, this is the largest deer on earth, with dark brown hair, humped shoulders, and thin legs (seeming too slender to hold such a large body). Not to mention that huge, pendulous muzzle, hanging and swinging, and that awful smell coming off them during mating season. The males have large palmate antlers, spreading four to five feet. Yes, they seem ugly, but at heart, they are very tender. Moose make marvelous parents, for about six months. Two calves are born, then swim at two weeks, spending all their initial days with their doting parents. Just before the birth of new calves, the previous arrivals are driven away by their parents. The terrible smell comes from both male and female during rut. Strutting his stuff, the male urinates and then wallows in the mud. The female also rolls in it. Fortunately, there's usually a swamp nearby, for a bath. I think my love for these creatures comes from my attachment to the spruce forests, marshes, and swamps they live in.

Western Jumping Mouse
Zapus princeps
Sometimes it runs on all four feet, but more often it moves through a series of jumps, especially when startled. This talented mouse also climbs and swims. It has yellow

sides and a white belly that is sometimes tinged with yellow. There is a dark, almost black, band running down the middle of the back. Its hind feet are larger than its front feet. This mouse is often a bog resident, fashioning its nest in the sphagnum moss. It also lives in moist meadows and woods and at the edges of lakes, ponds, or creeks. It is found from the southern Yukon, through B.C. and the Rocky Mountains, to the Oregon and California Cascades.

AMPHIBIANS

Northern Alligator Lizard
Gerrhonatus coeruleus
This lizard has several subspecies, including San Francisco (*G. c. coeruleus*), and Shasta (*G. c. shastensis*). This one, just called "northern" (*G. c. principis*), lives in the Cascades of Oregon and Washington, and into Idaho and western Montana. It is olive to bluish, with dark eyes. It has vague bands across the back, very indistinct on this subspecies. It is a diurnal creature, active throughout the day, looking for snails and insects. It lives under rocks or rotten logs in cool, wet woodlands, at an elevation of just over 10,000 feet.

Northern Pacific Rattlesnake
Crotalus viridis oreganus
This poisonous snake lives west and east of the Cascades, but it is not widely found on that range. It is a subspecies of the much more widespread western rattlesnake. This snake is found in south-central

British Columbia, eastern Washington and Oregon, and in west-central Idaho—Salmon River Country. It also lives east of the Sierra Nevada in California. It has brown blotches down the middle of its back. The blotches are surrounded by a white border. The markings narrow to rings near the tail. Its habitat is conifer forests and woodlands, including oak chaparral and rocky places, as high as 11,000 feet.

Western Skink
Eumeces skiltonianus
Found throughout Idaho and western Montana, this harmless snake has a brown band on its back between white stripes. It also shows a broad, dark band on its side between white stripes. The four light stripes extend to the tail. The tail is gray or brown, with juvenile tails a bright blue. When mating, the male has orange on the sides of the head. The subspecies found in Idaho (*E. s. skiltonianus*) has a dark border on the light side stripe. A diurnal creature, this skink feeds on insects, earthworms, and spiders. It lives in forests, open woodlands, and on meadows with some rocks. Its eggs hatch in July and August.

Western Toad
Bufo boreas
With nocturnal habits, this large toad lives in burrows it has made, or borrowed from rodents, preferring to nest near streams, springs, and on meadows. Not having vocal sacs, it merely peeps. It is gray to green, with a light stripe down the middle of its back. Its warts have a

reddish tinge, and are surrounded by black blotches. The male toad has a lightish throat. Its range is from southeast Alaska to Baja California and inland through southern B.C., all of Idaho, western Montana, and to central Colorado. At higher elevations, where heat stress is not a problem, this toad comes out during the daytime.

TREES, SHRUBS, AND UNDERSTORY PLANTS

Rocky Mountain forests are quite different in their understory features. While most of the same major trees are found in the Idaho and Montana Rockies as in the Cascades and coastal ranges (ponderosa pine, Douglas fir, spruce, western hemlock), the smaller trees and shrubs under the canopy vary from those found farther west. Here are some of the most common understory shrubs.

Creambush
Holodiscus discolor
Also known as mountain spray and ocean spray, the most commonly used name describes the creamy white flowers clustered in pyramid shapes. This large shrub is found in western coastal and inland forests, as far east as the Salmon River drainage region. Its range extends from British Columbia to Southern California. The shrub, growing to about 20 feet, has many branches with shreddy bark. The green leaves have some hairs above, with prominent veins beneath. The bark is light brown or gray, shredding as the tree matures. Although the individual flowers are tiny, the clusters make an impressive show. There are five petals and five sepals to each flower. They are clustered in panicles at the end of the branchlets.

Black Hawthorn
Crataegus douglasii
Growing in mountain valleys near streams, this small, compact tree bears black fruits, which are food for partridges, quail, pheasants, and other birds. It can be as tall as 30 feet but is usually shorter in the understory of a conifer forest. It has shiny, dark green leaves (paler below), shiny red twigs (usually with spines), and half-inch-wide flowers with five white petals and 10 to 20 pink stamens. The flowers form in clusters at the top of long stalks. The fruit (hawberry) is shiny black, about half an inch in diameter, containing yellow pulp and three to five nutlets. The major population of this tree is along the Pacific Coast from southeast Alaska through British Columbia, and as far south as central California. It is found in the B.C. and Idaho Rockies. There are isolated stands in the Southwest and near Lake Superior.

Kinnikinnick
Arctostaphylos uva-ursi
The name is a Native American word for tobacco-like smoking and chewing materials. It is a low, matted plant, with rusty brown trailing stems, small, leathery, dark green leaves, and pink, lantern-shaped

flowers. The fruit is a red berry. A common plant on the forest floors of the Idaho and Montana Rockies, kinnikinnick not only was used in place of tobacco but was considered a powerful medicine by Native Americans, who used it for many purposes, including as a treatment for sexually transmitted diseases.

Western Serviceberry
Amelanchier alnifolia
Found on both sides of the Canada/U.S. border, this small tree or shrub is usually seen with several trunks, making it easy to identify. It can grow to 30 feet but is often in the smaller shrub form. The alternate leaves are about two inches long and just about as wide, often nearly round, but sometimes oval. The thin bark is gray or brown. The hairless twigs are reddish-brown. The tree bears white, star-shaped flowers with five narrow petals in terminal clusters. The fruit has the appearance of a tiny apple, a half-inch in diameter, purple or almost black, with several seeds. The shrub provides browse for deer and other animals. Songbirds also feed on the serviceberry tree. People have long used the fruit in baking and making puddings. Its range is from central Alaska southwest to Manitoba and Minnesota, and south to Colorado and Northern California. It is an understory plant in the coastal forests and in the Idaho Rockies.

Birchleaf Spiraea
Spiraea betulifolia
This low shrub has clusters of small white flowers and small fruit pods. It grows to a height of 32 inches, al-though in the Rockies it is usually much shorter. The alternate leaves are a glossy green above and paler below. The leaves are usually toothed above the middle. The flowers are arranged in flat-topped clusters, first white when they appear in July and August, and then turning brown. It is one of several species of spiraea found in western mountain forests, and the flowers of other species have a stronger scent than those of the birchleaf. Other forest spiraea do not have flat-topped flowers. The many galls seen on this shrub are caused by insects laying eggs inside the flowers.

WILDFLOWERS

Bitterroot
Lewisea rediviva
Also called tobacco root, this little plant has given its name to a river and two mountain ranges. Deep mauve or pink-to-white flowers grow on short stalks, close to and in rosettes of small succulent leaves. Each flower has 12 to 18 petals, and six to eight sepals. At the middle of each stalk are five to eight bracts. Bitterroot is the translation for the Shoshone name for this herb, which is Montana's state flower. When boiled, the plant's root has the strong scent of tobacco, and it was used as a substitute for chewing tobacco. The plant is also found in the Tobacco Root Mountains far to the east.

Bunchberry
Cornus canadensis
You'll see this ground cover across North America, along coasts, and in

moist forests. Its range extends as far south as northern New Mexico and Northern California. The plant grows to eight inches, with long, narrow, oval-shaped leaves and bright red berries found in little clusters. The flowers are light green with four petals and four sepals in clusters surrounded by four oval-shaped, pink or white bracts. The bunchberry is widely cultivated for home gardens.

Explorer's Gentian
Gentiana calycosa
This lovely mountain wildflower is found on subalpine and lower meadows throughout the mountain ranges of the west, from the Coast ranges to the Montana Rockies, but not north of British Columbia. The plant has several leafy stems, bearing one to three flowers. The blue flower is 1.5 inches long and funnel-shaped, with a blue to yellow-green corolla, usually with green

streaks. The calyx has five lobes. Growing to a height of about 12 inches, this gentian is usually found beside streams and in mountain meadows.

Meadow Goldenrod
Solidago canadensis
You should know that this species of goldenrod is not usually the one that causes allergic reactions. The guilty party is commonly called ragweed (*ambrosia* species). When found on a meadow near the end of summer, in full yellow profusion, the meadow goldenrod is a delightful sight. It grows as tall as 20 inches and has tall, hairy stems that bear very small heads of flowers in a cluster, either long or flat-topped. The leaves grow to about five inches long, have fine hairs, and have three veins. The seed-like fruit has bristles on the top. The plant grows on mountain slopes and meadows from low woodland to subalpine elevations.

CHALLIS

Challis Hot Springs Campground
P.O. Box 1779
Challis, ID 83226
(208) 879-4442

Two pools (warm and hot) are beside the campground. There are RV hookups, a play area, and fishing nearby. Drive three miles south from Challis on Highway 93 and then onto Hot Springs Road and drive four miles north.

Challis Valley RV Park
P.O. Box 928
Challis, ID 83226
(208) 879-2393

This medium-size RV park is in the town of Challis, with hookups, dump station, and propane service.

KETCHUM AND SUN VALLEY

Elkhorn Resort and Golf Club
P.O. Box 6009
Sun Valley, ID 83354
(208) 622-4511 or 800-355-4676

This newer and modern resort has several restaurants, deluxe rooms and suites, golfing, and a ski base. It's just south of Ketchum. **($$ to $$$)**

The River Street Inn
100 River Street West
P.O. Box 182
Sun Valley, ID 83340
(208) 726-3611

This cozy B & B inn has suites with Japanese soaking tubs and a noted breakfast. It's close to downtown, shopping, and fine cafes. **($$)**

Sessions Lodge
P.O. Box 9696
Ketchum, ID 83340
(208) 774-3366

This is a small motel with overnight units, trailer spaces with hookups, a store, gas station, and cafe. **($)**

Sun Valley Resort
Sun Valley Road
Sun Valley, ID 83340
(208) 622-4111 or 800-635-8261
(outside Idaho) or 800-632-4104
(in Idaho)

Located on Sun Valley Road, just east of Ketchum, this is the oldest, and many say the finest, of the ski and summer destination resorts. The inn and the lodge provide varied accommodations, the dining in the lodge is superb, and there are more restaurants and lounges, along with golf courses, ice skating, swimming pools, and all the expected resort amenities. **($$ to $$$)**

Sun Valley RV Resort
P.O. Box 548
Ketchum, ID 83353
(208) 726-3429

This large RV park has trailer and RV spaces with full hookups, whirlpool, pool, mini golf, and more. It's located south of Ketchum.

MCCALL

Hotel McCall

P.O. Box 1778
McCall, ID 83638
(208) 634-8105

This 1930s-vintage hotel in downtown McCall has a warm atmosphere, aided by complimentary wine and free breakfast for guests. Most rooms have private bath. **($ to $$)**

McCall Campground

190 Krahn Lane
McCall, ID 83638
(208) 634-5165

Located 1.5 miles south of town, on Payette Lake, the campground has sites with scenic views. Facilities include hookups, dump station, laundry, and store.

Shore Lodge

501 West Lake Street
P.O. Box 1006
McCall, ID 83638
(208) 634-2244 or 800-657-6464

This large lodge is on the shore of Payette Lake, just west of downtown McCall. It features heated pools, a dock, a dining room, and an informal cafe. To get there, take Lake Street west along the south shore of the lake to the lodge. **($$ to $$$)**

SALMON AND AREA

Heritage Inn Bed & Breakfast

510 Lena Street
Salmon, ID 83467
(208) 756-3174

Located in the built-up area of Salmon, this B & B home evokes the aura of the late 1800s. **($ to $$)**

Lost Trail Hot Springs Resort

P.O. Box 37
Sula, MT 59871
(406) 821-3574

In the historic area explored by Lewis and Clark, this inn is just north of the Idaho/Montana border on Highway 93. It's not far from the Big Hole National Battlefield. The resort has rooms, hot spring pools, sauna, a restaurant, RV hookups, and campsites. **($ to $$)**

Motel Deluxe

112 South Church Street
Salmon, ID 83467
(208) 756-2231

This is a standard motel in downtown Salmon, with rooms, some kitchenette facilities, large beds, and a barbecue pit. **($)**

North Fork Motel

P.O. Box 100
North Fork, ID 83466
(208) 865-2412

This is a small, fairly new two-story motel in a scenic setting beside the river, next to a more-than-decent restaurant. The village of North Fork is a 21 miles north of Salmon. **($ to $$)**

Salmon Meadows Campground

P.O. Box 705
Salmon, ID 83467
(208) 756-2640

This is a large campground with full hookups, tent sites, and dump station on St. Charles Street, two blocks north of the junction of Highway 93 and St. Charles.

Smith House Bed & Breakfast
49 Salmon River Road
Shoup, ID 83469
(208) 394-2121

Located in Shoup, a small town near Salmon, this home is in a superb setting on the Salmon River. There's a hot tub, and restaurants are nearby. It's a "country inn" that's in the country. **($ to $$)**

Twin Peaks Guest Ranch
P.O. Box 774
Salmon, ID 83467
(208) 894-2290

In the mountains with a large rustic lodge, this guest ranch offers trail rides, evening barbecues, and fishing adventures. There are cabins to stay in, a pool, and whirlpool. **($$ to $$$)**

STANLEY

Idaho Rocky Mountain Ranch
P.O. Box 9934
Stanley, ID 83278
(208) 774-3544

This is an excellent place to stay, and it is located on Highway 75, 10 miles south of Stanley. Accommodations include cabin and lodge rooms. The summer season runs from June 1 to mid-September, and several cabins are kept open during winter months. Built as a hunting lodge in 1930, the walls of the lodge are constructed of logs. Full breakfast is served each morning with gourmet dinners in the evenings. A hot spring pool just adds to your relaxation. Picnic lunches are available, and there's a stocked fishing pond. **($$ to $$$)**

McGowan's Resort
P.O. Box 91
Stanley, ID 83278
(208) 774-2290

This resort has modern log cabins beside the Salmon River. The cabins have kitchenettes, fireplaces, and TV sets. Fishing is the focus of this resort. **($ to $$)**

Mountain Village Resort
P.O. Box 150
Stanley, ID 83278
(208) 774-3661

This is a large operation (for Stanley) with accommodations, gas, store, and dance hall near the main highway junction. It is open year-round, unlike some of the other motels in and around Stanley. **($)**

Sunbeam Village & RV Park
P.O. Box 310
Stanley, ID 83278
(208) 838-2211

This is a cabin operation with a small campground, located downriver from Stanley via Highway 75, near the historic Yankee Fork Dredge. Several cabins are also available.

WILDLIFE CHECKLIST

Birds of the Northwest

The following list of birds is provided as a selective guide to the bird species that are permanent, seasonal, and transient residents of the Northwest, particularly along the Pacific Coast. Bird names are organized by the standard order of species.

Shorebirds and Seabirds

☐ Red-throated Loon
☐ Arctic Loon
☐ Common Loon
☐ Pacific Loon
☐ Yellow-billed Loon
☐ Pied-billed Grebe
☐ Red-necked Grebe
☐ Horned Grebe
☐ Western Grebe
☐ Eared Grebe
☐ Least Grebe
☐ Short-tailed Albatross
☐ Black-footed Albatross
☐ Laysan Albatross
☐ Northern Fulmar
☐ Scaled Petrel
☐ Pink-footed Shearwater
☐ Sooty Shearwater
☐ Short-tailed Shearwater

☐ Manx Shearwater
☐ Leach's Storm Petrel
☐ Fork-tailed Storm Petrel
☐ Brown Pelican
☐ Double-crested Cormorant
☐ Brandt's Cormorant
☐ Pelagic Cormorant
☐ Red-faced Cormorant
☐ American Bittern
☐ Snowy Egret
☐ Great Egret
☐ Great Blue Heron
☐ Whooper Swan
☐ Trumpeter Swan
☐ Tundra Swan
☐ White-fronted Goose
☐ Snow Goose
☐ Emperor Goose
☐ Canada Goose
☐ Brant (Black)
☐ Wood Duck
☐ American Wigeon
☐ Gadwall
☐ Green-winged Teal
☐ Mallard
☐ Northern Pintail
☐ Blue-winged Teal
☐ Cinnamon Teal
☐ Northern Shoveler
☐ Canvasback
☐ Redhead
☐ Ring-necked Duck
☐ Tufted Duck

- ☐ Greater Scaup
- ☐ Lesser Scaup
- ☐ Common Eider
- ☐ King Eider
- ☐ Spectacled Eider
- ☐ Steller's Eider
- ☐ Harlequin Duck
- ☐ Oldsquaw
- ☐ Black Scoter
- ☐ Surf Scoter
- ☐ White-winged Scoter
- ☐ Bufflehead
- ☐ Barrow's Goldeneye
- ☐ Common Goldeneye
- ☐ Hooded Merganser
- ☐ Red-breasted Merganser
- ☐ Common Merganser
- ☐ Ruddy Duck
- ☐ Osprey
- ☐ Sandhill Crane
- ☐ Sora
- ☐ American Coot
- ☐ Black Oystercatcher
- ☐ Lesser Golden Plover
- ☐ Black-bellied Plover
- ☐ Semi-palmated Plover
- ☐ Snowy Plover
- ☐ Mongolian Plover
- ☐ Killdeer
- ☐ Eurasian Dotterel
- ☐ Black-tailed Godwit
- ☐ Hudsonian Godwit
- ☐ Marbled Godwit
- ☐ Whimbrel
- ☐ Bristle-thighed Curlew
- ☐ Long-billed Curlew
- ☐ Upland Sandpiper
- ☐ Spotted Redshank
- ☐ Greater Yellowlegs
- ☐ Lesser Yellowlegs
- ☐ Common Yellowlegs
- ☐ Solitary Sandpiper
- ☐ Wood Sandpiper
- ☐ Willet
- ☐ Common Sandpiper
- ☐ Spotted Sandpiper
- ☐ Wandering Turnstone
- ☐ Ruddy Turnstone
- ☐ Black Turnstone
- ☐ Ruby Turnstone
- ☐ Wilson's Phalarope
- ☐ Northern Phalarope
- ☐ Red Phalarope
- ☐ Red-necked Phalarope
- ☐ Common Snipe
- ☐ Short-billed Dowitcher
- ☐ Long-billed Dowitcher
- ☐ Surfbird
- ☐ Red Knot
- ☐ Sanderling
- ☐ Semi-palmated Sandpiper
- ☐ Western Sandpiper
- ☐ Little Stint
- ☐ Long-toed Stint
- ☐ Least Sandpiper
- ☐ White-rumped Sandpiper
- ☐ Baird's Sandpiper
- ☐ Pectoral Sandpiper
- ☐ Sharp-tailed Sandpiper
- ☐ Rock Sandpiper
- ☐ Dunlin
- ☐ Curlew Sandpiper
- ☐ Spoon-billed Sandpiper
- ☐ Stilt Sandpiper
- ☐ Buff-breasted Sandpiper
- ☐ South Polar Skua
- ☐ Pomarine Jaeger
- ☐ Parasitic Jaeger
- ☐ Long-tailed Jaeger
- ☐ Ivory Gull
- ☐ Ring-billed Gull
- ☐ Mew Gull
- ☐ Herring Gull
- ☐ Thayer's Gull
- ☐ California Gull
- ☐ Western Gull
- ☐ Slaty-backed Gull
- ☐ Glaucous-winged Gull

☐ Franklin's Gull
☐ Bonaparte's Gull
☐ Ross' Gull
☐ Black-legged Kittiwake
☐ Red-legged Kittiwake
☐ Sabine's Gull
☐ Caspian Tern
☐ Common Tern
☐ Arctic Tern
☐ Thick-billed Murre
☐ Common Murre
☐ Black Guillemot
☐ Pigeon Guillemot
☐ Marbled Murrelet
☐ Kittlitz's Murrelet
☐ Ancient Murrelet
☐ Cassin's Auklet
☐ Parakeet Auklet
☐ Crested Auklet
☐ Least Auklet
☐ Whiskered Auklet
☐ Rhinoceros Auklet
☐ Horned Puffin
☐ Tufted Puffin

Doves and Pigeons
☐ Mourning Dove
☐ Band-tailed Pigeon

Raptors
☐ Turkey Vulture
☐ Bald Eagle
☐ Golden Eagle
☐ White-tailed Eagle
☐ Steller's Sea Eagle
☐ Marsh Hawk
☐ Goshawk
☐ Sharp-shinned Hawk
☐ Swainson's Hawk
☐ Red-tailed Hawk
☐ American Kestrel
☐ Eurasian Kestrel
☐ Merlin

☐ Gyrfalcon
☐ Peregrine Falcon

Fowl-like Birds
☐ Ring-necked Pheasant
☐ California Quail
☐ Mountain Quail
☐ Willow Ptarmigan
☐ Rock Ptarmigan
☐ White-tailed Ptarmigan
☐ Ruffed Grouse
☐ Sharp-tailed Grouse
☐ Spruce Grouse
☐ Blue Grouse

Rail
☐ Virginia Rail

Owls
☐ Western Screech Owl
☐ Great Horned Owl
☐ Snowy Owl
☐ Northern Spotted Owl
☐ Hawk Owl
☐ Northern Pygmy Owl
☐ Barred Owl
☐ Great Gray Owl
☐ Long-eared Owl
☐ Short-eared Owl
☐ Northern Saw-whet Owl

Goatsuckers
☐ Common Nighthawk
☐ Whip-poor-will

Swifts
☐ Black Swift
☐ Vaux's Swift
☐ White-rumped Swift

Hummingbirds
☐ Ruby-throated Hummingbird
☐ Anna's Hummingbird
☐ Rufous Hummingbird

Kingfishers and Woodpeckers

- ☐ Belted Kingfisher
- ☐ Red-breasted Sapsucker
- ☐ Yellow-bellied Sapsucker
- ☐ Acorn Woodpecker
- ☐ Downy Woodpecker
- ☐ Hairy Woodpecker
- ☐ Pileated Woodpecker
- ☐ Northern Three-toed Woodpecker
- ☐ Black-backed Woodpecker
- ☐ Northern Flicker

Flycatchers

- ☐ Say's Phoebe
- ☐ Black Phoebe
- ☐ Belted Kingbird
- ☐ Western Kingbird
- ☐ Olive-sided Flycatcher
- ☐ Western Wood Pewee
- ☐ Yellow-bellied Flycatcher
- ☐ Alder Flycatcher
- ☐ Hammond's Flycatcher
- ☐ Western Flycatcher

Larks and Swallows

- ☐ Horned Lark
- ☐ Tree Swallow
- ☐ Violet-Green Swallow
- ☐ Purple Martin
- ☐ Northern Rough-winged Swallow
- ☐ Bank Swallow
- ☐ Barn Swallow
- ☐ Cliff Swallow

Jays, Magpies, and Crows

- ☐ Steller's Jay
- ☐ Gray Jay
- ☐ Scrub Jay
- ☐ Black-billed Magpie
- ☐ Clark's Nutcracker
- ☐ American Crow
- ☐ Northwestern Crow
- ☐ Common Raven

Chickadees and Titmice

- ☐ Black-capped Chickadee
- ☐ Mountain Chickadee
- ☐ Gray-headed Chickadee
- ☐ Chestnut-backed Chickadee
- ☐ Bushtit

Nuthatch

- ☐ Red-breasted Nuthatch

Creeper

- ☐ Brown Creeper

Wrens

- ☐ Bewick's Wren
- ☐ House Wren
- ☐ Marsh Wren
- ☐ Winter Wren
- ☐ Wrentit

Dipper

- ☐ American Dipper

Kinglets, Gnatcatchers, and Thrushes

- ☐ Siberian Rubythroat
- ☐ Bluethroat
- ☐ Mountain Bluebird
- ☐ Townsend's Solitaire
- ☐ Whiteear
- ☐ Varied Thrush
- ☐ Gray-cheeked Thrush
- ☐ Swainson's Thrush
- ☐ Hermit Thrush
- ☐ Eye-browed Thrush
- ☐ Fieldfare
- ☐ American Robin
- ☐ Arctic Warbler

☐ Ruby-crowned Kinglet
☐ Golden-crowned Kinglet

Wagtails and Pipits
☐ Yellow Wagtail
☐ Olive Tree Pipit
☐ Red-throated Pipit
☐ Water Pipit

Waxwings
☐ Bohemian Waxwing
☐ Cedar Waxwing

Shrikes
☐ Brown Shrike
☐ Northern Shrike

Starling
☐ European Starling

Vireos
☐ Red-eyed Vireo
☐ Warbling Vireo
☐ Solitary Vireo

Wood Warblers
☐ Orange-crowned Warbler
☐ Yellow Warbler
☐ Nashville Warbler
☐ Townsend's Warbler
☐ Yellow-rumped Warbler
☐ Blackpoll Warbler
☐ Bay-breasted Warbler
☐ American Redstart
☐ Northern Waterthrush
☐ Common Yellowthroat
☐ MacGillvray's Warbler
☐ Wilson's Warbler

Tanagers
☐ Scarlet Tanager
☐ Western Tanager

Buntings
☐ Snow Bunting
☐ MacKay's Bunting

Towhees and Sparrows
☐ Rufous-sided Towhee
☐ Fox Sparrow
☐ Song Sparrow
☐ Lincoln's Sparrow
☐ White-crowned Sparrow
☐ Golden-crowned Sparrow
☐ Dark-eyed Junco
☐ Savannah Sparrow
☐ Tree Sparrow
☐ Chipping Sparrow
☐ Lapland Longspur
☐ Smith's Longspur

Blackbirds and Orioles
☐ Northern Oriole
☐ Red-winged Blackbird
☐ Western Meadowlark
☐ Common Grackle
☐ Rusty Blackbird
☐ Brewer's Blackbird
☐ Bobolink

Finches
☐ Brambling
☐ Pine Siskin
☐ Common Redpoll
☐ Hoary Redpoll
☐ Gray-crowned Rosy Finch
☐ Purple Finch
☐ Pine Grosbeak
☐ Red Crossbill
☐ White-winged Crossbill

Other Animals of the Northwest

Fish
☐ Anchovy, northern
☐ Cabezon
☐ Cusk-Eel, spotted
☐ Dogfish, spiny

Flounder, starry

Hake, Pacific

Halibut, California

Halibut, Pacific

Halfmoon

Herring, Pacific

Kelpfish, giant

Lamprey, Pacific

Ling Cod

Loed, red Irish

Mackerel, chub

Mackerel, jack

Opaleye

Ratfish, spotted

Rockfish, black

Rockfish, blue

Rockfish, brown

Rockfish, China

Rockfish, copper

Rockfish, kelp

Rockfish, quillback

Rockfish, vermilion

Rockfish, widow

Rockfish, yelloweye

Rockfish, yellowtail

Sablefish

Salmon, chinook (king)

Salmon, coho (silver)

Salmon, sockeye

Sanddab, Pacific

Sculpin, buffalo

Sculpin, grunt

Sculpin, snubnose

Seaperch, rainbow

Shark, leopard

Shark, Pacific angel

Shark, white

Sheephead, California

Sole, English

Sole, rock

Steelhead

Surfperch, redtail

Sunfish, ocean

Thornback

Tomcod, Pacific

Trout, coastal cutthroat

Whitefish, ocean

Wolf-eel

Yellowtail

Seashells and Seashore Creatures

The following seashells and sea creatures are those found in protected marine environments, usually found in quiet Pacific Coast waters, in estuaries, bays, and between islands. They are the creatures often encountered on Pacific Coast beaches and in tidal pools.

Anemone, green

Angel Wing, eastern

Barnacle, giant acorn

Barnacle, goose

Beach Hopper

Bloodworm

Bubble, California

By-the-Wind Sailor

Chiton, black katy

Chiton, hairy

Clam, amethyst gem

Clam, razor

Cockle

Cockle, giant Pacific

Clam, common Pacific littleneck

Clam, Japanese littleneck

Clam, razor

Crab, Dungeness

Crab, blue-handed hermit

Crab, Pacific rock

Crab, Pacific shore

Crab, sharp-nosed

Dogwinkle, frilled

Drill, Atlantic oyster

Egg, common Pacific

Forreria, giant

- [ ] Geoduck
- [ ] Glass Mya, California
- [ ] Jungle Shell, false Pacific
- [ ] Horn Shell, California
- [ ] Jellyfish, moon
- [ ] Limpet, finger
- [ ] Macoma, Baltic
- [ ] Macoma, bent-nosed
- [ ] Melampus, California
- [ ] Musculus, black
- [ ] Mussel, blue
- [ ] Mussel, fan-shaped horse
- [ ] Neptune, common Northwest
- [ ] Olive, purple dwarf
- [ ] Oyster, giant Pacific
- [ ] Periwinkle, checkered
- [ ] Periwinkle, eroded
- [ ] Periwinkle, Sitka
- [ ] Pheasant Shell, California
- [ ] Piddock, flat-tipped
- [ ] Piddock, giant
- [ ] Sea Cucumber, red
- [ ] Sea Gooseberry
- [ ] Sea Lemon
- [ ] Sea Urchin, green
- [ ] Shipworm, common
- [ ] Snail, purple olive
- [ ] Star, core
- [ ] Star, giant sea
- [ ] Star, sunflower
- [ ] Tagelus, California
- [ ] Tusk, Indian money
- [ ] Venus
- [ ] Whelk, eastern mud
- [ ] Worm, Agassiz's peanut
- [ ] Worm, lug

Mammals

- [ ] Bat, big brown
- [ ] Bat, California myotis
- [ ] Bat, little brown (myotis)
- [ ] Bat, red
- [ ] Bat, silver-haired
- [ ] Bear, black

- [ ] Bear, brown
- [ ] Beaver
- [ ] Beaver, Mountain
- [ ] Bobcat
- [ ] Chipmunk, Allen's
- [ ] Chipmunk, Siskiyou
- [ ] Chipmunk, Townsend
- [ ] Coyote
- [ ] Deer, black-tailed
- [ ] Deer, Columbian black-tailed
- [ ] Deer, mule
- [ ] Dolphin, common
- [ ] Dolphin, Pacific white-sided
- [ ] Elk, Roosevelt
- [ ] Fox, gray
- [ ] Hare, snowshoe
- [ ] Lynx
- [ ] Marmot, hoary
- [ ] Mink
- [ ] Mole, California
- [ ] Mole, Pacific
- [ ] Mole, Townsend
- [ ] Moose
- [ ] Mountain Goat
- [ ] Mountain Lion
- [ ] Mouse, California
- [ ] Mouse, deer
- [ ] Mouse, Pacific jumping
- [ ] Mouse, western harvest
- [ ] Mouse, western jumping
- [ ] Otter, river
- [ ] Otter, sea
- [ ] Pika (cony)
- [ ] Pocket Gopher, valley
- [ ] Porcupine
- [ ] Porpoise, Dall's
- [ ] Porpoise, harbor
- [ ] Rabbit, brush
- [ ] Raccoon
- [ ] Sea Lion, California
- [ ] Sea Lion, northern
- [ ] Sea Lion, Steller
- [ ] Seal, Pacific harbor
- [ ] Seal, northern elephant

Shrew, marsh
Shrew, Pacific
Shrew, Trowbridge
Shrew, vagrant
Shrew-mole
Skunk, spotted
Skunk, striped
Squirrel, California ground
Squirrel, Douglas
Squirrel, golden-mantled
Squirrel, northern flying
Squirrel, red
Squirrel, western gray
Vole, California
Vole, Oregon
Vole, Townsend
Vole, white-footed
Weasel, long-tailed
Whale, finback
Whale, gray
Whale, killer (orca)
Whale, minke
Woodrat, bushy-tailed
Woodrat, dusky-footed

Reptiles

Alligator Lizard, northern
Alligator Lizard, southern
Fence Lizard, northwestern
Garter Snake, coast
Garter Snake, common
Garter Snake, northwestern
Garter Snake, Oregon
Gopher Snake, Pacific
Kingsnake, California mountain
Pond Turtle
Racer, western yellow-bellied
Rattlesnake, northern Pacific
Ringneck Snake, northwestern
Skink, western

Amphibians

Bullfrog
Frog, foothill yellow-legged

Frog, northern red-legged
Frog, red-legged
Frog, tailed
Frog, Pacific tree
Newt, roughskin
Salamander, arboreal
Salamander, black
Salamander, brown
Salamander, California slender
Salamander, clouded
Salamander, Del Norte
Salamander, long-toed
Salamander, Olympic
Salamander, Pacific giant
Salamander, painted
Toad, boreal
Toad, western

Plants of the Northwest

Trees

Alder, mountain
Alder, red
Alder, Sitka
Alder, white
Ash, Oregon
Aspen, quaking
Birch, dwarf
Birch, paper
Cedar, Alaska yellow
Cedar, incense
Cedar, Port Orford
Cedar, western red
Chinquapin, golden
Club Moss
Club Moss, running
Cottonwood, black
Crabapple, Pacific
Cypress, Baker's
Dogwood, dwarf
Dogwood, Pacific
Dogwood, red osier

- [ ] Douglas Fir
- [ ] Douglas Fir, coast
- [ ] Douglas Fir, Rocky Mountain
- [ ] Fir, amabilis (balsam)
- [ ] Fir, grand
- [ ] Fir, noble
- [ ] Fir, Pacific Silver
- [ ] Fir, Shasta red
- [ ] Fir, subalpine
- [ ] Fir, white
- [ ] Gingko
- [ ] Hawthorn, black
- [ ] Hazelnut, California
- [ ] Hemlock, mountain
- [ ] Hemlock, western
- [ ] Juniper, common
- [ ] Juniper, Rocky Mountain
- [ ] Juniper, western
- [ ] Larch, alpine
- [ ] Larch, western
- [ ] Laurel, alpine
- [ ] Laurel, California
- [ ] Laurel, mountain
- [ ] Laurel, swamp
- [ ] Madrone, Pacific (arbutus)
- [ ] Maple, bigleaf
- [ ] Maple, Rocky Mountain
- [ ] Maple, sugar
- [ ] Maple, vine
- [ ] Mountain-ash, European
- [ ] Myrtle, Oregon
- [ ] Oak, California black
- [ ] Oak, canyon
- [ ] Oak, coast live
- [ ] Oak, Garry
- [ ] Oak, huckleberry
- [ ] Oak, Oregon white
- [ ] Pine, bishop
- [ ] Pine, foxtail
- [ ] Pine, jack
- [ ] Pine, Jeffrey
- [ ] Pine, knobcone
- [ ] Pine, limber
- [ ] Pine, lodgepole

- [ ] Pine, ponderosa
- [ ] Pine, shore (shorepine)
- [ ] Pine, sugar
- [ ] Pine, western white
- [ ] Pine, western yellow
- [ ] Pine, whitebark
- [ ] Poplar, balsam
- [ ] Redwood, coast
- [ ] Redwood, dawn
- [ ] Selaginella, Oregon
- [ ] Spruce, Engelmann
- [ ] Spruce, Sitka
- [ ] Spruce, white
- [ ] Tamarack
- [ ] Tanbark Oak (tan oak)
- [ ] Willow, Pacific
- [ ] Willow, Scouler's
- [ ] Willow, Sitka

Shrubs and Understory Plants

- [ ] Arborvitae
- [ ] Azalea, Cascade
- [ ] Azalea, mock
- [ ] Azalea, western
- [ ] Blackberry, California
- [ ] Blackberry, Himalaya
- [ ] Blackberry, Pacific
- [ ] Blueberry, Alaskan
- [ ] Blueberry, dwarf
- [ ] Blueblossom
- [ ] Burning Bush, western
- [ ] Cascara, sagrada
- [ ] Ceanothus, redstem
- [ ] Coffeeberry
- [ ] Coyote Bush
- [ ] Cranberry, bog
- [ ] Cranberry, high bush
- [ ] Creambush (ocean spray)
- [ ] Current, red flowering
- [ ] Devil's Club
- [ ] Elderberry, coast red
- [ ] Fern, California polypody
- [ ] Fern, coastal wood

- ☐ Fern, common wood
- ☐ Fern, deer
- ☐ Fern, five-fingered
- ☐ Fern, giant chain
- ☐ Fern, goldenback
- ☐ Fern, Indian's dream
- ☐ Fern, lady
- ☐ Fern, leather
- ☐ Fern, licorice
- ☐ Fern, spreading wood
- ☐ Fern, sword
- ☐ Gooseberry
- ☐ Hazel, California
- ☐ Honeysuckle, hairy
- ☐ Huckleberry, black
- ☐ Huckleberry, red
- ☐ Kinnikinnick
- ☐ Labrador Tea
- ☐ Labrador Tea, bog
- ☐ Manzanita, hairy
- ☐ Moss, mountain fern
- ☐ Moss, sphagnum
- ☐ Ninebark, Pacific
- ☐ Oregon Grape
- ☐ Osoberry
- ☐ Poison Oak
- ☐ Rhododendron, Pacific
- ☐ Salal
- ☐ Salmonberry
- ☐ Serviceberry, western
- ☐ Snowberry
- ☐ Skunk Cabbage
- ☐ Spirea, birchleaf
- ☐ Thimbleberry
- ☐ Twinberry
- ☐ Wax Myrtle, western

Wildflowers

- ☐ Alum root
- ☐ Anemone, western wood
- ☐ Aster, alpine
- ☐ Aster, Cascade
- ☐ Aster, Chilean

- ☐ Avens, large-leaved
- ☐ Avens, mountain
- ☐ Baby Blue Eyes
- ☐ Baneberry
- ☐ Balsamroot, arrowleaf
- ☐ Beadlily (clintonia)
- ☐ Beargrass
- ☐ Bedstraw, sweet scented
- ☐ Bell, yellow
- ☐ Bellflower, round-leaved
- ☐ Bitterroot
- ☐ Bleeding Heart, western
- ☐ Blue Blossom
- ☐ Blue Dicks
- ☐ Blue-eyed Grass
- ☐ Blue-eyed Mary, Torrey's
- ☐ Brodiaea, Douglas
- ☐ Brodiaea, harvest
- ☐ Brodiaea, white
- ☐ Brooklime, American
- ☐ Bunchberry
- ☐ Buttercup, Cooley's
- ☐ Buttercup, creeping
- ☐ Buttercup, little
- ☐ Buttercup, subalpine
- ☐ Buttercup, western
- ☐ Butterweed, Canadian
- ☐ Camas, blue
- ☐ Checker-mallow, Henderson's
- ☐ Cinquefoil, fanleaf
- ☐ Cinquefoil, shrubby
- ☐ Cinquefoil, slender
- ☐ Cinquefoil, snowbed
- ☐ Cinquefoil, sticky
- ☐ Clintonia, red
- ☐ Coltsfoot, western
- ☐ Columbine, red
- ☐ Corn Lily
- ☐ Cow Parsnip
- ☐ Daisy, seaside
- ☐ Daisy, wandering
- ☐ Darlingtonia
- ☐ Dirty Socks

- [ ] Dogtooth-violet
- [ ] Douglasia, red
- [ ] Dryas, yellow
- [ ] Evening Primrose, beach
- [ ] Fairybell, Hooker's
- [ ] Fairybell, Smith's
- [ ] False-hellebore, green
- [ ] False-hellebore, white
- [ ] Farewell-to-spring
- [ ] Fetid Adder's Tongue
- [ ] Fireweed
- [ ] Fireweed, dwarf
- [ ] Fleabane, golden
- [ ] Fleabane, shaggy
- [ ] Foam Flower
- [ ] Foamflower, trefoil
- [ ] Foxglove
- [ ] Gentian, explorer's
- [ ] Gilia, blue-headed
- [ ] Gilia, globe
- [ ] Gilia, scarlet
- [ ] Gilia, small-flowered
- [ ] Ginger, wild
- [ ] Goldenrod, dwarf
- [ ] Goldenrod, meadow
- [ ] Grass, European beach
- [ ] Groundsel, arrowhead
- [ ] Groundsmoke, dwarf
- [ ] Harebell, California
- [ ] Hawkweed, white-flowered
- [ ] Heather, mountain
- [ ] Hedge nettle, Cooley's
- [ ] Hopsage, spiny
- [ ] Horsebrush, gray
- [ ] Indian-tea
- [ ] Inside-out Flower
- [ ] Iris, Douglas
- [ ] Iris, western
- [ ] Isothecium
- [ ] Knotweed, Newberry's
- [ ] Lady's Tresses
- [ ] Larkspur, Menzies'
- [ ] Lilies, mariposa
- [ ] Lily, avalanche
- [ ] Lily, chocolate
- [ ] Lily, glacier
- [ ] Lily, leopard
- [ ] Lily of the Valley, false
- [ ] Lousewort, coil-beaked
- [ ] Lovage, Gray's
- [ ] Lupine, alpine
- [ ] Lupine, large-leafed
- [ ] Lupine, miniature
- [ ] Lupine, riverbank
- [ ] Lupine, silky
- [ ] Lupine, velvet
- [ ] Marsh-marigold, elkslip
- [ ] Marsh-marigold, twinflower
- [ ] Menziesia
- [ ] Milkmaids
- [ ] Milkwort
- [ ] Mission Bells
- [ ] Monkeyflower, chickweed
- [ ] Monkeyflower, Lewis'
- [ ] Monkeyflower, seep-spring
- [ ] Monkeyflower, sticky
- [ ] Monkeyflower, subalpine
- [ ] Monkeyflower, toothed
- [ ] Monkeyflower, Torrey's
- [ ] Monkeyflower, yellow (common)
- [ ] Monkshood, Columbian
- [ ] Morning Glory, beach
- [ ] Moss-campion
- [ ] Mountain Balm
- [ ] Mountain-heather, Alaska
- [ ] Mountain-heather, four-angled
- [ ] Mountain-heather, red
- [ ] Mountain-heather, white
- [ ] Mountain-heather, yellow
- [ ] Mountain Lover
- [ ] Mousetail
- [ ] Mustard, tansy
- [ ] Needle and Thread
- [ ] Nettle, stinging
- [ ] Ninebark, mallow

- ☐ Old Man's Beard (lichen)
- ☐ Olympic Onion
- ☐ Orchid, bog
- ☐ Orchid, calypso
- ☐ Orchid, rattlesnake
- ☐ Owl's clover, paintbrush
- ☐ Paintbrush, Indian
- ☐ Parsley, desert
- ☐ Parsnip, cow
- ☐ Pasqueflower, western
- ☐ Penstemon, Cardwell's
- ☐ Penstemon, coast
- ☐ Penstemon, Davidson's
- ☐ Penstemon, little
- ☐ Penstemon, meadow
- ☐ Penstemon, Siskiyou
- ☐ Phalacia, Bolander's
- ☐ Phlox, spreading
- ☐ Phlox, tufted
- ☐ Pickleweed
- ☐ Piggyback Plant
- ☐ Pink, California Indian
- ☐ Pitcher Plant, California
- ☐ Plantain, rattlesnake
- ☐ Plantain, seaside
- ☐ Pond-lily, yellow
- ☐ Prairie Star
- ☐ Pussy Ears
- ☐ Pussypaws
- ☐ Pussytoes, alpine
- ☐ Pussytoes, woolly
- ☐ Pyrolas
- ☐ Rose, Nootka
- ☐ Rose, woods
- ☐ Saltsage
- ☐ Sand Verbena, beach
- ☐ Sand Verbena, yellow
- ☐ Sandwort, arctic
- ☐ Saxifrage, Alaska
- ☐ Saxifrage, Oregon
- ☐ Saxifrage, Tolmie
- ☐ Sea Rocket
- ☐ Sedge, beaked
- ☐ Sedge, black
- ☐ Sedge, elk
- ☐ Sedge, Holm's Rocky Mountain
- ☐ Sedge, showy
- ☐ Sedge, Sitka
- ☐ Sedge, slough
- ☐ Sedge, water
- ☐ Sedge, woodrush
- ☐ Sheepfat
- ☐ Shooting Star, Jeffrey's
- ☐ Sibbaldia
- ☐ Silktassel, Fremont's
- ☐ Silverweed, Pacific
- ☐ Skyrocket (gilia)
- ☐ Solomon's Plume, starry
- ☐ Solomon's Seal, false
- ☐ Sorrel, redwood (Oregon oxalis)
- ☐ Sorrel, wood
- ☐ Spikenard, California
- ☐ Spiraea, white
- ☐ Spring Beauty, western
- ☐ Squawbush
- ☐ Squaw Carpet
- ☐ Starflower
- ☐ Stickseed, western
- ☐ Stonecrop
- ☐ Strawberry, beach
- ☐ Strawberry, wood
- ☐ Sundew, round-leaved
- ☐ Sunflower, little
- ☐ Sunflower, woolly
- ☐ Tansy, dune
- ☐ Toothwort, giant
- ☐ Trillium, western
- ☐ Twinflower
- ☐ Valerian, Sitka
- ☐ Vanilla Leaf
- ☐ Violet, redwood
- ☐ Violet, smooth yellow
- ☐ Violet, two-eyed
- ☐ Violet, wedge-leaved
- ☐ Violet, western dog
- ☐ Violet, yellow montane

- ☐ Water-lily, white
- ☐ Water-parsley
- ☐ Water-plantain
- ☐ Whisker Brush
- ☐ Wild Cucumber
- ☐ Willowherb, alpine
- ☐ Willowherb, red
- ☐ Windflower
- ☐ Winter Fat
- ☐ Wintergreen, white-veined
- ☐ Wood Nymph
- ☐ Wormwood, three-forked
- ☐ Yampah, Gairdner's
- ☐ Yarrow
- ☐ Yerba de Salva
- ☐ Yerba Santa
- ☐ Youth-on-age

Admiralty Island (AK), 321
Alaska. *See* Southeast Alaska
Alpine Creek Trail (ID), 354
Ancient Groves Nature
    Trail (WA), 197
Annie Creek Trail (OR), 157
Auger Point Loop Trail (BC), 263
Avenue of the Giants (CA), 39

Bandon (OR), 75
Bald Hills (CA), 21
Bald Hills Road (CA), 7, 21
Bartlett Cove (AK), 317
Bartlett River Trail (AK), 320
Bastendorff County Park (OR), 74
Beach and Nature Trail,
    Glacier Bay (AK), 320
Bedwell Lake Trail (BC), 266
Big Beaver–Little Beaver
    Trail (WA), 127
Big Creek Nature Trail (WA), 206
Big Creek to Salmon River
    Trail (ID), 360
Big Tree Grove Nature
    Trail (WA), 202
Boiling Springs Lake Nature
    Trail (CA), 164
Boulder Chain Lakes Trail (ID), 356
Boy Scout Tree Trail (CA), 27
Broken Group Islands (BC), 248
Brown Creek–Rhododendron
    Trail (CA), 30
Bumpass Hell, Mt. Lassen
    (CA), 162
Buttle Lake (BC), 260

Cal-Barrel Road (CA), 20
California
    north coast, 9
Cape Arago Highway (OR), 74

Cape Arago State Park (OR), 75
Cape Scott Provincial
    Park (BC), 268
    how to get there, 269–270
    hikes, 271–274
    camping, 274
Cape Scott Trail (BC), 271
Carl G. Washburne State
    Park (OR), 73
Cascades, Northern (OR)
    accommodations, 148–150
    climate, 119–121
    field guide, 141–147
    hikes, 125–129
    how to get there, 123–124
Cascades, Southern (OR/CA). *See
    also* Crater Lake National Park,
    Lassen Volcanic National Park
    accommodations, 175–179
    field guide, 168–174
    geology, 151–153
Cascade River Road (WA), 126
Chicagohof Island (AK), 310
Chilkoot Trail (AK), 322
Chilula, settlement (CA), 8
Cinder Cone Nature Trail (CA), 163
Cleetwood Trail (OR), 156
Climb to the Summit Trail (WA), 138
Coastal Drive (CA), 18
Coastal Trail (CA), 33, 35
Crater Lake National Park (OR), 153
    hikes, 156–159
    how to get there, 154
    rim drive, 155
Crescent Beach area (CA), 16

Damnation Creek Trail (CA), 28
Davison Road (CA), 20
Della Falls (BC), 262
    backcountry trail, 265

Del Norte Redwoods State
    Park (CA), 16
Devil's Elbow State Park (OR), 73
Doe Bay Village (WA), 98
Dolason Prairie–Emerald Ridge
    Trail (CA), 37
Dosewallips (WA), 204
  day-hike (WA), 205
Douglas–McKenzie Lakes
    Trail (BC), 264
Dungeness Spit and Wildlife
    Refuge (WA), 210

Eastsound (WA), 98
Ecola State Park (OR), 70
Ecology
  Glacier Bay National
      Park (AK), 318
  Northern Cascade
      Mountains, 120
  Olympic Peninsula (WA), 184
  Oregon Dunes, 63
  Pacific Rim National
      Park (BC), 241
  Redwoods National
      Park (CA), 12
  Rain Forest, 182
  Southeast Alaska, 302
  Strathcona Provincial
      Park (BC), 259
Elwha Valley (WA), 190
  day-hikes, 191

Ferries
  to San Juan Islands (WA), 93
  to Southeast Alaska, 306
  to Vancouver Island (BC), 239
Five Minute Trail (CA), 25
Fern Canyon Loop Trail (CA), 25
Forbidden Plateau (BC), 261
Frank Church–River of No Return
    Wilderness (ID), 357
Friday Harbor (WA), 94

Geology
  California North Coast, 10
  Mount Lassen (CA), 160
  Mount Rainier National
      Park (WA), 132
  Olympic Peninsula (WA), 185
  Southern Cascades (OR/CA), 151
  Strathcona Provincial
      Park (BC), 257

Gifford Pinchot National
    Forest (WA), 139
Glacier Bay National Park (AK), 315
  hikes, 320
  wildlife, 318–320
Golden Gate Trail (WA), 136
Gold Mine Trail (BC), 247
Gold River (OR), 76
Gospel Hump Wilderness (ID), 352
Graves Campground Nature
    Trail (WA), 203
Griff Creek Trail (WA), 192
Gustavus (AK), 317

Haida settlement (AK), 304
Haines (AK), 313
Hall of Mosses Nature
    Trail (WA), 198
Hidden Beach Trail (CA), 33
High Bluff Trail (CA), 26
Hiouchi Trail (CA), 27
Hoh Rain Forest (WA), 197
  day-hikes, 198
  Hoh Trail, 199
Holter Ridge–Lost Man
    Bike Trail (CA), 38
Hoonah (AK), 310
Horsfall Dunes and Beach (OR), 68
Hot Springs
  Olympic (WA), 191
  Sol Duc (WA), 195
Howland Hill Drive, 15
Humboldt Redwoods State
    Park (CA), 39
Humbug Mountain State
    Park (OR), 75
Hurricane Ridge (WA), 189
  day-hikes, 190
Hyndman Creek Trail–North Fork
    Trail (ID), 355

Ibex Pass, trail to (ID), 355

James Irvine Trail (CA), 29
Jedediah Smith Redwoods State
    Park (CA), 15
Jessie Honeyman State
    Park (OR), 66
Juneau (AK), 311

Kalaloch Lodge (WA), 204
Karst Creek Loop Trail (BC), 263
Ketchikan (AK), 307

King Range Wilderness (CA), 40
Klamath Basin National Wildlife
    Refuge (OR/CA), 159
Klamath River area, 17
Krause Bottom Trail (WA), 192
Kwai Lake Trail (BC), 264
Kwakiutl settlement (BC), 237

Lady Falls Trail (BC), 262
Lake Crescent (WA), 192
    day-hikes, 194
    Lake Crescent Lodge, 193
Lake Ozette (WA), 203
Lakes Trail (WA), 137
Lady Bird Johnson Grove (CA), 21
    loop trail, 24
Lassen Volcanic National
    Park (CA), 160
    hikes, 163–166
    how to get there, 161
    peak trail, 164
Lava Beds National
    Monument (CA), 160
Lime Kiln State Park (WA), 96
Lodge Trail (WA), 203
Long Beach (BC), 244
Lopez Island (WA), 98
Lopez Village (WA), 99
Lost Coast (CA), 40
    trail, 41
Lummi settlement (OR), 92
Lupin Falls Loop Trail (BC), 262

Madison Falls Trail (WA), 192
Makah Reservation (WA), 187
Marymere Falls Trail (WA), 194
Mather Memorial
    Highway (WA), 135
Metlakatla (AK), 307
Mill Creek–Nickerson Ranch
    Trail (CA), 28
Miner's Ridge Trail (CA), 29
Mink Lake Trail (WA), 196
Misty Fjords National
    Monument (AK), 320
Moraine Trail (WA), 136
Moran State Park (WA), 97
Mountain Lake to Cascade Lake
    Trail (WA), 101
Mount Becher Trail (BC), 264
Mount Constitution (WA), 97
Mount Fremont Lookout
    Trail (WA), 137

Mount Lassen (CA), 152, 160
Mount Mazama (OR), 151
Mount Rainier National
    Park (WA), 130
    day-hikes, 136
Mount St. Helens National Volcanic
    Monument (WA), 140
Mount Storm King Trail (WA), 194
Mount Young Trail (WA), 103
Myra Falls Trail (BC), 263

Nathan B. Drury Scenic
    Parkway 7, 20
Nez Perce National Forest
    (ID), 349
Nisqually View Trail (WA), 136
Nootka settlement (BC), 237, 248
North Cascades National
    Park (WA), 122
Northern Puget Sound Island State
    Park (WA), 100
North Fork Skokomish (WA), 206
North Shore Road (WA), 201

Orcas Island (WA), 97
Odlin County Park (WA), 98
Olympic Hot Springs
    Trail (WA), 192
Olympic National Park (WA)
    accommodations, 227–232
    attractions and hikes, 189–210
    field guide, 211–226
    how to get there, 188–189
Olympic Seashore (WA), 203
Oregon Coast
    accommodations, 86–90
    beaches, 72
        north, 69
        south, 74
    dunes, 63–69
    trails, 68–69
    field guide, 79–85
    history, 61–63
Orick area (CA), 23
Ozette Reservation (WA), 187

Pacific Crest Trail 129, 158, 165
Pacific Rim National
    Park (BC), 240–256
    Broken Group Islands, 248
    Long Beach Unit, 244–248
    West Coast Trail, 250–256
    wildlife, 241–244

Paradise Glacier Trail (WA), 136
Paradise Meadows Loop
    Trail (BC), 264
Pelican (AK), 310
Petersburg (AK), 309
Phillips Ridge Trail (BC), 263
Pig War historic sites (WA), 92
Prairie Creek Redwoods State
    Park (CA), 19
Prince of Wales Island (AK), 308

Queets Rain Forest (WA), 199
    day-hike, 200
Quilute settlement, 186
Quinault Rain Forest (WA), 200
    loop trail, 202

Radar Station Trail (CA), 26
Raft Cove Provincial Park (BC), 275
Rain Forests
    defined, 181
    rain forest trails (BC), 247
Redwood Creek Backcountry
    Trail (CA), 34
Redwood National Park (CA)
    accommodations, 52–58
    climate, 11
    field guide, 42–51
    geology, 10–11
    hikes, 24–38
    history, 9–10
    how to get there, 6
    wildlife, 12
Reedsport (OR), 67
Reflection Lake Trail (ID), 359
Requa Road (CA), 17
Revelation Trail (CA), 26
Rim Drive, Crater Lake (OR), 155
Robson Bight (BC), 276
Roche Harbor (WA), 95
Rocky Mountains, western front
    ranges, 116
Rogue River Country (OR), 76
    trail, 76
Ross Lake National Recreation
    Area (WA), 124

Salmon River (ID), 351
Salmon River Country (ID)
    accommodations, 368–370
    field guide, 362–367
    hikes, 354–361
    history, 349–351

San Josef Bay Trail (BC), 273
San Juan County Park (WA), 96
San Juan Island (WA), 94
San Juan Islands. *See also*
    specific islands
    accommodations, 109–113
    how to get there, 93–94
    field guide, 104–108
    hikes, 101–103
    uninhabited islands, 99–101
San Juan Islands National Wildlife
    Refuge (WA), 100
San Juan Preserve (WA), 100
Sawtooth National Recreation
    Area (ID), 353
Schooner Trail (BC), 247
Selway-Bitterroot
    Wilderness (ID), 349
Shady Lane Nature Trail (WA), 207
Shaw Island (WA), 99
    county park, 99
Shepherd Creek Loop
    Trail (BC), 263
Shore Acres Botanical Gardens State
    Park (OR), 74
Shoreline Bog Trail (BC), 247
Short Cathedral Trees Loop
    Trail (CA), 26
Siltcoos Recreation Area (OR), 66
Sitka (AK), 309
Skagway (AK), 313
Skyline Trail (WA), 136
Sol Duc River (WA), 195
    day-hikes, 196
    hot springs, 195
Sourdough Ridge Nature
    Trail (WA), 137
South Beach Trail (BC), 245
South Beach Trail (WA), 103
South Shore Road (WA), 201
Southeast Alaska
    accommodations, 337–344
    field guide, 326–336
    history, 304–305
    how to get there, 305–306
Spencer Spit State Park (WA), 98
Spruce Fringe Trail (BC), 246
Spruce Nature Trail (WA), 198
Spruce Railroad Trail (WA), 194
Staircase (WA), 206
Staircase Rapids Trail, 207
Stehekin Valley (WA), 126
    day-hikes, 126

Stout Grove Loop Trail (CA), 24
Strathcona Provincial
    Park (BC), 256–268
  camping, 267–268
  geology, 257–259
  hikes, 262–267
  how to get there, 257
  wildlife, 259–260
Sunset Bay State Park (OR), 74
Sun Valley (ID), 354

Tall Trees Grove (CA), 21
  loop trail, 32
Telegraph Cove (BC), 276
Thunder Creek–Park Creek
    Trail (WA), 128
Tlingit settlement (AK), 304
Tongass National Forest (AK), 321
Trail of the Shadows (WA), 137
Tree Capes area (OR), 71
Twin Lakes Trail (WA), 102
Trails. See also specific trails
  Alpine Creek (ID), 354
  Ancient Groves Nature (WA), 197
  Auger Point Loop (BC), 263
  Bartlett River (AK), 320
  Beach and nature trail,
      Glacier Bay (AK), 320
  Big Beaver–Little Beaver
      (WA), 127
  Big Creek Nature (WA), 206
  Big Creek to Salmon
      River (ID), 360
  Big Tree Grove (WA), 202
  Boiling Springs Lake (CA), 164
  Boulder Chain Lakes (ID), 356
  Boy Scout Tree (CA), 27
  Brown Creek–Rhododendron
      (CA), 30
  Cape Scott (BC), 271
  Cinder Cone (CA), 163
  Cleetwood (OR), 156
  Climb to the Summit (WA), 138
  Damnation Creek (CA), 28
  Della Falls (BC), 265
  Dolason Prairie–Emerald Ridge
      (CA), 37
  Dosewallips (WA), 206
  Douglas–McKenzie Lakes (BC), 264
  Fern Canyon Loop (CA), 25
  Five Minute (CA), 25
  Golden Gate (WA), 136
  Gold Mine (BC), 247

Graves Campground (WA), 203
Griff Creek (WA), 192
Hall of Mosses (WA), 198
Heart of the Forest (WA), 190
Hidden Beach (CA), 33
High Bluff (CA), 26
Hiouchi (CA), 27
Hoh (WA), 199
Holter Ridge–Lost Man (CA), 38
Hurricane Hill (WA), 190
Hurricane Ridge (WA), 190
Hyndman Creek (ID), 355
Ibex Pass (ID), 355
James Irvine (CA), 29
Karst Creek Loop (BC), 263
Krause Bottom (WA), 192
Kwai Lake (BC), 264
Lady Bird Johnson
    Grove Loop (CA), 24
Lady Falls (BC), 262
Lakes (WA), 137
Lassen Peak (CA), 164
Lodge (WA), 203
Lupin Falls Loop (BC), 262
Madison Falls (WA), 192
Marymere Falls (WA), 194
Meadow Loop (WA), 190
Miner's Ridge (CA), 29
Mink Lake (WA), 196
Mill Creek–Nickerson
    Ranch (CA), 28
Moraine (WA), 136
Mount Becher (BC), 264
Mountain Lake to Cascade Lake
    (WA), 101
Mount Storm King (WA), 194
Mount Young (WA), 103
Myra Falls (BC), 263
Nisqually View (WA), 136
North Fork (ID), 355
Olympic Hot Springs (WA), 192
Pacific Crest 130, 158, 165
Paradise Glacier (WA), 136
Paradise Meadows Loop (BC), 264
Phillips Ridge (BC), 263
Quinault Loop (WA), 202
Radar Station (CA), 26
Rain Forest (BC), 247
Redwood Creek (CA), 34
Reflection Lake (ID), 359
Revelation (CA), 26
Rogue River (OR), 76
San Josef Bay (BC), 273

Schooner (BC), 247
Shady Lane (WA), 207
Shepherd Creek Loop (BC), 263
Shoreline Bog (BC), 247
Short Cathedral Trees 26
Skyline (WA), 136
Sol Duc Falls (WA), 196
Sourdough Ridge (WA), 137
South Beach (BC), 245
South Beach (WA), 103
Spruce Fringe (BC), 246
Spruce (WA), 198
Spruce Railroad (WA), 194
Staircase Rapids (WA), 207
Stehekin trails (WA), 126
Stout Grove Loop (CA), 24
Tall Trees Loop (CA), 32
Thunder Creek–Park
    Creek (WA), 128
Trail of the Shadows (WA), 137
Twin Lakes (WA), 102
Upper Myra Falls (BC), 263
West Coast (BC), 250
Wickaninnish (BC), 246
Willowbrae (BC), 246
Wizard Island (OR), 156
Wonderland (WA), 137

Upana Caves (BC), 277
Upper Myra Falls Trail (BC), 263

Vancouver Island (BC). *See also*
    Pacific Rim National Park,
    Strathcona Provincial Park,
    Cape Scott Provincial Park
accommodations, 290–301
field guide, 279–290
how to get there, 239–240
native cultures, 235–239

Washington State Ferries, 93
West Coast Trail (BC), 250
Wickaninnish Trail (BC), 246
Willapa National Wildlife
    Refuge (WA), 208
William M. Tugman State
    Park (OR), 68
Willowbrae Trail (BC), 246
Wizard Island Summit
    Trail (OR), 156
Wonderland Backcountry
    Trail (WA), 137
Wrangell (AK), 308

Yurok settlement (CA), 8